EPHESIANS
A SHORTER COMMENTARY

EPHESIANS

A SHORTER COMMENTARY

ERNEST BEST
*Emeritus Professor of Divinity and Biblical Criticism
in the University of Glasgow*

T & T CLARK
A Continuum imprint
LONDON • NEW YORK

T&T CLARK LTD

A Continuum imprint

59 George Street
Edinburgh EH2 2LQ
Scotland
www.tandtclark.co.uk

470 Lexington Avenue
New York 10017–6504
USA
www.continuumbooks.com

First published 2003

ISBN 0 567 08819 7

British Library Cataloguing-in-Publication Data
A catalogue record for this book is available from the British Library

Typeset by Fakenham Photosetting Limited
Printed and bound by Bookcraft, Midsomer Norton

To my wife
Sarah Elizabeth
for her care and enthusiasm
for my work

CONTENTS

DETACHED NOTES

ESSAYS

PREFACE

Ephesians is not an easy book on which to write a commentary. Goodspeed describes it as 'the Waterloo of commentators. It baffles them.' The second of these sentences is undoubtedly true; how the first is to be understood depends on whether one is British or French! Protestant scholars on the whole prefer to write on Romans and Galatians and when, often reluctantly, they turn to Ephesians they regularly evaluate it in Pauline terms. It is however true that Protestants have given greater attention to Ephesians in recent years as a result of the ecumenical movement. If the nature of the church is to be discussed, then Ephesians can hardly be ignored. Catholic scholars have been much more happy with Ephesians for the church has been traditionally central to their theology, and it has been a Catholic scholar, H. Schlier, who has done most to direct and inspire modern discussion of Ephesians, even though his main positions have not always been acceptable.

All commentators stand on the shoulders of those who have preceded them. I am grateful to the many who have previously written on Ephesians, most of all to Gnilka and Schnackenburg, though I have not always agreed with them. The number of times their names appear in the index of authors bears no relation to the way their thought has penetrated and excited my own. Quotations from them or other commentators are few and far between because I have tended to read them, the relevant monographs and the learned articles, think about what I read and then formulate what I wanted to say in my own words.

All exegesis is controlled by the situation of those who write. They will necessarily view the text on which they work from the angle of the age in which they live and this may lead them to see new aspects of it and put fresh questions to it. They will also be affected by their church allegiance, if any, and, since Ephesians has much to say about the church, in its case this will be important. The coloured glasses we wear, usually without realising we do so, affect the way we read texts. I have not always agreed with the majority of commentators but when I have dared to disagree it has only been after long thought and with great hesitancy, though the latter may not always appear in the way I have expressed myself. A number of minor variations in an approach can in the end modify the total view and so if I have made some kind of contribution in respect of an overall view of Ephesians it is only because of a multitude of minor differences. Perhaps more than most commentators I have tried to observe what is *not* said in Ephesians for I believe that this can be a real help in putting what is said into its proper perspective.

I have employed a number of unusual abbreviations. In particular I have referred throughout to the writer of the letter as AE. There are two reasons for doing this. To write 'the author of the letter' each time would use up too much paper and too many trees. By using AE I have left it to readers to expand it as they will, substituting, if they wish, Paul's name or that of some other of their choice. I have become increasingly convinced that Paul did not write Ephesians; on many occasions I have been compelled to say that Paul could have been the author if he had changed, developed, or otherwise modified what we know from his major letters; there is a limit to the number of times this can be done and it remain reasonable. Only in the third chapter does a decision about authorship affect in any major way what is deduced as the meaning of the text. For similar reasons to my use of AE for the author of the text I have used A/Col for the author of Colossians. There are naturally many references to the *Haustafel*, Household Code (5.22–6.9) and I have used for this the abbreviation HT. The abbreviations for biblical books are those of the series; I have also used Ψ and Kgdms where I have wished to draw special attention to the Greek text of the OT.

I need to explain the differences between this commentary and my commentary on Ephesians in the ICC series. Unlike my commentary on Ephesians in the ICC series which was designed for the academic reader, this briefer commentary is intended for more general readers. Consequently much of the detail beloved by academics has been dropped here. There is thus no discussion of the Greek text and the commentary is based on the English translation provided in the ICC volume.

The chronological list of Commentaries from the ICC has been reproduced, to remind the reader that scholars have devoted themselves to explaining the Epistle to the Ephesians from the third century down to the present day. Information about many of these authors can be found in such reference books as *The Oxford Dictionary of the Christian Church*. Whenever a scholar is referred to by name in the text of this commentary, that name will be found either in the chronological list of commentaries or in the succeeding alphabetical list of works referred to that are not commentaries on Ephesians.

Most people when they see a building being erected see it surrounded by a mass of scaffolding. It is only when the scaffolding is removed that the true shape and beauty of the building are revealed. The academic detail can be likened to the scaffolding. All the beauty and importance of the letters are fully revealed within.

Finally my thanks are due to all at T&T Clark for their careful preparation of my material for the printers, and to my daughter Dr Mary Popple, and her husband Andrew, for continual assistance with computing problems, and to Professor J. C. O'Neill for assistance in the abbreviation from the ICC commentary.

LITERATURE

Commentaries in Chronological Order

Origen: J. A. F. Gregg, 'The Commentary of Origen upon the Epistle to the Ephesians', *JTS* 3 (1901–2) 233–44, 398–420, 554–76

Marius Victorinus: MPL 8, 1235–94

Ephraem of Syria: *S. Ephraemi Syri commentarii in ep. D. Pauli*, Venice, 1893, 140–56

Ambrosiaster: CSEL 81, 71–126

Chrysostom: MPG 62, 9–176; and *Interpretatio Omnium Epistolarum Paulinarum*, IV, Oxford, 1852, 104–419

Jerome: MPL 26, 467–590

Theodore of Mopsuestia: MPG 66; and H. P. Swete, *Theodore of Mopsuestia on the Minor Epistles of S. Paul*, I, Cambridge, 1880, 112–96

Severian of Gabala: K. Staab, *Pauluskommentare aus der griechischen Kirche*, Münster, 1983, 304–13

Pelagius: *Texts and Studies* IX, Cambridge, 1922, 344–86 (ed. A. Souter)

Theodoret of Cyrrhus: MPG 82, 505–58

John of Damascus: MPG 92, 821–56

Oecumenius: MPG 118, 1169–256

Theophylact: MPG 124, 1031–138

Oecumenius of Tricca: Staab, op. cit., 448–52

Primasius: MPL 68, 607–26

Photius of Constantinople: Staab, op. cit., 611–21

Thomas Aquinas, *Opera Omnia* (ed. S. E. Fretté et P. Maré), XXI, Paris, 1876, 260–343

Grotius, Annotationeas Novi Testamenti, 1624

Erasmus, D., *Opera*, VI, Leiden, 1705, 831–60

Calvin, J., CR 79, 141–240

Beza T. de, *Annotationes majores in Novum Testamentum*, 1594

Zanchius, H., *Commentarius in Epistolam Sancti Pauli ad Ephesios*, c. 1605, (reprint) Amsterdam, 1888

Locke, J., *A Paraphrase and Notes on the Epistles of St Paul to the Galatians, 1 and 2 Corinthians, Romans, Ephesians*, 1707 (reprinted, Oxford, 1987, II, 607–61)

Bengel, J. A., *Gnomon Novi Testamenti* (Tübingen, 1773): Textis recusa adjuvente J. Steudel, Tübingen, 1850, III, 256–84

Harless, G. C. A., *Commentar über den Brief Pauli an die Ephesier*, Erlangen, 1834

Meyer, H. A. W., *An die Epheser* (KEK), Göttingen, 1843

Eadie, J., *Commentary on the Epistle to the Ephesians*, 1854[1], 1883[3] (reprinted Minneapolis, 1977)

Hofmann, J. C. K., *Der Brief Pauli an die Epheser*, Nördlingen, 1870

Ellicott, C. J., *The Epistles of Saint Paul*, 1854[1] (reprinted Andover, 1884)

Barry, A., *Galatians, Ephesians, and Philippians*, London, n.d.

Hodge, C., *A Commentary of the Epistle to the Ephesians*, 1856 (reprinted Grand Rapids, 1980)

Alford, H., *The Greek Testament, Ephesians*, 1849–61, with revision by E. F. Harrison, Chicago, 1968, III, 6–26, 68–151

Beck, J., *Erklärung des Briefes an die Epheser*, Gütersloh, 1891

Macpherson, J., *Commentary on St. Paul's Epistle to the Ephesians*, Edinburgh, 1892

Findlay, G. G., *The Epistle to the Ephesians*, London, 1892

Soden, H. von, *Die Briefe an die Kolosser, Epheser, Philemon; die Pastoralbriefe* (Hand-Commentar zum NT), Freiburg, 1893[2]

Wohlenberg, G., *Die Briefe an die Epheser, an die Colosser, an Philemon und an die Philipper ausgelegt*, Munich, 1895

Abbott, T. K., *The Epistles to the Ephesians and to the Colossians* (ICC), Edinburgh, 1897, 1–191

Haupt, E., *Die Gefangenschaftsbriefe* (KEK), Göttingen, 1897

Dale, R. W., *The Epistle to the Ephesians*, London, 1901

Gore, C., *St. Paul's Epistle to the Ephesians*, London, 1902

Robinson, J. A., *St Paul's Epistle to the Ephesians*, 1903[1], 1904[2]

Westcott, B. F., *Saint Paul's Epistle to the Ephesians*, 1906 (reprinted Grand Rapids, 1979)

Belser, J., *Der Epheserbrief des Apostels Paulus*, Freiburg, 1908

Henle, F. A. von, *Der Epheserbrief des hl. Apostels Paulus*, Augsburg, 1908

Ewald, P., *Die Briefe des Paulus an die Epheser, Kolosser und Philemon*[2], Leipzig, 1910, 1–262

Salmond, S. D. F., *The Epistle to the Ephesians* (Expositor's Greek Testament III), London, 1910, 201–395

Dibelius, M., *An die Kolosser, Epheser, an Philemon* (Handbuch zum NT 12), 1913[1], Revised edn of H. Greeven, Tübingen, 1953, 54–100

Murray, J. O. F., *The Epistle to the Ephesians*, Cambridge, 1914

Vosté, J.-M., *Commentarius in Epistolam ad Ephesios*, Rome and Paris, 1921

Lock, W., *The Epistle to the Ephesians*, London, 1929

Scott, E. F., *The Epistles of Paul to the Colossians, to Philemon and to the Ephesians*, London, 1930, 117–257

Erdman, C. R., *The Epistle of Paul to the Ephesians*, Philadelphia, 1931

Synge, F. C., *St. Paul's Epistle to the Ephesians*, London, 1941

Könn, J., *Die Idee der Kirche. Bibellesungen über den Epheserbrief*, Cologne, 1946

Huby, J. S., *Paul. Les Épîtres de la captivité*, Paris, 1947, 127–259

Asmussen, H., *Der Brief des Paulus an die Epheser*, Breklum, 1949

Masson, C., *L'Épître de saint Paul aux Éphésiens* (CNT IX), Neuchâtel, 1953, 133–228

Beare, F. W., *The Epistle to the Ephesians*, Interpreter's Bible, X, 1953, 595–749

Rendtorff, H., *Der Brief an die Epheser* (NTD 8), Göttingen, 1955, 56–85

Simpson, E. K. (with F. F. Bruce), *Commentary on the Epistles to the Ephesians and Colossians* (NICNT), Grand Rapids, 1957, 15–157

Allan, J. A., *The Epistle to the Ephesians*, London, 1959

Benoit, P., *Les Épîtres de Saint Paul aux Philippiens, à Philemon, aux Colossiens, aux Éphésians*[4], Paris, 1959, 74–108

Grosheide, F. W., *De Brief van Paulus aan de Efeziers*, Kampen, 1960

Rienecker, F., *Der Brief des Paulus an die Epheser*, Wuppertal, 1961

Zerwick, M., *Der Brief an die Epheser*, Düsseldorf, 1962

Foulkes, F., *Ephesians*, Leicester, 1963

Schlatter, A., *Der Brief an die Epheser*, Stuttgart, 1963 (first edn 1909)

Staab, K. (with J. Freundorfer), *Die Thessalonicherbriefe, die Gefangenschaftsbriefe, die Pastoralbriefe* (RNT), Regensburg, 1965, 114–66

Dahl, N. A. et alii, *Kurze Auslegung des Epheserbriefes*, Göttingen, 1965

Gaugler, E., *Der Epheserbrief*, Zürich, 1966

Hendriksen, W., *Ephesians*, Carlisle, Penn, 1967

Thompson, G. H. P., *The Letters of Paul to the Ephesians, to the Colossians and to Philemon*, Cambridge, 1967

Houlden, J. H., *Paul's Letters from Prison*, London, 1970, 233–341

Gnilka, J., *Der Epheserbrief* (HTK), Freiburg, Basel, Vienna, 1971

Schlier, H., *Der Brief an die Epheser*[7], Düsseldorf, 1971

Conzelmann, H., *Die kleineren Briefe des Apostels Paulus* (Das Neue Testament Deutsch 8), Göttingen, 1972, 56–91

Hugedé, N., *L'Épître aux Éphésiens*, Geneva, 1973

Καραβιδοπουλος, Ι. Δ. Ἑρμηνεία τῆς πρὸς Ἐφεσίους τοῦ Ἀποστόλου Παύλου, Thessalonica, 1973

Bouwman, G., *De Brief aan de Efesiërs*, Bussum, 1974

Ernst, J., *Die Briefe an die Philipper, an Philemon, an die Kolosser, an die Epheser* (RNT), Regensburg, 1974, 245–405

Barth, M., *Ephesians* (Anchor), 2 vols., New York, 1974

Taylor, W. F. (with J. Reumann), *Ephesians, Colossians*, Minneapolis, 1975

Roon, A. van, *De Brief van Paulus aan de Epheziers*, Nijkerk, 1976

Caird, G. B., *Paul's Letters from Prison*, Oxford, 1976, 9–94

Mitton, C. L., *Ephesians* (NCB), London, 1976

Stott, J. R. W., *The Message of Ephesians*, Leicester, 1979

Bratcher, R. G. and Nida, E. A., *A Translator's Handbook on Paul's Letter to the Ephesians*, London, 1982

Mussner, F., *Der Brief an die Epheser*, Gütersloh, 1982

Schnackenburg, R., *Die Brief an die Epheser*, Neukirchen-Vluyn, 1982 (ET *The Epistle to the Ephesians*, Edinburgh, 1991)

Patzia, A. G., *Colossians, Philemon, Ephesians*, San Francisco, 1984, 102–276

Bruce, F. F., *The Epistles to the Colossians, to Philemon and to the Ephesians* (NICNT), Grand Rapids, 1984, 227–416

Lindemann, A., *Der Epheserbrief*, Zürich, 1985

Penna, R., *La Lettera agli Efesini*, Bologna, 1988

Lincoln, A. T., *Ephesians* (Word), Dallas, 1990

Roberts, J. H., *Die Brief aan die Efesiërs*, Kaapstad, RSA, 1990

Bouttier, M., *L'Épître de saint Paul aux Éphésiens* (CNT IX), Geneva, 1991

Martin, R. P., *Ephesians, Colossians and Philemon* (Interpretation), Louisville, 1992, 1–79

Pokorný, P., *Der Brief des Paulus an die Epheser*, Leipzig, 1992

Kitchen, M., *Ephesians*, London, 1994

Best, Ernest, *A Critical and Exegetical Commentary on Ephesians* (ICC), Edinburgh, 1998

Muddiman, John, *The Epistle to the Ephesians* (Black's), London, 2001

Other Literature Cited by Author's Name

Adai, J., *Der Heilige Geist als Gegenwart Gottes in den einzelnen Christen in der Kirche und in der Welt*, Frankfurt am Main, 1985

Allen, T. G., 'The Body of Christ Concept in Ephesians' (unpublished Ph.D. thesis, University of Glasgow, 1982)

Arnold, C. E., *Ephesians: Power and Magic* (SNTSMS 63), Cambridge, 1989

Bankhead, R. C., *Liturgical Formulas in the New Testament*, Clinton, S. Carolina, 1971

Barton, S. C. and Horsley, G. R. G., 'A Hellenistic Cult Group and the New Testament Churches', *JAC* 24 (1981) 3–41

Batey, R. A., 'Jewish Gnosticism and the "Hieros Gamos" of Eph. v. 21–33', *NTS* 10 (1963/4) 121–7

Berger, K., *Formgeschichte des Neuen Testaments*, Heidelberg, 1984

'Hellenistiche Gattungen im Neuen Testament', *ANRW* II 25.2, 1031–1432, 1831–85

Theologiegeschichte des Urchristentums, Tübingen and Basel, 1994

Best, E., *One Body in Christ*, London, 1955
1 Peter, London, 1971
1 & 2 Thessalonians, London, 1972
'Ephesians i.1', *Text and Interpretation* (FS M. Black, ed. E. Best and R. McL. Wilson), Cambridge, 1979, 29–41*
'Dead in Trespasses and Sins (Eph 2.1)', *JSNT* 13 (1981) 9–25*
'Ephesians 1.1 Again', *Paul and Paulinism* (FS C. K. Barrett, ed. M. D. Hooker and S. G. Wilson), London, 1982, 273–9*
'Paul's Apostolic Authority – ?', *JSNT* 27 (1986) 3–25*
'Recipients and Title of the Letter to the Ephesians: Why and When the Designation "Ephesians"?', *ANRW* II 25.4, 3247–79
'The Revelation to Evangelize the Gentiles', *JTS* 35 (1984) 1–30*
Paul and His Converts, Edinburgh, 1988
The Temptation and the Passion (SNTSMS 2), 2nd edn, Cambridge, 1990
'Ephesians 2.11–22: A Christian View of Judaism', *Text as Pretext* (FS R. Davidson, ed. R. P. Carroll), Sheffield, 1992, 47–60*
'The Use of Credal and Liturgical Material in Ephesians', *Worship, Theology and Ministry in the Early Church* (FS R. P. Martin, ed. M. J. Wilkins and T. Paige), Sheffield, 1992, 53–69*
'Thieves in the Church', *IrishBS* 14 (1992) 2–9*
Interpreting Christ, Edinburgh, 1993
Ephesians (New Testament Guides), Sheffield, 1993
'Ephesians: Two Types of Existence', *Int* 47 (1993) 39–51*
'Ministry in Ephesians', *IrishBS* 15 (1993) 146–66*
'The Haustafel in Ephesians', *IrishBS* 16 (1994) 146–160*
'Who used Whom? The Relationship of Ephesians and Colossians', *NTS* 43 (1997) 72–96
Those marked * have been reprinted in *Essays on Ephesians*, Edinburgh, T&T Clark, 1997
Bultmann, R., *Theology of the New Testament*, London, 1952

Buscault, A. F., 'The "Preparation" of the Gospel of Peace', *ExpT* 9 (1897) 38–40

Caragounis, C. C., *The Ephesians Mysterion: Meaning and Content*, Lund, 1977

Carrington, P., *A Primitive Christian Catechism*, Cambridge, 1940

Cross, F. L. (ed.), *Studies in Ephesians*, London, 1956

Díaz, J. R., 'Palestinian Targum and New Testament', *NT* 6 (1963) 75–80

Dupont, J., *Gnosis. La connaissance religieuse dans les épîtres de saint Paul*, Louvain, 1949

Engberg-Pedersen, T., 'Ephesians 5, 12–13: ἐλέγχειν and Conversion in the New Testament', *ZNW* 80 (1989) 89–110

Fee, G. D., *God's Empowering Presence: The Holy Spirit in the Letters of Paul*, Peabody, Mass., 1994

Feuillet, A., *Le Christ, Sagesse de Dieu*, Paris, 1966

Fischer, K. M., *Tendenz und Absicht des Epheserbriefs* (FRLANT 111), Göttingen, 1973

Gewiess, J., 'Die Begriffe πληροῦν und πλήρωμα im Kolosser- und Epheserbrief', *Vom Wort des Lebens* (FS M. Meinertz), Münster, 1951, 128–41

Goodspeed, E. J., *The Meaning of Ephesians*, Chicago, 1933

Gordon, T. G., ' "Equipping" Ministry in Ephesians 4?', *JETS* 37 (1994), 69–78

Halter, H., *Taufe und Ethos: Paulinische Kriterien für das Proprium christlicher Moral*, Freiburg, 1977

Hamann, H. P., 'The Translation of Ephesians 4:12 – A Necessary Revision', *Concordia Journal* 14 (1988), 42–9

Hanson, A. T., *The New Testament Understanding of Scripture*, London, 1980
The Wrath of the Lamb, London, 1957

Harris, W. H., 'The Ascent and Descent of Christ in Ephesians 4:9–10', *BSac* 151 (1994), 198–214

Kirby, J. C., *Ephesians, Baptism and Pentecost*, London, 1968

Knox, W. L., *St. Paul and the Church of the Gentiles*, Cambridge, 1939

Kuhn, K. G., 'Der Epheserbrief im Lichte der Qumrantexte', *NTS* 7 (1960/1) 334–45

Larsson, E., *Christus als Vorbild*, Uppsala, 1962

Lemmer, H. R., 'Pneumatology and Eschatology in Ephesians – The Role of the Eschatological Spirit in the Church' (D.Th. dissertation, University of South Africa, 1988)

Lincoln, A. T., *Paradise Now and Not Yet* (SNTSMS 43), Cambridge, 1981
'Ephesians 2:8–10: A Summary of Paul's Gospel?', *CBQ* 45 (1983) 617–30

Lindemann, A., *Die Aufhebung der Zeit. Geschichtsverständnis und Eschatologie im Epheserbrief*, Gütersloh, 1975
Paulus im ältesten Christentum, Tübingen, 1979

Lyall, F. *Slaves, Citizens, Sons: Legal Metaphors in the Epistles*, Grand Rapids, 1984

Maillet, H., 'ALLA ... PLÉN ...', *ETL* 55 (1980) 566–79

Mare, W. H., 'Paul's Mystery in Ephesians 3', *BETS* 8 (1965), 77–84

Merkel, H., 'Der Epheserbrief in der neueren exegetisch Diskussion', ANRW II 25.4, 3156–246

Merklein, H., *Das kirchliche Amt nach dem Epheserbrief*, Munich, 1973
Christus und die Kirche, Stuttgart, 1973

Meuzelaar, J. J., *Der Leib des Messias*, Kampen, 1979

Miletic, S. F., *'One Flesh': Eph 5.22–4, 5.31. Marriage and the New Creation* (AnBib 115), Rome, 1988

Mitton, C. L., *The Epistle to the Ephesians*, Oxford, 1951

Moffatt, J., *Introduction to the Literature of the New Testament*[3], Edinburgh, 1918

Morton, A. Q., *Literary Detection*, Bath, 1978

Moule, C. F. D., *The Epistles to the Colossians and to Philemon*, Cambridge, 1957
An Idiom Book of New Testament Greek, Cambridge, 1953

Mussner, F., *Christus, das All und die Kirche*, Trier, 1955
'Beiträge aus Qumran zum Verständnis des Epheserbrief', *Neutestamentliche Aufsätze* (FS J. Schmid), Regensburg, 1963, 185–98

Nock, A. D., 'Early Gentile Christianity and its Hellenistic Background' in A. E. J. Rawlinson (ed.), *Essays on the Trinity and the Incarnation*, London, 1928, 51–156

Penna, R., *Il 'Mysterion' Paolino*, Brescia, 1978

Percy, E., *Der Leib Christi: In den paulinischen Homologumena und Antilegoumena*, Lund, 1942
Die Probleme der Kolosser und Epheserbrief, Lund, 1946

Pfammatter, J., *Die Kirche als Bau. Eine exegetisch-theologische Studie zur Ekklesiologie der Paulusbriefe*, Rome, 1960

Pokorný, P., *Der Epheserbrief und die Gnosis*, Berlin, 1965
Der Brief des Paulus an die Kolosser, Berlin, 1987

Reynier, C., *Évangile et Mystère. Les enjeux théologiques de l'Épître aux Éphésiens* (LD 149), Paris, 1992

Roberts, J. H. *Die Opbou van die Kerk volgens die Efese-brief*, Groningen, 1963

Roels, E. D., *God's Mission: The Epistle to the Ephesians in Mission Perspective*, Franeker, 1962

Romaniuk, K., *L'Amour du Père et du Fils dans la sotèriologie de Saint Paul*, Rome, 1961

Sanday, William and Headlam, Arthur C., *A Critical and Exegetical Commentary on the Epistle to the Romans* (ICC), Edinburgh, 1895, 5th edn., 1902

Sanders, J. T., 'Hymnic Elements in Ephesians 1–3', *ZNW* 56 (1965) 214–32
The New Testament Christological Hymns. Their Historical and Religious Background (SNTSMS 15), Cambridge, 1971

Schlier, H., *Christus und die Kirche im Epheserbrief*, Tübingen, 1930

Schlier, H. and Warnach, V., *Die Kirche im Epheserbrief*, Münster, Westfalen, 1949

Schmid, J., *Der Epheserbrief des Apostels Paulus. Seine Adresse, Sprache und literarischen Beziehungen*, Freiburg, 1928

Schubert, P., *Form and Function of the Pauline Thanksgivings* (BZNW 20), 1939

Selwyn, E. G., *The First Epistle of St. Peter*, London, 1946

Spicq, C., *Agape in the New Testament*, St Louis, MO, 1968 *Notes de lexicographie néotestamentaire*, 3 vols., Fribourg, 1978, 1982

Steinmetz, F. J., *Protologische Heils-Zuversicht. Die Strukturen des soteriologischen und christologischen Denkens im Kolosser und Epheserbrief*, Frankfurt am Main, 1969

Studies in Ephesians, see Cross, F. L.

Sullivan, K, 'The Mystery Revealed to Paul – Eph. 3:1–13', *Bible Today* 1 (1963), 246–54

Usami, K., *Somatic Comprehension of Unity. The Church in Ephesus* (AnBib 101), Rome, 1983

Van Roon, A., *The Authenticity of Ephesians* (SupNT 39), Leiden, 1974

Vermes, G., *The Dead Sea Scrolls in English*[3], London, 1987

Vielhauer, P., *Oikodome. Das Bild vom Bau in der christlichen Literatur vom Neuen Testament bis Clemens Alexandrinus*, Karlsruhe, 1939, and Munich, 1979

Wengst, K., *Christologische Formeln und Lieder des Urchristentums*, Gütersloh, 1972

Wink, W., *Naming the Powers*, Philadelphia, 1984

ABBREVIATIONS

Special Abbreviations

A/Col = Author of Colossians
AE = Author of Ephesians
DSS = Dead Sea Scrolls
FS = Festschrift (volume of essays dedicated to named persons)
HT = *Haustafel* or Household Code

General Abbreviations

AnBib	Analecta biblica
ANRW	*Aufstieg und Niedergang der römischen Welt* (ed. H. Temporini and W. Haase), Berlin
BETS	*Bulletin of the Evangelical Theological Society*
BSac	*Bibliotheca Sacra*
BZNW	Beihefte zur *ZNW*
CBQ	*Catholic Biblical Quarterly*
CNT	Commentaire du Nouveau Testament
CIL	*Corpus inscriptionum latinarum*
CR	Corpus Reformatorum
CRINT	*Compendium Rerum Iudaicarum ad Novum Testamentum* (ed. S. Safrai and M. Stern), Assen, 1974
CSEL	Corpus scriptorum ecclesiasticorum latinorum
ETL	*Ephemerides theologicae lovanienses*
ExpT	*Expository Times*
FRLANT	Forschungen zur Religion and Literatur des Alten und Neuen Testaments CIL *Corpus inscriptionum latinarum*
GCS	Griechische christliche Schriftsteller
HTK	Herders Theologischer Kommentar zum Neuen Testament
ICC	The International Critical Commentary
Int	*Interpretation*

IrishBS	*Irish Biblical Studies*
JAC	*Jahrbuch für Antike und Christentum*
JETS	*Journal of the Evangelical Theological Society*
JSNT	*Journal for the Study of the New Testament*
JTS	*Journal of Theological Studies*
KEK	H. A. W. Meyer, Kritisch-exegetischer Kommentar über das Neue Testament
LCL	Loeb Classical Library
LD	Lectio Divina
MPG	J.-P. Migne, *Patrologia graeca*
MPL	J.-P. Migne, *Patrologia latina*
NCB	The New Century Bible Commentary
NICNT	The New International Commentary on the New Testament
NT	*Novum Testamentum*
NTD	Das Neue Testament Deutsch
NTS	*New Testament Studies*
RNT	Regensburger Neues Testament
SNTSMS	Society for New Testament Studies Monograph Series
SupNT	NT Supplement Series
ZNW	*Zeitschrift für die neutestamentliche Wissenschaft*

INTRODUCTION

Ephesians was written to believers; these did not necessarily live in Ephesus (see on 1. 1f) but were either (a) members in a group of Christian communities which we cannot identify but which probably lay in Asia Minor (cf 1 Peter) and may possibly have included the community at Ephesus, or (b) Christians in general, though probably those in a restricted area like Asia Minor. The letter itself does not supply us with sufficient information to make a final decision between these possibilities, let alone to determine the exact geographical location of the readers. In favour of (a) is the implication that Tychicus was sent with the letter (6. 21f) and must have known where he was going; but the reference to Tychicus may only be part of AE's pseudonymous framework. In favour of (b) are the absence of any kind of greeting, the very general nature of both the address ('to the saints and faithful') and the conclusion ('peace be to the brothers'). Hypothesis (b) is probably, but by no means certainly, to be preferred. If however (a) is chosen then the communities AE has in mind were probably a number of churches in different cities rather than a number of house churches in one particular city.

AE's use of the OT might imply his readers were Jewish Christians but since a large portion of the argument of the letter relates to the acceptance of Gentiles as believers and since the readers are addressed in the second plural as Gentiles who have forsaken pagan ways (2.1f; 3.1; 4.17), the majority of them must have been Gentiles. Were there however no Jewish believers among them (cf Barth)? Many of the terms used about the readers (e.g. 1.1, saints, faithful) had been first applied by Jewish Christians to themselves. Gentiles are sometimes referred to in the third person (3.6, 8) (cf Roels). The author himself was a Jewish Christian. There was indeed a large Jewish population in Asia Minor, the probable area of destination of the epistle. It is difficult to believe that even by the end of the first century, if Ephesians is as late as that, there were churches in which there were no Jewish Christians.

Already long before the rise of the historical-critical method, Erasmus in the brief introductory sentences to his commentary remarked on the difference in style between Ephesians and the other Paulines. There is a large number of long sentences: Moffatt lists 1.3–14; 1.15–22; 2.1–7; 2.11–13; 2.14–16; 2.19–22; 3.1–7; 3.8–12; 3.14–19; 4.1–6; 4.11–16; 4.17–19; 4.22–4; 5.3–5; 5.18–23; 5.25–7; 6.1–3; 6.5–8; 6.14–20. Many of these are difficult to disentangle because of the multitude of clauses within them. Noticeable also are the number of sequences of genitives: Percy lists 1.9; 1.13; 1.17; 1.18; 2.2; 2.3; 2.12; 2.15; 3.2; 3.7; 3.9; 3.11; 3.21; 4.3; 4.4; 4.12; 4.13; 4.14; 4.22; 4.24; 4.29; 4.30; 5.6; 5.8; 5.9; 5.11; 5.26; 6.12; 6.15; 6.19. There is only one question in Ephesians (4.9), though questions are frequent in Paul.

Sanday and Headlam (*Romans* ICC, 1v), who accept the authenticity of Ephesians, summarise well the difference between Ephesians and Romans:

> The difference is not so much a difference of ideas and of vocabulary as a difference of structure and composition ... The sense of dissimilarity reaches its height when we turn from the materials (if we may so speak) of the style to the way in which they are put together. [In contrast to the vivacity of Romans] we have a slowly-moving onwards-advancing mass, like a glacier working its way inch by inch down the valley. The periods are of unwieldy length; the writer seems to stagger under his load.

Can objective tests be devised? Those who counted the proportion of *hapax legomena* in the Pauline letters believed this was an objective test but this test is of no help in relation to Ephesians. The objectivity of this test derives from the element of counting. Are there other factors in writing which can be measured in a similar objective manner and are not dependent on content or the age of the author? It has long been recognised that such factors probably exist, e.g. sentence length, but in the past they were too difficult to calculate because of the immense labour in counting every item individually. The use of the computer has changed this. The first to realise this and to employ the computer was A. Q. Morton; in a series of books and articles, many in conjunction with S. Michaelson, he has discussed among other ancient writings the Pauline letters. Morton has widened the type of tests he has initially used but has seen no reason to alter his original position that the only genuine Paulines are Romans,

1, 2 Corinthians, Galatians, with the possible addition of Philemon (its brevity makes a definite decision impossible).

If AE is not Paul, why does he write in Paul's name? Is this not dishonest? Pseudonymity undoubtedly existed in the ancient world; it needs to be distinguished from: (1) anonymous authorship (it should be recognised that books which we regard as anonymous may originally have had a name attached to them which has not survived); (2) the use of a pen-name, i.e. the adoption by authors of names other than their own under which to write; (3) plagiarism, where authors take something written by someone else and apply their own names to it. Pseudonymous writing takes place when authors choose to write under the names of people whom their readers already know and respect, and who, normally, are dead.

It cannot be denied that pseudonymous writing existed in the ancient world: the disciples of Pythagoras wrote much which they attributed to him; plays were written in the names of the earlier great Greek dramatists; it is widely held that Plato did not pen all the letters attributed to him, though it is not agreed which are genuine.

It is generally accepted that many OT books were not written in their entirety by their supposed authors; Isaiah may have written part of the prophecy attributed to him but others made additions. First-century Christians were hardly aware of this. However they were familiar with later Jewish pseudonymous writings which came into being in or around their period. Among them were apocalyptic writings like the Enochic literature and 4 Ezra and some writings in the wisdom tradition; though it is not explicitly said that Solomon composed the Wisdom of Solomon this can be deduced from its contents (it is written by a king who built a temple and describes events which happened in Solomon's lifetime); also pseudonymous are the Sentences of Pseudo-Phocylides written around the turn of the era in Ionic dialect. The process of creating pseudonymous literature was thus in being among Jews at or near the time Ephesians was being written and its author was a Jew.

In the century after Christ Christians created pseudonymous literature. The *Kerygma Petri*, of which only fragments remain, was intended to be an account of Peter's preaching and for a time some believers accepted it. The last few verses of the *Gospel of Peter* attribute that writing to him. Col 4.16 led to the composition of a letter allegedly by Paul to Laodicea. The *Protevangelium of James* is attributed to James. The *Gospel of Thomas* may in its present form be much later than these but it has clearly evolved from an earlier form.

If Christians lived in the Jewish atmosphere which produced pseudonymous literature and in the second century themselves produced that kind of literature, we have to ask whether it is impossible that they should have done so in the first century. 2 Th 2.2, whether 2 Thessalonians is by Paul or not, proves the existence of such literature in the first century.

If AE, or other first-century Christian pseudonymous authors, had been asked to justify what they did, they might have replied that they were doing nothing other than what their contemporaries did and that they wrote to help other believers with no personal gain for themselves. AE in particular might also have defended himself on the grounds that at times when Paul was unable to visit his churches he sent someone from the circle of his assistants to represent him; AE might even have been at one time a member of that circle and gone on missions for Paul. Moreover AE does not write with the intention to deceive, but only to instruct Christians in the new situations in which they were finding themselves in the way Paul would have done had he still been alive. That AE's teaching diverges at times from Paul's does not invalidate such a conclusion, for all the writings of the NT differ in points from one another. Had Tertullian been told that Ephesians had been written by a disciple of Paul he would have had no difficulty in accepting it, for he accepted the Gospels of Mark and Luke because they were written by the disciples, respectively, of Peter and Paul, saying that the works which disciples publish belong to their masters (*adv Marc* II 5.3–4).

It is important to point out that though we shall be examining possible differences between Ephesians and the generally accepted Paulines this should not be taken to imply that there are not also great similarities. Since most, if not all, of the writers of the NT held to a set of central beliefs there is bound to be very much which will be common between Paul and any NT writing;

thus to prove a similarity of thought on some particular point between Ephesians and Paul tells us very little.

The church forms one of the main themes of Ephesians and it is appropriate to begin with it (for full details see Essay: The Church). While AE's teaching on it can be said to be in line with Paul's and not to depart from his major emphases but only to represent a development, yet there are considerable differences. There is a change of emphasis because Ephesians writes about the universal church rather than individual congregations and the head is no longer one member among others but is Christ. The latter difference is shared with Colossians; as for the former, Colossians is interested both in the local church and the universal. Significant also is the way in which the church rather than Christ occupies the centre of attention. Whereas Paul relates the eucharist to the unity of believers (1 Cor 10.16f; 11.17ff) and Ephesians stresses unity, especially in 4.4–6, AE does not mention the eucharist. While Paul's genuine letters show him as the historical founder of particular churches, in Ephesians apostles and prophets are depicted theologically as the foundation of the universal church (2.20); in Paul the foundation was Christ (1 Cor 3.11) and the prophets function as guides to the existing church (1 Cor 14.3, 5, 6, etc.) and not as part of its foundation. This is a variation which Ephesians does not share with Colossians. Ephesians differs significantly from the earlier Paulines in the place given to the continuance of Israel in which unlike Paul AE has no interest (see Detached Note: Israel and the Church); yet it must be acknowledged that Paul had once before changed his position, as a comparison of 1 Th 2.14–16 and Rom 9–11 shows.

Already in Paul there are signs that he saw the whole cosmos as the object of God's redeeming love (Rom 8.19–21; Phil 2.9–11); this becomes much clearer in Colossians and Ephesians (see on 1.10). In line with this Christ is given a greater cosmic role, again in both Ephesians and Colossians, than in the earlier Paulines (see on 1.10, 22f; 3.10; 4.10). This cosmic interest may account for the proportionally greater prominence given to the powers than in the earlier Paulines. Interestingly Ephesians and Colossians present a cosmos without an underworld whereas one is customary in Paul (e.g. Phil 2.10). The essence of Paul's teaching on salvation through God's grace and not through works is seen in 2.8–10, but the terms in which it is expressed are recast and at one point 'works' is used with a good sense. This is a theme, however, which is hardly mentioned in Colossians.

In Ephesians salvation as present fact is stressed much more strongly than in Paul in that believers are viewed as already raised from death and seated in the heavenlies (2.6). Future expectation accordingly receives much less attention though it does not disappear (1.18; 4.4; the reference to hope in 1.12; 2.12 do not relate to a final future hope but to the expectation of Gentile Christians that they have the same position in God's plan as Jewish Christians); the parousia is not mentioned. Ephesians does not echo Paul's sense of the transitoriness of the world (1 Cor 7.31). In other letters Paul shows himself, and by inference all believers, as weak and in continual need of the grace and strength of God (2 Cor 4.7ff; 6.3ff; 12.9); AE never mentions this element in his depiction of the Christian life. Equally missing is any trace of an internal struggle in believers which is set out so eloquently in Rom 7.7ff; AE does not feel obliged to grapple with the place of the Law in God's plan of salvation or with the continuance of Israel (see on 2.15).

Perhaps the most significant variation from the earlier Paulines lies in the ethical area (see Essay: Moral Teaching). In the light of the restriction in Ephesians of the HT to households consisting entirely of believers it is very difficult to see Paul as either compiling such a code or, if he received it in the tradition, embodying it in what he writes (see Best, 'Haustafel'). It would be equally difficult to see him ignoring the relation of believers to the world in which they live; Ephesians however shows them neither as under pressure from it nor as affecting it in any way; in particular Ephesians lacks a missionary impulse; in this it also contrasts with Colossians (see Col 4.5f). While Paul sees all sections of humanity as standing in an equal relation to God (1 Cor 12.13; Gal 3.28) AE is only concerned about the reconciling of Jews and Gentiles.

The external data suggest a date between AD 60 and AD 90. The lack of evidence for knowledge of Ephesians until Ignatius and Polycarp and certain internal data would suggest a date towards the end of that period.

Is Ephesians a genuine letter? Many alternative suggestions have been made. Roughly speaking the views of those who do not regard Ephesians as a genuine letter may be classified as follows: (a) a tractate, with which should be associated a theological essay as being similar (Schlier), (b) a liturgical writing (e.g. Kirby), (c) a meditation (Conzelmann), (d) a speech, (e) a homily, with which should be included the possibility that it is a sermon. In each case it is assumed that for some reason it has been turned into a letter.

(a) is justified because of the detailed theological discussions of the nature of the church and the reconciliation of Jewish and Gentile believers, yet it fails to account for the presence of extensive passages of devotional and paraenetic material. Advocates of (b) stress the extensive devotional material. Too little is known of the liturgies of the period for a firm conclusion to be drawn here, and a distinction has to be made between the use of liturgical language and a liturgy itself; the references to baptism are too few for it to have been a baptismal liturgy; since baptism would have been seen as a significant event in their lives by Christians who had been converted from paganism, it would not be surprising to find some references to it in any Christian writing. The presence of only one direct baptismal reference (4.5) also renders it unlikely that it represents a sermon preached at the baptism of new converts (cf Caragounis). Had it been a eucharistic sermon there would have been some reference to the eucharist, yet there is none. (c) fails for the same reason as (a), the amount of paraenetic material. (d) is supported by the final main section, 6.10–17, which resembles a peroration and by the material in the main body of the letter which instructs and persuades to action; yet the prayer in the middle (3.14–21) and the opening eulogy would have been inappropriate to a speech; praise of the addressees at the start would be, but not praise of God.

This leaves (e) as the most probable, for a homily could contain devotional material, theological discussion, narrative and moral counselling. A homily would also normally lack precise reference to the circumstances of the recipients for they would never be the same. A homily could of course have originated as a sermon from which for purposes of wider circulation passages relevant to the original delivery would have been removed. The NT contains other homilies: Hebrews, James, Jude, though in some way they are made to appear as letters. It should be remembered that NT letters, with the possible exception of Philemon, were never intended for private reading; they would be read aloud at gatherings for worship and so the characteristics of 'letter' would be forgotten, especially if, as in the case of Ephesians, these characteristics were not emphasised. But is it possible to regard Ephesians as a homily which has later been turned into a sermon by the addition of epistolary openings and conclusions? Certainly the introductory address (1.1f) bears little relation to the content of the letter, and could have been added later but the conclusion, 6.18–24, flows easily from what precedes and thus does not appear to be a later addition. It seems best then to think of AE as intending to write a homily but, realising that Paul normally wrote letters, deliberately disguising his homily as a letter. It is consequently of mixed genre.

Although Ephesians contains only one verse (4.14) which sounds polemical this has not prevented suggestions as to false positions against which AE may have directed his letter. Following on the work of the *Religionsgeschichtliche Schule*, many have seen Ephesians as intended to refute a growing gnosticism. Evidence of this was seen in gnostic belief in a wall dividing heaven and earth; if however AE found and changed a reference to such a wall in the supposed hymn underlying 2.14–18 he was not supporting gnosticism but eliminating it (see on 2.14–18). Gnostic tones have been detected in other passages and are discussed in the relevant notes (see on 2.19–22; Detached Note: The Body of Christ; on 5.22–33). If there appear to be gnostic elements in Ephesians it is much more likely that AE has used some terms which, if not then, later became current in gnostic thought in order to express his own ideas, because these terms were known to his readers and their use would enable them to understand his message.

Because the letter pays so much attention to the relationship of Jewish and Gentile Christians, many view it as intended to deal with that relationship. At the time of its composition there was a considerable Jewish population in Asia Minor, some of whom naturally became Christians. All the first believers also had been Jews and many of them had opposed the acceptance of Gentiles as their equals in the church. Arguments about this may not have wholly died down by AE's time and so he writes both to reassure his Gentile readers that they have a full and legitimate place in the church and to justify Paul's work in arguing for their admission. It cannot be denied that AE may have been thinking of Jewish-Gentile relationships as he wrote and this may have been a subsidiary purpose, yet it occupies too small a proportion of the letter to be its main purpose.

Was there a general situation which provoked the letter? We can only hazard a guess. All those entering the church from paganism came from membership in various groups, either from groups related to their work such as trade guilds or groups concerned in different ways with the ongoing life of the community or cult groups. They would have participated in at least some of these. Now as Christians they have entered a new group and it is important that they should realise its nature and the conduct required of them in it.

I

SALUTATION

(1.1–2)

**¹ Paul, apostle of Christ Jesus by the will of God
to saints and believers in Christ Jesus,
² grace to you and peace
from God our Father and the Lord Jesus Christ.**

Paul, at least from the time of his earliest extant letter, used with modifications the ancient letter form, approximating more closely to Near Eastern than to Hellenistic usage. Later Christian letter writers followed him in this (1.1f; Col 1.1f; 1 Pet 1.1f; 2 Pet 1.1f; Jude 1f; cf 1 Clem 1.1; the letters of Ignatius). The genuine Paulines differ in minor ways from each other. That Eph 1.1f differs slightly from the others thus gives no clue as to whether Paul wrote it or not. If it is not Pauline its author certainly knew Colossians and some of the other letters, e.g. Romans, 1 Corinthians, Philemon, and would have picked up the form from them. Similarity to Colossians is most noticeable through the use of **believers**, yet Ephesians differs from that letter in (i) the non-use of 'brothers' and (ii) the absence of a co-author. The address is less extensive than in some of Paul's other letters (Rom 1.1–7; Gal 1.1–5; 1 Cor 1.1–3). AE must have deliberately chosen the epistolary form to introduce what he writes even though it is probably not a genuine letter and certainly not a personal letter addressed to a single person or group of people and dealing with their problems. It is equally not a letter addressed to people in general, for it is assumed that all its readers are Christians, and probably that they are of Gentile and not Jewish origin. AE could have in mind all believers or all believers in a particular area. It has a certain air of impersonality as can be seen in the concluding benediction where the recipients are addressed in the third person and not the second as elsewhere in Paul. It is doubtful if AE was thinking of a precise group of people, other than Gentile Christians.

1. If Paul did not write the letter then its author has given it at the outset his authority, and in particular his authority as apostle. The use of a title lends a kind of official nature to the letter (Schlier), though of course only to those who acknowledge the title. This 'official' nature goes well with the unique position accorded Paul in 3.3, 7ff. **Apostle** has a considerable range of meaning. At one extreme it indicates a member of the Twelve, among whom there was no place for Paul; Rev 21.12–14 with its twelve gates also understands it in this way. In Luke and Acts **apostle** generally designates one of the Twelve, though in Acts 14.4, 14 Paul is termed an apostle, but Barnabas is described as an apostle at the same time. At the other extreme the word simply means 'messenger' (Jn 13.16; Phil 2.25; 2 Cor 8.23). Between these extremes Andronicus and Junia are counted as apostles (Rom 16.7) and Paul describes himself as an apostle but places alongside himself in the same category Silvanus and Timothy (1 Th 2.6). In Rom 1.1 and Gal 1.1 he terms himself an apostle and also in 1 Cor 1.1; 2 Cor 1.1 where, though associating others with himself, he does not apply the word to them. In Phil 1.1; 1 Th 1.1; 2 Th 1.1 (if genuine); Philem 1 he does not use the term at all. In what circumstances does he then use it? He may have used it in the first instance in 1 Th 2.6 because it indicated he had been sent by Christ; elsewhere he seems to use it whenever he feels his position is challenged by those who say he is inferior to other leaders, in particular inferior to the Twelve (1, 2 Corinthians, Galatians). He makes the same claim in Romans, but by the time he wrote this letter to people he had never visited he was aware that there were those who challenged his position and he therefore needed to tell them that he was in no way inferior to those who regularly used the term of themselves. It appears that he found it more and more necessary to apply the term to himself, yet at no point where he does so does he issue commands or directions to those he addresses. It is arguable that if he had been asked to choose a word to describe himself he would have preferred 'father' or 'parent' (1 Cor 4.14ff; Gal 4.19; 1 Th 2.7, 11; 2 Cor 6.13; 12.14; Phil 2.22; Philem 10). AE has probably used 'apostle' in Eph 1.1 because he knows Paul used it in the addresses of some of his letters, and because by the time AE wrote the word signified someone of importance and authority in the church. Yet AE's use of the terms is inconsistent, for in 3.5 (see notes there) he names a group, the apostles and prophets, of which Paul (see 3.3) is clearly not a member and where the apostles are the Twelve. The same is probably true of 2.20 (see notes there); Paul was not a part of the foundation of the church as were the Twelve who had been selected by the incarnate Christ. All this makes it difficult to know what AE means when in 1.1 he calls Paul an apostle. He certainly regards his apostleship as derived from Christ Jesus; Paul is not someone who stands alone and whose authority lies within himself. He also appears to assume that an apostle is someone with authority so that he becomes a guarantor of the tradition (Merklein).

Whether or not the Christian use of apostle derives from Hebrew *shaliach*, Paul viewed himself as the representative or ambassador of Christ; it was not a position to which he had appointed himself; God chose him (Gal 1.1, 12f; cf Eph 4.11). He represents Christ because it is God's will. His authority does not rest on his claim to be equal with Peter, John and James but on God's appointment.

According to ancient epistolography once a writer has identified himself he also identifies those to whom he is writing and AE does this here, yet the identification is uncertain for the textual tradition varies. The vast majority of manuscripts and Fathers read 'to the saints, the ones being in Ephesus, and believers in Christ Jesus' (the A text), but the uncorrected reading of two excellent early manuscripts (Codex Sinaiticus; Codex Vaticanus) gives, 'to the Saints, the ones being, and believers in Christ Jesus' [and this is scarcely possible to translate]. The excellent early Chester Beatty Papyrus reads, 'to the saints being [there, in some locality] and believers in Christ Jesus'. In addition it should be noted that all the textual traditions give the superscription as 'To the Ephesians'. As we begin to assess this evidence it is important to realise that AE was someone who was able to write intelligibly and therefore must have written something sensible which people could easily understand; also whatever he wrote must accord with the general non-specific nature of the content of the letter.

Although the A text can be translated it is very difficult to find a satisfactory meaning for it. It relates the place name only to

3

'saints' (contrast Col 1.2) and so creates two groups, the saints who are in Ephesus and the believers who are in Christ Jesus. There are no traces elsewhere in the letter of two groups apart from Jews and Gentiles, or Jewish Christians and Gentile Christians. It is however impossible to equate these with the two nouns, for when AE uses **saints** elsewhere it includes both Jewish and Gentile Christians (1.18; 3.8; 4.12; 5.3); there is also no reason why one group should be given a geographical location and the other a theological. It is even more difficult to accept this reading with its reference to Ephesus if we assume Paul is the author, for he was largely responsible for the existence of the church in Ephesus, yet the author of this letter neither knows his readers nor do they know him (1.15; 3.2; 4.20f). The limitation of the readers to one church also runs into difficulty with the non-specific nature of the letter's content. Almost all this applies equally even if with Marcion we assume the letter was written to Laodicea. To overcome these problems it has been suggested that the letter was a circular letter and that there was a gap where 'in Ephesus' appears; when Tychicus carried the letter from one church to another he filled in the gap with the appropriate name, which would have been Laodicea in the copy Marcion possessed. Most of the difficulties listed above still apply. In addition, no examples can be found from the ancient world containing such a gap.

The non-specific nature of the letter and the absence of identifiable communities suggest the original address was general and we conjecture a reading not found in any manuscript: 'to the saints and believers in Christ Jesus'. This would fulfil the requirement that AE wrote intelligibly.

Another problem however still remains in relation to the word Ephesus in the address. If the letter had no original geographical identification, why was Ephesus chosen when it was decided that a name was necessary? There is no reason to assume that the scribe who inserted the name did not believe that Paul wrote the letter. Did he not realise that the author is supposed to have no knowledge of the community, or communities, to which it was written, and Paul had a close association with the Ephesian church? Other scribes may have inserted the names of other cities. Marcion either inserted Laodicea or found it in the manuscript he used. It is possible other manuscripts contained other names. Why was Ephesus inserted in some manuscripts and why has it survived as the most common identification? A number of suggestions have been made, none very satisfactory. Presumably when the Pauline letters were first brought together as a whole, Ephesus was already present in the manuscript in use, but how did it get there? (1) When the letter had been written it was sent to Ephesus for copying and distribution and the name then became associated with it. (2) Ephesus was the most important city in Asia but no letter had been written to it, so it was picked for the nameless letter. (3) The letter was written in Ephesus and distributed from there and so the name of that city was applied to it. (4) Ignatius wrote a letter to Ephesus which has some similarities with our letter; in writing his letter he must have used ours and therefore our letter must have been sent to Ephesus. (5) Paul had written a letter to Ephesus but it was lost; our letter without a geographical identification was known and it was assumed it must have been the lost letter.

Returning now to the proposed original address 'to the saints and believers in Christ Jesus', we can see that there is no suggestion of two groups but of one described with two words (they have a common article). **Saints** is a term frequently used of all Christians (for other possible meanings see on 1.18; 2.19), especially in the addresses of letters (Rom 1.7; 1 Cor 1.2; 2 Cor 1.1; Phil 1.1; Col 1.2). It derives from the OT where God is often termed the Holy One; his people are then also holy or saints. **Believers** is much less frequent as a description of Christians, appearing mainly in the later NT writings (Acts 10.45; 2 Cor 6.15; Col 1.2; 1 Tim 4.3, 10, 12; 5.16; 6.2; Tit 1.6). Since the words saints and believers are linked in Col 1.2, they may have been an accepted description of Christians in the Pauline school. 'In Christ Jesus' applies to both nouns and not to 'believers' only (Bouttier). Its meaning here is similar to that in Phil 1.1; 2 Cor 12.2; Rom 8.1 implying a personal relationship to Christ, if not necessarily a relationship of believers as a whole, though the plural may suggest the latter.

2. AE uses here a stereotyped wish that God should bless his addressees. **Grace** and **peace**, two basic concepts of Pauline theology, had been united in the earliest of Paul's epistles (1 Th 1.1).

Whether he or someone else (the origin of the formula does not concern us) had brought them together, he continued to use them as his standard form (2 Th 1.2; 1 Cor 1.3; 2 Cor 1.2; Gal 1.3; Phil 1.2; Philem 3; Rom 1.7; Col 1.2) and AE, if he is not Paul, has simply taken over the form. AE is not the source of the grace and peace he desires for his readers; these come from God and Christ (no attempt should be made with Jerome to relate grace to God and peace to Christ) and a similar double expression is found in all the letters apart from 1 Th 1.2; in Col 1.2 there is no reference to Christ. There are equivalent greetings in Jewish writings (*2 Bar* 78.2; *Jub* 12.29; 22.8f) but of course they lack the mention of Christ; the presence of his name makes clear that our greeting is Christian. In secular letters the opening wish might have no reference to God at all and the sender is then the source of the greeting. Christ and God the Father are here apparently put on a level (cf 6.23); normally in the NT God's gifts come through Christ rather than directly from God. God is defined here as the Father (see on 1.3) of believers; this term became for Christians their most characteristic description of him; Jews and some pagans also described him in the same way but with varying understanding. That the whole of v. 2 appears so regularly in early Christian letters suggests it may have been used in worship.

II

GOD, THE BLESSED, BLESSES

(1.3–14)

³ **Blessed is the God and Father of our Lord Jesus Christ**
   who has blessed us with every spiritual blessing
      in the heavenlies
      in Christ:
⁴ **according as he chose us in him**
      before the foundation of the world
      to be holy and blameless before him,
  in love ⁵ **foreordaining us**
      as his adopted children [sons] through Jesus Christ
      according to the good pleasure of his will,
⁶   **to the praise of the glory of his grace,**
      with which he graced us in the beloved;
⁷ **in him we have deliverance through his blood,**
      the forgiveness of trespasses,
      according to the riches of his grace
⁸   **which he made to abound to us;**
  in all wisdom and understanding ⁹ **making known to us**
      the mystery of his will,
      according to his good pleasure
      which he purposed in him
¹⁰   **for the administration of the fullness of times,**
  to sum up all things in Christ,
      the things in heaven and on earth;
  in him ¹¹ **in whom also we were given a lot,**
  being foreordained according to the intention
      of him who works everything
      according to the desire of his will,
¹² **that we might be to the praise of his glory,**
      we who had [previously] hoped and continue to hope

because of Christ;
13   **in whom also when you had heard the word of truth,**
          the gospel of your salvation,
          in whom also when you had believed
      you were sealed with the Holy Spirit of promise,
          who is the earnest of our inheritance,
14   **for the deliverance,**
          the acquiring of the inheritance,
          for the praise of his glory.

(i) The cry **Blessed is** (are you) **God** is found in isolated form in the OT, and is a response to something in the context (cf Ps 41.14; 68.36; 89.53;106.48; 119.12; Neh 9.5; 1 Chron 16.36; Tob 3.11). It is also found in the OT and in other Jewish writings in more structured form where it is followed by a clause, or clauses, giving the ground for the cry. There are brief cries of thanksgiving to God for deliverance from enemies (Exod 18.10; 1 Sam 25.39; 2 Sam 18.28; Ps 31.21f; 124.6; Jth 13.17; 1QM 14.4). Deliverance however is not only from physical enemies (1QM 18.6ff). Other circumstances can lead to a Berakah ('blessing', 'eulogy'): the gift of a son as successor to David on the throne of Israel (1 Kgs 1.48; 5.21(7); 2 Chron 2.11, 12; cf 1 Kgs 10.9; 2 Chron 9.8), the gift of wisdom, revelation and understanding (1 Esdr 4.40, 60; 1 QS 11.15; 1 QH 10.14; 11.27, 29; cf Ezra 7.27), help in time of need (Ps 28.6; 1 QH 5.20; Tob 11.13), unspecified blessings (Ps 66.20; 72.19f; 144.1f; *Ps Sol* 6.6; 1QH 16.8). As responses to the activity of God eulogies are phrased in both the second and third persons. There are a number of extended Berakoth ('blessings') in which several areas of response to God are covered and more than one reason supplied (1 Kgs 8.15ff, 56ff; 1 Chron 29.10ff; 2 Chron 6.4ff; Tob 8.5ff, 15ff; 13.1ff; Dan 3.26ff (LXX), 52ff (LXX); 1 Macc 4.30ff; Lk 1.68ff; 1QApocGen 20.12ff; 1QM 18.6ff). In extended Berakoth the 'blessing nuance' may be lost as the passage continues and passes into other areas of prayer; this is so in the case of the two other epistolary Berakoth in the NT (2 Cor 1.3ff; 1 Pet 1.3ff). Eph 1.3–14, though straying towards the end, keeps more consistently within the area of blessing.

Berakoth were regularly used in Jewish worship (e.g. Shemoneh Esreh), above all at meals. Jesus would have used one when he fed the multitudes or ate with his disciples, in particular at the Last Supper (Mk 14.22; Mt 26.26). In this way they passed into Christian worship including that of the eucharist.

Berakoth may have been employed eucharistically in AE's community and this may have prompted him to use one here or he may have imitated 2 Cor 1.3ff. The latter is less probable because even if he knew 2 Corinthians Eph 1.3ff is developed differently from 2 Cor 1.3ff and unlike the latter is followed by a normal thanksgiving section. If there is any relationship with 1 Pet 1.3ff, dependence lies on the part of 1 Peter. Elsewhere AE displays knowledge of Jewish ways and a Jewish form would have come naturally to him. There are a number of Jewish letters outside the NT which begin with a Berakah (1 Kgs 5.21f [5.7f]; 2 Chron 2.10f; Euseb *Praep Ev* 9.34; Josephus *Ant* 8.53). Although these all derive from 1 Kgs 5.21f (5.7f), this does not mean that they would have appeared, as Gnilka suggests, as a single example to an ancient reader. Gnilka is however correct in saying that they do not indicate a fixed epistolary form, yet their existence shows that the Berakah was an accepted way of beginning a letter. If, as is probable, 1 Pet 1.3ff is dependent on neither 2 Cor 1.3ff nor Eph 1.3ff, this increases the probability that the form was in use among Christians.

How far does the eulogy extend? While most Berakoth pass almost imperceptibly into other areas, 1.3–14 continues to supply grounds for the original benediction. Although the tenor changes after v. 10 and even more in vv. 13f where the liturgical style is less evident, vv. 11–14 continue to contain reasons for blessing God. The whole passage holds together so well that it is probably better to regard all of it as eulogy.

(ii) 1.3–14 is one long sentence with a complex array of subordinate clauses and phrases whose exact relation to one another is often difficult to determine. Many have spoken harshly of it, e.g. E. Norden '... the most monstrous conglomerate of sentences that I have ever met in Greek ...'. There have also been more appreciative verdicts, e.g. 'a work of art of high beauty' (Rendtorff).

That the eulogy is carefully constructed can be seen from v. 3 where the verb 'to bless' appears three times though after the first appearance synonyms could have been used and there are recurring phrases, 'according to the desire of his will' (vv. 5, 9, 11), 'to the praise of his glory' (vv. 6, 12). With these as clues many attempts have been made to discern within vv. 3–14 a strophic structure. No general agreement has been reached and Sanders' verdict, '... every attempt to provide a strophic structure for Eph 1.3–14 fails', still stands. Given this failure and the repetition of phrases, did AE adapt to his own purpose a hymn containing them? Reconstructions of such a hymn have been so diverse and so subject to individual opinion that none has proved generally acceptable. If AE did not adopt and modify an existing hymn then it is unlikely that he has employed a Berakah extracted from a baptismal or eucharistic liturgy. The eulogy may be suitable for either purpose, and AE may have presided in the worship of his own community and been influenced by what he did there, but that is not the same as asserting that the eulogy belongs to a liturgy. Sonorous and dignified language may be spontaneous, produced by the occasion, rather than deliberately drawn from a source.

(iii) If then AE neither adapted an existing hymn nor created one, we must seek the structure of the eulogy in its content rather than in a formal pattern. There are a number of leading ideas and these provide the most satisfactory basis for an analysis, though we should avoid the over-isolation of leading ideas from one another. The eulogy hangs together as a whole, beginning and ending with praise of God. The note of praise sounds throughout as the reasons for it, in the final issue lying in God's loving purpose, are introduced from different angles. Ideas pile up on top of one another; part of the difficulty of dismemberment lies in the flow of almost synonymous words.

Verse 3 introduces the theme of God's blessing; the way he blesses is detailed in what follows. This verse also shows that he is the real subject of all that is subsequently said. His will is repeatedly stressed, a will governed not by arbitrariness but by love and grace. God then has a plan for the cosmos, which has been hidden but is now revealed through his son (Acts 22.14f; Mt 11.25–7; cf Wisd 9.13–18; 2 Esdr 6.20); his plan refers not only to history but includes the cosmos and its redemption. One aspect of the plan, the acceptance of the Gentiles, is not mentioned in the eulogy but appears in 2.11–22; 3.1–13. V. 3 also indicates that it is the members of the church who are the recipients of his blessing activity. Christ for his part mediates God's blessings to us as is emphasised by the repeated references to him, mainly through personal and relative pronouns, and Christ is depicted both in his redemptive and cosmic roles: God's eternal will is executed through Christ and the cosmos summed up in him; salvation comes through his death.

(a) God's blessings began prior to history (vv. 4f), for in his love, and his will is governed by his love, he chose and foreordained us that we should have a position before him as his children. (b) In order to have such a position our sins must be forgiven (vv. 7, 8a); this is again an act of God's grace. (c) But God's blessings include more than a position before him as his redeemed; he imparts to us an understanding (vv. 8b–10) of his total purpose for the cosmos, previously a secret hidden from all. Here the eulogy reaches a kind of summit and this once achieved the climb begins again, as it were from half-way up the hill (vv. 11–14). (d) While everything may be summed up in Christ, believers need reminding that they have been given a place in all that God does (vv. 11f) so that their hope may be reinforced. (e) Finally AE applies all he has said to his readers by changing from the first person to the second (vv. 13f), at the same time bringing out further aspects of God's blessing. As believers his readers have received the Spirit which is a first instalment of yet greater gifts to come. So we move from the blessings of God initiated before time, through the present, to those which are yet to come in their fullness.

3. As we have seen, AE has taken over and re-shaped a Jewish liturgical formula. Jewish Berakoth may speak of God *simpliciter.* 'Blessed is (be) the Lord' (e.g. Exod 18.10; 1 Sam 25.39), or may identify him more precisely, 'Blessed is (be) the Lord, the God of Israel' (e.g. 1 Sam 25.32; 1 Kgs 1.48); 1 Chron 29.10 introduces God as father into a eulogy. In Eph 1.3 he is identified as **the God and Father of our Lord Jesus Christ**, i.e. in Christian terms. The Christians worship the same God as the Jews but view him in a new way. There is thus both continuity and discontinuity between the faith of the Old and New Testaments.

The whole blessing is said to be spiritual because it belongs to the sphere of the Spirit, who has worked, is working and will continue to work until God's plan is complete and who himself belongs to that plan's eschatological fulfilment. It is not spiritual in the popular charismatic sense but in the sense in which the gifts of Gal 5.22 are ultimately from the Spirit. The blessing is enjoyed now and does not belong only to the future for (1.13) every Christian is sealed with the Spirit. **In the heavenlies** is a further qualification. The sense is local, but the phrase serves also to reinforce the divine origin of the blessings. Christ sits in the heavenlies (1.20) and believers sit with him because they have been made to live with him (2.6). What belongs to the heavenlies is therefore already ours (for fuller discussion see Detached Note: The Heavenlies). Christians are blessed because they are united to Christ. V. 3 is a very general statement setting the tone for what follows but leaving the nature of the spiritual blessing unidentified. This is filled out in vv. 4ff: God's past eternal election (vv. 4–5a) realised in present existence (5b–8, 11–14) is to be consummated in the future (9–10). Although God, Christ and the Spirit all feature in v. 3 it would be wrong to think that AE deliberately created a Trinitarian formulation. He cannot however adequately describe God's blessing without introducing all three persons of the Trinity.

DETACHED NOTE I
THE HEAVENLIES

The NT contains no unified concept of heaven. It cannot be defined as the place where God dwells or where the righteous dead live. It is understood differently in different NT books and sometimes differently within the same book. In Heb 8.1 (cf 9.24) Christ is said to sit at the right hand of God in the heavens, but in 4.14 he passes through the heavens to God and in 7.26 he is above the heavens. Both plural and singular are used to say apparently the same thing (Heb 9.1 and 9.24). In accordance with Jewish thought in which there can be many heavens, the plural can also be signified (2 Cor 12.2). Since, again according to Jewish thought, there is to be a new heaven and a new earth (Isa 66.22), heaven need not be regarded as perfect.

Whatever our modern views of heaven, no believers in the ancient world would have doubted the statement of 1.20 that Christ sits at God's right hand in heaven for the heavenly session was part of accepted belief. Those believers would also not have been surprised to learn that the cosmic powers were active in heaven and that there was warfare between them and humanity (6.12). Such warfare would make it necessary for the wisdom of

God to be made known to the powers in heaven (3.10). What is surprising is that this should be taking place now (see on 3.6). However, this is not out of accord with the consummation of all in heaven and earth in Christ (1.10). The reference to the heavenlies in 2.6 may most easily be understood along the lines: believers died with Christ (a common Pauline idea), they have been made alive with him (either a Pauline idea or a development of it, see on 2.6), they sit with him in the heavenlies. If this final statement is true then since they sit in heaven they must enjoy the blessings of heaven. This brings us back to 1.3 where the reference to Christ can be seen to be appropriate: we sit with him in heaven as members of his body.

Verse 3 therefore assumes that the readers already accept what is found later in the letter in respect of the heavenlies. AE is not giving new teaching but using acknowledged teaching and adapting it to his own ends.

4. AE now begins to spell out the spiritual blessings and supply the reasons why God can be called blessed, and commences, not from a call to believers to remember their conversion experience, but from the position that God has given believers in that he has chosen them. This is the firm foundation on which all the blessings such as adoption and forgiveness are erected, and from which they flow.

God is called blessed, not because we decide to turn to him nor because he foresaw that we would be deserving of salvation, but because he chose us and his choice preceded creation. Although the verb 'to choose' is rarely used in the NT of God's eternal choice the concept is present (Rom 8.28f; 2 Tim 1.9; Tit 1.2; Jn 15.16; 17.24; 1 Pet 1.1f). It, of course, goes back into the OT (Deut 7.6f; 14.2) and was continued in Judaism (*Jub* 18.30; 22.9; *1 En* 93.2; 2 Esdr 3.13; *2 Bar* 48.19f; 1QS 11.7; 1QSb 1.2; 1QM 10.9). Election and predestination in our passages are not related primarily to individual salvation but to God's purpose. AE displays no interest in those who are not chosen, though as the remainder of the letter shows he is clearly aware that there is a difference between those in and those not in the church. A eulogy of praise and context of love is not the place in which to refer to the damnation of unbelievers. The seemingly logical deduction that when some are chosen others are rejected is not worked out in the NT, though later it came to be discussed widely in the church. Depending on how 1.10 is understood, it may be that AE does not believe that there will be any who will be ultimately rejected; all will be brought together in Christ. There is no clear statement here as to the purpose of God's election of believers; no immediate task ('saved to serve') is laid before them. Their election however gives them a new status; they are holy and blameless and have become God's children (v. 5).

The church is elect. We tend in thought to distinguish the church from those who from time to time are added individually to it; this is a distinction which cannot be made in a pre-temporal situation. All the elect were elected pre-temporally and the church is comprised of all the elect. The stress on election should reassure Gentile believers that they are in no inferior position to Jewish believers.

'Before' is a familiar concept since events are regularly apprehended in temporal sequence, but it is difficult to give a precise meaning to 'before creation'. AE uses it to emphasise God's sovereignty, an idea appearing again in the stress on his will in vv. 5, 9, 11. Nothing that has happened since creation led God to elect his people; his election was not a response to human sin (first mentioned in v. 7) or the failure of Israel, but was intended from the time he intended the universe. God is not a chess player who makes his next move only after he has seen the last move of his opponent. He works to a plan (cf 1QH 13.10; CD 2.7; Philo, *Opif Mundi* 16ff) and that plan always included the church. The church is not then simply a sociological phenomenon appearing under appropriate conditions. Yet if we say God works to a plan we must allow that for AE God is not primarily a great architect but a loving Father. The pre-temporal election of his people is only one side of a complex picture of God.

The election is said to be 'in Christ', a connection not made in Rom 8.28–30. What does it signify? In relation to Christ it implies he had a role wider than that of redeeming humanity through his incarnation, death and resurrection. As in Col 1.15ff he has a role in creation (cf 3.9); v. 4 thus prepares the way for v. 10. Christ's pre-existence is found in many parts of the NT, in particular in the hymn of Col 1.15ff which AE probably knew as tradition (cf Jn 17.5; 1 Pet 1.20). If then the church is chosen in Christ and he existed prior to creation, does this imply the church's pre-temporal existence? Behind this could lie the idea of Christ as a representative or inclusive figure (see Detached Note: In Christ) and this may supply the reason why AE thought of 'election in Christ'. However, an instrumental interpretation of 'in Christ' would also be possible. Whatever interpretation is chosen, the conclusion that the church pre-existed does not necessarily follow (Essay: The Church §5). It is in any case improbable that 'in Christ' is meant by way of contrast with the choice of Israel in Abraham (*Gen R.* 44 (27a), see SB III, 579); that choice was not pre-temporal but took place in history and Jews come within it because of their physical descent from Abraham.

The introduction of the reference to Christ has further significance. Election is related to the one who died, rose and ascended. This makes his love known and God's action seen as one made in love (cf Rom 9.18, 25). The introduction of Christ thus brings together what may seem two incompatible ideas: God elects us before we exist and without our consent; we respond freely to his activity in Christ. Christ is the unifying factor in this.

God does not act aimlessly and his choice must have a purpose or result and in v. 4 this is that believers are holy and without fault and become his children. Though 2.10 suggests that 'good works' have been prepared in advance for Christians there is no suggestion that God saw that particular people would be good and so chose them. Both **holy** and **blameless** are terms drawn from the cultus (for the second see Num 6.14; 19.2; Exod 29.37f; Heb 9.14); in time both were used more generally of moral behaviour (again for the second see Ψ 14.2; 17.24; Sir. 31.8; 40.19; Eph 5.27; Phil 2.15; Jude 24; Rev 14.5). Yet their cultic origin is not totally lost here, for the holiness and faultlessness is a holiness and faultlessness before God.

What does AE mean by his use of the adjectives? Are they to be understood in a realised sense – believers are already holy and faultless even as they are already justified – or do we have an implied exhortation – believers have been elected so that they may strive to be holy and faultless? A statement counselling moral behaviour would not be appropriate in a eulogy though one affirming the status and position before God of those who are elect would be. The general drift of the passage suggests AE in using the phrase wished to emphasise the present position of Christians. Believers are already holy and without fault before God, as is the church (5.27). This accords with the cultic sense of the words and follows on their election by God.

If God has elected believers this should give them confidence in the face of opposing cosmic powers (6.12ff) and should free them from any idea that they are at the mercy of a faceless fate. Often when people who appear inadequate for an important position are elevated to it they suddenly reveal new capabilities; they respond to their new position and gain confidence from it. So AE's Gentile believers are given a new confidence as God's elect to meet whatever comes to them. As the following reference to love shows, God's election, or his foreordination, is linked to his love (5.2). Realising God loves them and has chosen them makes them new people (4.24) fit for new tasks.

5. This and the following verse extend the thought of v. 4 and election is seen to be a foreordination to adoption.

Believers have not only been chosen before the foundation of the world, they have also been foreordained (**foreordaining us**) to be adopted. Because foreordination as AE uses the concept applies here to people it is to be distinguished from a general predestination of all that happens. The members of the group who are foreordained are identical to those who are chosen and presumably their election and foreordination are to be thought of as simultaneous, though it is doubtful if simultaneity is a concept relevant to a pre-temporal period. The reference to **love** implies that God's purpose originates in and is controlled by his love; it is not an arbitrary exercise of power. Nothing is said here about the perseverance to final salvation of those who are foreordained and their relation to what happens in 1.10 is left unexamined. Neither election nor foreordination in AE's eyes cuts out the need for moral effort. Had they done so he would never have gone on to lay down in 4.1ff guiding lines for conduct and encouraged his readers to live by them, nor would he have threatened them with the judgement of God (5.5f).

Foreordination though not mentioned explicitly in the OT is found in the Qumran writings (1QH 4.31; 15.13–22) and in Paul (using the same verb as here) at Rom 8.29f; 1 Cor 2.7; the idea is probably also present in 1 Th 5.9; Rom 9–11; it is found again in

1 Pet 1.1f; 2.8; Ign *Eph* (address). Jeremiah (1.5) was called before his birth and was therefore predestined to fulfil his mission. Foreordination and election are to be distinguished from the impersonality of Greek concepts of fate (e.g. it is all written in the stars) because a personal and loving God operates them. Without the knowledge that foreordination is the result of God's love foreordination would be wholly inexplicable. Like v. 4, v. 5 exists to say something positive about believers. AE in referring to their election and foreordination, and in common with most Jewish references to them, does not enter into the philosophical and religious issue of the relation of the human will to the divine plan; Stoicism was already alert to this problem but it was some time before it attracted the detailed attention of Christians (cf Schnackenburg). AE is clearly not aware of it for he counsels believers to pray for others (6.18f) and their prayer could have no effect if everything is already arranged. AE's paraenetic section shows he does not ignore the place of the human will; probably those to whom he wrote were not worried by the problem in the way the later church became. Again AE does not discuss election as implying an intervention of God into the historical process; his readers in common with almost all in the ancient world would not have been worried by such a question.

Believers have been adopted by God and have not made themselves his children; God has foreordained them to this. It was a common theme of primitive Christianity that God was the Father of believers and they his children. From this the concept of adoption developed and apparently was first employed by Paul (Rom 8.15; 9.4; Gal 4.5; in Rom 8.23 the text is uncertain). Adoption is a legal rather than a religious term and Paul probably derived it from Roman rather than Jewish or Near Eastern law; in the latter it was much less clearly developed. AE took it over as an idea which his readers knew and, whatever its origin, which they would probably have understood in the light of Roman law. It may have been a pre-Pauline idea for Gal 3.26 treats it as if it was known. In Rom 9.4 Paul applies it to Israel but not all Israelites were sons (Rom 9.6). In Roman law 'the adoptee was taken out of his previous state and was placed in a new relationship of son to his new father, his new paterfamilias. All his old debts were cancelled, and in effect the adoptee started a new life as part of his new family' (Lyall). He was now under the control of his new father and responsible to him alone. But he could, and usually did, also become his new father's heir (1.11).

Since AE uses adoption metaphorically we must be careful not to press the idea too far. It is not set in opposition to 'children of wrath' (2.3) and we cannot deduce from it anything about the 'previous' family of believers ('Satan's slave-camp', Simpson) nor that Paul has only male believers in mind because normally only males were adopted among the Romans. There are also clear differences between human and divine adoption. The father who adopted a son did so out of his own need, wishing either to continue his family or to provide himself with an heir; he is concerned with his own interests. God however does not adopt in that way for he already has a son and heir; he adopts because he loves those he adopts. The contemporary human father usually adopted someone from a social status similar to his own; God adopts believers to lift them up into a new status, similar to that of his own son. The adoption indeed takes place through that son (in Rom 8.15 through the Spirit) and the adoptee is chosen so that he may become like that son and bear his image (Rom 8.29; 1 Cor 15.49; 2 Cor 3.18). This is another point where the metaphor breaks down for no one mediated the adoption in Roman law. Since adoption takes place through Christ this implies that the sonship of believers is different from his, though AE would not have disagreed with Paul in describing Christ as firstborn among his brothers (Rom 8.29).

Verse 5b is solemn and Hebraic in tone; similar phrases are found in CD 3.15; 1QH 4.32f; 5.4; 11.9 and the genitival linkage of synonyms is a characteristic of AE (Percy). The phrase emphasises both God's freedom in foreordination and that he is the source of foreordination. **Good pleasure** is rarely found outside the LXX, the NT and literature influenced by them (Spicq; Schrenk; Romaniuk); Origen says the word was coined by the LXX translators. In addition to it our passage contains a number of other words denoting God's will. In the LXX the Greek word 'good pleasure' renders a range of Hebrew words and has two basic meanings: favour (this is the more frequent in the NT) and purpose. The reference to love suggests the former here and would reinforce the graciousness of God's will; it also appears to be the most satisfactory meaning in v. 9; so the sense 'favour' should probably be accepted here. Whichever the meaning, the totality of God's will is to be seen in this passage, moving from a pre-temporal determination to a post-temporal consummation (1.10). Behind all that happens is a personal God, not just arbitrary fate.

6. God foreordains so that the glory of his grace should be praised.

Alford comments 'beware of the miserable hendiadys "*his glorious grace*", by which all the richness and depth of meaning are lost'.

God's foreordination began in his love; it results in the praise of his grace (AE stresses God's grace, 1.7; 2.5, 8). The initiating love is now depicted as undeserved; this naturally follows from foreordination; the idea of an undeserved gift moreover is basic to 'grace' in 1.7; 2.5, 8 (though not in 3.2, 7, 8; 4.7). God's fore-ordination has not been forced on him by anything in those whom he elects. Realising this they will praise him. Blessed by him, they bless him (v. 3). God has acted so that he may be praised. AE wishes to show here the proper response to God's fore-ordaining love and is as little concerned to deal with the moral question of reconciling God's love with its purpose in leading to his praise as he was in squaring foreordination with human freewill. The praise which is the desired outcome of God's goodness is stressed again in vv. 12, 14, though there without the mention of grace. At first sight the praise may appear only to be offered by 'us', i.e. the believing community, but 3.10 may suggest it is also offered by the 'powers'. That all creation worships God has been a constant theme of Christian hymnody and earlier of the Psalms.

The repetition of v. 6a in vv. 12, 14 would suggest that we have now completed a stage in the argument; we are however immediately driven on by the relative clause; v. 6b is a transition clause following a kind of chorus line at the end of a stanza; it continues the theme of God's all-embracing grace but also prepares us for its manifestation in history (vv. 7ff). In the relative clause of v. 6b two key terms reappear in different guises: 'grace' as **grace with which he graced us** and 'love' as the love shown **in the beloved**.

The double use of the root 'grace' reinforces the idea of the free abundance of God's grace. It is grace which controls his ordaining power and it is this grace which is displayed to us 'in the loved one'.

Through its use in the baptismal and transfiguration narratives the verbal adjective **beloved** became a technical title for the Lord which continued to be used in early Christian literature, e.g. 1 Clem 59.2f; Ign *Smyrn* preface. Its particular significance in the Gospel stories is debated, being seen as derived either from Isa 42.1 and so connected to the Isaianic servant or from Gen 22.2 and linked to Isaac as type of Christ in his sacrifice.

7. From the pre-temporal election of believers AE moves to its historical realisation through the redemption which God has effected for them 'in Christ'. This might indicate Christ as the means of redemption, but since this is expressed through the reference to blood it more probably implies inclusion in him: believers have their redemption in living fellowship with Christ. There is a temporary change here in the verb to the first plural; elsewhere God is the subject of the verbs in vv. 3–10. The verb moreover is in the present tense contrasting with the prevailing aorists. The present tense implies redemption and forgiveness are present possessions and this is in keeping with AE's stress on the present nature of salvation.

The word translated **deliverance** is used in two ways: (a) of release, e.g. of a prisoner, where a price is paid, (b) of deliverance in a general way. Though infrequent in non-biblical Greek it normally has meaning (a) which it obtains from the basic root. When we turn to biblical Greek the picture changes. Due to the influence of context and the underlying Hebrew, **deliverance** and its cognates regularly have meaning (b), though there are possible exceptions, e.g. Mk 10.45; 1 Pet 1.18.

If AE used **deliverance** here without envisaging the payment of a price that does not mean that his readers would have understood it in that way. If they normally thought of the word in relation to a price to be paid and if they have only been Christians for a short period and have not picked up the special Jewish understanding of the term, they may have thought of 'blood' as the price to be paid for their redemption. Those who had been Christians for a longer period and had come to know more of the OT would gradually have moved from this interpretation to that which sees it as a term signifying deliverance without thought of payment.

The second phrase of v. 7, which refers to the forgiveness of sins, is parallel with the first and may serve to explain it as in Col 1.14 'the forgiveness of sins' explicates the meaning of 'deliverance'. The connection with repentance is not made here and would be inappropriate in a section concentrating on God's initiatory action. Forgiveness may appear to deal only with the past through the removal of guilt but such a removal enables the one who is freed to live a new life set free from the burden of the past. AE may have chosen 'forgiveness' rather than the justification language of Paul as being more easily appreciated by Greek readers.

If 'blood' does not indicate the price paid, what does it signify? As a term it entered Christian usage prior to Paul (Rom 3.25), and though he did not use it regularly (Rom 5.9) apart from his references to the eucharist (there is no need to see such a reference here) it gradually came to be employed more widely (Col 1.20; Eph 1.7; 2.13; 1 Pet 1.2; 1 Jn 1.7; 5.6–8), above all in Hebrews. It always carries some reference to the death of Christ but it is unlikely that it simply indicates that death as bloody and violent. In most cultures it carries overtones of power, defilement, cleansing, etc. (e.g. 1 Kgs 22.38, the taurobolium, the drinking of blood, menstrual blood) and in particular is linked to sacrifice. It was the sacrificial association which led Christians to use it of Christ's death. Its overtones would have helped Gentiles to see it as possessing effective power to deliver and forgive sins. Unlike the death of Christ the deaths of the two who were crucified with him were bloody and violent but were not sacrificial. The thought of 1.7 is thus not far different from that of Rom 3.24f, though expressed in much less 'Jewish' terms. The deliverance AE has in mind is possessed now (in 4.30 it has a future aspect) and this is not out of accord with the general realised eschatological position of the letter. AE makes no attempt to explain how Jesus' death and sin are related; he simply accepts this as true; it had been a part of Christian thinking from the beginning (1 Cor 15.3).

The foreordination of believers was to the praise of the glory of God's grace; it is God's grace and not 'Christ's', for in v. 6 the grace was certainly God's and v. 8 continues with God as subject. God's grace is also the cause of the deliverance of believers. Of that grace there are inexhaustible and boundless 'riches'. 'Riches' is one of AE's favourite terms (1.18; 2.7; 3.8, 16). It may have been in use in the Pauline school for A/Col also uses it (1.27; 2.2); it is not frequent in Paul (only six times). The Qumran writings emphasise the wealth of God's mercy and grace (1QS 4.3–5; 1QH 4.32; 7.27; 11.28; 12.14; 18.14; frag 2.5). Not only does God deliver through his grace but those delivered are able to praise him for that grace and for the depths of his compassion; their deliverance is not the result of their own activity but of God's; all Christian existence begins and ends in grace.

8. God being rich in grace has bestowed it in abundance on all believers; **to abound** though only here in Ephesians is a Pauline favourite. Paul affirms the abundance of grace in Rom 5.20.

Words dealing with wisdom go fittingly with a word indicating the making known of a mystery (v. 9). 'The revealer of (a mystery) wisely selects his audience, and prudently chooses the proper time, place, and method for his disclosures' (Eadie). If this is so it seems wiser to associate the reference to wisdom with v. 9 and regard it as God's wisdom and not human wisdom. Whatever God does he does with wisdom and insight.

9. The verb 'to make known' is regularly used in connection with revelation (Rom 16.26; Eph 3.3, 5, 10; Col 1.27) and associated with the disclosure of mysteries. It represents a new step in the eulogy. Believers, foreordained and already possessing their deliverance, are now told about the secret of the ultimate destiny of the cosmos. This knowledge is made known to all believers and is not restricted to Paul or the apostles whatever may be true of the revelations of 3.3, 5. Even in 3.3, 5 it is implied that the apostles and prophets did not keep to themselves the understanding of the mystery they had received but made it known to all believers.

What is made known in the mystery may be the understanding of a dream or vision (e.g. Dan 2.19), a description of how and when the end will come (Dan 2.27–9; 2 Bar 85.8ff; 1QpHab 7.1–5), an unveiling of the divine structure of the cosmos (1 En 71.4; 2 Bar 48.2f), an explanation of God's activity in human affairs (1 En 63.3; 1 QM 14.14; 1QH 9.23f), or, outside Judaism in the Mystery Religions, knowledge of ceremonies and ritual that lead to salvation (cf also 1QS 9.18f).

When mysteries are made known they are made known not to humanity as a whole but to privileged sections within it; in the Mystery Religions, the initiates; in Judaism and Christianity, the people of God. The promise is not that at some future time, e.g. after death, a disclosure will be made to believers but that they are put in possession of the secret now, although they may not fully understand it now (cf Col 1.26–8; 1 Cor 2.6–10). The mystery may also be disclosed beyond humanity to the 'powers' (3.10) and (potentially) to all people (Rom 16.25–7) though they may only come to understand it when they become Christians.

Mystery in the NT often relates in some way or other to membership in the people of God (Rom 11.25; 16.25–7; Col 1.26f; 1 Tim 3.16; Eph 3.3, 4, 9), and this may colour other passages where the content is not made clear (Col 2.2; 4.3). This is not surprising for Paul asserts (Gal 1.11f) that it was as a result of divine revelation that he evangelised the Gentiles. Indeed, generally speaking, the early church believed its mission to the Gentiles was not the result of reflection on the OT (Rom 16.25f may be an exception) or on the inner significance of the life of Jesus, but came through a direct command or revelation of God (e.g. Mt 28.16–20; Lk 24.47–9; Acts 1.8; 9.15; 10.1ff; cf Best 'Revelation') and was thus a disclosure of something previously hidden. The explicit linking of 'mystery' to the Gentile mission as in 3.3ff (see notes there) is mainly post-Pauline. Paul uses the word with other connections (1 Cor 2.7; 4.1; 13.2; 14.2; 15.51; 2 Th 2.7). It was the fact that he used the word when joined to his belief that he occupied a special place in God's plan for the admission of Gentiles that led his disciples to employ it to connect him with that admission. Mystery is also linked with Christ, more in Colossians (1.27; 2.2; 4.3) than in Ephesians (3.4); the two ideas however fit easily together since it is the new fact of Christ which permits Gentiles to be members of the church.

As the 'all' of v. 10 shows, the 'mystery' of v. 9 relates to something more comprehensive than the salvation of individual believers or the acceptance of Gentiles, though their acceptance was itself a first step towards an even greater comprehensiveness. The use of the word 'mystery' in v. 9 may also have been influenced by its eschatological associations in Judaism for v. 10 has an eschatological flavour. But why has AE used the word at all?

The thought would run just as easily without it, 'God had made known to us his will ...' (the same is true in 6.19 where all that would be strictly required would be '... to make known the gospel'). Its employment reinforces the idea of revelation – what God had intended for the eventual fate of the universe lay hidden and unknown, a mystery, until revealed to Paul or other followers of Christ. The redemption which it involves was not then some afterthought but part of God's plan from the beginning (Bouttier). So in 6.19 it emphasises that what Paul proclaims is not something he has himself devised but a revelation of God to him.

It is common to speak with Robinson of a mystery as 'a secret which God wills to make known and has charged his apostles to declare to those who have ears to hear it'. This needs to be given more precision. When initiates joined a Mystery Religion they came to know certain secrets which were never made public. Because the NT has been widely published it appears as if the mysteries of which it speaks were intended to be open to all who could read or listen; there is nothing hidden about them. The message of the original preachers of the gospel was not 'We have mysteries to reveal' but 'there is salvation in Christ'. Once those who responded to this message had been baptised, they learned, perhaps only after a lengthy period, that God had revealed new aspects of salvation (e.g. the admission of Gentiles to the church). They were still however only a tiny group in possession of precious knowledge otherwise not widely known; as an elite they may have thought themselves important. The mystery was not deliberately kept secret but it was not made widely known. In contrast to initiates into the Mystery Religions, no oaths bound Christians to keep secret what they knew, though Paul is not permitted to reveal what he learnt in his rapture (2 Cor 12.1ff). If their friends in other religions boasted of their secret knowledge the Christians could boast of theirs, yet unlike their friends they could reveal what they knew; but since there were few believers there was no widespread proclamation of the secrets.

What AE affirms has been made known is the mystery of God's will in relation to the summing up of the All in Christ (v. 10b). Before reaching that climax, however, an intervening clause (vv. 9b, 10a) has to be fitted into the argument. Vv. 9b and 10a are to be treated as a unit. While this unit could be taken with v. 10b (so Haupt) it would be clumsy. It goes better with v. 9a (so Schlier; Gnilka; Schnackenburg). It functions like a refrain, though not appearing at the end of a stanza. God has acted not with dictatorial freedom but with a freedom conditioned by goodwill.

God's goodwill is further defined through the relative clause. The verb here would normally mean 'to plan, purpose', and in view of AE's love of the heaping up of synonyms there is no need to render it with the NRSV as 'set forth'.

10. As we have seen v. 10a goes with v. 9b. In 1.10 the activity or plan is not Paul's but God's. We may assume that if God administers he does so in accordance with his own inner plan, a plan which incorporates the choice and redemption of believers (vv. 4–7) as well as the summing up of the All.

The fullness of times is not the same phrase as that of Gal 4.4 and carries no reference here to the incarnation. 'The times' can be either the events which occur in time (Schlier) or the periods of time which together comprise time (so almost all other commentators). These periods may themselves be either the days, months and years into which time is divided (Haupt) or, more probably, the periods mentioned in the apocalyptic writings (Gnilka; Schnackenburg; cf Tob 14.5; 2 Esdr 4.37; *2 Bar* 14.1; 20.6; 40.3; 81.4; 1QpHab 7.2, 13f). The 'times' in this sense cannot properly be distinguished from the events which must take place before the end. Ephesians, unlike the apocalyptic writings, says nothing about these events. Their fullness denotes a completion or an endpoint to time which will be identical with the summing up of all things in Christ. It is in the fullness of the times that time attains its meaning (Asmussen).

Verse 10b picks up and discloses the content of the mystery which has been known (9a); this disclosure forms the peak to which the eulogy has been building up.

In 3.9 **all things** indicates the whole creation (see 3.9 and Detached Note: The Heavenlies) and we should not reject that meaning here (cf 1.22; 4.10; Rom 11.36; 1 Cor 8.6; 15.27; Phil 3.21; Heb 1.3; 2.10; Rev 4.11). Neither should we restrict it to sentient beings, least of all to the 'good'; the things in heaven include not only the angels but also the evil powers and the things on earth include unbelievers.

The emphasis of the verb 'to sum up' lies more on the idea of 'summing up' than on reconciliation. But what does summing up in Christ mean? It might be regarded as implying that Christ is the 'head' of the All, and undoubtedly this is true. Yet when we recall the sense of *résumé* we might do better (to play on words) to describe him as 'the heading'. This retains the rhetorical sense of the verb, except that a heading is normally found at the beginning of an argument rather than the end. In what way would Christ be the 'summing up' of the universe? Perhaps in the way an architect's plan sums up what is built; the shape of what comes into existence is both summarised in the plan and determined by it.

Christ's relation to the cosmos gradually came to concern the early Christians and they saw his importance as lying in areas beyond the simple forgiveness of sin. The cosmic nature of OT thought began to appear in passages like Isa 11.6–9 and Ezek 34.25–7 and became more explicit in the concept of a new heaven and a new earth (Isa 65.17; 66.22). In the light of this Christians began to connect Christ both to creation (Jn 1.3; 1 Cor 8.6; Col 1.15–17; Heb 1.2) and to the end. Rom 8.19–23 does not make the latter connection explicit but it lies in its context; it becomes explicit in 1 Cor 15.20–8; Phil 2.9–11; Col 1.20; Eph 1.10, though in each case in different ways. In v. 10 the sense of 'in Christ' (see Detached Note: In Christ) may be that Christ carries out the summing up but more probably that everything comes together in him; what is divided is unified in him. The significance of the cosmos is made known in him. The cosmic nature of their faith might have been appreciated by Gentiles as echoing the thought of a future Golden Age (Virgil, *Eclogues* iv 11.4–11, 21.9; Ovid, *Metamorph* 1.84ff; Horace, *Epode* 16). As far as early Christianity is concerned it must be allowed that there is also a strain, a more widely found strain, in scripture which sees part of creation as finally remaining outside the love and care of God and Christ, perhaps acknowledging his sovereignty but not willingly offering any allegiance; where this holds, the stress lies on the defeat of evil and not on its summing up in Christ. The existence of both strains must be accepted, yet we need to ask which represents more closely the central drive of the NT. Eph 1.10 seems to do so.

In 1.20–3 Christ already holds the powers in subjection; in 2.6 believers already sit with him in the heavenlies. It is not out of keeping with these passages if then we say that the universe *is*, and not *will be*, summed up in Christ. The consummation of the All is as much an event outside the normal parameters of time as are the choice and foreordination of believers (vv. 4f).

11. In him at the end of v. 10, though appearing redundant, creates the bridge to the next stage of the eulogy in which attention returns from the cosmic to blessings granted more directly to believers; the two are related through the entrance of a more eschatological strand in relation to believers. If v. 10 was the peak to which we climbed through vv. 3–10, we now appear to descend from it, yet this is not so, for a climb begins now to a new peak.

But does the change here to the first person plural indicate attention as focussed now on some believers only and no longer on all? A first plural can be understood in various ways: 'we and you', 'we in contrast to you', 'we, my own special group' (e.g. if a plurality of authors had been named in 1.1f), or the authorial 'we'. The context must determine its precise meaning on each occasion.

The vast majority of commentators see the alternatives as lying only between Jewish believers and all believers. Many from Pelagius onwards (e.g. Abbott; Beare; Barth; Hugedé) consider that the first person plural which has obtained from v. 3 and meant all believers now changes its reference and applies only to Jewish Christians. In response to this we would argue that if a change of referent were intended at v. 11 AE would have brought this out more clearly as he does at 2.11; there is nothing in 1.11 to suggest the 'we' has any other reference than in 1.3–10; it is true that one of the themes of the letter is the unity of Jewish and Gentile Christians but this is a deduction we draw after we have read it; scholars may have it in mind as they read v. 11; AE however wrote Ephesians expecting it to be listened to, not worked over in the study! Only at the end of v. 12 would hearers have a clue that Jewish Christians were intended; they would then have to go back in their minds and rethink what they had heard and would wonder if they should read the new significance back to vv. 3–10. For the same reason any attempt to limit the 'we' of vv. 11f to Paul and his associates fails. It is not inappropriate that at the end of the eulogy AE should turn his attention more specifically to his readers and tie in what he says to them; the same variation between 'we' and 'you' occurs in the eulogies of 2 Cor 1.3ff and 1 Pet 1.3ff. Finally it is important to note that there is nothing in vv. 13f which is specifically oriented towards the way in which Gentiles rather than Jews become Christians. So we conclude that there is no change of the referent of 'we' in v. 11 (e.g. Haupt; Ewald; Dibelius; Dahl; Cambier).

We were given a lot *or* portion signals the new area into which the eulogy has turned. The verb, applied originally to the casting of lots, obtained the more general sense of allotting or assigning and came to be used in an allied way in its two (three) appearances in the LXX, 1 Kgdms 14.41; Isa 17.11; Esth 4.11(A). The Israelite tribes were allotted portions of land which became their inheritance (Num 26.52ff; 36.1ff; Josh 12.7); thus the word is linked to the idea of inheritance. This has led to it being understood in our passage as indicating either that we have been given a 'lot' (inheritance) by God or that we have been allotted to God as his inheritance. The concept of Israel as the 'lot' or chosen portion of God among the nations is found regularly in the OT (Deut 9.29; 32.8–10; Zech 2.12 [LXX v. 16]) and is emphasised in Qumran (1QS 2.2; 1QM 1.5; 13.5) where opponents of the community are known as the lot of Belial (1QM 1.5; 4.2; 1QS 2.4f) or of darkness (1QM 1.11; 13.5). So the church might be described as the 'lot' of God. Yet since the concept of inheritance is explicitly present later in vv. 14, 18 it may seem better to see it already in v. 11. 'Adoption' (v. 5) also harmonises with the reception of an inheritance.

What then is the nature of the inheritance which Christians receive? If that of Israel was physical Palestine that of the Christians might well be 'heaven' (cf Col 1.12), but it is more probably their adoption, forgiveness, sealing with the Spirit, that is to say all the blessings intended in v. 3. In the NT it has eschatological associations (Mt 5.5; 1 Cor 6.9f; 15.50). In Ψ 15.7 (cf Dan 12.13) it is God himself. Thus it may be equated with salvation (Pokorný). Whatever its nature they have not obtained it through their own efforts; they were foreordained to receive it.

12. The **we** who are to be to the praise of God's glory are now further defined as those who had previously hoped and still continue to hope in Christ. 'In Christ' retains here its formulaic significance and relates either to the togetherness of Christians in Christ (Gnilka) or gives the reason for hope (Masson; cf Phil 2.19). Since conversion all Christians have hope (see further on 1.18 and 4.4 for its nature). It is not simply a hope in the parousia or a hope that all humanity may have in a future Golden Age; that all Christians continue having a hope is seen in passages like 1 Cor 15.19; 2 Cor 1.10; 1 Tim 4.10.

13. While the main line of thought of this verse is clear the repeated **in whom** causes considerable difficulty in working out the details. Its first occurrence picks up the same phrase in v. 11 with the same antecedent, Christ: the Christ in whom we are sealed is the one in whom we received our lot. The second occurrence can be taken as resuming the first, the intervening words being parenthetical and/or parallel, or as a fresh step in the argument with Christ still the antecedent, or as with some word (e.g. 'gospel' or 'word') in 13a as antecedent. In view of the continual use throughout the eulogy of phrases with **in** referring to Christ, the last possibility is unlikely. Only an examination of the content will indicate which of the others is to be preferred.

If, as we have already argued (see v. 11), the change to 'you' in vv. 13f does not indicate that AE now specifically addresses only Gentile Christians, why did he make the change? Has he in mind the newly baptised among his readers? Even if we reject the general thesis that the letter is a baptismal tract it is true that v. 13 uses evangelistic language and may be directed at new converts, but almost all Christians at that time were new converts. Some, believing AE used an existing hymn as the basis for his eulogy, account for the change of person by supposing that vv. 13f are his addition to it, an impossible solution if all the eulogy is attributed to AE. More probably AE wishes to bring home to his readers that he is not simply describing God's activity as in a vacuum but wishes them to see their own place in it. The change between first and second persons recurs repeatedly in the letter and probably represents the kind of change which every preacher makes in the course of a sermon.

The terms of v. 13, 'hear, believe, word, truth, gospel, salvation', are those of Christian mission. The gospel is preached, people hear, respond and are sealed with the Spirit. 'The word of truth' means the word whose content is truth and not 'the truthful word'; the phrase is found also in other post-Pauline literature (Col 1.5; 2 Tim 2.15; Jas 1.18) and implies an objectification of the gospel.

There are two ways of hearing: some hear and pay no heed; others hear and are saved (Mk 4.9; Acts 3.22ff; 4.19; Gal 3.2, 5; Rom 10.14–18; 1 Jn 4.6; Rev 2.7). It is the latter hearing of which AE writes; he does not think of a chance physical hearing in the market-place which is quickly forgotten, but of the hearing which becomes belief. Because believing hearing is implied throughout v. 13a, little new is said in the description of readers as believing; this summarises and repeats v. 13a. Those who believe have heard the word of truth, the gospel of salvation.

Is however sealing a reference to baptism or some element within it like the laying on of hands? The image of sealing has little in itself which would lead us to accept or reject either idea. Seals are used to indicate ownership (Rev 7.3–8; 9.4), to authenticate (Jn 3.33; 6.27; 1 Cor 9.2) and to protect what is sealed (Mt 27.66; Rev 20.3). Hellenistic religion has little to teach about the Christian usage of the image, though, whatever AE may have had in mind, the possibility cannot be ignored that his readers may have understood the seal as some form of magical protection (cf *Pistis Sophia* 195–7). The image was used in Christianity prior to Ephesians; in 2 Cor 1.22 it is connected as here with the **earnest** of the Spirit. The argument supporting the view that sealing means baptism in 1.13 is complex and depends more on allusion than direct evidence; explicit evidence is not found until after the time of Ephesians (2 Clem 7.6; 8.6; Hermas, *Sim* 8.2.3f; 6.3; 9.16.3–7; 17.4; *Acts of Paul and Thecla* 25; *Testim Truth* IX, 3 69.7–11). However: (i) in Rom 4.11 (cf *Barnabas* 9.6) circumcision is termed a seal and though the Jewish evidence comes from much later, it is not unreasonable to suppose that Paul employs an idea to which he had been accustomed in his Jewish days (the description of circumcision as a 'sign' goes back as far as Gen 17.11–13). (ii) In Col 2.11f baptism and circumcision are drawn closely together but commentators are by no means agreed on their equivalence (*pro* Gnilka; Lohse; Pokorný; *contra* O'Brien; Schweizer; Martin); even if they are not equivalent in Col 2.11f AE might have assumed they were. (iii) The giving of the Spirit is regularly associated with baptism (Acts 2.38; 1 Cor 12.13) but is also associated with the laying on of hands in an action distinct from baptism (Acts 8.16; 19.6). In the case of Cornelius the coming of the Spirit, revealed in glossolalia, was the sign for him to be baptised (Acts 10.44–8). In missionary activity this was probably the normal pattern; people who showed signs of the Spirit were baptised. Such people, as Cornelius, might well have been described as 'sealed' with the Spirit prior to baptism.

None of this compels acceptance of sealing as a metaphor for baptism in v. 13. If the letter were a baptismal tract there would be stronger grounds for making the equation; failing this the issue must remain in doubt. If AE intended us to understand that he had baptism in mind why did he not simply use the word? In the absence of the actual word we are left with the impression that for AE the divine aspect of becoming a Christian lies not in the act of baptism but in the coming of the Spirit to believers. From the first moment of faith Christians believed the Spirit was with them. If the direct connection of sealing with baptism is in doubt there is less reason to connect it (with Schlier) with the laying on of hands, for the supporting allusions to circumcision are now irrelevant and there is no certainty that the laying on of hands accompanied baptism in this period.

The Spirit can be regarded as either the tool which leaves the mark of the seal on the object being sealed or the mark which is left. It is here almost certainly the latter. The activity of the Spirit should not be limited to charismatic gifts in the narrow sense but seen in the fruit of the Spirit (Gal 5.22f). Their sealing indicates to believers (cf 2 Cor 1.22) that they belong to God and are under his protection. A promise is related to the Spirit; this may be either that of the OT and Judaism (cf Acts 2.17; Gal 3.14; Lk 24.49 for this idea) which is now fulfilled ('the promised Spirit') or, slightly more probably, the promise of a future fullness of God's blessings to be given in eschatological times (cf 3.6).

14. 'Earnest', is a legal and commercial term of Semitic origin adopted into Greek which commits both giver and recipient to the completion of a deal under penalty. Yet the earnest is not just a pledge or guarantee that something will be given later; it is itself a partial gift, and is perhaps better translated as 'first instalment'.

Sealed with the Spirit, Christians have begun to participate in their inheritance of salvation and have a legal claim to inherit it fully; the metaphor perhaps breaks down at this point for heirs do not receive part of their inheritance in advance but all when the testator dies. The life of the church in which Jew and Gentile are now reconciled is an earnest of life in the world to come when all will be summed up in Christ. The concept of inheritance has already been introduced (v. 11) and is implicit in sonship (v. 5). In Paul the idea is used in connection with the relationship of Jewish and Gentile believers (Rom 4.13f; 8.17; Gal 3.18, 29; 4.1, 7, 30) and, in a more normal and less theological way, of the inheritance of future salvation (1 Cor 6.9, 10; 15.50; Gal 5.21). These two aspects reappear in Ephesians: Gentile Christians are fellow-heirs with Jewish (3.5); all Christians (v. 14) have yet to enter on their full inheritance of salvation. We can observe here the tension that runs throughout the epistle, for Christians already sit with Christ in the heavenlies (2.6) and therefore appear to enjoy full salvation.

DETACHED NOTE II
IN CHRIST
Throughout the eulogy the phrase 'in Christ' has recurred repeatedly, eleven times in the twelve verses, though it has been in variant forms; while this high rate is not maintained throughout the remainder of the letter the phrase appears twice as frequently (in all thirty-three times, Schmid) as in the genuine Paulines. Does AE employ it in the same way as Paul?

For Paul the phrase may be said to have two main thrusts, the instrumental and the local, each predominating from time to time but neither ever totally absent. These two thrusts still appear in Ephesians but with variations. In the instrumental usage God is now much more often introduced explicitly as the subject of action in Christ which benefits believers; this is found in Paul only at 2 Cor 2.15; 5.19 (but see also Col 1.19; 2.9, 15) but in Ephesians at 1.3, 4, 6, 9, 10, 20; 2.6, 7; 3.11; 4.32. Often also in Ephesians God is the real subject where the verb is passive (Maurer); this is found four times in Paul, four times in

Colossians, and there are also a number of passages in Paul where God is clearly the subject (Rom 6.23; 8.2; Gal 3.14); this variation must not then be over-exaggerated. The frequent use of God as subject produces a triangular relationship (God – Christ – the church) and here the usage is clearly instrumental. This sense is not only very frequent in Ephesians but also goes beyond Pauline usage in that it may refer to God's pre-temporal activity in Christ (1.4, 11) and to his cosmic activity (1.9, 10).

The number of instances in which the local sense predominates are fewer than with Paul; this is at least partly accounted for by the absence from Ephesians of a section of personal greetings and because there are no passages in which Paul is under pressure to defend himself (4.1 is the closest). Yet the local sense does occur and mostly in corporate form. When, 6.1, children are told to obey their parents 'in the Lord' (for the reading see on 6.1) only an obstinate insistence that 'in the Lord' must be taken imperatively with the verb, and we have seen that not all instances in Ephesians are imperatival, forbids us seeing the phrase as connecting parents and children; children are addressed as members of the Christian community and as such should obey their parents (cf 1 Cor 7.39). When in 4.17 AE testifies 'in the Lord' he does so because he and his readers are members of the church; he would not have used the phrase if addressing non-Christians. When in 6.21 it is said that Tychicus, the beloved brother and servant in the Lord, will give the readers information, 'in the Lord' goes more easily with servant and brother than with the verb; Tychicus will tell them because he is a brother to them and serves them in the church. For the local sense see also the notes on 2.13, 15, 21. The local significance, and in particular the corporate, has not then disappeared from Ephesians and there is no reason to suppose it may not lie in the background in many cases where the instru-mental sense predominates; only the interpretation of individual texts can show if it is present.

III

A PRAYER FOR KNOWLEDGE

(1.15–23)

[15] So I for my part when I heard of your loyalty
    to the Lord Jesus and to all the saints
[16] do not cease returning thanks for you
    mentioning you in my prayers,
[17] that the God of our Lord Jesus Christ,
    the Father of glory,
    should give you the Spirit of wisdom and revelation,
    in knowledge of him,
[18] the eyes of your heart having been enlightened
    to know him so that you may understand
    what is the hope of God's calling,
    what are the riches of the glory of the inheritance
    he provides among the holy ones,
[19] and what is the exceeding greatness of his might
    towards us who believe,
    in accordance with the power of the vigour of his
    strength
[20] with which he empowered Christ,
    in that he raised him from the dead
    and seated him at his right hand in the
    heavenlies
[21] above every rule and authority and power
    and dominion or whatever they are termed,
    and that not only in this age
    but also in the coming age;
[22] and has set in subjection all under his feet
    and given him who is head over all to the
[23] church, which is his body,
    the fullness of him who is being totally filled.

This paragraph is again one long sentence comprising thanksgiving (vv. 15f), intercession (17–19), and leading to theological statement (20–3).

In most Pauline letters a thanksgiving and intercession follow the address; Ephesians instead begins with a eulogy in praise of God (1.3–14). Thanksgivings and intercessions refer more directly to the condition of the recipients. Because of its nature intercession would not flow naturally out of eulogy; the brief thanksgiving creates a suitable transition. In providing thanksgiving and intercession AE conforms to the general Pauline pattern, though 2 Corinthians differs in moving directly from a much briefer eulogy to the body of the letter without thanksgiving or intercession. Sometimes the whole of 1.15–3.21 is taken as the prayer because 3.14–21 is again explicit prayer; but 2.1–22 and 3.1–13 are not prayer. 3.14–21 should be taken as a separate prayer section; as Paul in Rom 11.33–6 adds a doxology to his doctrinal section so AE adds a prayer and doxology to his. The brief thanksgiving contains most of the elements usually found in a Pauline thanksgiving. Vv. 15f set out the relation between writer and readers. In vv. 17–19 interest centres on the readers and the benefits the prayer will bring them. In vv. 20–3 attention centres on Christ.

1.20–3 have sometimes been regarded as a hymn or as based on one. Certainly the verses contain a number of phrases drawn from the catechetical and/or liturgical traditions which with some careful editing could be made to resemble a hymn or credal statement. It is however more likely that instead of using a preformed piece of tradition AE has simply drawn from the tradition those elements which suit his particular purpose (cf Gnilka). There are similar sets of traditional theological statements in 1 Pet 3.18–22; Polyc *Phil* 2.1f; Ign *Trall* 9.1f and, more diffusely, in 1 Cor 15.20, 24.8. Each of these has its own peculiarities: 1 Pet 3.19 brings in the preaching to the spirits in prison; our passage has no reference to the death of Christ (present in the context of 1 Cor 15); it also ends (v. 23) with a statement about the church. There is also an important connection in thought between 1.20–3 and 2.1–6.

Eulogies are by their nature impersonal without direct relation to the situation of the readers. AE, realising he must attract their attention after the eulogy's stiff theological thought now turns directly to them with a brief thanksgiving for their Christian existence (vv. 15f) and a longer intercession for their deeper insight into God's ways (vv. 17–19). God's ways are ways of power and might so his intercession leads him on to say something about what God did in raising Christ and taking him into heaven; the result was a triumph over the supernatural hostile powers which readers fear may control them (vv. 20–2). This in turn leads AE finally to introduce explicitly one of the most important themes in the letter, namely the church (vv. 22f), and at the same time to return to the letter's cosmic setting.

15, 16. Paul now speaks, or is made to speak, in the first person: 'I also give thanks, make mention', or 'I who have uttered the eulogy have more to say'.

AE's (Paul's) informants (**when I heard**) are not identified; the absence of a reference accords with the general nature of the letter; the reference to hearing indicates that Paul, or AE, had never visited the readers. According to Acts 19.1ff Paul spent a considerable time in Ephesus on his main visit, though there had been a brief initial visit, 18.19–21. The inference from our verse that the author had never visited the recipients cannot be countered by arguing that AE only refers here to the faith of those who have been converted since he left Ephesus (so Hodge) or that a long period had elapsed since his final visit and that therefore he needs to be updated; nothing in the text implies he had fresh converts in mind and nothing in the text implies the lapse of a long period of time. AE's phrases are stereotyped and sufficiently general to fit a circular or general letter. If AE implies Paul has not heard of their faith, does he also mean that he himself has not had that information or is it just a part of the framework of pseudonymity?

Similarities have been pointed out between 1.15f and sections of Colossians; if there is dependence of one letter on the other it is more probably that of Colossians on Ephesians. But more probable than the dependence of one author on the other is the dependence of both on a pool of words and phrases belonging to their Pauline school. See Best 'Who used Whom?'

Quite a number of manuscripts insert in v. 15 a reference to love, 'love to all the saints'. If it was not originally present it may have been introduced to create the frequent triad, faith, hope (v. 18), love. In the manuscripts where it appears its exact position varies. This suggests that if we can find a satisfactory meaning for the phrase without the reference to love we should accept it as the harder reading. We note first that faith is related to 'the Lord Jesus' whereas the normal relation is to Christ; 'Lord' is rather the title of confession. Faith however can be given the sense of 'loyalty, faithfulness'; it does not refer to an initial act of faith but to a continuous activity. Loyalty or faithfulness towards fellow Christians could be important in many difficult situations; fellow members must be upheld. Somewhat hesitantly we suggest what is meant is that the recipients should have loyalty based in the Lord Jesus and directed towards all the saints (cf Barth; Scott; Ewald; etc.) and that therefore the reference to love should not be read.

Whether we accept or reject the reading which includes love, a dual reference is present: to be a Christian involved being related both to Christ and to fellow Christians (**saints**).

AE says that he does not **cease** some activity; is it giving thanks (the thanks would be directed to God and not to the readers) or interceding? Probably both. Elsewhere Paul in his opening sections, expressing himself in a variety of ways, continually prays for his readers (Rom 1.9; Phil 1.3f) or gives thanks for them (1 Cor 1.4; 1 Th 1.2; 2 Th 1.3; Philem 4). For AE to say Paul does not cease praying is a typical exaggeration, and should not be taken literally as if Paul were never off his knees!

17. The intercession commences with two solemn descriptions of God, both probably derived from liturgical usage. There are no similar solemn descriptions elsewhere in the genuine Paulines in the movement from thanksgiving to intercession, but what is found here fits the style of Ephesians (the nearest parallel is Col 1.3). **The God of our Lord Jesus Christ** identifies the God who is addressed as the Christian God but not however in deliberate contrast to the OT's 'the God of Abraham, Isaac and Jacob'. This kind of evocation of God when pleading with him became normal in Christian prayer from 1 Clem 64 onwards. **Father of glory** picks up **glory** from v. 14. Normally 'father of' would be followed by the name of a person, however a metaphorical use of father is found in Jas 1.17; 2 Cor 1.3 (cf Heb 12.9) with the sense 'source of'; thus here he is the source of glory to those who are his children. The phrase may be derived from liturgical usage (cf Ψ 23.7; 28.3; Acts 7.2; 1 Cor 2.8) and is not then an indirect reference to Christ, he being equated with **glory** since God is his father. Two meanings for **glory** are possible here: (i) 'might, power' (as in 3.16; Rom 6.4); God's power is emphasised in v. 20 and linked as in Rom 6.4 with his might in the resurrection; (ii) 'splendour', since 'glory' is taken up in v. 18 where the connotation is 'splendour'; v. 18 is closer than v. 20 and so (ii) is probably its significance here. 'Splendour' with its implication of 'sight' is appropriate to the impartation of knowledge and the enlightenment of the eyes. It is difficult to find an English word which carries both senses but perhaps 'majesty' may do so, as an old term for royal beings who have, or had, both power and splendour.

Two parallel requests (17b and 18a), both concerned with knowledge, give the content of the prayer. The readers' loyalty (faith) and love (if the word should be read) are not in question; what they need is more knowledge (contrast Phil 1.9). **Knowledge**, a theme already present in vv. 8f, is of great importance to AE; what follows indicates the areas where he believes his readers' knowledge should grow. God is requested to give them **the Spirit of wisdom and revelation**. This is not simply a prayer that they should be more intellectually alive, though they should be, but goes much deeper for the biblical concept of wisdom does not relate to intellectual processes alone: the fear of the Lord is the beginning of wisdom. The revelations AE prays for his readers are not insights into scientific or artistic truth, but relate to the way they are to live their lives.

Is the **Spirit** here God's Spirit or the human spirit? Of course if it refers to the human spirit, then for believers it is the human spirit as inspired by the divine Spirit. Since the readers have already been sealed with God's Spirit (v. 13) and may be presumed to possess it, many commentators take the human reference pointing out that **Spirit** lacks the article in Greek and that there are many parallel phrases to a spirit of wisdom (= a wise spirit), e.g. Exod 28.3; Num 5.14; Deut 34.9; Zech 12.10; Lk 13.11; 1 Cor 4.21; Gal 6.1. Yet **Spirit** when referring to the divine Spirit in the NT often lacks the article (Mt 12.28; Mk 1.8; Lk 1.15,

35, 41, 67; Rom 1.4; 1 Pet 1.2). Moreover while a spirit of wisdom can mean a wise spirit, a spirit of revelation can hardly mean a revelatory spirit (it means more probably a spirit open to revelation). That the Spirit is said to be given is more appropriate to something handed over from outside and is in accord with contemporary Jewish usage (e.g. Wisd 7.7). Believers are not immediately made completely wise when converted and sealed with the Spirit; an area exists then where enrichment is necessary and it can only come from the Spirit (cf 1 Cor 2.12, 14; 12.8). We note that in this verse all three persons of the Trinity are mentioned though AE has no developed Trinitarian theology. If the Spirit of wisdom stood alone here it would suggest direct dependence on Isa 11.2, but because of the addition of 'revelation' any dependence is probably indirect; Isa 11.2 affected later Jewish thought extensively and wisdom and the Spirit are regularly related. When the Spirit is absent there is no true **wisdom** (for the meaning of wisdom see on 3.10); human speculation cannot bring knowledge of God; wisdom is hidden in God (Col 2.3) and he alone can make it known (1 Cor 2.10–11); although there is considerable agreement here with 1 Corinthians (1.18–2.5), Ephesians lacks the idea of wisdom as the foolishness of God.

What is the **Spirit of revelation**? If the Spirit of wisdom imparts wisdom presumably the Spirit of revelation imparts revelations; the origin of true knowledge in God is thus again stressed. Ephesians differs here from Colossians which, while it has much to say about wisdom, has nothing to say about revelation. The charismatic discussion of 1 Cor 14 refers to 'revelations' (vv. 6, 26, 30); these are revelations or disclosures of some particular matter. In 3.3 AE speaks of a revelation given to Paul relating to the admission of the Gentiles and though this is much more general it is still the disclosure of a particular truth. There is nothing in our context which enables us to tie down the content of the revelations

The final phrase of v. 17, **in knowledge of him** (i.e. God), can be attached to what precedes and regarded as supplying God's purpose in giving the Spirit or to v. 18 and mean that believers would have their spiritual eyes enlightened through the knowledge of God. This interpretation provides a point of departure for further insights (Gnilka). What AE prays for his readers is not understanding of human nature but an understanding of God; he is not setting out an anthropology but a theology. The precise word for knowledge here is rather unusual and is found again both in Ephesians and Colossians but is infrequent in Paul. It was probably a word current in the Pauline school which Paul may have derived from Hellenistic thought where it was an important concept. The knowledge that is given is not knowledge of the nature of the world or of human nature; it does not refer primarily to theoretical knowledge; it is not the disclosure of the mystery of 3.3, 5 since this has already been made known to apostles and prophets; it is practical and experiential knowledge and should lead to obedience to and love for God and human beings. In the light of what follows it probably also relates to knowledge of God's calling, the believer's inheritance and God's might. If this is so, in what way does an understanding of God differ from an understanding of music or art? Neither Paul nor AE ever discusses the existence of the arts and so it is vain to seek in them an answer to a question like this.

18. As so often in AE's long and complex sentences the meaning is clear though the construction is not. The **enlightenment** of the **eyes of your heart** is probably another gift (**give**, v. 17). It stresses in AE's manner that true understanding comes from God alone and is the Spirit's work.

The **heart** is the centre of personality. It should neither be contrasted with the mind, as if mental processes are to be suppressed, nor equated with it, as if a mere intellectual grasp of the issues is all that is needed. The metaphor of the eyes of the heart appears elsewhere (*CH* 4.11; 7.1; 1 Clem 36.2; 59.3) and the enlightening of the eyes was also widely used metaphorically (Ps 19.8; Ezra, 9.8; Bar 1.12; 1QS 2.3; 4.2). Despite his impressive intellectual ability Paul would have remained a Pharisee had his eyes not been opened through his Damascus Road experience and what AE prays for here is a similar enlightenment of his readers. The hearers of a sermon need enlightenment as much as its preacher; if they do not have it, or do not obtain it during the sermon, they will not be able to appropriate what is being said.

By the second century **enlightenment** had become a technical term for baptism (Justin, *Apol* I, 61.12; 65.1; *Sib Or* 8.247, 271). This meaning may already be present in Heb 6.4, but since there is no obvious link in our context to baptism there is no need to see it alluded to in v. 18. The insight believers gained when they heard the gospel continued with them; they became children of light (5.8; 1 Th 5.5) and shone as lights in the world (Phil 2.15). The metaphor of enlightenment was so frequent in the ancient world that there is no need to suppose AE derived it from the Mystery Religions or gnosis; his readers, however, may have seen a connection, yet they will also have been aware of the differences between Christian enlightenment and any other. For AE salvation includes knowledge as well as those elements like adoption and the forgiveness of sin which we normally associate with it (Pokorný).

The purpose of the enlightenment of the heart is now presented in three parallel clauses introduced by **what** and further aspects of the salvation of which AE spoke in the eulogy are brought forward. Three of the leading ideas (hope, inheritance, power), one from each clause, are also found together in 1 Pet 1.3–5.

(a) The first clause speaks of the hope which comes to light through God's calling of believers; 4.4 again associates hope and call, an association found only in Ephesians. Because their call was pre-temporal (see on 1.4f) and not simply the result of subjective experience, the hope of believers is soundly based; enlightened knowledge brings it about. Hope is an important theme in Paul (Gal 5.5; Rom 5.2–5; 8.24f; 15.4; 2 Cor 3.12) and this provides the background for AE's use of the concept. In v. 18 the emphasis does not lie primarily on the expectant hoping of believers for, as Eadie comments, it would not require enlightened eyes to produce the emotion of hoping. Instead the emphasis lies on the content of what is hoped for; if this is the sense of hope here, it is not seen as one member of the triad, faith, hope, love, and so provides no reason for reading 'love' in v. 15. The actual content of the hope is not spelt out but has to be gleaned from the rest of the letter. Gentile, though not Jewish, believers were without hope before they believed (2.12); now they possess hope. Their hope is not then that of redemption, even if redemption is understood as being with God or Christ in heaven, for they have already been raised and sit with Christ in the heavenlies (2.6). If this appears to eliminate any future sense from hope, believers should remember that they are summoned to live worthily (4.1), are instructed in how to do so (4.2ff) and still require defensive armour against the assaults of the devil (6.10ff). A tension then exists between the certainty of attained salvation and the need to live as those who have not fully attained it; already heirs of salvation because they have received the first-fruits of the Spirit (1.14), they have not yet fully entered into their inheritance. Even if the content of their hope is not spelt out it needs to be distinguished from the hope of better conditions on earth, of a new social order, of attaining great wealth, or of winning a lottery or of a contented mind.

(b) The second clause explains the knowledge God has given us into **the riches** (see on 1.7) **of the glory of the inheritance** (see 1.14 for the word); as in 1.14 the church is not God's inheritance but the inheritance is what the church receives. Even though the phrase is wordy it is better as in v. 17 not to treat **glory** (for the word see on v. 17) as if it were an adjective and render 'glorious riches' or 'glorious inheritance'. The phrase 'riches of glory' probably belongs to the Pauline school for it appears again in Col 1.27 where it relates to the universality of salvation as including Gentiles. Believers are not just in the position of looking forward to their inheritance; they already partake of it since even now they sit with Christ in the heavenlies (2.6).

Who are **holy ones**? The normal rendering of the Greek word is 'saints' meaning Christian believers (cf 1.1 and the frequent Pauline use of the word in this sense). If this is its sense here nothing is added to the meaning of the verse. An increasing number of commentators, especially since the discoveries at Qumran, understand the saints here to refer to the 'heavenly ones' or 'angels' (e.g. Pokorný). Extensive evidence exists for this sense of the word, stretching back into the OT (e.g. Job 15.15; Ψ 88.6, 8; Isa 57.15; Amos 4.2; Ecclus 45.2; Dan 8.13) and appearing more regularly in the inter-testamental literature (e.g. *1 En* 1.9; 12.2; 39.1; *Jub* 31.14; 1QM 12.1; 1QH 3.22f; 11.11f). 1QS 11.7f, 'God has given them [various spiritual blessings] to His chosen ones as an everlasting possession, and has caused them to inherit the lot of the Holy Ones' (ET from Vermes) moves in the same area as Eph 1.18 in linking the members of the earthly community with the holy ones in heaven in relation to spiritual blessings (cf Wisd 5.5; 1QH 3.21f). According to 2.6 believers already sit in the heavenlies. There is then no reason to reject the interpretation of the saints as the heavenly ones in 1.18; it is also the probable meaning in 2.19 and is possible in 3.18; it was already present in Paul (1 Th 3.13); the saints on earth share their inheritance with the angels. This sharing exists now and does not belong to the future.

19. (c) The third clause relates to God's **power** and, though not a climax, is probably put last as supplying a link from v. 18 to vv. 20–3. Without God's power we would not have any certain hope, resurrection or inheritance. In typical manner AE stresses the exceeding greatness of his power. A reference to God's grace rather than his power might have been expected, but the two are not far apart; God's grace is not his amiability but his power to save. His power operates on us. AE sees himself as much in need of help as other believers; God's power works in him as in other Christians. The first person also leads appropriately into vv. 20–3 which contain credal-type statements. While it is true that God's power operates within believers, it also operates on them as it were from outside. Its external nature is confirmed here by the reference in v. 20 to God raising Christ. It is not however introduced here as a power which will eventually raise believers for they have already been raised with Christ (2.5f). The power is active now just as the hope and the inheritance exist now. When the readers appreciate the meaning of these three prayer clauses (18, 19a) they will 'be better equipped to fulfil their responsibilities and tasks in living and being to the praise of God's glory' (Roels).

Verse 19b with its multiple words for power begins the movement from intercession to theological statement. The concept of power is picked up, developed and made the basis for what God has done in Christ (20–3). V. 19b depends on v. 19a and continues the theme of v. 19a, God's power (Abbott; Schlier).

Three words for power, typical of AE's redundant style, now emphasise God's might. While many religions stress the power of the deity, what is more important is the nature of that power and the way it is exercised. For AE the power of God is closely related to his grace and love (love was related to his electing power in 1.4f), and in our present passage God's power is exercised in the raising and exalting of Christ and in the raising, exalting and delivering from sin of believers (2.1–10). V. 19b then both picks up what has been said and throws us forward to what will be said. Missing from AE's discussion of God's power is the way Paul relates it to the weakness of Christ in the cross (1 Cor 1.17ff) and his abandonment of power in his incarnation (Phil 2.6ff). AE only alludes to the incarnation in 4.9f and does so there only as a foil to the ascension on which his stress lies. Our present passage emphasises the majesty of Christ and not his humiliation. It needs also to be said that the power of God is not seen in 'miracle'; despite God's power, Paul remains a prisoner.

It is probable that the prayer ends here, to be briefly resumed at 3.1 and then, at length, in 3.14–19.

20. This verse continues the theme of power with a play on words which it is difficult to reproduce in English; **empowered** is an approximation. God's power is exercised in four specific acts: he (i) raises Christ, (ii) seats him at his right hand, (iii) subjects all things to him, (iv) makes him head of the church. The article is again found with Christ. It may serve here to prepare readers for the OT allusion and is more appropriate than 'the Lord'; the latter is the christological term usually associated with Ps 110.1, but it would be improper to speak of the empowerment of the Lord. We probably do not have here another instance of the 'in Christ' formula; 'in' denotes the place of God's activity.

(i) That God raised Christ from the dead was a basic belief of the first Christians; it is found in early confessional statements (e.g. 1 Cor 15.4; 1 Th 1.10; Rom 10.9) and in all strata of the NT. The particular phrase **raised from the dead** is also widespread (e.g. Rom 4.24; 6.4; 8.11; 10.9; Gal 1.1; 1 Pet 1.21). The resurrection of Christians is also regularly related to that of Christ. The connection is not explicit here but 2.6 refers to both the resurrection of believers and their heavenly session and is to be linked in thought to 1.20.

(ii) God has seated the one whom he raised **at his right hand in the heavenlies**. Whether or not Christ's ascension and resurrection were originally distinguished (cf Rom 8.34; Phil 2.9; Col 3.1; 1 Tim 3.16), by the time of Ephesians they are envisaged as distinct events. Once it was accepted that Christ appeared in physical form after his resurrection it was necessary to devise some means to move him to heaven where it was believed he now dwelt. This led to the separation of resurrection and ascension. The ascension (and/or theheavenly session) is sometimes simply stated as a fact; sometimes, as here, attention is drawn to the activity of the Exalted One as ruling (cf 1 Pet 3.22) or interceding (Rom 8.34); it is only in Acts 1.9–11 that the ascension is described physically. At times Christ is said to sit down at God's right hand (Heb 1.3; 10.12) and at other times God is said to seat him (Acts 2.33–5; 5.31); the latter accords better with Ps 110.1 and fits the flow of the present passage. While Psalm 110 was probably not taken as messianic prior to Christianity, believers rapidly gave it this sense. It is the Psalm most frequently quoted or alluded to in the NT, especially in relation to the heavenly session, and was early associated with Ps 8 (see on v. 22). Whether Ps 110 originally created, shaped or was simply used to express belief in the heavenly session, by AE's time it was accepted as prophesying it and used to express it. Probably AE simply accepted from the tradition both the heavenly session and its connection with Ps 110.

The session at God's right hand is made more precise in two ways: (a) it is in the heavenlies (see Detached Note: The Heavenlies); (b) in the heavenlies Christ is above the 'powers' (v. 21). 'Above' is a spatial term like 'in the heavenlies', 'right hand', and 'under' (v. 22). It is difficult to know whether AE took these spatial terms literally or metaphorically. Origen, probably influenced by Philo, is certainly aware of the problem. The association of 'aboveness' with a position of power is natural; a royal throne is set on a dais. So if Christ is set above some other beings he may be assumed to have power over them. His power and authority are also implied in the reference to the right hand. In the ancient world to be seated at the right hand was to be given the position of honour and the one who occupied it was the one closest in power to the one beside whom he sat, here God. The imagery involved, if it be imagery, is spatial rather than temporal. Since Christ already sits in the heavenlies he already has authority and power. The setting of the powers above the earth accords with AE's general view of the cosmos. In 4.10 Christ is above the heavens rather than in the heavenlies; the difference may be accounted for since 'heaven' was not a precisely defined term in the ancient world (see Detached Note: The Heavenlies); there is then no major inconsistency between 4.10 and 1.21.

21. The superiority of Christ to the powers is depicted here in a different manner from Phil 2.9–11; there those below Christ hail him as Lord. Only those whose subjection is willing and not the result of a forced defeat can offer a genuine and acceptable 'hailing' of Christ. However, in Eph 1.21 defeat is probably envisaged for there would be no point in referring to Christ's ascension as one indicating superiority to good angels; that would be obvious. The powers are then to be regarded as hostile; only in overcoming hostile powers would Christ's might be displayed. But does that not create a conflict with 1.10? The summing up of all things in Christ suggests a willing submission rather than the subjection of hostile elements. The NT in fact contains two strains of thought (see on 1.10): a belief that Christ conquered the powers; a belief that all who oppose him will eventually be won over. That the latter view only emerges briefly at various points in church history and is always speedily overcome by the former in ecclesiastical thought is not surprising, but does nothing to invalidate its truth.

Four 'titles' are applied here to the powers but there is no need in view of the following **whatever they are termed** (literally 'named') to see in that an attempt at their exhaustive enumeration (four winds, four points of the compass, etc.; compare the use of 'four' in Revelation). Equally we should not suppose that they are set in either a descending or ascending order of importance. In 1 Cor 15.24ff the subjection of the powers is in process and not yet complete but has a purpose, that God may be all in all; in vv. 21f the subjection is already complete and is an end in itself (Lindemann). Since AE is not sure he has named all the powers or classes of powers (the names he gives are not standard definitions) he adds a clause to ensure none has been excluded. Had he not done so, some of his readers who knew them by other names might have worried if the powers they knew had in fact been overcome. The clause is not a scornful rejection of the powers as if they had no real existence nor does it indicate their worth or value. In the ancient world a name was more than a verbal symbol; it was believed to have a genuine relation to the reality to which it was attached; to know the name of a demon gave power over it (Gen 2.19f; Mk 5.9). In the Philippian hymn God gives Christ a new name, Lord, indicating a new position of superiority.

By listing names and implying there are other names for the powers, AE is not however claiming that knowledge of names gives Christians superiority to the powers but saving his readers from possible doubts. It is Christ alone who has superiority.

The final clause of the verse teaches that Christ is above the four named powers and any others that may exist, whether belonging to this age or the age to come. The word underlying **age** (aeon) can be taken either spatially (= world) or temporally (= age); here because it is the **coming** age it almost certainly has temporal significance. The first Christians derived the doctrine of the two ages from Jewish apocalyptic but modified it since the Messiah with whom the coming age was associated had already come. The reference to **the coming age** is a little strange here since Ephesians has on the whole a realised eschatology (cf Introduction) and since Christ is already above all the powers; the phrase, though not in Paul, is found in Mt 12.32 (cf Heb 6.5) and has probably been drawn from the liturgical or catechetical tradition. Such tradition tends to be conservative and to continue to employ phrases after their original significance has been abandoned. AE probably therefore uses a well-known phrase without seeking to align it with his general eschatological position. Whether this is so or not, he is certainly asserting that Christ rules the powers now and will continue to do so; there are no limits to his rule. Believers need not fear the powers since they are already delivered, at least potentially, from them, though they still need to wage war against them (6.12), a war for which they are divinely equipped.

DETACHED NOTE III
THE POWERS

Prior to Ephesians Paul had employed terms similar to those of 1.21 (Rom 8.38f; 1 Cor 2.6–8; 15.24–8; and perhaps Gal 4.9); these had been taken up in Colossians (1.16; 2.9f, 13–15). AE did not then invent the terms of 1.21 and we do not need to trace their origin. It is in fact obscure. The names suggest beings with authority. It is probable that Paul derived both the terms and the ideas which they represent from Judaism, although similar ideas, if designated with different terms, existed in the Hellenistic world as the many references to them in the Fathers and in gnostic writings show. It came naturally to both Fathers and gnostics to use them. There were of course other names for supernatural beings in Judaism in addition to those in Ephesians (cf *1 En* 61.10f; *2 En* 20–2). Given AE's adoption of the terms the number of times he refers to them suggests that they were important for him or that he believed them important to his readers. Satan was originally an angel in the heavenly court and these supernatural powers were believed, at least by some, to inhabit the air or heaven (2.2; *1 En* 61.10).

To what then did AE take them to refer and to what did his readers? In considering this we have to realise that while a word or title may be used throughout a period the understanding of its referent may alter. 'Satan' remained a name in Judaism but though originally referring to an angel at the court of Yahweh (Job 1.6ff) it came to designate the supernatural opponent of God. The referents of AE's terms were in Judaism: (a) political, in the widest sense, persons or bodies, those people or bodies who control other people and bodies; (b) supernatural beings who exercise or attempt to exercise control over one another and over the created world including humanity. 'Supernatural' is used here for lack of a better word; in the ancient world the natural and supernatural were not clearly distinguished as with us but closely interwoven. In the messages to the seven churches (Rev 2.1–3.22) the angel of each church is addressed, yet it is the church itself which hears the message and is summoned to take action. Folk angels and the nations to which they were attached were similarly capable of being confused. In this way basically political terms can be applied to spiritual powers. In their earliest use the terms of 1.21 appear to have referred to good supernatural beings, in so far as they referred to such beings at all; however as in the case of Satan they came in time to denote evil supernatural beings, and this change took place prior to Paul (cf Wink). The myth of the fallen angels probably contributed to this change. Within Judaism we encounter demons who require to be exorcised (cf 1 Sam 16.14; 18.10–12; 19.8–10 and the Gospel exorcism stories) and spirits associated with Satan (e.g. 1QM). That these two aspects cannot be considered separately is seen in the phrase 'unclean spirits' which can denote both demons and associates of Satan.

The Jews and the first Jewish Christians saw their lives as affected by, if not under the control of, both hostile supernatural beings and earthly rulers and governments. It is this which may have led them to apply political terms to the evil supernatural powers. Assisting this identification would have been Jewish belief in folk angels. The latter might be regarded as friendly or hostile as the nations over which they were placed were friendly or hostile to Israel. Such a view is supported by the ambiguity of 1 Cor 2.6–8. If the terms came into use in some such way this would account for their application to both friendly and hostile powers. In Col 1.16 Christ is said to create the powers but this does not entail their friendliness; in Judaism, and Christianity, there is no ultimate dualism; Satan did not come into existence apart from God; hostile angelic powers must have also had their origin in him. Like Satan they may have been originally thought of as non-evil. The hymn of Col 1.15–20 ends with a reconciliation of all to Christ; there is no reason to conclude the 'all' of v. 20 excludes the powers of 1.16; if they require to be reconciled they must have been to some extent hostile. In the Philippian hymn, 2.6–11, the final result of Christ's work is that everything in heaven, on earth and under the earth bows down to him; if so, there must have been a time when they did not bow, a time when some of them must have been hostile.

When the Hellenistic readers of Ephesians heard the terms of 1.21 what came into their minds? Clearly they may have thought of political and social power in its many forms. That can hardly have been all, though some older exegetes did attempt to sustain this position. The terms do not normally have a supernatural reference in Greek and this must therefore have been carried over from Jewish Christianity. Of what then did Jewish Christians, and later Gentile Christians, think when they heard the words? It is impossible to be precise. There is no doubt they believed in all kinds of supernatural evil. Paul views the opponents who seek to undo his work in Corinth as controlled by Satan (2 Cor 11.13–15); so also Luke (22.3) and John (13.2) regard Judas as controlled by him. There were demons who made people sick and needed to be exorcised. Paul personalises law, sin, death, the flesh and so turns them into supernatural forces, but this does not mean that we should 'internalise' the powers and transform them into psychological forces. The power of the state is regarded as friendly in Rom 13.1–7 but not in Rev 13 where its hostility is traced to supernatural forces. In addition to this, magic with its dependence on supernatural force was an ever-present reality in the Hellenistic world (e.g. Acts 19.19). It was easy to explain the forces operating in it as demonic (Justin, *Apol* I 56). Christians had to account for idolatry and they claimed the gods whom others worshipped were demons (1 Cor 11.20). In so far as the emperors became the objects of a cult, they will have been seen as an evil supernatural influence with the double understanding of 'ruler' as heavenly and earthly. The pagan gods were related to the stars as were the powers (Rom 8.38f), and astrology was an ever-present and potent factor in directing behaviour. Fate, in so far as the Greek world saw it as controlling life, was supernatural and so could be taken to be a power. Many of these ideas came to be more clearly stated in the second century, in particular the astrological connections of the powers and the demonic under-standing of pagan worship. That does not mean that these connections were not being made at the time of Ephesians. Any or all of the forces which perverted the good and even course of the universe and, in particular, made life difficult for Christians could be seen as supernatural. These did not need to be identified with specific names, as AE indicates when he adds to his list in 1.21 the reference to other 'names'.

There are inconsistencies between the various references to the powers in the NT. We have already dealt with one apparent incon-sistency (creation by God) in relation to Col 1.16. A more significant inconsistency exists in relation to the time when the powers are overcome. In 1 Cor 15.24–8 they become subject to Christ at the parousia while in Rom 8.38f Christians are assured they need not fear them now. In Col 2.14f they are already defeated because they have been nailed to the cross (cf Col 1.20; Jn 12.31; 16.11) but in Eph 1.21f their defeat follows on the ascension of Christ. Christian thought was in process of formation at this period and consistency should not be expected. All the passages agree in seeing the defeat of the powers as related to the Christ-event. Though the powers have been defeated (Eph 1.20f) their influence has still to be fought (Eph 6.10ff). This apparent contradiction within Ephesians is part both of the inconsistency in relation to the time of their defeat and of a general biblical tension and similar to that of the indicative-imperative contrast. Christians are sons and daughters of God, therefore they should behave as such. The power of death has been destroyed, yet Christians still die. Granted Christ's victory over the powers Christians are not subject to them in the same way as they were prior to conversion for they are now equipped with spiritual weapons (Eph 6.10ff) with which to fight them. Just as those who are called to be children receive the Spirit so those who know of the defeat of Satan and his powers receive the means to fight him.

Can we explain the powers in twentieth-century terms either as political, social and economic forces, or as the power of tradition, ethical custom, race, or as psychological psychoses or forces like sex within us which we cannot control? Even if we were able to explain the powers in this kind of way in respect of some NT passages, it is not possible to do so for Ephesians for in it the powers are related to heaven (1.20f; 3.10; 6.12; cf Stott). For AE's readers the powers are supernatural and cannot be reduced to, and explained in, natural terms. Yet even if some in the West today do not believe in such supernatural powers it is necessary to remember that there remain those in the West and in other parts of the world who do. Though the powers may be connected to the heavenlies and thus to the stars and can therefore be regarded as controlling the lives of people, there is however an important difference between those who believed in them in the first century and those who read astrological columns in newspapers and magazines today; in the ancient world a real relationship was believed to exist between the stars and the gods; astrology was then a part of religion in a way it is not for the normal Westerner interested in astrology today.

This is not to deny that people today do not at times feel themselves frustrated by forces over which they have no control; these forces may be political or economic; they may be part of the culture and ethos in which they live. People may believe themselves under the uncontrollable power of a lust for food or sex, or the desire to have more and more possessions or power over others. They may see their jobs as controlled by remote financial forces or their lives as unfulfilled because of a faulty gene. They may be ambitious to perform tasks for which their physique renders them incapable; a five-foot, seven-stone young man will never be an international rugby-football forward; a woman lacking imaginative power will never be a successful novelist. People are affected by events that without their consent intrude into their lives. They may be destroyed by an accidental infusion of blood from someone who was HIV positive. They may die young without realising their full potential. In other words the same kind of tragedies happen to us as happened in the ancient world, but we attribute them to natural and not supernatural causes; we seek rational, not magical, explanations for them and, in so far as it is possible, scientific means for their cure.

This in an odd way shows up the difficulty of understanding 1.20–3. While AE and his readers might in some way accept the concept that supernatural beings are already subject to Christ their conqueror, we cannot understand, to take an example, the car accident in which some innocent person dies as an event subject to Christ; it is a stubborn fact and it and others like it will go on recurring while the world lasts. Once we have transformed spiritual beings into facts and observable forces we cannot see them as already overcome by Christ. Again it is difficult for us to take seriously the idea that the church proclaims the wisdom of God (3.10) to facts and observable forces. On the other hand when we encounter unpleasant facts and forces we may be able to face them better if we equip ourselves with the spiritual armour offered in 6.14–17. It is probably therefore wrong to attempt to transform the powers into anything which we can observe and measure, though many of the things we can observe and measure affect us in unexpected ways.

22. (iii) The central thought continues: God's action in relation to Christ. If Christ sits at God's right hand (v. 20), a position of authority, then the universe has been made subject to him and this is now expressed with a vivid metaphor drawn from Ps 8.6 which continues the spatial imagery. What applied originally to 'man' is especially applicable to the Son of man (cf Heb 2.6f). Christ has, as it were, his foot placed triumphantly not only on the necks of the powers but on everything within the universe. It is not suffi-cient to say (v. 21) that Christ is superior to the powers in the same way as a duke is to an earl, for the earl may not be subject to the duke though the latter ranks higher. The powers are not merely inferior to Christ, they are subject to him. Ps 8.6 is used also at 1 Cor 15.27; Heb 2.6–8. Ps 110.1 is also quoted in 1 Cor 15.25 and the Psalm is cited regularly in Hebrews; Ps 110 and Ps 8 were then probably linked early in Christian thought, even prior to Paul, and given messianic significance. 1 Cor 15.24–7 and Eph 1.20–3 have a number of common features but there are also important differences. 1 Cor 15.23ff concentrates on the sequence of events within the End, Eph 1.22 on the totality of Christ's lordship; unlike 1 Cor 15, Eph 1.22 represents a realised eschatology in keeping with other parts of the letter (see on 1.10); in Eph 1.22f God is the subject while in 1 Cor 15.20–8 it is Christ. If direct dependence is excluded, it can be said that AE is indebted to the same tradition as Paul, a tradition also reflected in 1 Pet 3.22; Phil 2.5–11. AE does not identify the nature of the subjection; the Psalm quotation implies its present existence as fact and that it is both total and absolute (Belser); yet as we go on through the letter we find that all is not subject to Christ for evil still exists to perplex believers.

(iv) The fourth and final action of God (v. 22b) introduces the **church** and relates Christ to it; with this half verse we begin one of the most difficult sections (vv. 22b–3) of the letter. God has given Christ as, or 'to be', **head** of the church. It is possible to translate **has given** as 'has appointed' but the idea of a gift contrasts better with v. 22a. Christ is said to be head over all; his headship is not then over the church which is his body (as in Col 1.18) but headship over the cosmos. There is no idea that there are alternative heads to Christ for the church. He is thus given a cosmic position.

Why has 'head' been introduced here? (On 'head' see Detached Note: The Body of Christ). It is possible Christ's headship over both cosmos and church is in mind. God in his graciousness has given the Christ, the cosmic head, to the church and he is then naturally its head; the nature of that headship is not worked out here but comes later in 4.15f; 5.22f. It is certainly not simply one of overlordship as with the cosmos, for that would not entail the church being his body. The church, however, for its part might be said to come under Christ's cosmic headship in view of its organic union with him (cf Caird). Yet the headship of Christ over it would be different.

23. The difficulties of this verse have long been recognised. There are three basic interrelated problems: (i) How does the **fullness** clause relate to the rest of vv. 22, 23? (ii) What is the meaning of **fullness**? (iii) How are we to take the final words **totally filled**? However, before we turn to these questions we must look at the brief introductory clause. Paul had already identified the church with the body of Christ in Romans and Corinthians and while in those epistles it is not entirely clear if the body of Christ denotes the whole church or individual congregations, this ambiguity has disappeared in Ephesians where it is applied to the whole church. Is however v. 23a parenthetical or part of the main argument? This brings us to question (i).

Does the **fullness** (pleroma) clause relate directly to v. 23a or does it refer back to v. 22, in which case it might be in apposition to either **church** (this would be very little different in meaning from the former suggestion) or to **him**? The last is rendered difficult by the remoteness of the clause from **him** and is clumsy. It would also imply that what is being explained is the nature of Christ rather than the nature of the church – which is the main theme.

Questions (ii) and (iii) are closely linked and we turn to (iii) first. The translation **who is being totally filled** seems preferable to 'who is totally filling', which is possible but unlikely because of the words rendered 'totally'. It is then wiser to accept it as a passive. As a passive it means someone or something is being filled with someone or something. It is natural to understand the words as meaning Christ was being filled. Elsewhere in the NT Christ is spoken of as 'full of grace and truth' (Jn 1.14) and of the Holy Spirit (Lk 4.1); in Col 2.3, though the verb is not used, it is said that all the treasures of wisdom and knowledge are hidden in him and this idea is very much the same; in 1 Cor 1.24 he is said to be the wisdom of God which must mean that God's wisdom fills him. In Col 1.19; 2.9 all the fullness of God dwells in Christ and this is again very much the same idea.

If then Christ is being filled, with what or whom is he being filled? This is not stated. In Col 1.19; 2.9 it is God who is said to dwell in him. Given this, it is not difficult to see AE conceiving of Christ as being totally filled with God, though it would also be possible to view him as filled with every grace and blessing. The present **being filled** would indicate a constant filling, and thus a dynamic rather than a static relation between Christ and God, and the adverbial phrase **totally** would obviate any idea that Christ was inadequately related to God.

The understanding of **fullness** (pleroma) is also difficult. Is it to be taken passively (that which is filled) or actively (that which fills). The word is found in the NT with a number of meanings. Appearing twice in Colossians (1.19; 2.19) and four times in Ephesians (1.10; 23; 3.19; 4.13) it is sometimes argued that in these epistles it has a technical meaning and this is often related to its origin. A number of sources have been suggested in respect of its origin:

(a) Gnosticism (so Schlier). The word is found as a technical term in some of the gnostic systems of the second century, in particular in Valentinianism. These references are too late to impart any certainty to the supposition that AE and A/Col borrowed the term from them; the reverse process is more likely

(b) Assuming Col 1.15–20 was a hymn adopted by the author of Colossians then the word possessed a theological use prior to Colossians. If it has the same meaning in Ephesians, and this is not certain, and if Ephesians was in some way a general letter, then since AE does not define it, there is a good chance its theological usage would have been understood without explanation by a fairly wide circle of believers in Asia Minor who would have known the Colossian hymn. It was then already an accepted term before AE came to write.

(c) Stoicism or Jewish Hellenism dependent on Stoicism. Here it is important to distinguish between the word and the concept. The word is not found in early or middle Stoicism but appears in *CH* 16.3; 12.15; 6.4. However, the idea that 'God' fills all things with his presence so that the cosmos is completely full with no vacuum in it is a basic doctrine of Stoicism. Such an explanation of the term's origin is more appropriate to Colossians where the interest is cosmic than to Ephesians where it is ecclesiological.

The word is found in the LXX (e.g. Jer 8.16; Ezek 19.7) and in Philo (e.g. *Praem et Poen* 65, *Spec Leg* 2.200, 213), and the idea of God as filling the universe would be pre-Stoic in Jer 23.24 (LXX). Jewish Hellenism, in keeping with Judaism, however, clearly distinguished between God and the universe.

From this it results that when we come to examine the meaning of pleroma in 1.23 we have to accept it as a term which was already in theological use but was also widely used without such significance. It is associated with its cognate verb 'to fill' at 1.23; 3.19; Col 2.9f and this suggests its meaning must be closely related to that of the verb. At 3.19; Col 1.19; 2.9 we have 'the total fullness' or 'all the fullness'; since this phrase first appears in the Colossian hymn (1.19) and since it is partially redundant, for pleroma itself can carry the sense of totality, the phrase in distinction from the word may well be 'technical'. Conversely the absence of 'the total' ('all the') at Eph 1.23; 4.13 may suggest non-technical usage. We cannot then begin from the assumption of a unitary meaning for the word in Ephesians (cf 1.10), let alone Ephesians and Colossians. In 4.13 the pleroma is that of Christ but in 3.19 that of God (cf Col 2.9; in Col 1.19 it is undefined). This suggests that the defining agent in 1.23 might be either Christ or God; it is in fact determined by the cognate participle **filled** whose subject (see above) is probably Christ.

One solution to the whole phrase of v. 23 sees Christ as filled and completed by the church. This understanding was popular with the Fathers (e.g. Chrysostom; Oecumenius; Ambrosiaster), with some of the Reformers (Calvin; Beza) and more recently with many English-speaking scholars under the influence of Robinson. Head and body are a unit; a head is incomplete without a body; the church completes Christ. This interpretation does not transgress in any way the grammar of the verse. Objections to it are based on: (i) The lack of support for it elsewhere in Ephesians and in the NT; it is not possible to support it from Col 1.24 for its meaning (the church, or Paul, completes Christ's sufferings?) is too uncertain (see the commentaries) for the basing of any argument on it. (ii) The immediate context of Eph 1.23 does not favour the idea of the completion of Christ since the stress has been on Christ's greatness and it would be surprising if it was now said that he needed completion (Grosheide). (iii) Though head and body may form a whole, v. 22 did not refer to Christ's headship of the body but to his headship of the cosmos and it would be inappropriate to introduce the church as a completion of that headship. (iv) More generally in the biblical pattern it is people who are filled by God or Christ (e.g. Eph 3.19); they are never depicted as filling him. (v) If the church completes Christ it is difficult to see how he can be its head and the source of its life (4.16), and also love it and give himself for it (5.25). Some of the theological difficulty of the theory might seem to be taken away if 'complement' were substituted for 'completion'; head and body complement one another; the body is the instrument for the execution of the head's will. This again is not the way in which AE views the relation of head and body, especially in this passage where we are not concerned with the activity of believers, either individually or as a whole, in the world.

Attempts have been made to overcome the objection to any idea of the church as the completion or complement of Christ by viewing Christ as an inclusive personality. Christ is being totally filled, i.e. made complete, as reconciled believers are incorporated into him. They are then his filling out or completion (pleroma) in the world as they represent him through his body the church. This is an ingenious solution but the introduction of believers as those who fill Christ comes from nowhere. When Christ and believers are brought together in relation to filling it is he who fills them (Col 2.10) and not they who fill him. An inclusive personality is not 'filled' with others; he is others.

There is no easy solution to the exegesis of v. 23. All that can be said is that our translation is probably better than any other; the pleroma is filled by Christ who is himself being filled by God. Christ is both head to the church and fills it as his pleroma. As we go on to examine other passages in which AE explains his concept of the church as Christ's body, we shall see that this interpretation is not inconsistent with them. Presumably AE has introduced pleroma as a further explanation of the relation of Christ and the church to obviate any idea of the body being interpreted primarily in a 'political' sense, as a collection of members working together for a common purpose, and to root his concept of Christian community firmly in christology. The fullness is an accomplished fact, as is the existence of the church.

DETACHED NOTE IV
THE BODY OF CHRIST

When AE wrote he was aware already of the use of the term 'body of Christ' as a designation for the church. The origin of Paul's conception of the church as the body of Christ lies deep in his theology and is to be connected among other things to his view of the relation of believers to Christ beginning in conversion/baptism and continuing through participation in the eucharist. Though the phrase 'body of Christ' is not used, the idea is present in 1 Cor 6.15 and 10.17. Whether in the latter passage body has the same connotation as in 10.16 or not, it indicates that believers form a body. In 1 Cor 6.15 the bodies of believers, which in Paul's terminology simply means 'believers', are members of Christ. This togetherness also underlies Paul's thinking when he uses phrases like 'in Christ', 'with Christ', and those which depict him as our representative and when he thinks of Christ as the Second Adam. We note also that in 1 Cor 12.13 believers are said to have been baptised into one body and in Gal 3.27 baptism is into Christ. In the light of all this it is not surprising to find the reference to Christ in 1 Cor 12.12 and to discover the first explicit occurrence of the phrase 'body of Christ' in 1 Cor 12.27. The most significant factor in its use is not then that of a unity embodying diversity, but the relation of the church to Christ. Believers are together with one another and with Christ. Paul can use the phrase because for him 'body' is not a simple physical concept; it is often equivalent to the personal pronoun. The concept of the body of Christ then existed prior to its expansion in 1 Cor 12.12ff and Rom 12.4ff along the lines of the fable of Menenius Agrippa. The image was in use in the Pauline school of which AE was a member as Colossians shows. We can assume that the phrase had been much talked over within that school. There are however differences between the way it is used in Ephesians and its earlier usage in 1 Corinthians and Romans; most of these differences Ephesians shares with Colossians. Before discussing them it should be noted that the differences do not of themselves prove non-Pauline authorship; authors regularly adapt their imagery to suit new situations and contexts. The main differences are:

a. The body is envisaged as growing (4.15f). The concept of the growth of the church, or of Christians, is found in 1 Cor 3.6f; 2 Cor 9.10; 10.15. In the second and third of these passages, and probably also in the first, it refers to a maturing, that is a growth in quality rather than quantity. This is true also of its use in Eph 2.21; 4.15f where it relates to both the building imagery and that of the body (4.16). Being a general concept (Christians mature) which has come to be associated with the body image it has no special significance in respect of the body.

b. The body has cosmic connections (3.9f; 1.22f).

c. Stress on diversity among members is missing, though Christians are still regarded as related to one another in the body (4.25; 5.30). The absence of stress in Ephesians on the use of the image to display diversity among members may simply be due to the lack of need to bring out this aspect; it was emphasised in 1 Cor 12.12ff because of division in the Corinthian church over charismatic gifts; if no clear divisions needing correction exist within a community there is no need to draw out this aspect. The fable's theme of diversity is not prominent in Ephesians (the 'member' element still survives in 4.25; 5.30); AE does not depart from the original Pauline drive.

d. Another possible variation is frequently suggested: in 1 Corinthians and Romans the body of Christ is the individual congregation while in Ephesians and Colossians it is the whole church. Yet Paul knew that the church was the continuation of the people of God, for since there was only one people of God there could be only one church; he must then have conceived of the church as neither a group of individuals sharing a common interest nor a collection of congregations. That instead he saw the church as a whole emerges from time to time: for example in Gal 1.13; 1 Cor 15.9; in some of the descriptions of it in the addresses of his letters where he writes 'to the church which is *in* ...' and not 'to the church *of* ...' (1 Cor 1.2; 2 Cor 1.1). If a contrast then exists between the earlier epistles and Ephesians and Colossians in respect of emphasis it is not an absolute one.

e. The major variation in the presentation of the body imagery in Ephesians compared with that of the earlier epistles lies in the identification of Christ as head. Since this variation is also found in Colossians we may assume that it appeared in the Pauline school to which the authors of Ephesians and Colossians belonged rather than being thought up individually by the authors of the two letters. **Head** is used physically of the uppermost part of the body and then in a similar way applied to such things as the tops of mountains. How is it used metaphorically? Here it ranges in meaning from overlordship to source or origin, e.g. of a river. In a patriarchal society the husband in a family functions as both its biological source and its ruler. In discussing Christ as head of the church two questions then face us: What led to the identification of Christ as head? What is the significance of the identification?

It is easiest to assume that the idea of Christ as head arose out of a discussion among believers on his relation to the church as his body. For Greek thought the body is not the person, as it could be for Jews (cf Rom 12.12; 1 Cor 13.3; Phil 1.20, etc.), but a less important part of the person. Body and soul make up the whole, but of the two the body, being physical matter, is inferior. To prevent this inherent inferiority of body being carried over into the representation of the church as the body of Christ, it was necessary to define Christ's position in relation to his body. The use of head might seem to be excluded since in the expanded image of 1 Cor 12.12ff ordinary members of the church had already been identified with the head of the body (12.21), as had the eyes and ears which are parts of the head (12.16). Greek thought would indeed have been happier with the idea of Christ as, say, soul and not as head. The cosmos was regularly pictured as a body in Greco-Roman literature and as such viewed as an 'ensouled body'. But if Christians were to describe Christ as the soul of his body which is the church, this might have implied a dualism with a consequent belittling of the body. 'Soul' carries neither the idea of origin, nor of overlordship, both of which can be associated with head. Possibilities other than soul were the eyes, heart, brain. However none of these terms is frequent and AE may not have been aware of them as possibilities.

In beginning our answer as to the reason for the choice of head, we need to observe how head is used in Ephesians and Colossians other than in relation to the body. In Eph 5.23 it relates husband and wife but we can safely ignore this as the origin of its use, since in the discussion at this point it is linked to the Christ–church relationship. In 4.15 and Col 2.19 it is again the Christ–church relationship which is at issue. But in 1.22 Christ's headship relates to the cosmos and not directly to the church and the same seems true of Col 2.10. In Col 1.18 the reference is to a headship over the church but most commentators argue that in the hymn underlying Col 1.15–20 the headship was one over the cosmos. It may signify origin here since it is to some extent set in parallel to 'beginning' and 'firstborn' (Col 1.18); its significance would thus differ here from Eph 1.22. Since it is in the hymn its usage must predate both Ephesians and Colossians. This may suggest that within the Pauline school Christ was first described as head in relation to the cosmos and the idea then transferred to the church. There is evidence in the Greek world for the cosmos being regarded as a body with a head and also for the leading or ruling member of the state being termed its head. Similar ideas appear in the OT and Judaism: Deut 28.13; Judg 10.18; 11.8f, 11; 2 Sam 22.44; Isa 7.8f; 9.13f; *Jub* 1.16; *1 En* 103.11; *T Zeb* 9.4; Philo, *Praem Poen* 114, 125; *Vit Mos* 2.30; *Spec Leg* 3.184. Once 'head' had been introduced into the discussion it would have been possible for Christians to choose this as the word to describe Christ's own position in relation to the church, his body.

Of the occasions when Christ is described as head in Ephesians he is clearly depicted as overlord in 5.23 and 1.22. Probably this holds also for 4.15 even if Christ, and not the head, is to be viewed as the source of the body's growth and development.

IV

FROM DEATH TO LIFE

(2.1–10)

[1] And you [he made alive] who were dead
    in your trespasses and sins
[2] in which you used to walk
      according to the aeon of the world
      according to the ruler of the kingdom of the air
        the spirit who is active now in the sons of disobedience
[3] among whom we also all once spent our lives
    in the desires of the flesh
      doing the wills of the flesh and of the intentions
      and were by nature children of wrath like everyone else –
[4] But God who is rich in mercy
    because of his great love with which he loved us
[5] [and] we who were dead in trespasses he made alive with
                                   Christ,
    – by grace you have been saved –
[6]   in that with Christ he has raised us
    and made us to sit in the heavenlies in Christ Jesus
[7] so that he might exhibit in the coming aeons
    the overflowing riches of his grace
    by means of his kindness in Christ Jesus.
[8] For you have been saved by this grace through faith;
    this has not come from yourselves;
    it is the gift of God –
[9]   not from what you have done
    so that no one should boast –
[10] we are his making, created in Christ Jesus
    with a view to good works prepared by God beforehand
    so that we should walk in them.

Three sections of 'narrative' now follow: 2.1–10 tells the story of the move of Gentile believers from paganism to Christianity, 2.11–22 that of their move into the people of God, 3.2–13 that of Paul's special position in respect of their move.

AE commences 2.1–10 with a reference to the condition of his readers before they believed (v. 1) and seems to have intended to go on at once to speak of God's remedy for their condition when he realises he has not described that condition adequately; a simple reference to sin is insufficient. So he breaks off from what he was about to say to describe the pre-Christian condition of his readers, not only as one of sin (v. 1), but also (v. 2) as one of control by supernatural evil forces; in sinning they were not their own masters but were under external control. The digression continues in v. 3 stressing that actual wrong desires governed them in acting sinfully, and pointing out that in so acting they had made themselves subject to God's judgement. With v. 4 AE begins to pick up again one of his main themes, salvation, which, had he not made his diversion, would have been the main clause of the sentence which began in v. 1. With the theme of salvation expressed, he repeats in v. 5 the thought of v. 1, adding the essential statement that those who were dead have received new life in Christ. That new life is defined in v. 6 in terms which link it to what was said in 1.20 about Christ's resurrection and heavenly session. Believers have been brought to life in that with Christ they have been raised and like him given seats within the heavenlies. The dead condition of unbelievers differs, however, from that of Christ; his death had been physical, theirs spiritual. It is this difference which occasioned v. 1 and its expansion in vv. 2f. But there is a similarity between the risen condition of believers and Christ for they were raised with him when they believed or were baptised. Their new position serves to exhibit the grace of God to the approaching 'aeons' and thus they have a role in making salvation known on a cosmic scale. The theme of their salvation, enunciated first in v. 5b, is (vv. 8–10) expanded and explained in a way that both generalises what Paul had taught and yet retains essential contact with it. Their salvation is not the result of their own efforts but is God's gracious gift; none of them can boast of what they contributed to their present position as believers. They are God's creation and even the good works they perform as Christians were prepared for them by him beforehand.

The argument thus flows from a negative description of the earlier position of the readers as held by sin and the powers of evil to a positive description of their present position as saved. It is a kind of narrative of the life of a typical believer. This change in their position results from their being caught up in what happened to Christ. In a sense AE leaves here his major theme of the togetherness of Christians to take it up again in 2.11–22, but he does so because it is essential to explain before going further how his readers have become Christians; togetherness in the church is only possible for Christians. This passage is thus a necessary preparation for what is to follow.

Attempts have been made without success to discover liturgical and credal material within 2.1–10 The passage is held together internally by the repetition in v. 5 of phrases from v. 1 and by the repetition in v. 8 of the final clause of v. 5, 'saved by grace'. Its unity is however marred by the lengthy parenthesis of vv. 2f.

1. The verse lacks a verb and it has to be supplied from v. 5 where part of v. 1 is repeated. The initial **and** of both verses creates a problem and is best left untranslated. There is no close link in v. 1 with what precedes; probably the use of **and** should be related to its use in Col 2.13a where it is also difficult. Wengst has therefore suggested that AE used a traditional couplet:

> **and you being dead in trespasses**
> **he [God] made to live with Christ.**

The couplet was one current in the Pauline school and part of a larger passage to which it was linked through the **and**.

In Col 2.13 circumcision is mentioned, probably implying a baptismal reference. By omitting the reference to circumcision AE has reduced the baptismal colouring here, if not removed it altogether, though he does refer explicitly to baptism in 4.5; and probably in 5.26. His addition of a second word, **and sins**, is in keeping with his normal love of synonyms. In each case the plural indicates actual sins as distinct from a sinful condition.

This brings us to the crux of the verse: What does it mean to be **dead in sins**? It is the pre-Christian condition in which both Jews and Gentiles exist. Though v. 6 introduces the idea of a resurrection with Christ there is no idea in v. 1 of a 'death with Christ' as in Rom 6.3ff. A connection between death and sin gradually appeared in Jewish theology through reflection on Gen 3 (cf Ezra 3.7; Wisd 2.24; Ecclus 25.24; etc.) and on the idea that the soul that sins dies (Ezek 18.20; cf 4 Ezra 3.25f; 8.59f; Baruch 54.15, 19; etc.). V. 1 offers a realised eschatological conception of death, an idea present also in 5.14; Col 2.13; Jn 5.24; 1 Jn 3.14 (cf *Sentences of Sextus* 7) which is consistent with the idea of 'new birth'; if at some stage believers come to life they must have been previously dead. The idea of a pre-conversion death continued among the early Christians (Ign *Philad* 6.1) and was developed in gnosticism (e.g. Hipp *Ref.* 6.35.6; *CH* I 19; VII 2; Clem Alex, *Exc Theod* 58.1; 80.1).

The **sins** which produce death are not those of Adam nor are they particularly heinous sins. They are those words, deeds and thoughts which separate from God (cf 2.12; 4.18). The idea is not that people are born alive and slowly die through sinning and are then made alive again at conversion. Still less is there any suggestion that people begin by being spiritually alive and then die because of sin. AE does not have in mind a process of slow dying or moral degeneration. In using his phrase he is not passing a moral judgement on society (contrast 4.17–19; Rom 1.18ff) but making a theological judgement on the pre-conversion existence of all. He is not indicating that there is a certain point in the development of human life at which 'death' takes place (e.g. when sin comes to be recognised as sin). The lifestyle of the non-Christian is one which may be described as one of death or as one of sins and trespasses. People are born dead and remain so until they come to believe (Calvin). Those who are dead in this way cannot come to life of their own accord; only God can make them live; so the passage goes on to speak of the way God gives life (vv. 5, 6). But before it does this it approaches the life of the unbeliever from another angle, as one under the control of alien supernatural forces.

2. At this point AE breaks off into a parenthesis, mangling the grammar, for v. 1 had not described fully the nature of the pre-Christian life of believers and so he qualifies it with vv. 2f which is in line with what he said in 1.21; people are subject to the control of the powers. He now he takes up this aspect of pre-Christian life.

The Christians took over from their Jewish background the metaphor of **walking** to describe behaviour. In proportion to their length both AE and A/Col use it more regularly than Paul and it was therefore probably a word of their Pauline school learnt first from him. Believers do not now walk under the control of the devil though they once did. In the Pauline corpus Christians are regularly reminded of their pre-Christian condition (cf Rom 5.8–11; 6.19–21; 7.5; 11.30; 1 Cor 6.9–11; Gal 4.3, 8; Eph 5.8; Col 1.21; 2.13; 3.7; Tit 3.3). **Once** they lived in such and such a way; **now** they live differently.

Aeon normally indicates a period of time whether brief or lengthy (the two ages) but occasionally the universe (Heb 1.2; 11.3). However both prior to and after the beginning of the Christian movement it was used of deities. How then is it used in 2.2? Its association with **world** might suggest it had the same meaning; AE loves to put synonyms together. On the other hand if **ruler** in the next phrase indicates a personal being would not the parallelism require its identification with this being? (Satan had many names in the contemporary period and another would not be surprising.) The latter seems the simpler solution. If it is objected that it had a temporal sense in 1.21 and may have in 2.7, that does not require rejection of the personal sense; when words have more than one meaning the correct meaning must be determined from the actual context; **flesh** is used with two different senses even within one verse (v. 3). The essential meaning of the cosmic and temporal interpretations hardly differs.

While it is clear in the next phrase that **ruler** refers to the devil, it is not obvious why AE chose this particular phrase or what is its peculiar flavour. It is used elsewhere in the NT and early Christianity of a personal power of evil (Jn 12.31; 14.30; 16.11; Ign *Eph* 17.1; 19.1; *Magn* 1.2; *Trall* 4.2; *Rom* 7.1; *Philad* 6.2). It was thus perfectly natural for AE to choose the word to designate the devil rather than a Jewish name like Satan; he knows it will be understood in the Greek world. The **air** is the region, or part of the region, between heaven where God dwells and the earth (see Detached Note: The Heavenlies) and is peopled with evil beings; from another point of view it is the sphere in which the evil powers are active (*T Levi* 3.1–3; *T Benj* 3.4; 2 *En* 7.1–5; 18.3–6).

The most difficult word in the second phrase is **kingdom**. It could be taken adjectivally, 'the powerful ruler of the air' or 'air' could be adjectival, 'the ruler of the airy power', or all three nouns could be given their full value as nouns: 'the ruler with authority over the air' or 'the ruler of the power which the air exercises'; of these the first two have little to commend them and the second two require us to read too much into the way the words are associated. The whole phrase is most easily understood if the word has the sense of the sphere or area in which authority is exercised (cf Gnilka; Schlier; Ewald; Schnackenburg; Lincoln), a meaning which it probably gathered from its use in the LXX; it has this sense in Lk 6.4; 22.53; 23.7; Col 1.13. Before their conversion believers therefore lived lives controlled by the ruler of the demonic spirits or evil angelic beings who inhabit or control the space above the earth and below heaven. As spirits **of the air** they are near to man and can easily lead him into evil.

The **spirit** in the final clause is then an (the) evil spirit, a regular meaning of the word in Jewish Greek derived from its Hebrew significance. It is much more appropriate to the context to take it in this way with many of the early Fathers than with some moderns as 'spiritual influence'. This evil spirit is active **now**. With what does this **now** contrast? There is nothing in the passage which suggests a past free from the activity of this spirit; it was the spirit in which believers once (v. 4) walked; now at least they are partly set free from it, and in their future when Christ is all in all it will have lost all its power. While this understanding is possible, it is more likely that AE is reflecting on the present condition of the world outside the Christian community rather than contrasting past and future (for the usage cf 1 Tim 6.17; 2 Tim 4.10; Tit 2.12).

The evil powers exercise their present activity in **the sons of disobedience**; the form of the phrase is Semitic; it is found regularly in the NT (Mk 3.17; Lk 10.6; 16.8; 20.34; Acts 4.36; Eph 5.8; 1 Pet 1.14). It is equivalent here to 'disobedient [or unbelieving] sons'. The Spirit of God now works in believers but the evil spirit among all others. Disobedience and unbelief are closely related; disobedience is not just disobedience to a set of moral rules, but disobedience to God in the rejection of the salvation offered in Christ and is therefore unbelief.

In breaking the structure of his sentence at 2.2 AE must have felt that to characterise the past life of his readers and the present life of unbelievers solely in terms of a death in sins and trespasses was not sufficient. Although AE says **once** he may not be thinking primarily in terms of time but rather in terms of area or sphere. His readers were under the control of external forces when they were outside the church; now within it they are under other influences. AE does not refer to forces acting on people to excuse them (so Chrysostom). Those who, like AE, accept a dualistic view of existence in which God is opposed by a personal evil spiritual power, even if that power is ultimately subject to God, must characterise life apart from God as in the control of that power. There may be more than one aspect to the control exercised by that power if, for instance, we take the **aeon of this world** as indicating the totality of existence and not referring directly to the evil power. This would suggest pressure from both natural and supernatural forces but this is a distinction which would not have been so clear to early Christians as to us. Over and above the separation from God caused by sins and trespasses another factor exists: the power evil beings exercise on human life. AE does not picture this power as coming from the 'material' nature of existence as with some gnostics; nor is it present because of creation by an evil god.

How should those who no longer accept the idea of super-natural evil powers as affecting human life understand what AE is saying? Ought they to speak of the *Zeitgeist* or the spiritual and moral atmosphere of society? Such a simple substitution cannot be made, not only because the *Zeitgeist*, since it is the product of human thinking and action, is not a personal being, but because the atmosphere of society is not wholly evil, as by definition spiritual forces opposed to God are. In Christian or post-Christian society Christianity has affected society and encouraged factors operating for good within it; only if we deny the existence of goodness apart from Christianity can we assert the wholly evil atmosphere of paganism. Such negative judge-ments may be implied in what AE says (cf 4.17–19), but if so we should regard him as making a theological and not a sociological judgement on society. How then are we to understand what AE is saying in respect of control by external evil powers? He appears to be claiming that the life of pagan society is dominated not only by a personal will towards sin but also by supernatural forces driving it to evil. Such forces still exist, though we may not term them supernatural. They are the pressures of society, which if not wholly evil are not wholly good: poverty, upbringing and environment, genetic constitution, physical disability, economic decisions taken at a distance. These are wider than the spiritual atmosphere of a culture and they exercise a compulsion on those who are subject to them so that the end result may seem the same as for those who believe they are trapped by supernatural forces. Only those who wear the armour of God (6.12ff) can resist them.

3. The digression is continued but with a return to the human aspect of sin and a sudden change from the second person plural to the first; thus questions are raised about who is intended by the first plural and how the verse relates to what precedes. The combination **we all** renders difficult the interpretation of the first person plural. Stress on the **we** implies a contrast with the 'you' of v. 2 suggesting that Jewish Christians may now be in mind (so Abbott; Barth; Schlier; Ernst; Bruce; etc.); stress on the **all** suggests it is to be understood of both Jews and Gentiles ('you Gentile Christians once lived in sin … in fact we all, Jews and Gentile Christians, did so; so Gaugler; Grosheide; Ewald; Schnackenburg; Lindemann; etc.). This is preferable, and it is this understanding of the first plural which is continued from here through the remainder of 2.1–10.

There is nothing in v. 3 which is particularly relevant to Jews; it cannot be said that Jews unlike Gentiles are subject only to the desires of the flesh and not to the devil. Certainly in vv. 4f the first person plural must mean 'all Christians'; a sudden change in reference between v. 3 and v. 4, though possible, would be difficult. There is however a third way of understanding the first plural where the contrast is drawn between readers (vv. 1f) and writer (v. 3); AE's tact leads him in v. 3 to associate himself with his readers in sin (so Mitton; Simpson; Masson); this way of taking it however removes the writer from ever having been under the control of the devil.

All were among the sons of disobedience because all once lived in conformity with the desires of the flesh. It is wrong to regard v. 3 as an unmythological interpretation of v. 2 (so Lindemann). Such a change from v. 2 may accord with modern ideas of the causes of sin but AE would have accepted the descriptions of both v. 2 and v. 3 as valid. **Desire**, strictly a morally neutral word (e.g. 1 Th 2.17; Phil 1.23), regularly carries an evil connotation in the NT, probably under Jewish influence. Greek readers would however have easily picked this up since, though for a different reason, the word also has a bad sense in Stoic philosophy being one of the passions which reason ought to control, if not eliminate. The desires of Jews and Christians however are evil because they are opposed to God's will, not because they disturb 'calm reason'. The evil sense of **desire** in v. 3 is made clear through its connection with 'flesh' (cf Gal 5.16; 1 Jn 2.16; 2 Pet 2.18). While evil desires are often used to describe non-Christian existence (1 Pet 1.14; Tit 3.3; 1 Th 4.5) they are also present in Christians (Rom 13.14; Gal 5.16; Eph 4.22). It is not indicated here what they are, but AE would probably have included those he lists in 5.3–5.

The desires of our flesh sounds a characteristically Pauline phrase but Paul rarely uses a personal pronoun with **flesh**. When the pronoun is present, flesh cannot be understood as a power from outside affecting human existence. Before we determine more exactly its meaning in v. 3a, we must examine v. 3b where it is again found.

Verse 3b is apparently parallel to v. 3a and explanatory of it. **Wills** is an unusual plural which AE may have used in parallel with the plural **intensions** to create a feeling of comprehensiveness: all we intend is evil. Sin belongs not only to the human body but also to the mind and the will. Returning now to the meaning of flesh in v. 3a, the parallelism between v. 3a and v. 3b suggests that in v. 3a flesh must apply to the whole of human existence, indicating a life lived apart from God, or, in less religious terms, a life governed by human desires whose main aim is self-expression. That between v. 3a and v. 3b **flesh** should to some extent have changed its sense is not surprising for this regularly happens when writers use a word with a wide range of meaning. In neither case has the word its characteristic Pauline sense; this is true also of the use of sin and death in v. 1; thus we have Pauline language in these verses without Pauline thought.

The third clause of the verse is neither a further explanation of v. 3a nor a consequence of either it or v. 3b but is coordinate with both. It was not that Christians became **children of wrath** because they sinned. V. 3c provides a parallel or alternative description of non-Christian existence. V. 3a and v. 3b together describe the activity of non-Christians and therefore of the readers before they became Christians; v. 3c is a statement of status. At first sight **children of wrath** appears to employ a similar idiom to 'sons of disobedience' (2.2) but the genitive functions differently; sons of disobedience are disobedient people; children of wrath are not angry people but people subject to the wrath of God; for this form of the idiom see Jn 17.12; Lk 20.36; 2 Th 2.3; 2 Pet 2.14. The idiom of v. 3c is probably Semitic in origin (cf 1 Kgdms 20.31; 2 Kgdms 12.5; Ψ 78.11; 101.21; Isa 57.4) but is not unknown in non-biblically oriented Greek. Almost exact parallels to our expression appear in Apoc Mos (see *Life of Adam and Eve*) 3.2 where Cain is described as a 'son of wrath' and in *Sib Or* 2.309, 'children of anger'; those so termed end in eternal perdition. These parallels suggest that in 2.3 the wrath in mind is the eschatological wrath of God, though as such this wrath is not necessarily future and may be experienced now (cf Rom 1.18ff; 13.4f and see on 5.6), for AE has a realised eschatology. It should be understood as personal wrath rather than impersonal, though the parallel with human wrath should not be drawn too closely for unlike human anger God's anger is neither malicious nor spiteful. The absence here of an explicit reference to God is no more surprising than the similar absence in the references to grace in vv. 5, 8. That believers were once, and unbelievers are now, subject to the eschatological wrath of God coheres with their being once dead in trespasses and sin.

How does the qualification **by nature** affect the phrase? The term **nature** has no equivalent in biblical Hebrew and is found only in later Jewish Greek. Within our context it could mean either 'character' or 'constitution': children of wrath because of behaviour or children of wrath as human beings. If the former we would expect an ethical quality to be stated and the understanding of the whole phrase as 'subject to wrath as human beings' accords better with v. 1. Unbelievers are 'dead', not because of a succession of sins which brought death, but because they have never come alive as believers. As dead they are subject to judgement (cf Jn 3.36) and so may properly be described as 'subject to wrath'. 'Children of wrath by nature' thus describes 'a permanent condition' (A. T. Hanson) in the relation of unbelievers to God. It is not a judgement on the factual degree of their sin. If any parallel or contrast is intended with the actual world, it may be with Stoic teaching where living according to nature is true living; such living for AE would be subject to the judgement of God. Granted that what we have here is not Stoic teaching, the theological distinction between nature and grace should not be read into the phrase; if there is a contrast it lies between what men are, left to themselves, and what they become when God makes them to live, that is, the contrast is between 'then' and 'now' or between those outside the church and those within it and not between the ways in which each state is attained.

Has that 'outside' state been created by 'original sin' as the use of 'children' might suggest? In the idiom however 'children' is not used literally. There are a number of possibilities: (i) original sin in the traditional hereditary sense; (ii) an involvement in sin through 'constitution' or 'nature', regarded either as providing an innate capacity for sin or as belonging to human nature as such, whether considered individually or socially; (iii) the person who lives without God is subject to God's wrath; (iv) an involvement with sin through actual sins so that 'character' becomes sinful. (iii) and (iv) seem excluded as referring to actual behaviour and not taking **by nature** sufficiently seriously; (ii) is probably what is being said but there is nothing which would render (i) untenable and equally nothing demanding its acceptance. In either case the use of **nature** implies that unbelievers left to their own devices cannot escape God's judgement. When does God's judgement takes place? If for AE it is possible to envisage believers as already sitting in heavenly places (v. 6) it seems possible to conceive of unbelievers as already under the judgement of God, even though that judgment is eschatological and has not yet fully taken place.

2.1–3 explain non-Christian human existence in two ways: as governed internally by sin and externally by evil supernatural powers. Can these two approaches be reconciled? While economic pressures on people may come from outside as a result of the human greed of others, a person's genetic constitution cannot be blamed on the sin of others. AE had probably not thought much about economic pressures as such; their results on individuals he would probably have put down to evil supernatural forces; as for sins, he would also probably have put these down both to human nature and, with much traditional theology, to outside powers like the devil.

Does a hymn or credal fragment underlie vv. 4–10? It is very difficult to work out any proper strophic structure for this supposed hymn. The idea of **being made alive** (v. 5) picks up that of being dead in v. 1 and the idea of being raised and given a seat in the heavenlies with Christ follows on the resurrection and ascension of Christ in 1.20. Thus the passage fits easily into its context, suggesting it was written for it.

4. If unbelievers were once dead in sin, under the power of evil supernatural beings, controlled by their own wicked desires and subject to God's wrath, they could expect no mercy from God, yet surprisingly, that is not so, for God is rich in mercy. Thus the parenthesis of vv. 2, 3 not only elaborates v. 1 but also sets off more strongly the contrast appearing with v. 4. The new position of believers is a result only of the nature and activity of God. As in chap. 1 so here again the initiative in salvation lies with God and we have a *theo*logy rather than a *christo*logy. It is probably wrong to overstress here the contrast between the 'wrath of God' (v. 3) and his 'mercy'. When AE began v. 1 he had v. 4 in mind; v. 3c is not then a climax carefully built up through vv. 1–3b to be contrasted with v. 4. The real contrast lies between 'death' (vv. 1, 5) and 'life' (v. 5). It is introduced with a general statement of God's nature: **rich** (a favourite term of AE, see on 1.7) **in mercy** which leads on naturally to a succession of active verbs.

Some commentators (e.g. Schlier; Conzelmann; Gnilka) have seen a connection between the use of **mercy** and baptism and instance 1 Pet 1.3 and Tit 3.5 as parallels. The connection is certainly present in Tit 3.5, but it is not immediately so in 1 Pet 1.3 unless that letter is taken to be a baptismal sermon or liturgy; this is unlikely. **Mercy** is also used in 'election' contexts (Rom 9.23; 11.30–2; 1 Pet 1.3) and since this is a theme prominent in

1.3–14 it may have determined its choice here. It is more probable, however, that AE chose the word because it is one occurring frequently in the OT, and is a synonym for **love** which he is just about to use. V. 4b is a connecting link between v. 4a and v. 5. God's love in the death of his son is a part of his merciful attitude towards people which reaches its climax in that death, so that through that death those who are dead in sin are made to live. The new life of Christians is then related directly to God's action in Christ rather than to his nature as merciful.

5. Here as at v. 1 the initial **and** is difficult and probably due to the use of preformed material (see on v. 1). It is probably best left untranslated. Our verse repeats the essential content of v. 1 with the omission of 'sins', which was an addition in v. 1 to the preformed material; it also alters the second person to the first. **Made alive with** is the new element in what AE is saying. Paul does not speak of **being made alive with Christ** but often speaks of **being made alive** and does this almost always in resurrection contexts (Rom 4.17; 8.11; 1 Cor 15.22, 36, 45), using it of the future resurrection of believers (Rom 8.11; 1 Cor 15.22) and as describing the activity of God or Christ (Rom 4.17; 1 Cor 15.45). All his references may be understood as relating to the future final resurrection, whereas here and in Col 2.13 the act of making alive lies in the past. Resurrection is however also its primary significance here where the verb's reference to 'life' contrasts vividly with the concept that those outside the Christian community were previously dead.

In v. 5 we have the first of three steps, the verbs of v. 6 denoting the second and third: **made alive**, **raised**, **seated in the heavenlies**. Dead people cannot bring themselves back to life (Könn) and so the first step here, and the following two, come from God. We can arrange neither to be born nor to be reborn.

The antithesis between death and life in v. 5 is not however the same as that in Romans 6 where a past dying with Christ is usually understood as contrasting with a future rising with him, and of course it is not the same as in those passages where 'with Christ' refers to a final future existence. What we have here must have arisen independently, for the death is one existing from the time of birth, is one in sin (see v. 1) not one with Christ. There is much in the NT, e.g. the new creation in Christ (2 Cor 5.17) or the concept of the new birth, testifying to the present new life of believers. Those born anew commence, as it were, a new life just as dead unbelievers begin to live when they are made alive by God. The new life must have begun at some point, as is indicated here (cf Col 2.13) by the use of a past tense.

When do believers begin to enjoy this new life? (a) at the resurrection of Christ? (b) at the moment when faith began? (c) at their baptism? (a) is a possibility (cf Caird; Lock) in the sense that when Christ who was a representative or inclusive figure was raised all were potentially raised with him; the past tense **loved** in v. 4, which can be referred to the Christ-event, gives some support to this view. Yet believers were dead in an entirely different way from Christ and therefore can hardly have been 'included' in him when he was made alive. The choice must then lie between (b) and (c). The readers, once dead, have been made alive and this would have taken place at the moment they became Christians. But is this the moment when faith began or the moment when they were baptised? The reference to 'faith' (v. 8) would support (b); the reference to baptism is clear in the similar passage of Col 2.13. But the distinction later theologians have drawn between the moments of faith and baptism, derived from the post-New Testament practice of enforcing a lengthy catechumenate, would have been unreal to the primitive church. Acts shows that once belief had been affirmed baptism followed directly as the first act of obedient faith (cf 2.41; 8.36; 10.47f; 16.31–3); Acts probably represents in this respect both what originally happened and the practice of its own period which was more or less contemporary with that of Ephesians. It is probably then incorrect to ask whether AE had faith or baptism in mind; for him they would have been an indissoluble unity.

A brief parenthesis now breaks the sequence of thought: **by grace you have been saved**. If AE's readers have been made alive and so saved this is not through any effort or goodness on their part but only because of the grace of God. AE develops this thought in vv. 8–10 but he cannot wait until then to express his wonder at what God has done. The parenthesis as such stands out from the ongoing argument through the sudden change from the first person to the second; there are changes in person again at v. 8 and v. 10. It is unlikely that AE wishes to distinguish in v. 5b between himself and his readers or between Jewish and Gentile Christians as if either he or Jewish Christians were not saved in the same way as others. The parenthesis is an interjection of the author into his argument in which by a change of person he drives home his point more forcefully; at the same time it could also be a quotation of a phrase regularly used in worship.

The past tense of **saved** is unusual in the Pauline corpus. Paul normally uses the verb in the future (e.g. Rom 5.8, 9; 9.27; 1 Cor 3.13) or with a future reference (e.g. Rom 11.14; 1 Cor 5.5), though he also speaks of salvation as an ongoing process (1 Cor 1.18; 15.2; 2 Cor 2.15) and uses the cognate noun to describe that process (Rom 10.10; 2 Cor 6.2). Only once (Rom 8.24) does he set salvation in the past and there it is qualified by a reference to hope. Moreover he does not elsewhere connect **grace** with **save** relating it instead to justification. In view of these differences from Paul's normal usage, it is surprising to find Foulkes describing the present clause as Paul's 'favourite summing up of the gospel'. Bruce is surely more correct when he says the clause 'departs from *distinctively* Pauline usage' (italics as in Bruce). The actual tense AE uses suggests that the 'state of salvation' is in mind; 'life' will now be continuous since death is past.

6. In Col 2.13 being made alive with Christ is explained as the forgiveness of sin and the cancellation of the legal bond; Eph 2.6 relates it to the resurrection and ascension. This appears to create a temporal sequence with ascension with Christ following on resurrection with him, but this is an illusion so far as AE is concerned; believers once raised are in heaven and are there immediately seated. So the two verbs of v. 6 do not follow chronologically on one another or on the being made alive of v. 5. It is better to regard all three verbs as aspects of the same act of God, **made alive**, **raised**, **seated**. **Made alive** comes first because nothing can happen without the dead being made alive. Paul usually describes the passage from pagan to Christian life by speaking of dying and rising with Christ. AE follows the same way of thinking, but expresses it differently using the same verbs as those of 1.20, verbs drawn from the Christian credo. 2.6 thus offers from a different angle what it means to be a Christian. It is interesting that at this point his sequence of events differs from that of Col 2.12f where burial and resurrection with Christ precede being made alive from the death of sin and the latter is apparently the explanation of the former. AE can have a different order because his primary focus is not on baptism. For AE rising with Christ and sitting with him in heaven explain the significance of being made alive.

By the time of Ephesians the idea of dying and rising with Christ was part and parcel of Pauline imagery; in Paul the verbs relating to resurrection are normally in the future. However, in our verse resurrection with Christ is set in the past and with it is linked the heavenly session with Christ, both seen as accomplished facts. The change to the past tense in respect of resurrection with Christ had already been made in Col 2.12; 3.1. It is not unnatural. The present nature of new life with Christ following on a past death with him is certainly indicated in the genuine Pauline letters (Rom 6.4, 10, 11, 13; 7.4; Gal 2.20; 2 Cor 4.10, 12; 5.17); there is no point in exhorting believers to live a new life if that life belongs only to the future. In Rom 6.1ff dying and rising with Christ is associated with baptism; baptism was a past fact for believers; it was inevitable that some who had been baptised should eventually come to think of their resurrection as past fact since they were already enjoying the new life that resurrection would bring; indeed we find that when the pastness of resurrection with Christ is first positively stated in Col 2.12 it is linked to baptism; the author of Colossians may however have had some hesitation about this, since in 3.5 he writes of the new risen life as hidden with God. In Eph 2.6 there is no explicit reference to baptism and it is difficult to argue for an implicit one, since AE does not use the verbs denoting dying and being buried with Christ which are particularly linked with it in Rom 6; the absence of a reference to baptism is not unreasonable, since from the beginning expressions relating to new life with Christ were not exclusively associated with the rite (cf Gal 2.19f; 6.14; 2 Cor 4.10; 5.14; Phil 3.10); Christians of that period did not distinguish so clearly between the moment when faith began and baptism took place as we do (see on v. 5). The past nature of Christ's own resurrection would also lend momentum to the acceptance of the past nature of that of believers. The idea may also be implicit in the pre-Ephesian and probably non-Pauline hymn of 5.14.

The transfer of believers from the death of sin and the realm of the devil is expressed more strongly in v. 6 than elsewhere in the

NT when it is said that believers have sat down with Christ in the heavenlies. In other places their reign is set in the future (2 Tim 2.12; Rev 3.21; 5.10; 20.4; 22.5; cf 1 Cor 6.2f; 1 Pet 2.9; Mt 13.43; Rom 8.17, 30). Believers are distinguished from Christ in that they are not said to sit at God's right hand.

Colossians and Ephesians share the idea of a past resurrection of believers with Christ, and in Ephesians it is impossible to decide whether AE thought the moment when this took place was that of faith or baptism (see v. 5). In accepting a past ascension of believers, AE goes beyond Colossians which in 3.3 says only that believers are now hidden with God. It is however logical to accept ascension with Christ once a past resurrection with him has been accepted; it is also in keeping with AE's belief that the church is active in the heavenlies (3.10), where it has access to God (2.18), and with 2.19, if the 'saints' there are the inhabitants of heaven. However, in 1 Cor 4.8 Paul spoke scornfully of some who believed that they were already reigning as kings. In 2 Tim 2.18 the belief that resurrection is already past is condemned as heretical. The realised nature of the heavenly session of believers goes so much against what we would expect and so differs from Paul that it is not surprising that Bratcher and Nida suggest that translators should insert a phrase like 'as it were', but there is no justification for this. Would Paul if he had still been alive have condemned what AE writes here?

What is missing in Ephesians is any suffering of believers (Rom 8.17) and dying (Rom 3.4, 6) with Christ. This leaves the impression that AE is concerned too much with seeing Christians as in a position of glory without first passing through suffering (Rom 8.17), an impression reinforced by his failure when he later discusses the behaviour of believers to say anything about what they may have to endure.

In considering this it is wise to remember the particular flavour AE gives to 'in the heavenlies' (see Detached Note: The Heavenlies). These are not the perfect heaven of later Christian thought, but a place where evil powers still fight to maintain their position (6.10ff). AE does not then see believers who sit in the heavenlies as freed from the struggle with evil and sin, and in the second part of his letter he has much advice and exhortation to give to them for this struggle. His teaching on the heavenlies is then consistent. The background to Paul's attack in 1 Cor 4.8 on those who claim to reign already is their spiritual enthusiasm. Nothing AE writes suggests he saw this as a danger for his readers. Whatever defence however is put up to explain the meaning of AE's words within his context, it cannot be denied that they are open to wrong deductions; our verse is quoted in gnostic contexts in support of a present spiritual resurrection (*Treat Res* I, 4 45.27; cf 49.16–28). Ephesians may thus be on the way to what ended as gnosticism.

What does AE mean by sitting in the heavenlies? In 1.20 Christ's seat in the heavenlies implies his superiority to the powers; he occupies a position of authority and reigns. We should expect the same to be intended of Christians; they reign, or rather, they participate in Christ's reign. Yet it is not said that believers are exalted to the right hand of God as was Christ. Their position in the heavenlies is not then identical with his. In 6.10ff believers are offered equipment for exercising authority over evil spiritual powers, for, unlike Christ, Christians so long as they live are still threatened by these powers. It would seem that AE in following through the apparent parallel of rising with Christ and sitting with him has not been able to express adequately what he wished to say and has left himself open to misunderstanding, and that not only in a too realistic sense by gnostics. More usually as with the Fathers the realism has been undervalued. The problem of what sitting in the heavens means is not new to Christianity for no one supposes that when in Ps 110.1 the king is said to be at God's right hand he was actually sitting there, yet it is basic to the description of the Christian life; on the one hand believers are still plagued by sin; on the other they already reign (Rom 5.17) in a new type of existence. AE is faithful to both sides of this paradox but throughout the letter he tends to stress its second element and 2.6 taken out of the context of the letter is open to serious misunderstanding. Those who stress the first element also look forward more consistently to a future eschatological realisation of the second. The future is not stressed by AE but it has not fully disappeared (e.g. 1.14, 18; 2.21; 4.4, 15f, 30; 5.5, 16, 21).

7. God does not raise believers to the heavenlies merely for their own good but that he might exhibit, or prove, the wealth of his grace to (in) **the coming aeons**. Since **aeons** is plural here it can hardly mean 'the coming age'. If the plural is to be taken as a genuine temporal plural it is better to understand it as suggesting that the future consists of a number of periods of time (so Origen, *de Princip* II 3.5). The aeons would be the future history of this age and of the age to come as they approach from the future (so Gnilka; Gaugler; Ernst; Bruce). It would however be wrong to attempt to identify the aeons as particular periods of history or as implying the rise and decay of civilisations. God, by what he has done for the writer and readers of the letter, is able to exhibit or prove his grace to future ages.

The main difficulties in referring **aeons** to the 'coming ages' are these: (i) It gives a unique position to the writer and readers. It is easy to see how God's grace towards them could be displayed to those among whom they live but an approaching aeon will shortly be an aeon which is past and it will have within it believers, as well as those in AE's aeon, in whom God's grace will be seen and it would have been better to refer to these. (ii) Human beings will not be aware that writer and readers have sat down in the heavenlies unless they have spiritual perception; in that case they will be believers and will not require God's grace to be exhibited to them in this way. To avoid these difficulties the aeons have been understood as supernatural personal beings. The evidence for this use of the word is widespread in second-century gnosticism and the aeons could be viewed either as friendly or hostile. In either case such an understanding follows on well from v. 6: the aeons inhabit the heavenlies in which the believers sit. It is more natural to regard the aeons as hostile since if they were friendly they would not require God's grace to be shown to them. If hostile, then they could be conceived of as coming against or attacking. 3.11 may be said to present a similar idea for there the divine mystery is made known through the church to the supernatural powers. However, this whole view runs into several difficulties: (i) the Greek verb translated **exhibit** never means 'to show, or prove, to'. (ii) In 3.21 the aeons are related to the temporal term 'generations'.

There is no easy solution. It may be that AE plays on the ambiguity of **aeons** and wishes to say that the exaltation of reader and writers to their position in the heavenlies will indicate the grace of God to the future ages which contain personal supernatural beings. This makes the primary significance of the word temporal. Whatever meaning is chosen for **aeons** the verse again suggests that AE sees a cosmic significance in Christian salvation; God is concerned with more than the salvation of individuals or even of the church as a whole.

What God exhibits or proves is **the overflowing riches of his grace**. AE uses a similar phrase in 1.7. **Grace** picks up v. 5 and prepares for v. 8. To have been made to live and been raised to sit with Christ in the heavenlies is the result of God's grace and of that alone (v. 8b). It might seem that AE had said all that needed to be said but he goes on to add in his customary style a seemingly superfluous reference to God's **goodness**. It is probably best to take it as dependent on **grace** and understand it either causally, 'God exhibits the overflowing riches of his grace because of his goodness', or instrumentally, '... by means of his goodness'. If the former, God's goodness is the cause of his grace; this is unlikely since grace is the more fundamental term for Paul and his school. Since God's action and purpose are never unrelated to Christ the sentence is rounded off by referring to him. There is nothing vague about God's grace; it is anchored in Christ.

We have now come to the end of the flow of argument which began at 2.1, was interrupted by vv. 2f, but picked up again by v. 4. With v. 8 a fresh sentence begins.

8. Resurrection and heavenly session are essential parts of salvation for AE and he now states this explicitly by picking up the phrase he had already used in v. 5c, developing it, returning as he does so to the second plural, and supplementing it by introducing the reference to **faith**. Vv. 8f have a high concentration of Pauline concepts. Paul developed the themes of grace, faith, salvation, boasting and works during his struggle to ensure that Gentile Christians did not have to observe the Jewish Law to be saved, and AE has derived them directly from Paul.

To whose **faith** does AE refer? That of Christ or that of believers? It can be argued, though probably incorrectly, that when Paul uses the phrase he intends the former. Whether that is so or not, it does not appear to be the case here (*pace* Barth); AE introduces and stresses references to Christ so regularly that if he had Christ in mind we should have expected 'faith of Christ'. In 3.12, 17 the phrase refers to the faith of believers. Since in vv. 8b–10 the place of believers is stressed, v. 8 probably also refers to their faith. The object of faith is not here defined but in 1.13, 15; 3.12 it is Christ and we may assume it is the same here. Faith is the response of believers to what God has done; it represents their openness to his activity. God's activity and human receptiveness are two sides of one coin.

In v. 8b AE picks up and develops v. 8a. This refers to the whole of v. 8a and not simply to **faith**. It indicates a new step in the argument: believers are not the source of their own salvation; it is God's gift. This emphasis is already present in the OT (e.g. Isa 31.1; 42.5f; 43.3, 11; Hos 1.7; Ps 33). A new aspect of the meaning of grace is also drawn out here; in v. 7 it was related to God's goodness; now it is seen as God's gift, freely given and not called forth in any way by what its recipients have said or done, or by any quality or talent that lies within them, or by anything which results from their natural powers (AE would have in mind human effort towards salvation in Stoicism and in contemporary religion and magic). God alone is the cause of salvation and it is a gift. Faith is not one among a number of gifts which believers may receive but is a basic gift underlying all others.

9. Both v. 8b and v. 9 are comments on v. 8a (cf Lincoln) and are similarly structured: a negative statement followed by another which either adds more information to it (v. 8b) or qualifies it (v. 9). V. 9 uses terms, 'works' (**what you have done**), 'boasting', drawn from the Pauline polemic. In that polemic the 'works' are those of the Law (e.g. Rom 3.20, 28; Gal 2.16; 3.2, 5, 10); they are not so defined or restricted here; indeed there is little to suggest that the Jewish Law is in mind; it is indeed only mentioned once in Ephesians (2.15). Paul refers often to **boasting**. There is a legitimate boasting in God and what he has done (e.g. Rom 5.2, 11; 1 Cor 1.31) and in the Christian success of one's converts (e.g. 2 Cor 7.14; 9.2), but there is also an illegitimate boasting in works and activity (e.g. Rom 4.2; 2 Cor 11.16; Gal 6.13) and in the Law (Rom 2.23); the Law itself may be the content of such boasting (Rom 3.27; 4.2, 4; 1 Cor 1.28–31). In v. 9 boasting is clearly wrong. Boasting about themselves and their religious activities is excluded for those who depend on grace for their salvation. There is a change in v. 9 from the second person plural of v. 8 to the third person singular, due either to a desire to drive home the point by individualising it or because a well-known Pauline 'tag' has been employed.

It would appear as if AE having stated his position in v. 8 now restates it in v. 9 in more Pauline terms or, if Paul is the author, that he drops back in v. 9 into his traditional terms. These terms, with others (justification, faith, grace, works of the law), were originally derived from the Jewish perspective of Paul's polemic. Underneath that perspective is a much wider issue of the relation of humanity to God, of which the judaising problem is only one aspect. Does salvation come from moral living, intellectual appreciation of the truth as in philosophy or gnosticism, or from passing through certain rites? AE's changes have put the question in universal terms which would be more quickly appreciated in the Hellenistic world: **grace** and **faith** cannot easily be changed but they ought to be understood by everyone, and in case grace is not it is interpreted as 'gift of God'; 'justification', the Jewish legal word, is replaced with the non-specific 'salvation'; the idea that obedience to the Law is not a factor in gaining salvation or justification is replaced by the all-embracing **not from what you have done**: there is nothing people can do for themselves which can be a factor in their salvation. Then having universalised the problem of the Law as a way to God, AE falls back in v. 9b into the traditional language in order to show the continuity of his thought with that of Paul, though even here by not defining **works** as those of the Law he lets us see that he is widening the original issue. It cannot be denied that Paul himself may have seen the need to widen the issue as he continued to be rejected by synagogues and increasingly turned to evangelising only Gentiles. Yet that he continues to use the traditional terms in Philippians (see 3.2–11) which cannot be dated much earlier than Ephesians (if he is the author) suggests he may never have seen the need to widen the issue. Whether Paul wrote Ephesians or not, vv. 8f represent a transplanting of the Pauline doctrine of justification into Hellenistic soil; it is in this sense that we should understand the many statements of commentators that in vv. 8f we find the heart of Paul's Gospel. With the widening of the issue the original tie to the Jewish Law has been lost and a more basic and profound issue brought to the fore. In consequence there is no reason to suggest (*pace* Barth) that either v. 9 or its immediate context is polemically oriented. As time went by the salvation vocabulary took over in the later parts of the NT (Acts 2.47; 4.12; 15.1, 11; 2 Tim 1.9; Tit 3.5; Heb 7.25).

10. If v. 9 is parenthetical because it adds nothing to the argument but only recalls Pauline terminology, then we must see the introductory **for** of v. 10 as going back beyond it to pick up v. 8, or rather as picking up both v. 9 and v. 8. The return in v. 10 from the second person of v. 8 to the first person of vv. 3–7 is made easier through the indefinite **no one** of v. 9. The word we have translated as **making** is rendered as 'workmanship' in many EVV; this is unfortunate since it suggests a play on 'works' but there is no facile connection between our works and God's work. The English 'making' is a good rendering since it is as colourless as the Greek. In the biblical tradition God's creative activity did not cease with creation but continued in history (e.g. Ps 64.9; 92.4; Isa 29.16). God is always 'making' and his 'saving' is just an aspect of his 'making' (cf Isa 41.11–20; 45.7f; 51.9–11 in each of which the thought moves easily between the two aspects). Thus what this word brings out here is not that salvation is a second creation but that it is God who creates it and not we ourselves; this is another way of expressing the same truth as v. 8b where salvation is God's gift.

If salvation is to be regarded as a second creation this idea comes with **created**. Those who become Christians are new creations (Gal 6.15; 2 Cor 5.17; Eph 2.10, 15; 4.24; Col 3.10). To be saved is to be created anew by God; those who were dead in sins have been brought to life (2.1, 5). This gives salvation a wider significance than merely a forgiveness of sin; believers are created anew (cf 4.24 and 2 Cor 5.17). The first creation contained distinctions; one was that between Jew and Gentile, and since God called Abraham he can be said to have created that distinction. If the distinction is to be abolished then God must create again and this idea is developed in 2.14ff with 'create' being used at 2.15 (cf Gal 6.15). It may however be wrong to envisage a second creation in Ephesians; for AE the creation of believers is the only genuine creation, just as in John's Gospel the only genuine life is eternal life; 2.1–10 draws no contrast between the first creation and the creation of believers. There are not two creations, only one; salvation is creation reaffirmed; there has been no change in God's original plan; rather it is now carried fully into effect; we have here the completion of God's creative activity (cf Findlay; Caird). **In Christ Jesus** brings Christ into the process of creation.

Since God never acts purposelessly, he creates believers **with a view to** the good works which they will perform, not that his original creation did not have this end in view. In so far as people exist they exist to carry out God's will, and though they may be dead in sins (v. 1) it cannot be said that God created them to be dead in this way; he created them, whether as believers or unbelievers, to **walk in good works**. The same word is used here as in v. 2, perhaps deliberately, to bring out the contrast. The lifestyle of the believer has changed from one of sins under the power of Satan to one of good works. The plural **good works** corresponds to the plural 'trespasses and sins'. Paul normally speaks of works pejoratively, e.g. as part of the phrase 'the works of the law' (Rom 3.20, 27f; Gal 2.16, etc.); but even where there is no explicit reference to the Law it still carries a bad connotation (Rom 13.12; Gal 5.19). While the singular may be similarly used (1 Cor 5.2), it more often has a good sense (Rom 2.7; 1 Cor 9.1; 15.58, etc.). In the later NT writings the plural is used regularly with a good sense (e.g. Mt 5.16; Jn 3.21; Acts 9.36; Heb 10.24; 1 Pet 2.12; Rev 2.19) and is especially frequent in this sense in the Pastorals. No Greek reader encountering the phrase **good works** would have been put off by it. All in all, while Paul might have used the phrase, especially in a new context, it is easier to understand its use here if Paul is not the author. The concept of the life of believers as new and good is not however un-Pauline. **Good works** represents a reinterpretation for Gentile Christians of phrases such as 'newness of life' (Rom 6.4), 'sanctification' (Rom 6.19, 22; 1 Th 4.3), 'the fruit of the Spirit' (Gal 5.22). Good works are never the cause of salvation but ought to be its fruit.

All this is straightforward, but the same cannot be said of **prepared beforehand**. It would not be surprising to find a reference to the 'preparation' or 'election' of believers (Rom 9.23), or to their being prepared for good works (2 Tim 2.21; 3.17; Tit 3.1), and this is the way in which some commentators (e.g. Masson; Abbott) and translations (NEB 'the good deeds for which God has designed us') have understood it. However the Greek cannot really be made to have this sense. The need for the present clause is caused perhaps by the very vagueness of 'good works' and is intended to indicate that there is something new in the Christian life.

It is **beforehand** which causes the problem. It can be taken either narrowly within the verse as indicating preparation before the conversion of believers, or widely from the letter as a whole as indicating preparation before the foundation of the world. In view of the regularity with which the idea of 'beforeness' is used in Ephesians (1.4, 5, 9, 11) with the pre-creation connotation (cf Rom 9.23) the wider understanding is preferable, though clearly the more difficult to understand. The clause stresses that good works do not derive from believers themselves and are therefore not meritorious. God is the sole cause of the good deeds of believers. This is an idea which is often found elsewhere, e.g. Gal 5.22; it is the present form of its expression which is strange. Yet when the idea of human activity as coming from God is combined with that of believers as chosen beforehand to be holy (1.4f), it seems a natural consequence. When however we move into the area of election and predestination, natural consequences of previous statements often appear difficult, if not illogical.

If the **good works** of believers have been created in advance, have believers become automatons? Do they just slip into, or put on like a coat, a set of good works which lie in advance along the sequence of their lives? Believers were once dead in sins and trespasses and under the control of Satan (vv. 1f) and might equally then have been considered to be automatons. So v. 10 corresponds in a way to vv. 1, 2. It may be that by using the plural 'works' instead of a unified concept like 'sanctification' AE indicates the possibility of the freedom of believers to accept or reject any one particular good work which has been prepared **beforehand**. Since AE goes on in chaps. 4–6 to urge his readers to good works he cannot, if he is consistent, be imagining here that they will always perform them, yet if they do fulfil the prepared good works they have no cause to boast and v. 10 thus picks up v. 9.

V

JEW AND GENTILE: ONE IN CHRIST

(2.11–22)

[11] You should remember then
    that you were once Gentiles by birth
    belonging to those who are called 'uncircumcision'
      by those called 'circumcision'
        which is a physical matter,
[12]   that you were at that time
      apart from Christ,
      separated from the community of Israel,
      and strangers in respect of the covenants of promise,
      with no hope,
      and without God in the world.
[13]   But now in Christ Jesus you who were once afar
      have become near through the blood of Christ.
[14] For Christ is our peace,
    he who made the two one
    and destroyed the middle wall of the fence which
                    separates,
      that is, the hostility (in his flesh),
[15]   inasmuch as he made of no effect the law
      consisting of commandments
      and expressed in regulations,
    so that he might create out of the two in himself
    one new (human) being,
      thus making peace,
[16]   and that he might reconcile
      both to God through the cross in one body
      after killing enmity by it.
[17]   And when he came
      he proclaimed the good news

of peace to those far off
and of peace to those near at hand;
18 for this reason
we both have through him access
in one Spirit to the Father.
19 For you are no longer foreigners and strangers
but are fellow citizens with the holy ones
and belong to God's household,
20 since you have been built on the foundation
consisting of the apostles and prophets
with Jesus Christ himself being the angle-stone,
21 in whom (Christ) all the building
being neatly fitted together
grows into a holy sanctuary in the Lord,
22 in whom also you have been built together
into a place which God indwells in Spirit.

The dispute in the early church about the admission of Gentile Christians as full and equal members with Jewish Christians had lost its virulence by the time of Ephesians; though the case no longer needed to be argued, it still continued to echo, brought to the fore from time to time by the vast numerical superiority of Gentiles in an area such as Asia Minor and the smaller numerical superiority of Jews to Christians. If Jews were God's chosen people and Gentiles were not, and if Gentile Christians were not Jews and yet the elect of God (1.4f), what were they? Did they form a new group distinct from Gentiles and also from both Jews and Jewish Christians and, if so, how should that group be characterised? If Jews and Gentiles are equal in Christ, do Gentile Christians take over some or all of the privileges and responsibilities of Jews? These are the kind of questions which lie behind 2.11–22; yet because we know so little of the churches to which AE wrote it is difficult to point to any actual situation in them which may have led to the raising of these questions.

The discussion unveils a new aspect of the work of Christ: the reconciliation of people not only to God but also to one another. Salvation is more than believers receiving forgiveness of their sins, deliverance from the grip of the powers, adoption as children of God, and union with Christ in resurrection and exaltation. Salvation means union with one another. 1.10 implied something of this but on a grander and less precise scale; in 2.11–22 the cosmic framework sinks into the background and the idea is expounded exclusively in terms of the Jew-Gentile distinction, though it clearly has a much wider reference in relation to division between groups of people all of whom are Christian. As presented here the framework is historical, the relation of Jews and Gentiles. Relations between them were never easy; Jews were proud to be God's people; Gentiles looked askance at their curious ways. From another angle we may say that while 2.1–10 was narrative in dealing with the redemption of the individual, 2.11–22 might be categorised as narrative recounting what happened to a group, the Gentiles. This naturally launches us into a discussion of the nature of the church. Since so many of the themes of the letter surface in 2.11–22 it has been termed its theological centre (cf Conzelmann; Merklein; Barth), but this can only be true if we ignore the large final paraenetic section where Jewish–Gentile relations never surface. Indeed this and other passages might be regarded as preparation for the paraenesis. The whole letter in fact holds together in such a way that it is impossible to speak of a centre or a key passage.

2.11–22 consists of three sections, vv. 11–13, 14–18, 19–22; the first and third are marked off from the second in being couched in the second person plural whereas the third is largely in the third person with God or Christ as subject. 2.11–13 describes the position of Gentile Christians before and after they became Christians. The contrast again uses the once-now (or inside-outside, now expressed as near-far) schema to make its point and is expressed in Jewish terms. General theological terms (sin, faith, resurrection, ascension) were used in 2.1–10; the choice of explicit Jewish terms is now forced on AE because he wishes to deal with the relation of Jewish and Gentile Christians within the church. In vv. 11–13 the contrast may appear to lie between Gentiles and Jews but in vv. 14–18 it is between non-membership of the Jewish people and membership of the church. The church is then more than a reformed Judaism. As well as the temporal contrast there is also a spatial (v. 13). The middle section, vv. 14–18, looks like an excursus; unlike the surrounding material it is either in the third person singular with God as subject or, when it becomes plural, largely in the first person plural.

The present position of Gentile Christians in contrast with their original place outside Israel is developed positively in the third section, vv. 19–22, through a description of the church with ever-changing imagery, though with only vague reference to the once-now schema. Verses 14–18 thus form the bridge between the original position of Gentile Christians and their present position and do so through the discussion of their reconciliation with Jewish Christians (vv. 14–18). In this way the connection between soteriology and ecclesiology is brought out.

There are clear parallels between the first and third large sections. Gentile believers were once alienated from God, in the flesh, without a Messiah, excluded from citizenship in Israel, now they are near God, in the Spirit, built together with a Messiah, fellow citizens within Israel. There is then a balance between the first and third sections; this has been brought about through Christ who has made peace and brought Jewish and Gentiles believers together in himself.

11. The once–now contrast is not concerned with the length of the period between conversion and the present and so tells us nothing about how long the readers have been Christian. There is also a change in the way the contrast is presented from that of 2.1–3; it is no longer stressed as that between once a sinner and now saved, but between once a Gentile outside God's people and now a Christian within that people. If in the communities to which AE writes there are still some Jewish Christians aware of their Jewish heritage and if there are Jews in the area whom the Christians may encounter, and there were a large number of Jews in Asia Minor, second- and third-generation Gentile Christians might still be forced through their contact with Jews to think about their origin. Few Christians today think of themselves as Gentiles but that should not lead us to think that those of AE's day were similarly unaware of their Gentile origin.

Whether they are recent converts or those of long standing, they are told to keep on remembering (the verb is in the present tense) the change in their position. Since what has happened in the past (the exodus, the cross) creates the present, remembering has always been important to both Jews and Christians; here however believers are not summoned to recollect the great things God has done externally in the past but what he has done in their own lives: once they were outside his people, now they are within.

The addressees are first identified physically as of Gentile birth. Left to themselves Gentiles would never have classified themselves as Gentiles, though they might have distinguished between themselves and barbarians or between nationalities. In their eyes Jews were simply one more race or nation. Only encounter with Jews would have made them aware of Jewish feeling on Gentile identity. Gentile Christians, even if they had met no Jews, would of course have become aware of the distinction through their use of the OT which would not have been so easily assumed then to be a Christian book as it is today. AE may have recalled his readers to the distinction here because of a possible tendency on their part to forget or ignore, as Marcion did later, their Jewish heritage. Apart from that, people always belong to large groups and AE reminds them of the two major human groups as seen by a Jew. The emotional involvement found in the case of Paul (cf. Rom 3.1f; 9.4f) is lacking here.

AE has no intention of emphasising **circumcision** as a main factor in the Jewish-Gentile contrast, yet it cannot be ignored. Its presence reminds us that what he is discussing is the pre-Christian existence of Gentiles and not of all people. As a physical distinction made in the flesh by human hands it no longer possesses for Christians any religious significance (cf Gal 5.6; 6.15; 1 Cor 7.19). The contrast is not then between a physical circumcision and one of the heart (Rom 2.28f). Underlying what AE writes is the mistaken, but widely held, assumption in the ancient world, that only Jews were circumcised. If Paul wrote our letter he would probably have been aware that it was also a custom among other Semitic peoples because of his sojourn in Arabia; his discussion of Ishmael in Gal 4.21–31 confirms that awareness.

Physical is the translation of a term which literally means 'made by hand'; this term was used in the LXX of idols (Lev 26.1, 30; Isa 2.18; Dan 5.4, 23; cf Acts 17.24) and in the NT of the Jewish temple (Mk 14.58; Acts 7.48; Heb 9.11, 24), always with the intention of stressing the inadequacy of its referent. Jews would never have applied it to their God-ordained circumcision, though like Paul they could (Rom 2.29) spiritualise it into a circumcision of the heart (Deut 10.16; Jer 4.4; Ezek 44.7, 9; Lev 26.41; 1QS 5.5; 1QH 18.20; 1QpHab 11.13; Philo, *De Spec Leg* 1.305); Paul indeed speaks of Christians as the true circumcision (Phil 3.3). The adjective is used in Col 2.11 and AE probably derived it from the Pauline school to which he and A/Col belonged. Col 2.11 relates it to baptism but there is no such reference in Eph 2.11. What AE says here about circumcision is similar to Paul's idea that neither circumcision nor uncircumcision is of value (Gal 5.6; 6.15); AE however does not go as far in devaluing it as does Paul in Phil 3.2. AE neither positively attacks circumcision, nor suggests baptism as a substitute (cf Percy), nor spiritualises it. Either of the last two positions would probably have taken him a step further than he would have wished in lining up Christians more directly as the successors of Jews.

Circumcision originally signifying the rite, came to mean, as here, the group of people, i.e. the Jews, who are circumcised (cf. Acts 10.45; Rom 3.30; Col 4.11; etc.).

The summons to the readers to remember resembles the Deuteronomic appeal to the Israelites to recall their former slavery in Egypt (Deut 5.15; 15.15; 16.12; 24.18, 22); it is more than an instruction to recollect particular facts or situations; once recollected they should be evaluated and the evaluation acted on, cf. Lk 17.32; Jn 15.20; Acts 20.35; Col 4.18; 2 Tim 2.8; Heb 13.7. Recollecting their past should then lead readers to consider the great change that has come over their position; v. 12 makes clear that this is much more than ignoring the absence of circumcision. Even when believers are not told to remember their past, it is often thrust on their attention (Rom 9–11; Gal 4.8–11, 21–31; 1 Pet 2.10).

12. Circumcision may be the obvious place to begin a discussion of the distinction between Jew and Gentile and it may be tactful to get it out of the way at the beginning as repulsive to Gentiles. Philo does the same in *Spec Leg* before turning to discuss the Law. But there are more important things to remember, and so AE now expresses the distinction in new ways. Verse 12 is parallel to v. 11 and introduces five descriptions of the Gentile condition. 4.17–19 throws a different light on that condition. For the present AE writes a description of the disadvantages which Gentiles suffered as seen, not by a Jew, but by a Jewish Christian. Paul's list in Rom 9.4f is in contrast a list of the advantages of being a Jew. The two lists are complementary: Rom 9.4f states the privileges of Israel and Eph 2.12 the disadvantages of the Gentiles. They also serve different purposes. AE as a member of the Pauline school may have known that Paul drew up lists and he selected the qualities he wished from among them. The list in v. 12, compiled by a Christian, would not necessarily be the same as one drawn up by a Jew.

The first phrase refers to Christ (**without, apart from**). Before becoming Christians Gentiles would probably not have known the term 'Christ', and a Jew would probably not have put it first in a list of privileges. Gentile Christians are now 'in Christ'. What would it mean to be without him? Christ can be conceived as present with Israel: (i) in his pre-incarnate state (e.g. 1 Cor 10.4; 1 Pet 1.11; Jn 12.41 (von Soden; Barth); (ii) as living and dying in historical Israel (Haupt; Merklein); (iii) as the Messiah for whom Israel hoped (Schlier; Gnilka; Mussner). Nothing elsewhere suggests AE believed in a pre-incarnate presence of Christ with Israel. Limiting the reference to the historical Christ makes only a trivial point and would have been true merely for a brief period. (iii) is to be preferred in the light of 1.12 which, whether its subject is Jewish Christians or all Christians, indicates that AE believed Jewish Christians had the hope of a Messiah. But once Jesus had come and been accepted as Messiah believers would not have been able to separate (iii) from (ii).

In the second phrase the word underlying **community** has a wide range of meaning. The term refers here neither to the 'way of life' of Israel (cf 2 Macc 8.17; 4 Macc 8.7) which would render 2.19 difficult, nor to the constitution of Israel (Josephus *Ant* 4.45; 13.245), but to membership in Israel, or, more exactly, to possessing the rights, privileges and duties which go with belonging to Israel as a defined political and religious community, though not in the modern sense a nation (2 Macc 13.14; 4 Macc 17.9); our rigid separation between politics and religion was unknown in the ancient world. From this community the Gentiles were excluded, **separated**. If Gentiles are in a state of exclusion from **Israel** (AE, like Paul, uses the title preferred by Jews) this does not imply that they were once included and then expelled or that they separated themselves; it was God who separated Jews and Gentiles through his choice of Abraham; neither 2.14ff nor 3.6 indicates the restoration of an original unity. **Israel** does not designate the church here but empirical Israel; when it denotes anything other than the Jewish people, or a part of it, this is made clear, e.g. Gal 6.16 (even there, it is doubtful if the church is intended).

Like the second phrase the third continues to express the condition of the Gentiles in Jewish terms: they are **strangers** in respect of the covenants of promise. There is no implication that they once belonged. The plural **covenants** is unusual, appearing in the NT only at Rom 9.4, where the singular is a variant, and Gal 4.24, which mentions two covenants of which only one refers to Israel. Normally God is regarded as having a covenantal relationship with Israel which was renewed or reaffirmed on a number of occasions. In Jewish literature the plural regularly means 'promises, decrees, oaths'. The sense 'promises' is impossible in 2.12 because of the following 'of promise' and while 'oaths' is possible both here and in Rom 9.4, there seems little reason to prefer it to the normal 'covenant'. It would be possible to understand the renewal of the covenant as indicating several covenants (cf 2 Macc 8.15; Sir 44.17–45.26) but it is more likely that Christians would have viewed the new covenant of Jer 31.31–4 in the light of its fulfilment in Christ and connection with the eucharist as a second covenant, different from that made with Abraham. AE speaks of a promise (singular) as associated with the covenants and though the term promise is not frequent in the OT, appearing almost as often in Ephesians as in the whole of the OT, there is a forward look in the covenants relating to the continuance of Israel which could be seen as indicating a promise. Gentiles are strangers in respect of that forward look and so to that promise. It is possible that AE has also in mind OT passages which imply that Gentiles will share in the future messianic period (Isa 42.6; 49.6) but unlikely since, if this were so, he would not have gone on to write of the Gentiles as being once without hope.

The final two phrases are couched in terms which appear to lack any reference to Israel yet to a Jew they would have been natural consequences of the preceding three in representing the 'spiritual' condition of Gentiles. But the latter, who would not have been troubled by the first three accusations, would have rejected these two as false because, with few exceptions, they did not regard themselves as atheists or **without hope**. AE's dismissal of Gentile hope springs from his different perspective. The reference to hope follows naturally on that to the promise, for hope arises out of promises. Jewish hope was wider than the expectation of a Messiah or an afterlife; it was essentially the hope that the Jewish people should continue to be God's people and he their God, though the hope might be expressed with varying emphasis in different periods and by different people. AE may have thought of it in terms of **inheritance** which has a future aspect (1.14) and is a privilege of the Jew in which the Gentile Christian will share (3.6; remember that AE is detailing Jewish privilege as seen from a Christian perspective). **In the world** probably relates to both the final two phrases but not as suggesting the world as the content of hope; while they lived in the world apart from Christ there was no real **hope** for Gentiles.

Atheists can mean: (i) those who do not believe in God; the word was used in this way against both Jews (Josephus *c. Ap.* 2.148) and Christians (*Mart Polyc* 3.2; 9.2) since they did not worship any of the gods recognised among the Gentiles; (ii) godless, impious; a moral rebuke which would hardly be in place here; (iii) abandoned by God or the gods. In using the word AE will have intended some combination of (i) and (iii). Neither charge could have been made to stick absolutely. Paul is not going against his Jewish upbringing when he allows that Gentiles have some knowledge of the true God (Rom 1.18ff; cf Acts 17.16ff), nor as a Christian had he completely abandoned them for he planned their ultimate redemption (Rom 9–11). Pagans might have laughed scornfully at AE's charges, but his Gentile–Christian recipients would have agreed with them. While AE associates hopelessness and godlessness many today who do not believe in God would deny that they were without hope, though their hope might lack a transcendental dimension.

The five phrases of v. 12 might be taken to represent what, from a Christian point of view, is good in Judaism, and good rhetorical practice would have amplified them in the following discussion. Yet AE has not done this. Vv. 14–18 could be regarded as an expansion of the first and v. 19 of the second, but nothing picks up the other three. We should note also the list's failure to mention either the temple or the Law; the absence of a reference to the former is surprising since in v. 21 the Christians are described as the new temple, but perhaps less surprising if it had been already destroyed.

13. **But now** picks up the **once** of v. 11 and the **at that time** of v. 12. Once they were **afar** but now they are **near**. While the implications of this change begin to be worked out here they are brought out more fully in vv. 14–18. Temporal terms have now been changed to spatial. The terms **near**, **afar**, are probably drawn from Isa 57.19, a text used more directly in v. 17. Ps 148.14 says Israel is near to God. In Isa 57.19 however a contrast is drawn between Jews in exile and those in the homeland (cf 43.6; 60.4; Ezek 11.16; etc.); this is probably also the meaning in Acts 2.39, though not in Acts 22.21. In later Judaism Isa 57.19, or at least its terms, are applied to proselytes who became Jews. While it is true Jewish proselyte terminology used the terms it is difficult to believe in the light of v. 17 that AE had not the Isaiah passage in mind. Gentiles were also at times regarded as 'afar' (*Num R* 8 [149d]). Those joining the Qumran community are said to draw near (1QS 6.16, 19, 22; 7.21; 8.18).

Afar and **near** are relative terms requiring a fixed point from which to be measured. This could be Judaism, the church, or God. It can hardly be the church even though the characteristics of Judaism which the Gentiles lack have been described in v. 12, since those described as 'near' are actually in the church and not just 'near' to it. The choice is then between Judaism and God; since 'the blood of Christ' is normally used in relation to redemption it may seem better to understand the nearness as that to God; yet the mention of nearness after v. 12 and the use of the terms in v. 17 leave us also with the thought of Gentiles as near to Israel. There is then a certain degree of ambiguity or ambivalence, and this runs right through vv. 14–18 in that it is difficult to separate the 'horizontal' relation of Gentiles to Jews from their, and also Jews', 'vertical' relation to God. For their part the Gentiles, once far off (Deut 29.22; 1 Kgs 8.41; cf Deut 4.7; Ps 148.14) and without God (v. 12), are now near to him. Echoes of this idea of nearness may lie in Acts 22.21; Lk 15.20 (Mk 12.34 suggests there can be a relative nearness but the terms in

Ephesians are used absolutely). Gentiles became near when they believed or were baptised. The phrase contains no clue as to when this happened nor does it imply that the writer has always been 'near', or 'nearer' for a longer period than his readers have. It is only a reminder of their change in position. It goes too far to say that the Gentiles have now gained what v. 12 implied they lacked. They have not become members of the community of historical Israel though they have of the new Israel; they are under a new covenant, not that made with Abraham. This verse contains a mixture of temporal and spatial terms; neither is fully adequate to express AE's meaning. What has taken place has taken place through **the blood of Christ**.

2.13 gives the first indication of a theme which is followed up in vv. 14–18, that Jews and Gentiles are reconciled to one another through the cross. In keeping with v. 8 AE does not say that the Gentiles have brought themselves near to God or Israel; it is God who has brought them near. It should be noted finally that no statement is made about when this took place; it may have been at baptism or at the moment of initial faith; but it is of God.

The second qualifying phrase, **in Christ Jesus**, suggests that believers are no longer apart from Christ but are with him, **in Christ** having the inclusive sense. This fits in with the spatial manner of AE's thought.

As we have already noted, vv. 14–18 stand by themselves because we change at v. 14 from the second person plural to the first and return to the former at v. 19 and because Christ becomes the subject of the verbs of vv. 14–18. Verses 14–18 are thus a unit within vv. 11–22 and many, following Schlier, have argued that this unit is based on an existing piece of tradition, probably, as Schille suggested, a hymn, which AE adapted.

The great majority of the points raised by those who see an underlying hymn are explicable on the basis of AE's authorship. It is not an unfair criticism of the many reconstructions of the underlying tradition to point out that no two attempts agree. Agreement is lacking even in respect of the verses chosen to form the base for any reconstructions. Since we do not accept the hymn there is no need to provide a separate exegesis of it or examine AE's alleged redaction for clues to his own meaning.

14. Verse 14a provides the theme or text for vv. 14–18, **peace**. The word itself appears three times and the theme is also expressed through the ideas of 'reconciliation', 'oneness' and their opposite 'enmity'. Although these emphases also appear in Colossians (1.20–3) and may belong to the Pauline school they are much more prominent in Ephesians. AE and A/Col probably derived them from their master (cf Rom 5.1; 15.33; 16.20; Gal 5.22), and behind him from the OT, and not from the *Pax Romana* in which they lived and from which in various ways they may have benefited nor from Jesus who had said that he had not come to earth to bring peace but a sword (Mt 10.34). Is AE then unfaithful to Jesus? We shall return to this after v. 18 when we have explored what he has to say about peace. Gentiles who were afar (v. 11) have now been brought near (v. 13) through the blood of Christ for he is our peace. The change here from the second person plural to the first means vv. 14–18 apply to Jews and Gentiles without distinction. 2.14a does nothing to resolve the ambiguity already observed in v. 13: Christ may be the creator of peace between Jew and Gentile, the horizontal relationship, or between God and both Jew and Gentile, the vertical relationship, or the creator of peace for both relationships. In stressing Christ as peace AE prepares for an important element in his later paraenesis, the need for unity within the community (4.3).

The identification of Christ with peace is at first sight surprising; we more naturally think of him as making peace (v. 15) or proclaiming it (v. 17) than being it; the identification parallels that in which he proclaims the word and is the Word, is life and gives life (Col 3.4; cf 1 Cor 1.30), or where believers are light and impart light (5.8). While peace may have been personified in the Greco-Roman world in relation to the *Pax Romana*, the ultimate origin of AE's description of Christ as peace probably lies in Isa 9.6 which he would have understood as a messianic passage (cf Mic 5.4; AE also plays in our passage on Isa 57.19; 52.7) and in Jewish expectations of eschatological peace. In v. 12 AE said Gentiles were without the Messiah, in v. 13 he viewed them as near and now (v. 14) as sharing with Jews in the one Messiah. But this does not explain how he understood Christ as peace.

Jewish and Greek thinking on peace differed. It was at this time an important concept in the Greco-Roman world following on the re-establishment of the *Pax Romana* after the quelling of the Jewish rebellion and the destruction of Jerusalem, for Vespasian had revived the ideas of Augustus on peace. This might have suggested a link with Gentile–Jewish relations, and perhaps an implicit comparison of Christ to the emperor who was regarded as the creator and maintainer of peace. Yet this cannot have been the sole factor, nor even the most important, for the word peace had been widely used from much earlier in Christian worship, e.g. 'the kiss of peace', and in Christian letters where it supplemented the Greek greeting (see on 1.2). We can assume AE's readers once they had been converted would quickly become alert to the cluster of new ideas which came with the word from Judaism. They would of course also have brought with them into their Christianity ideas of peace which belonged to the Greco-Roman world in which they lived; there peace signified a condition of non-war in which stability and good order flourished. While for a Jew it could signify the absence of conflict (6.15), it also meant much more. Since the theme of conflict between Jew and Gentile or between either and God is at best only implicit in 2.11–13, it is proper to understand peace here in its wider Jewish sense where it refers to both physical and spiritual well-being, comes close to meaning salvation and attains eschatological significance. Peace is the end of alienation; people can be alienated from God, from one another or internally alienated; the first two aspects are present here, the third is not. Peace as salvation is God's gift. After referring to blood in v. 13 AE might have gone on to say that Christ is our salvation but instead he says he is our peace; this provides him with an easy transition to the discussion of Jewish and Gentile relationships. He will also have been influenced by Isa 57.19 to which he alluded in v. 13 and will use again in v. 17 for it contains the word **peace**.

To what does **the middle wall** (v. 14) refer? Walls serve different purposes; they can be used to separate one group of people from another, sometimes erected for this purpose by a third group; they can be erected by one group to protect themselves from another group with emphasis either on excluding the other group or on preserving the identity of the erecting group, or erected in order to keep others out or to keep themselves in. Their existence can cause enmity when they exclude a group from what they regard as their legitimate position or prevent a group from being released from a position in which they are oppressed. Walls can be metaphorical or physical. It has been normal to understand the wall of v. 14 as non-material and referring to something else. With these possibilities in mind it is necessary to ask what the wall was which AE envisages Jesus as breaking down.

(i) An answer which became popular early this century suggests AE had in mind the stone balustrade which separated the area in the Jerusalem temple into which Gentiles were allowed to enter from the areas into which their entrance was prohibited. This balustrade was a 1.5m-high wall (cf Josephus *Ant* 15.417; *BJ* 5.193–4; cf *m Mid* 2.3) carrying inscriptions threatening death to Gentiles who crossed it. They were allowed into the outer court but no further. Two stones bearing the inscription in whole or in part have been discovered; their discovery led to the popularity of this solution. The balustrade represented in Jewish eyes a distinction between themselves and Gentiles, a distinction which in Christian eyes had been destroyed through Christ's death. This understanding of the wall fits the present context of the Jewish–Gentile distinction and prepares for the mention of the temple at vv. 21f. Paul, if the author of Ephesians, would have been aware of this wall since he had lived in Jerusalem and had been accused of bringing a Gentile, Trophimus, across it (Acts 21.29). It is said the animosity between Jews and Gentiles was very bad during the time of his imprisonment in Caesarea and if he wrote Ephesians from there then this would have been at the front of his mind. This solution is more likely to be true if Ephesians is Pauline. Whether it is or not, it encounters serious objections: (a) Would readers in Asia Minor have been aware of the balustrade and its significance? The temples of Asia Minor had no similar walls. (b) Neither in Josephus nor in the inscriptions is this balustrade termed a **middle wall**, (c) If Ephesians is not Pauline then by the time it was written the temple had been destroyed by the Romans and not by Christ; this would make the reference meaningless. (d) The destruction of the balustrade would only be relevant if the argument of 2.14–18 had been about the admission of Gentiles to ordinary Jewish privileges and this is not AE's argument; when elsewhere in the NT Christians are seen as enjoying Jewish privileges these are not ordinary privileges but those of the priesthood (e.g. Rom 12.1f; 1 Pet 2.5, 9). (e) While 2.11–22 looks forward to the building of a temple in v. 21, it is not a physical temple but a spiritual. An unimportant variation to this solution sees the middle wall as the curtain of the temple which was torn in two at the time of the death of Jesus (Mk 15.38); AE however refers to a wall and not a curtain. Finally we should note that if the wall is not the balustrade there is nothing to be learnt from it about the date of Ephesians.

(ii) The area in mind may be the whole cosmos and the wall one dividing the supernatural realm from the earthly. This solution was first advocated in detail by Schlier though the idea goes back to F. C. Baur published in 1845; it has since been accepted by many others (Dibelius; Pokorný; Fischer). Schlier argued that the gnostic Redeemer descends through the heavenly wall, encounters enmity from the heavenly powers and the Jewish folk angels (the heavenly powers and the Law are connected in Gal 3.19; Col 2.8, 10), destroys the wall and the enmity, and thus creates peace. This solution accounts for the ambiguity in relation to the nature of reconciliation; AE has used gnostic terms to which his readers are accustomed and which relate to God–human reconciliation and has superimposed on them a Christian interpretation dealing with the division between Jews and Gentiles. Schlier also drew in many of the other ideas of 2.14–22 arguing that they were gnostic.

Schlier's solution however encounters considerable difficulties: (a) The evidence offered is often late (e.g. the Mandean literature, the long recension of Ignatius) and when early is not exact, e.g. *1 En* 14.9 and parallel passages speak of a wall but never of its destruction; in *3 Bar* 2.1ff the wall has gates through which Baruch and the angels pass and thus does not need to be destroyed. (b) The crucial word translated **middle wall** is missing from all the literature, except where there has been Christian influence as in the long recension of Ignatius. (c) There is little certainty as to which gnostic concepts were current in the area to which Ephesians was addressed. (d) The connecting links in the various steps in the formulation of Schlier's argument are both complex and tenuous; if it was AE's intention to explain the relationship of Jews and Gentiles through the use of gnostic terminology he cannot be said to have done it very successfully. (e) As Schnackenburg notes, AE does not elsewhere separate heaven and earth in a way similar to that required by this theory (see also Detached Note: The Heavenlies). (f) The wall of the Law does not possess the alleged cosmic significance (Merklein). (g) Schlier's solution may explain the wall in an alleged underlying gnostic piece of tradition, but leaves too much unexplained in relation to the actual text and thus his interpretation provides no explanation for the latter.

(iii) If the 'area' which the wall divides is taken as the world of people then the Jews often regarded the Law as a wall which separated them from the Gentiles and protected them from Gentile impurities (*Ep Aristeas* 139, 142; *1 En* 93.6; 89.2; Prov (LXX) 28.4; Philo, *Virt* 186; *m Abot* 3.18). The origin of this idea may lie in Exod 19.12, 21–4 and a metaphorical use of **wall** in relation to division can be seen in CD 4.12; 8.12, 18 where some, probably the Pharisees, are accused of building a wall. Like the first solution this again fits easily into the context of a division between Jews and Gentiles; moreover v. 15 goes on immediately to refer to the Law as being rendered ineffective. Unlike the temple balustrade it is easier to assume that there would be Gentiles in Asia Minor who would have some notion of the Law as that which separated them from Jews, produced the impression that Jews were arrogant and exclusive, and caused Jews to despise Gentiles; Jewish adherence to the Law was then responsible for creating the barrier between them and Gentiles. Unfortunately, as with the other solutions, the key words are never found in connection with this supposed wall. This solution also seems to imply that the wall which represents the Law, or the Law itself, must be described as **enmity** and it is not easy to see a follower of Paul and one who quotes the Pentateuch approvingly (5.31; 6.2f) as accepting it. While it is true that some Gentiles who were well acquainted with Judaism might have accepted that the Law separated them from the Jews, by no means all Gentiles would necessarily have thought in that way. Strictly the wall only existed from the Jewish point of view.

(iv) None of these solutions is completely satisfactory. Each takes the wall to represent something; in (i) a physical wall in the temple at Jerusalem, in (ii) a 'spiritual' or non-material wall between heaven and earth, and in (iii) a spiritual concept, the Jewish Law. It may however simply be that we have an ordinary metaphor of a separating wall and are wrong to look for recondite meanings in it.

Cf Robert Frost's 'Mending Wall' (*Selected Poems*, New York, 1963, 23f),
Before I built a wall, I'd ask to know
What I was walling in or walling out,
And to whom I was like to give offense.
Something there is that doesn't love a wall,
That wants it down.

It is not unnatural for people when they disagree, or when they see others disagreeing, to speak as if there was a separating factor ('I can't get through to them; it's as if there was a wall between us'). The wall could then be regarded as purely metaphorical and not indicative of some theological idea. Jews and Gentiles are distinct groups; there was much keeping them apart. Greco-Roman literature shows that Jews were despised for their peculiar ways and their high opinion of themselves as the unique people of God. Their belief that they were God's people led them to look down on those who were not; they refused to assimilate themselves to the prevailing culture; they regarded the Romans who oppressed them as arrogant (cf *Ps Sol* 17 for the mutual attitude of Jews and Romans). On both sides there were inhibiting factors which led each to look down on and despise the other. In such circumstances it becomes perfectly natural for both sides, and not Jews only, to think of a wall dividing them. The walls of Mic 7.11; CD 4.12; 8.12, 18 are not the Law but metaphorical walls. But why is **middle wall** used? It is an ordinary architectural term without any necessary religious reference, except in so far as it may be used in describing religious buildings; as an architectural term it was well known in Asia Minor, being found seven times in the instructions for the erection of the temple at Didyma. It is used metaphorically in a non-Christian context in Athenaeus, *Deipn* 7.14. 281D (ed. G. Klaiber). Some of the Fathers seem also to regard it as metaphorical, though they are not unanimous about its reference (Origen; Theophylact; John of Damascus). The second word **fence** is a genitive of apposition and such a use of a synonym is fully in line with AE's normal plerophoric style. AE therefore uses both words to describe a real division between Jews and Gentiles, which both would have agreed existed, but which had no specific theological significance, though if Jews had been forced to think the matter through they would have agreed that their distinction from Gentiles rested on their being a holy people who had special rules of their own. Gentiles would have viewed the separation in quite a different way.

We now turn to the individual phrases. A reference to **enmity** is not unnatural after one to peace. Where enmity exists much more is needed than the cessation of hostility; healing is also needed; the Semitic concept 'peace' contains both ideas. As we have seen, an ambiguity exists in the passage in relation to the horizontal and vertical components of reconciliation and we therefore need to ask whether the enmity is that between humanity and God (cf Rom 5.10) or between Gentile and Jew; the flow of thought suggests the latter as the more important at this point; in addition the reference to the **middle wall** implies that the hostility is two-sided, lying on both its sides, and God cannot be the party on one side for he is not hostile to humanity. Yet is **enmity** not too strong a term to designate the difference between Gentile and Jew? It would be quite wrong to suppose that every Jew regarded every Gentile as an enemy, and vice versa, but the Jewish nation kindled hatred and scorn in many people and many Jews from their privileged position as God's people came to regard as enemies those who belittled God's Law. Moreover the statement about hostility is that of an outside observer, neither Jew nor Gentile (whatever he previously was AE is now a Christian), and the views of outside observers often differ from and are more harsh than those of participants. With the destruction of the middle wall the enmity disappears; the two belong together and it is impossible to say, especially if the wall is 'metaphorical', which precedes the other.

We have taken **in his flesh** as parenthetical, indicating where and how the action of the participles is achieved. It thus carries the same significance as blood in v. 13 and cross in v. 16. But why has AE used **flesh** and not a word like 'death' (cf Col 1.22)? Since there is no underlying hymn it cannot be the source of 'flesh' and flesh is not a reference to the incarnation as such, though it could be to Christ's human life taken as including his death (cf Thomas

Aquinas; Robinson; Mitton; Beare) since only those 'in the flesh' are able to die. Perhaps AE chose 'flesh' in preference to 'body' in view of his other use of body in this passage and the letter as a whole; his choice could also have been anti-docetic.

15. The phrase (v. 15a) about the rendering ineffective of the Law again evinces AE's love of a succession of similar words (Percy). **Law** is not law in general but, as the context indicates, the Jewish Torah; AE only uses the word here but since he shows indebtedness to Paul's teaching on justification (2.8–10) we can assume that he rejects any idea of salvation through the Law. **Commandment** is used again in 6.2 of one of the ten commandments, implying that these continue to have value for AE. In contrast to the singular **Law** the plural **commandments** refers to the individual prescriptions of the Law. **In regulations**, though omitted by some manuscripts, fits AE's style too well for it to be a gloss; it could easily have been dropped as apparently redundant. Col 2.14, a passage not unrelated to ours, also uses the noun, and both there and here it probably means 'legal decrees or regulations' (possibly a usage of the Pauline school for it is not used by Paul). As often in Ephesians it is impossible to differentiate fully between almost synonymous words coming in sequence. There is no reason to see a reference either to a new law given by Christ or to Christian doctrine as rendering the Jewish Law ineffective. Nothing AE writes suggests that he would differ from Paul in seeing the Law as abrogated by anything other than the cross; the whole context of 2.14–18 has that death in view. The two nouns AE has put in the plural suggest that he envisages here the actual regulations of the Law which showed up the differences between Jews and Gentiles and created hostility. There is nothing in the context to suggest AE is thinking only of circumcision and regulations about purity and food. It is therefore better to regard the whole law as at issue here.

As for **made of no effect**, the verb appears only here in Ephesians but is found regularly in the genuine Paulines, sometimes in relation to law (Rom 3.31; 7.2, 6). Presumably AE and his readers were aware of this usage. If in 6.2 AE quotes approvingly from the Decalogue and if he himself sets down moral rules in 4.1ff, it is unlikely that he would regard law as such as abolished or destroyed; yet it can no longer be a means of salvation (see 2.8–10) and used to enforce the separation of Jew and Gentile. AE thus expresses in his own way what Paul says about the ending of the Law through Christ (Rom 7.4; 10.4; Gal 3.13), but unlike Paul he makes no attempt to defend the Law or claim that it is good (cf Rom 3.31; 7.12, 14; 13.8–10). Has the Law then no continuing function? The Law as the duty of love remains and binds both Jews and Gentiles. Lastly in view of the horizontal–vertical ambivalence of the passage it may be that AE thinks at this point of the Law as separating Jew from Gentile and also both from God.

What Christ creates is **the one new (human) being** and he creates this person out of the two, i.e. Jews and Gentiles. But as individuals or groups? Are Jews and Gentiles made (i) as individuals into a new type of humanity, or (ii) as groups into a new corporate person? Either is grammatically possible and in both cases a new being comes into existence which did not exist prior to the death of Christ. The earliest support for (i) is found in Clem Alex *Stromata* 3.70.2, GCS 228.1 (cf Mussner; Henle; Grosheide; Masson; Meyer; Macpherson; Salmond). Those favouring it have argued that if a new corporate being were intended there was no need to speak of *one* new person. The one new person is of course neither superman nor sexless, and the idea is not derived from democratic idealism but from the cross.

Supporters of (ii) (e.g. Schlier; Gnilka; Schnackenburg; Barth; Roels; Lindemann) argue that in 5.22–23 the new Christian group of former Jews and Gentiles is pictured as a single individual, the bride, and in 4.13 as a mature person. In v. 16 the new group is depicted as 'one body' and this one body is not an individual but the church (cf 4.4). The corporate concept could have been derived from the new Adam understood corporately (Rom 5.15–21; 1 Cor 15.22) or the myths of the *Urmensch* redeemer. On balance (i) is to be preferred; (ii) in any case appears in v. 16. Whichever view is chosen there is again a realised eschatology since the new creation in Jewish thought belonged to the end time.

Christ has created the one new man **in himself**. What does the phrase mean? (i) It may be instrumental but it is difficult to see what this adds to the original 'he created …'. (ii) It is better to give the phrase its customary sense in which believers are 'in Christ' – that he might create in himself, that is, in his corporate existence. Those who are 'in him' are new beings, or if the one new human being is understood corporately Christ is seen as identifying himself with this new being. In either case Gal 3.28 probably foreshadows what we have, and it accords with the intimate relation between Christ and the church which runs through the whole of Ephesians.

The final **making peace** returns us to the opening words of v. 14 and the theme of peace. The creation of the new person takes place simultaneously with the making of peace. The peace is clearly that between Jew and Gentile. The good ruler in the ancient world created peace, e.g. *pax Augusta*, and so a recognisable virtue is transferred to Jesus though set in an entirely new context. Faust sees a soteriological connection with events in the Roman world in that Vespasian and Titus are made world rulers by Jupiter and overcome the division of the world which had come through the Jewish rebellion. The Romans were involved in the crucifixion of Jesus; in contrast it is his shameful crucifixion which actually brings peace.

16. This verse is not a consequence of v. 15b but parallel to it; terms are balanced (two–both, create–reconcile, in him–in one body, making peace–killing). Unlike v. 15b which spoke of the bringing together of Jews and Gentiles, v. 16 treats the relationship of both to God; thus the ambiguity of horizontal and vertical which commenced in v. 13 is continued and at the same time resolved. Not only do Jew and Gentile move towards one another; both move towards God. Neither movement may be said to be prior to the other or regarded as its basis, unlike Mt 5.23f (cf *m Joma* 8.9) where the horizontal precedes the vertical. Here the reconciliations are as inseparable as the two great commandments of love. The two groups are reconciled to God by Christ; it is not God who is reconciled to them.

The reconciliation of human beings to God is not expressed elsewhere in the NT so clearly as by Paul and his school (the LXX uses the verb for it in 2 Macc 1.5; 5.20; 7.33 where God, not humanity, is the object of reconciliation; in 2 Macc 8.29; Isa 9.4; Jer 31.39 the reconciliation is entirely on the human level); the idea may indeed have been introduced into Christian thought by Paul. The metaphor is derived from the social and political sphere where it is used of the bringing together of those who for some reason are apart and is used in this way in Mt 5.23f; Acts 7.26; 1 Cor 7.10f. AE was the first to use it to describe the new relationship of Jews and Gentiles, and it is a not inappropriate metaphor in the context of peace, but he does not use it directly of their being brought together; that was expressed in a different way in v. 15b; yet since he speaks of groups and not individuals as reconciled this cannot be far from his thoughts. Whatever advantages Jews may once have had (v. 12) no distinction is now made between the ways in which they and Gentiles are reconciled to God. In Col 1.20 the cosmos is said to be reconciled to God; AE is closer to Paul in restricting reconciliation to humans (in 2 Cor 5.18 the cosmos is the world of humanity), yet unlike Paul he speaks of the reconciliation of groups, though this will of course imply the reconciliation of the individuals within the groups who respond to the divine activity.

Christ reconciles the two groups **in one body** (cf the same phrase in Col 3.15 where already body is linked to peace). If we associate the reference to the body closely with that to the cross, the body in v. 16 might be the physical body of Christ which hung on the cross (so Chrysostom; Theodoret; Percy; Bengel; Harless; etc.). If this were so, we should expect 'in his body' or possibly 'in a (the) body'. Since AE uses 'body' in the singular elsewhere of the church he would probably have used 'flesh' here if he had meant Christ's physical body. The vast majority of commentators accept the reference here as to the church, and this is true even if the 'one new man' in v. 15b is understood individualistically. Accepting that the reference is to the church, we see that both vertical and horizontal relationships are fully present, Jews and Greeks being simultaneously reconciled to God and to one another. The former is the primary reference.

With the reference to **the cross** Christ's death, which has been underlying all that preceded, is now made explicit. Redemption is connected here to the cross and not to the resurrection, not that AE ignores the latter. The body which is the church came into existence through Christ's death. The enmity which is killed is that between Jew and Gentile (Eadie) as in v. 14 and not that between humanity and God (Haupt; Abbott) or both (Scott). It received its death blow in the cross. Christ is killed and he kills!

DETACHED NOTE V
ISRAEL AND THE CHURCH

The church is new for it did not exist prior to Christ, but how new is new? Do we have a third group, consisting of neither Jews nor Gentiles, standing alongside both and yet different from both? Has a new people of God, contrasting with Israel the old people, come into existence? Have Gentile Christians been absorbed into Israel so that they continue it? What, in short, is the relation of the church to Israel?

The NT writings provide varying answers to our questions. In Rom 9–11 Paul argued at length that Israel had not dropped out of God's sight and that the evangelisation of the Gentiles was a step on the way to its rehabilitation. This may represent a change in his original thinking for in 1 Th 2.14–16 he appears to see Israel as subject for ever to the wrath of God. Other parts of the NT reflect in greater or lesser degree his earlier position. Mark sees the cross as God's judgement on Israel, presumably because though the Jews had the Law and the prophets they had not recognised their Messiah. Matthew's form of the parable of the vineyard suggests that Israel loses its heritage and that it is given to another, the church (21.33–43). Acts 28.28 has often been read in the sense that God has turned away from Israel and in future salvation is to be offered to the Gentiles alone. Jn 8.44 sees Judaism as satanic in outlook. In Hebrews Judaism has had and perhaps still has its place, but it is an inferior place to Christianity. It is not easy to harmonise these statements with one another. It is not always easy to harmonise any one particular writer's statements. Paul's position changed between 1 Thessalonians and Romans. Within John, 4.22 sheds quite a different light on Jewish–Gentile relations from 8.44. The NT does not offer then a uniform picture in respect of the future position of Israel over against Christianity and at times there is also a lack of uniformity in particular writers.

It is clear that: (i) AE evaluates Israel positively in a way he does not evaluate Gentiles, as both 2.12 and his use of the OT and non-use of secular writings show; he implicitly agrees with Paul in that the Gospel is given first to the Jew and then to the Gentile. (ii) He can also be critical of Israel in so far as he downgrades circumcision (2.11) and speaks of the abrogation of the Law (2.15a), a criticism which remains even if his reference is only to the ceremonial law. His criticism of Israel does not extend to blaming her for the death of Jesus (contrast 1 Th 2.14–16). There is no polemic against the Jews in Ephesians; 2.11f implies God favoured them more than Gentiles. Since his interests lies elsewhere there was no point in him making a statement about their ultimate fate. (iii) While he associates Gentile Christians and Jewish Christians (3.6) there is no evidence that he associates Gentile Christians and non-Christian Jews. This means that at least for AE the church is continuous with Israel in a way in which it is not continuous with the Gentile world; 'the church without Israel would be an abstraction without a history' (Mussner). (iv) There is also discontinuity between Israel and the church for the church has an access to God through Christ which Israel did not have. (v) If the church is the continuation of Israel we might have expected AE to identify Israel as the church's foundation but instead he identifies this as the apostles and prophets (2.20). (vi) At no point does he make a direct comparison between Israel and the church and suggest the latter's superiority.

In comparison with Paul who argued in Rom 11 that God has not rejected unbelieving Jews, AE appears to ignore them. It cannot be argued that he was unaware of their continued existence for there were far too many Jews in Asia Minor for that to be possible. His different approach from Paul may perhaps have arisen because he was less personally involved with the Jews than Paul. It is however more probably a part of his general lack of interest in the world outside the church; equally he displays no interest in the survival of unbelieving Gentiles, not even suggesting that church members should seek to convert them. Since his main purpose is to build up the church and maintain its unity, he has no need to refer to the continuance of Israel; since also the Jews are not apparently disturbing the harmony of his communities he has no need to be anti-Jewish. In ignoring the future position of unbelieving Jews AE certainly does not go so far as *Barn* 13.1ff which explicitly excludes them from the covenant, and certainly not as far as the hostility expressed towards them in Melito, *On the Pascha* 42–3, 99. He can therefore be acquitted of any charge of anti-Semitism and also of one of anti-Judaism. It may be that our worries in respect of AE's position come from our realisation that the Jews have continued to exist through two millennia and therefore some explanation is necessary. For AE there are three groups of people, the Jews, the Gentiles and the church. AE would not then have rejected the traditional term for the church: the third race. The term goes back at least as far as *Kerygma Petri* (= Clem Alex *Strom* 6.5.39–41; cf *Diognetus* 1; in Aristides, *Apology* 2, the Syriac version adds a fourth group, the Barbarians).

17. AE now returns to the theme of peace first announced in v. 14a. In vv. 14b–16 he is said to have made peace, but being peace and making peace do not avail or benefit unless the peace is made known: AE brings this out by using Isa 57.19, to which he had already alluded in v. 13 (see there for the background to its use). In saying that Christ **proclaimed** peace AE goes beyond the choice of a simple word, such as 'to preach', which would merely mean that Christ announced it, and chooses instead 'to proclaim an evangel' which in itself contains a valuation of the proclaimed message as good news; he probably drew the verb from Isa 52.7 where it is connected to the concept of peace.

Peace is again understood with its Jewish significance (see on v. 14) in going beyond the cessation of hostility to the total well-being of those to whom it is offered. It is not merely, 'I am no longer angry with you', but more positively, 'I seek your well-being.' He splits the double reference in the OT, 'peace, peace', and applies 'peace' separately to the two categories, 'far off', 'near at hand', so that he sees peace as affecting both groups in the same way. 'You, **the far off**' are the Gentiles, to whom he is principally writing. As we saw in v. 13 **far off** and **near at hand** refer respectively to Gentiles and Jews (AE preserves the Isaianic order and this probably accounts for his placing Gentiles first). In v. 17 AE deals with the vertical aspect of the ambiguity running through our passage: the peace that is proclaimed is that between God and Gentile and between God and Jew and not that between Gentile and Jew. There is no distinction in the way God offers peace to Jew and Gentile or in the nature of the peace as it is described in v. 18.

When he came forms the main problem in v. 17: when did Christ preach peace? The participle could denote an action simultaneous with the main verb or one prior to it; the main verb has been understood in many different ways, resulting in a number of different solutions: (i) A preaching prior to the incarnation. (ii) The incarnation itself as a proclamation of peace (Harless; Hofmann); but AE shows little interest in the incarnation; for him the centre of Christ's earthly life is his death. (iii) Christ's earthly life as itself his preaching (Chrysostom; Mussner; Masson; Haupt; Rendtorff; Macpherson); those who adhere to (ii) usually (with Chrysostom) combine this view with it; the Gospels present Jesus as saying of himself that he has 'come' (Mt 5.17; 9.13; 10.34; Lk 19.10; etc.). (iv) The resurrection as Christ's preaching (Ambrosiaster; Aquinas; Bengel; Murray; Van Roon; Caird); the 'coming' is then an event after the death. (v) A preaching of Christ in the coming of the Spirit; this would post-date his death (Meyer; Westcott; Hodge; Salmond; Alford). (vi) Christ preaches in that he instructs and inspires those who then proclaim the Gospel to Jew and Gentile; since he is the content of what they preach he may be regarded as himself the proclaimer (Abbott; Gnilka; Schnackenburg). Such preaching post-dates his death and by AE's time was addressed to Gentiles as well as Jews; moreover a part of the task of missionaries will be the bringing of peace (Mt 10.13) and when missionaries are received it is as if Christ were received (Mt 10.40f; Lk 10.16). (vii) The ascent of the crucified saviour through the cosmic barrier represents his preaching and revelation (Schlier).

None of these solutions is wholly satisfactory and perhaps Barth is correct when he says that it is impossible to tie the reference down to any one solution. Attempts to combine more than one (Mussner; Vosté) do not appear to be any more successful. If we have to choose, (iii) and (vi) are probably least objectionable. Whatever the meaning it is the same gospel which is preached to those near, the Jews, and those afar, the Gentiles. Even if Jews are not within the church, they are not outside the range of the gospel; in this respect Jews and Gentiles are equal.

18. V. 18 summarises and explains what has gone before (Gnilka; Haupt): the Gospel of peace is the joint access of Jew and Gentile (note the first person plural as in v. 14a) to the Father. Such access is only possible once enmity has been removed, both have been made into a new type of being and form one body, and peace exists. We find in Rom 5.1 the same close association of peace with access and there as here a present tense indicates a continuing experience on the part of believers. What continues depends on what once happened in the death of Christ; Christ is the active agent of redemption.

Believers come to God only through what Christ has done for them or as he introduces them. The root of the word translated **access** was used in the contemporary world to describe the approach of people to a ruler and, more importantly, for the offering of sacrificial gifts (Lev 1.2, 3, 10, etc.). AE has then selected a word common in the cultus rather than drawn one from Rom 5.1f to use for his own purposes (Gnilka); Christ presents believers to his Father. If God is to be encountered the way must be opened, not from our end but from his (cf Pokorný). Despite the cultic background however, Christ is not depicted here as in Hebrews as High Priest, though as in Hebrews (9.12; 10.19–22) access is a consequence of the cross. The religious and philosophical systems of the ancient world offered different and unsatisfactory ways to God. Access is not conceived here individualistically, every man his own priest, but is an access of the whole church comprising both Jews and Gentiles, an access experienced in worship. Through their cultus Jews already had access, though of a limited nature; Gentiles had none; now both have the same free access. We come here to the climax of AE's argument. Though not explicitly mentioned, 2.6 already implied access for believers.

This access is said to be **in one Spirit**. Is this (a) the divine Spirit (Chrysostom; Gnilka; Schlier; Schnackenburg; Adai; Lemmer), or (b) the human spirit (Jerome; Scott; Haupt), or (c) the human spirit as affected by the divine Spirit? Those who hold to (b) probably mean (c) since the human spirit of believers is always one in which the divine Spirit dwells. If (c) is accepted (cf Phil 1.27) then we deal with the attitude in worship of those who are given access, or with their consciousness of being redeemed, or it is being suggested that Jews and Gentiles are engulfed in the same spirit, a kind of *esprit de corps*. There is a certain parallelism between v. 16 and v. 18 for both speak of a relation to God; in v. 16 it takes place 'in one body', here 'in one Spirit'. Where in 4.4 body and Spirit are again linked it is certainly the divine Spirit which is in mind, and we may therefore assume the same here. If then (a) is intended and a relation exists between the body of

Christ and the Spirit it would be too simple to envisage it as similar to that of the human spirit in the human body. The relation of the body (= the church) to Christ is complex, so also is that of the Spirit to him. The introduction of the Spirit at this point is not inappropriate for a writer of the Pauline school since Paul related the Spirit and adoption (Rom 8.14–16; Gal 4.6). Children have access to their fathers. Access to God the Father may be opened through the Christ-event but it is mediated through the Spirit. Believers enjoy the blessings of the Spirit (1.3), are sealed by the Spirit who is the initial instalment of full redemption (1.13f; 4.30), the Spirit works in them (3.16), and they are built into a dwelling-place of God in the Spirit (2.22). **One** is important because as Jews and Gentiles receive redemption through the one Lord so they have the same access in the Spirit to the one Father in worship and service. AE does not say that Gentiles have gained an access that earlier belonged to Jews alone, but that both Jews and Gentiles have a new access; there is an unresolved tension then here with v. 12 where AE set out Jewish privileges. The Spirit is a unifying power which gives here an upward movement to God in contrast to the downward of 1.3 (Adai). We note finally that many of the words here like **access** have spatial connotations. There is also here a triadic reference, Father, Christ, Spirit, which emerges naturally from AE's theology. God is described here as Father which, though Jews applied it to him, has a special ring for Christians because of the prominence given it by Jesus.

We can see then that AE has taken up Paul's use of the concept of reconciliation between God and man. Aware of its employment in the Colossian hymn in relation to the reconciliation of the all to God, and seeing the need to explain the relationship of Jews and Gentiles, he has applied it to this and in so doing has created the confusion between the vertical and horizontal ideas of reconciliation. At the same time in taking this step he has realised that these two aspects of reconciliation go together and that each is meaningless without the other. Though AE was not directly considering the general problem of racial or social reconciliation, he shows that its horizontal and vertical aspects cannot be separated. Such a twofold reconciliation moreover is achieved, not through education, social reform, military might, or revolution, but through the death of Christ.

At the beginning of the discussion of v. 14 the question was raised whether AE was faithful to Jesus in saying that Jesus was peace since Jesus had said he had not come to bring peace. The saying of Jesus relates to the calling of disciples; when someone heeds the call of Jesus the probable result will be the breakup of the family to which he or she belongs, so the peace to be expected within families will be destroyed; in that sense Jesus is a disturber of the peace. However, AE is not writing about the call of disciples but about what should happen within an existing Christian community. In saying that Jesus is peace he is not thinking of peace in general, or referring to peace between nations or tribes, between social classes or between races. In our passage as it developed we saw that the result of God's action in Christ was both the reconciliation of humankind to himself and that of Jewish and Gentile Christians to one another. This fits in with the general tenor of his writing. His paraenesis (4.1–6.20) treats the behaviour of believers towards one another, not their behaviour towards the world outside the church (see Essay: Moral Teaching). All that we know of the early church implies that there was no peace between it and the world; persecution, whether official or casual, affected believers. AE does not refer to the relationship of believers with the world outside the church. If peace and reconciliation go together there could not be reconciliation between the church and the world for the world would not permit it. What Jesus had said about himself and peace is not contradicted therefore by what AE writes. So when he says Jesus is peace he means loyalty to Jesus should result in peace within Christian communities. AE is not interested in peace or oneness between the nations; he has no passage equivalent to Col 3.11. The peace he espouses is not established by force of arms nor maintained by careful diplomacy as was the *Pax Romana*; it comes from the weakness of a crucifixion carried out perhaps to maintain the *Pax Romana*.

19. The discussion of the Jewish–Gentile relationship reaches its climax in vv. 19–22 (Penna). Jewish Christians and Gentile Christians are equally members of the church and in that light AE expounds a part of his understanding of the church. In doing this he returns to v. 12 for some of its words and ideas; they were used there to stress the superiority of the Jews and AE now modifies them for his present purpose. The Gentiles were once **foreigners** and **strangers**. It is difficult to distinguish between and define precisely the meaning of these two words because their significance varied in different communities. By and large they indicated those who living in a community did not possess full citizenship and AE is probably only seeking to say that Gentiles do not belong to a defined community. But to what community? The use of **foreigners** might suggest Israel was in mind but the community of which they are now members is the church, so AE is probably thinking of their previous non-membership of that body. But is it the church on earth or that in heaven?

The answer comes in v. 19b. Whereas v. 19a was negative, v. 19b is positive. The Gentiles are citizens together with others (all citizens are full citizens), but with which others? Who are **the holy ones**? A number of suggestions have been made: (i) The Jewish patriarchs and other celebrated Jews (Chrysostom; Theophylact); since this entails a most unusual meaning of the word it may be dismissed. (ii) Jewish Christians (Vielhauer; Dibelius; Grosheide; Caird; von Soden; Roels; Faust). (iv) Christians (Mussner; Pfammater; Haupt; Abbott; Ernst; Masson; Merklein; Gaugler). This is the word's usual meaning in the NT though at 1.18 we saw reason to believe AE was aware of another meaning, that of (v) below. (v) Angels, heavenly beings (Lindemann; Bouwman; Gnilka; Schlier; Van Roon; Schnackenburg allows this as a possibility). We have already argued that this is the probable meaning in 1.18. 2.6 supports it in that believers are already raised with Christ and sit with him in the heavenlies. The citizenship of members of the Qumran community was in the heavens with the sons of heaven (1QS 11.7f). In Judaism (2 *Bar* 4.2ff; *Ps Sol* 17.30; Philo *Conf Ling* 78) and early Christianity (Gal 4.26; Phil 3.20; Heb 11.9f; 12.22) the concept of the heavenly city appears regularly. (vi) Glorified believers; Schlier and some others rightly combine this view with the previous since believers raised to heaven cohabit with heavenly beings. This combination of (v) and (vi) seems the most satisfactory.

The image now changes to the warmer metaphor of the readers as members of a household, almost implying kinship: they **belong to God's household**. The house and the city were very similar concepts in the ancient world. In Philo a similar word is used to indicate nearness to God (*Cherub* 18; *Post Cain* 12, 135; cf *Qu Exod* II 29). This phrase then, unlike the first which referred to a relationship among believers, relates believers to God. Christians form a community related to Christ (Mk 3.33–5; 10.29f) or God (Heb 3.1–6; 1 Pet 5.17) behind which lies the concept of Israel as God's house (Exod 16.31; 2 Sam 1.12; Num 12.7; Ps 127; 1QS 8.5; CD 3.19; *1 En* 89.29ff). Believers are children of God (2 Cor 6.18), adopted as such (1.5) and given access to him (2.18), the head of the household. All this implies intimacy. Those who belong to God's household are members of the house, not necessarily kinsfolk but certainly not slaves; nor are they 'guests – here to-day and away to-morrow' (Eadie) – well treated when present but forgotten when gone. The extended family was an important unit in contemporary society and Cynic-Stoic preaching made use of the image of the family; AE's Gentile readers would then easily grasp his idea even if they were not aware of its OT background.

But where is God's household and who is in it? Does it consist only of living Christians and confined to this world or does it also exist in the heavenlies and contain angels and dead believers? We have already seen that the latter is the more probable; that it is the correct interpretation is supported here by the absence of a reference to Christ. In the letter elsewhere the relationship of Christians and Christ is stressed (e.g. they are in him, are raised with him, are members of his body), and that relationship to him is linked to his earthly existence, be it only his death and resurrection. The earthly link cannot predominate when we think of a relationship to God; this makes it fitting to take God's household as being in the heavenlies and including heavenly beings. AE has thus passed in this verse beyond the consideration of the place of Gentiles in the church and is working out the place of all, Gentile and Jewish, who form the one church of God. Gentile Christians, once refugees, are now neither homeless nor stateless (cf Stott). Those who were once outsiders are now insiders.

20. The imagery, having changed from membership of a city to that of a household, now changes to the building which contains the household, and those who dwell in the household (v. 19) are pictured as the bricks with which it is built. The use of building imagery was foreshadowed with the architectural term **middle**

wall (v. 14). The building has a **foundation, the apostles and prophets**, on which believers are built.

The metaphor of building is used in two distinct ways, statically, in depicting a group of people as an edifice, and dynamically, of the maturing of people in their faith. In the first case the implied subject of the erection of the edifice is God or Christ; in the second it may be either God or Christ, but is more usually believers who build up themselves or one another in conduct and faith. The image is used in 2.20–2 in the first way (cf 1 Cor 3.9, 16) and in the second in 4.12, 16, 29 (cf 1 Cor 10.23; 14.4–20; 2 Cor 10.8; 12.19; 13.10; 1 Th 5.11). In the second also there is normally no reference to the type of edifice which is being erected; it is either the church viewed as a community of believers (not a structure of wood and stone) or individual believers. This second dynamic usage is by far the more frequent in the Pauline corpus and probably derives directly from the OT and not from the static.

Like all buildings the edifice of v. 20 has a foundation. In 1 Cor 3.10 it is Jesus Christ and it is laid by Paul, not God. Even if Paul is the author of Ephesians there is no reason why he should not have modified his use of the building metaphor from 1 Cor 3.10; authors regularly vary their use of metaphors. The foundation is not of course the rock or ground on which the lowest stones or bricks are laid but the lowest level of the building on which the remainder rests. We might have expected AE to say that the foundation of the church was Israel rather than the apostles and prophets; in not doing so he indicates that the church is not just a simple continuation of Israel.

But who are the apostles and prophets and why are they introduced? They are certainly not introduced as great figures of the past who might act as role models for conscientious Christians (cf Ign *Eph* 11.2; 12.2; Polyc *Phil* 3.2; 11.3). Apostles and prophets are different groups and not the same group, defined by two different titles, apostles who are also prophets (in Rev 21.14 the apostles alone are the foundation). The two groups however are so tied together by the one article that those who wish to deduce from the reference to the apostles as foundation that the church is apostolic must equally be ready to accept that the church is prophetic.

Neither apostles nor prophets are precisely identified by their titles for both terms are used loosely. Apostle (see on 1.1) can have a wide sense with undefined edges and be somewhat equivalent to 'missionary' (Rom 16.7; 1 Th 2.6) and a restricted sense as indicating the Twelve or the Twelve plus Paul; it can denote missionary figures of the first generation and include Paul and Barnabas (cf Acts 14.4, 14). There is little in our context to indicate which sense is intended, but in 3.5 where there is a parallel usage it probably means the Twelve without Paul since he appears separately at 3.3. This sense would be supported if our understanding of prophets is correct (see below). It is relatively easy to see how the Twelve (= the apostles) could have been regarded as the foundation of the church; they are figures of the past; it was not simply that they were the first members of the church but it was from their preaching after the resurrection that the church grew; their preaching may also be said to have given the church its shape, though Paul and Barnabas did the same in accepting Gentiles as full members. Their (the Twelve, or the Twelve plus Paul and Barnabas) position would thus be analogous to some interpretations of Peter as the rock on which the church is built (Mt 16.18).

The prophets were taken to be those of the OT by Origen, *Cant* II 1, 11, GCS 8, 157, Chrysostom, Theodoret, Ambrosiaster, Calvin, Beza, Roberts; Marcion presumably understood them in this way for Tertullian, *adv Marc* V, 17, 6, says he omitted the reference to them. More generally, from Pelagius onwards, they have been assumed to be those of the early church who either foresaw the future (Acts 11.28; 21.10f) and/or proclaimed the truth of God in particular situations. Had the OT prophets been intended the order would have been 'the prophets and the apostles'. If AE had been wishing to refer to the OT since the foundation of the church is being considered, a better phrase would have been 'the law, the prophets and the apostles'. In 3.5 where we again have the double phrase it is early church prophets who are intended (see notes on 3.5) for OT prophets are hardly responsible for the command to evangelise the Gentiles. In 4.11 the prophets are charismatic figures who are listed among the ministers of the church and therefore must be NT prophets.

How however could NT prophets, who were certainly honoured in the early church (1 Cor 12.28; Rev 18.20) and were probably still a living force at the time of Ephesians (*Did* 10.7; 11.7ff), be regarded as the foundation of the church or as bearers of revelation? 3.5 provides a clue for it associates prophets with apostles in the transmission of the divine command to evangelise the Gentiles. This command is given in variant forms and to groups whose membership is defined in different ways in Mt 28.16–20; Lk 24.47–9; Acts 1.8; Jn 20.21b. Since contemporary prophets gave directions about the future activity of the church it is not difficult to see how some might have thought of them as involved in the original command to evangelise, and if they were, they were involved in the admission of the Gentiles and thus in a decision about the shape of the church; they could then be considered alongside the apostles as its foundation. In Acts 13.1–3 prophets were involved in moving the church into a new venture; in doing so they were shaping its nature; this was necessarily something belonging to the past of AE. It is also always difficult to dissociate activity from the people exercising it and so, though strictly it is the revelation which permits the admission of Gentiles, those who mediated the revelation could be taken to be its foundation. Another approach reinforcing this conclusion is possible. The book of Revelation describes itself as a prophecy (1.3; 22.7, 10, 18, 19); prophets predict the End in Mk 13.22; if 1 Th 4.15f, or some part of it, was a revelation to the church through a prophet, prophets again have an eschatological connection. May it not be that a part of the foundation of the church is the security of its end in God? If so, prophets have a role in its foundation.

Apostles and prophets are seen here, because of the single article, as one group, containing both apostles and prophets; whether AE has created this group for his own purposes or taken it from the tradition is difficult to say. Here and in 3.5 the group's function belongs to the past, not simply as first believers, which might be the case if apostles alone were mentioned, but as the basis for what follows in that its members were the channels of revelation. They are temporally prior to others and prior also in the reception of revelation (3.5) and therefore capable of sustaining the building, but not by themselves, as the final clause shows.

Verse 20b, while certainly implying that Christ has a special position within the building, does not, in terms of our present knowledge, make clear what that position is, for it is impossible to determine with any certainty the precise meaning of the word translated **angle-stone**.

Two main interpretations have been offered of: cornerstone, capstone. Luke may have been aware of the word's ambiguity for in 20.18 people can both fall over the stone and it fall on them! It is generally assumed that the word is used under the influence of Isa 28.16 where it relates to, or is a part of, the foundation. This has led some to regard it as a stone at a corner which is used in squaring off the building. This would imply a unique position for Christ. But it cannot be proved that such stones existed for none has ever been discovered in ancient buildings of the Greco-Roman world. All that has been found are long stones which run along the foundation, one end of which may be at a corner, but these do not jut out for people to stumble over and in any building there are a number of them so that no one can be regarded as unique. The further suggestion that Christ as the cornerstone unites the two walls of Jewish and Gentile Christians (Theod Mops; Chrysostom; Jerome; Thomas Aquinas; Calvin) is fanciful. If Christ is a stone in the foundation, even at the corner, does that distinguish him sufficiently from the apostles and prophets who also belong to the foundation? 1 Cor 3.10 makes clear Christ's unique position for he alone is the foundation. If the apostles and prophets are regarded as laying the foundation some of the difficulties are avoided but we have seen that this is not what is meant. In Mk 12.10f; 1 Pet 2.6–8 it is easy to take Christ as cornerstone because neither passage refers to the foundation.

It is these difficulties that have led to the acceptance of the alternative view of Christ as the capstone, the stone which locks an arch, not a dome, together. There are a number of instances of the use of the word where it implies a stone which is high above the ground: Isa 28.16 (Peshitta); 4 Kgdms 25.17 (Symmachus); *T Sol* 22.7–23.3; the background to these references is the Jerusalem temple. If the readers would not have known enough about the temple in Jerusalem to pick up a reference to the 'middle wall' as the balustrade, would they have picked up this as a 'high' stone in it? Tertullian, *adv Marc* 3.7, appears to think of a stone high in the building. A stone high in a building accords with the idea of Christ as the head of his body, the church. However, this solution to the meaning of the angle-stone is difficult in that it implies that the building is well on to completion for in the next verse the growth of the church is stressed; buildings do not grow up to stones above them. Has Christ moreover no place in the church until it is partly complete? Yet there must be a sense in which the church is already complete, for v. 22 says it is God's dwelling-place; can he be envisaged as dwelling in an incomplete building? There is a high degree of eschatological realisation in the letter and this may be yet another instance.

Both understandings of angle-stone can then be sustained with contemporary, but slender, evidence and both run into theological difficulties. Perhaps in the present state of our knowledge the problem is insoluble. However, the context shows clearly that AE wishes to allot to Christ a place in the building different from that of the apostles and prophets and more important than that of either of them.

21. The imagery again changes; the building is said to grow and is identified as a temple. It grows **in Christ**.

But what is it that grows 'in Christ'? AE is not thinking here of the growth of each separate congregation which receives his letter, still less of Jews and Gentiles being built together (Jerome; Aquinas), but of the one church of God. It would in any case be a little absurd to think of apostles and prophets as foundations of individual communities (Gaugler).

In important ancient buildings the stones were carefully **fitted together**, being smoothed where their surfaces met, dowel holes drilled and dowels inserted. The stones which are here being fitted together (present tense) are not the two groups, Jewish and Gentile Christians, but individual believers. Thus the argument which moved in v. 20 from believers as members of a household into the material with which the house was built and indicated the positions of apostles, prophets and Christ now depicts believers as harmoniously related to the believers beside, above and below them. No stone should be out of place (Origen). Since in fact believers do not always fit harmoniously together, as 4.25ff shows, the church is pictured as it ought to be rather than as it is.

The building is said **to grow**. While growth is something more normally associated with organic life it is not difficult to see it being transferred metaphorically to buildings in the course of erection and 1 Cor 3.6–17 (cf Jer 31.28) shows how easy it is to move from the organic to the building metaphor. 1 Pet 2.5 refers to 'living stones'. Growth (note the present tense of verb and participle) suggests that not all the stones have yet been built in; believers are added daily to the church and the growth is extensive in numbers rather than intensive in love as at 4.16. Growth implies incompleteness which conflicts with any idea of Christ as the final stone and with an over-realised eschatology. The builder is not identified; in 1 Cor 3.10 Paul as builder lays the foundation on which others build, though immediately prior to this God is described as the source of growth (1 Cor 3.6). We may assume then that in v. 21 God is the ultimate builder. However, both the fitting together and growth are **in Christ**, the angle-stone. It is difficult to see how stones are smoothly joined together by their relation to the angle-stone and we must assume a mingling of metaphors. Perhaps it is that believers are shaped, smoothed and joined together by their relation to Christ whom they are to resemble (2 Cor 3.18; Phil 3.21).

The imagery changes again and the building is viewed as a temple or **sanctuary**. The movement in metaphor from house to temple is made easier since the Jerusalem temple was sometimes termed the house of God and the idea of the temple had already been spiritualised in both Greco-Roman and Jewish thought, so that the world or man or a part of man (his mind or heart) could be termed 'temple'. Paul had already applied the image of the temple to the community (1 Cor 3.16f; 2 Cor 6.16; cf 1 Pet 2.4f); he had taught this during his first stay in Corinth (note the 'do you not know' of 1 Cor 3.16), and his disciples would know it; the idea probably also underlies Jn 2.13–22 and the Markan use of the logion of 14.58; 15.29. It can be traced to the Qumran Community (1QS 5.5f; 8.4–10; 11.8). Believers appear here as the material out of which the community is built. Gentiles who were once not allowed to enter the Jerusalem temple have become a part of this temple. As the material of the temple the position of believers contrasts here with 1 Per 2.4f where they serve within the temple as a spiritual priesthood (e.g. Rom 12.1f; 1 Pet 2.5;

Heb 13.15f). If Christians are already regarded by AE as inhabitants of heaven (see on v. 19) then he may also have the heavenly temple in mind. The Christians, Jews and Gentiles, as temple replace every earthly temple as the dwelling-place for God and at the same time are the realisation of the expected heavenly temple.

Finally the holy temple is said to be **in the Lord**; here as elsewhere in Ephesians the Lord is Christ and not God. The existence of the church is centred on Christ.

22. This verse is in part parallel to the preceding and in part develops it so that the temple is expressly identified as the place of God's dwelling. The verse with its sudden renewed direct address to the readers forms a suitable climax to the whole section, 2.11–22. What was theory in vv. 20f is now made relevant to the readers; they have not been left out, but have been built together with those already in the church on a foundation of the apostles and prophets and with Christ as the angle-stone.

The temple already exists and the readers are built into it, presumably by God. But if they are built **into** something already in existence, what is that something? (a) The Jewish people. It is unlikely that Gentile believers are added to the Jewish people to create the church. (b) The first Jewish Christians (Gnilka). In vv. 14–18 stress lay on the making one of the two groups of Jewish and Gentile Christians and so it might not be inappropriate here to regard Gentile Christians as built into the new Jewish–Christian people of God. Against the acceptance of this view is the present tense of the verb; when vv. 14–17 discussed the unity of Jewish and Gentile Christians past tenses were used with the unification envisaged as accomplished in the cross; the present tense here implies that Gentiles are built into a church already containing some Gentiles. (c) Apostles, prophets and Christ. It is improbable that AE thinks of his readers being added only to the foundation and angle-stone. (d) The existing church which consists already of Jewish and Gentile believers (cf Schnackenburg); the present tense of the verb suggests a process, believers are being built together with those who are already parts of the building, the existing Jewish and Christian believers. If the church is regarded as containing both heavenly and earthly members (see on v. 19) this interpretation is not affected. It is the most probable. (e) It is however just possible that the reference may be to Christ alone as in 2.5f.

The temple is now identified as the place of God's dwelling. Believers are built together for the purpose of being a place where God would dwell. That the gods inhabit earthly buildings is an idea found widely in the contemporary religions and is also present in the OT (Exod 15.17; 3 Kgdms 8.13; see also Mal 3.1) and elsewhere in the NT (1 Cor 3.16). The OT also has passages where God is said to be in his people (Exod 25.8; 29.45; Lev 26.11; Ezek 37.27). Once people and temple are identified the objection that God cannot dwell in a physical building is removed. If unbelievers point to their temples as the places where their gods live and ask Christians where theirs are to be found they can respond by saying that God dwells in their community. It is true he may also dwell in individuals and local house churches but the emphasis here is on his dwelling in the community as a whole. But can God live in what is incomplete? Presumably if the angle-stone, as a high-up stone, is in position there is a sense in which the building is complete.

God's dwelling is **in Spirit**. The parallelism of our verse with v. 21 together with this being its final phrase will imply that it is the Holy Spirit which is referred to here (cf Ps 18.6; 27.4f; 46.5, 7; 68.36). It does not suggest that the dwelling is simply metaphorical or non-material; such an understanding of **Spirit** would add nothing to an already metaphorical context. It is in any case clear that the temple of v. 21, unlike those of the OT and of the cities where AE's readers live, is non-material. **Spirit** does not indicate the builder but denotes the mode of God's activity or the way in which his dwelling is made possible. The Spirit is the Spirit of power and this lends a dynamic aspect to God's presence in the temple.

VI

PAUL AND THE GENTILES

(3.1–13)

¹ Because of this I, Paul, Christ's prisoner
    on behalf of you Gentiles –
² Surely you have heard of God's plan
    in respect of the grace given me for you,
³   namely that by revelation God made known
      the mystery to me,
        just as I wrote in brief above,
⁴   which when you read
      you are able to understand
    my insight into the mystery of Christ,
⁵   (a mystery) not made known
        in other periods to humanity
      as it has been revealed
        now to his holy apostles and prophets
          through the Spirit,
⁶   that the Gentiles are heirs together,
           members of the same body,
          sharers in the promise,
          in Christ Jesus
          through the gospel
⁷   of which I became a minister
      in accordance with the gift of the grace of God
      given me,
        in appropriate proportion
        by the working of his power.
⁸ To me this grace was given,
      me, lower than the least of all the saints,
    to proclaim to the Gentiles
      the unimaginable riches of Christ,

⁹   **and to enlighten all**
       as to the plan of the mystery,
        hidden from the ages
        by God who made everything,
¹⁰ **so that the much-variegated wisdom of God**
       might be made known now through the church
        to the rulers and authorities in the heavenlies,
¹¹   **according to his eternal intention,**
       which he resolved in the Messiah Jesus our Lord,
¹²   **in whom we have boldness and access with confidence**
       through his faithfulness.
¹³ **Therefore I beg you not to lose heart**
       at my tribulations on your behalf
       seeing that they are for your glory.

With his theological argument concerning the basis for the redemption of Gentile alongside Jewish Christians complete, AE moves on to intercede for the former (vv. 1, 14ff); prayer follows naturally after the reference to the temple (2.22). In approaching the prayer AE introduces the name of **Paul**. This leads him to break off the movement towards intercession in order to discuss how Paul had himself been instrumental in making known God's plan for the Gentiles. If Paul is himself the author then his emphasis on himself, **I, Paul**, reminds readers of his part in evangelising the Gentiles. 2.11–22 may have laid the theological basis for this, but there is also need to explain the historical process and so he (AE or Paul) breaks off to do this and inserts vv. 2–13, returning to the intercession at v. 14. Vv. 2–13 are thus a lengthy parenthesis; the style and language are sufficiently similar to that in the remainder of the letter to raise no suspicion that they are a later gloss. That vv. 2–13 are parenthetical does not mean they are unimportant. They give, in fact, the grounds for Paul's right to address the readers.

Paul was an apostle and his personal position has already been referred to: he was part of the foundation (2.20). This however only made him one among a number of apostles and prophets. Yet he was not just one among a number but had a unique position in relation to the Gentiles: he is the apostle to the Gentiles. What are the grounds for describing him in this way? It was neither his insight into the OT nor a brainwave on his part which led him to see that the gospel must include Gentiles. God had given him a revelation to that effect. The inclusion of the Gentiles had been part of God's plan from the beginning, but had previously been kept secret; it has now been made known to Paul (v. 3) and others (v. 5). Paul also had been empowered to be the primary instrument for its accomplishment (vv.7–8). Vv. 7, 8 hold together, though v. 7 is the conclusion of the first main sentence (vv. 2–7) and v. 8 the beginning of the second (vv. 8–12). They form the transition from the statement of Paul's place in God's plan to the outline of his fulfilment of his role. A revelation has been made whose content was the acceptance of the Gentiles into God's people (v. 6). God's plan has however an even wider cosmic ambit (v. 10), and this was his intention from the beginning through Christ (vv. 11–12). That Paul suffered was therefore of little importance and should not discourage the readers; in fact it was for their good (v. 13). The 'once-now' schema appears here again, though not now relating to a personal change in believers as in 2.1ff, but to God's action in withholding knowledge and then disclosing it.

This is the most personal section of Ephesians; if written by Paul it allows us to view Ephesians as a letter and not a homily or theological tractate. If it is post-Pauline, then the section must be seen as part of the theological argument in indicating how God chose one particular human being to work out his purpose. Whether Pauline or not, it contains some extreme statements in respect of Paul which accord him a very high, if not unique, place; these statements are matched only by his claim to have been the last person to see Christ (1 Cor. 15.8) and the possible claim in Col 1.24 that his sufferings are in some way related to those of Christ in benefiting the church. AE may have had in his mind a thought similar to Col 1.24 as he composed our section. Both AE and A/Col hold Paul in equal veneration and their school will have mulled over his significance. Merklein regards 3.1–7 as an interpretation of Col 1.24–8 while Bouwman argues that 2.11–22 takes up Col 1.21–3 and 3.2–13 plays on the idea of Paul as 'minister' and on the concept of mystery derived from Colossians. However, the idea that Paul's trials would benefit his converts is found more widely in his letters (1 Cor 1.3–7; 2 Cor 4.12) and so would have influenced his followers. The presence of the Gentiles in the church is indissolubly linked to Paul's position in God's economy.

It is not easy to tie down the genre of the passage. Though v. 1 heads what looks like being a liturgical section that section does not in fact commence until v. 14. Our paragraph is narrative, in so far as any part of Ephesians can be so described, for it recounts an action of the past, a revelation, and a continuing activity, a making known of the revelation. As narrative it is in part autobiographical (note the extensive use of the first person singular), though if Paul is not the author it might be better to describe it as pseudo-autobiographical. It is not, however, a 'testament' for there is no sign that Paul's death is near and no play on the idea that this might be his final writing to the readers. One of the main themes is 'revelation' but the revelation has already been disclosed and action in relation to it has already taken place. The genre is not then purely apocalyptic. It is perhaps a mixture of apocalyptic and pseudo-autobiography; genres do not need to be 'pure'. Although it may be correct to describe vv. 2–12(13) as a digression, it is not a carefully planned digression and cannot therefore be a *digressio* in the sense of ancient rhetorical criticism. As a digression in the ordinary sense of the word it fills an essential gap in the argument and it would be wrong therefore to look on it as a gloss (cf Kirby). That AE breaks into his argument here suggests that he had not cleverly planned what he was going to write.

1. This verse lacks a verb. The author broke off into a parenthesis (vv. 2–13), and the verb for this sentence is not given until v. 14: (**For this reason I)bow my knees to the Father ...** V. 1 is hardly a 'chapter heading'. AE broke off from the intercession he was about to make because the simultaneous mention of Paul and the Gentiles suggested a gap in his argument. Certainly Paul himself could have broken off in this way, for regularly in his certainly genuine letters we find anacolutha; there is also one at 2.1; the present break can therefore be regarded as neither favouring nor militating against Pauline authorship. Would a pseudonymist however have created anacolutha? Perhaps since AE is a good writer he did so in conscious imitation of Paul (Bouwman), being influenced by the words and ideas of the Pauline school as reflected also in Col 1.21ff. More probably it came about through the realisation that something important for the argument had been omitted. The presence of ancolutha in the letter probably indicates that it was dictated.

The double **I, Paul** stresses the identity of Paul. Paul uses similar phrases when he wishes to emphasise either an argument or his own position (2 Cor 10.1; Gal 5.2; 1 Th 2.18; Philem 19; cf Col 1.23). Only here and in Col 1.23 is it tied to his mission to the Gentiles. While the greater part of the letter will yield the same theological meaning whether Paul is regarded as author or not, that cannot be said of 3.2–13. If AE specifically mentions Paul as author he will be reminding his readers that Paul sealed his mission with a martyr's death in prison; in this way he will deepen the appeal of what he writes in setting out Paul as the architect of the church of Jews and Gentiles (cf Gnilka). When he wrote in Paul's name, AE played on his readers' knowledge that Paul wrote letters; now he plays on their knowledge that he was a prisoner; the very introduction of his name reminds them of everything they know about him. AE makes use of Paul's name in this way because his readers venerate Paul. The real emphasis of 3.2–13 however does not rest on Paul as prisoner but on him as God's instrument in bringing the gospel to Gentiles, yet his position as prisoner contrasts strongly with the position he is given later in the passage as the unique recipient of revelation. If it is Paul himself who writes, then he also draws attention to himself by using his name and referring to himself as prisoner; this would impress his readers with the importance of what he is about to say. If Paul wrote this, it is interesting that he does not say, 'I, Paul, the apostle and prisoner ...'. Whatever authority he may claim here he lets it rest on himself as one called by God, and not on some special position he may have been accorded in the church.

On other occasions when Paul introduces his own name he does so usually because he, his position as apostle, or his teaching have been attacked. Ephesians however contains no trace of any attack on him or his teaching; he is never on the defensive. He is introduced, or introduces himself, with the intention of being shown as the one who prays for the Gentiles; 3.14ff gives the prayer. Paul's name is introduced then with pastoral intent, but once introduced the discussion is given a new direction beginning from the reference to him as a **prisoner** on behalf of others.

Paul endured several imprisonments (2 Cor 11.23). On a number of occasions he refers to himself as in prison or in bonds (Phil 1.7, 13f, 17; Philem 1, 9, 10, 13) and these imprisonments become a standard theme of the post-Paulines (Col 4.10; 2 Tim 1.8; 2.9); AE reverts to the theme again at 4.1 and 6.20. But what does 'Paul, the prisoner of Christ' mean? If AE is indebted to Col 1.21ff, why did he not write of Paul the 'minister, 'servant' of Christ? In the light of Paul's actual imprisonments the reference cannot be taken as purely metaphorical as if Paul were simply Christ's captive, held by his love (cf Hodge). This may be true but would not entail the elimination of the idea of a physical imprisonment. In the literal sense he is a prisoner of Caesar, or of someone holding authority under Caesar. Yet he is kept a prisoner, not by physical restraint, but by his relation to Christ and his love for the Gentiles, on whose behalf he is a prisoner. He is Caesar's prisoner because he is first of all Christ's prisoner, not just a Christian who through some misfortune happens to find himself in prison; neither is he simply a prisoner of conscience, as are many because of their unwillingness to give up a cause to which their lives have been dedicated. His life is dedicated to a person. What in fact we have here is a christological use of **prisoner**, an idea already present in Phil 1.12–14; Philem 9. Paul's imprisonment is not then a sign of God's displeasure; whatever happens to him will be for the good of the gospel (Phil 1.12–26). His imprisonment contrasts strongly with his previous activity as a missionary (cf vv. 8ff).

If the historical Paul wrote these words, to which of his many imprisonments does he refer? Apart from those of which we are ignorant there are three possibilities, Caesarea, Ephesus, Rome. It will almost certainly be the latter, since if we credit Paul with the letter we will place it near the end of his life. A decision about the place of Paul's imprisonment does not affect the theological thought of the letter. Whether Paul wrote the letter or not, the reference to him as prisoner is much more vivid in recalling his life to others than would have been 'minister' (Col 1.25) or slave (Phil 1.1).

Paul is a prisoner on behalf of others, the Gentiles. It is historically true that he was frequently imprisoned because of his mission to the Gentiles, though he himself never expressly elsewhere connects the two. Acts recounts how when in his preaching in synagogues he spoke of God's interest in the Gentiles there were sometimes disturbances which led to imprisonment. His final imprisonments in Caesarea and Rome were basically the result of his mission to the Gentiles. Paul is Christ's prisoner **on behalf of you Gentiles**. Since the passage ends (v. 13) by speaking of his sufferings for the glory of the Gentiles (so Salmond) **on behalf of** can probably be given the more precise meaning 'to benefit you Gentiles' (for the meaning see Mk 9.40; Col 1.24; Rom 8.32; Heb 5.1; cf Salmond). On the significance of Paul's suffering for others see on v. 13. Paul played an essential role in the spread of the gospel and it is this, with other matters, which AE breaks off to bring out in vv. 2ff.

The reference to **you Gentiles** neither implies that this is a catholic letter to all Gentiles (Beare) nor indicates that it is addressed to individual believers (Hofmann) rather than a church or churches. What is written is intended for Gentiles in a number of churches, identifiable only in so far as Paul was not their founder.

2. The parenthesis, or digression, begins here. AE has already argued (1.3–14; 2.11–22) that the Gentiles are within the church because this was and is the way in which God has arranged his plan of salvation. Now he turns his attention to the human agent, Paul, through whom God carried out his plan and expands the phrase 'on behalf of you Gentiles' (v. 1). Paul first needed to receive the revelation of God's plan (vv. 2–7) before he could act on it (vv. 8–12). AE does not discuss whether there were Gentiles in the church prior to Paul's mission or, if so, its significance for the claim made about him here. Unlike statements Paul makes in other letters about his position in relation to the Gentiles, vv. 2–13 have no polemical edge.

It may be assumed that the readers already know something about Paul as apostle to the Gentiles; there would have been no point in AE writing in Paul's name if they had not heard of him, and knowledge about his activity among the Gentiles was the most likely item of information that everyone would have known. The readers' knowledge would have been indirect and not through personal acquaintance or AE would have said, 'if you remember'. Paul had neither evangelised them nor visited them in person.

Plan is the difficult word in the verse and it is best approached through the phrase accompanying it, **the grace given me**, a phrase which reappears in v. 7, suggesting v. 2 and v. 7 may form an *inclusio* (Reynier). **Grace** in Pauline writing normally denotes the amazing, redeeming love of God, manifest above all in the inclusion of the Gentiles in the church (cf Barth). It is by God's grace that people become Christians. But it is not the conversion of Paul which is related to grace here; instead the idea is that God gave Paul grace in relation to the Gentiles; they are the ultimate beneficiaries of the grace as **for you** indicates. Apart from its sense in relation to God's redeeming love, **grace** is sometimes used more concretely with a meaning similar to charisma (cf 4.7; 1 Pet 4.10). God has given Paul a gift to be used for the benefit of the Gentiles, though of course charismatic gifts are not restricted to work among them for at 4.7 there is no special reference to the Gentiles. The phrase about the gift of grace is Pauline (1 Cor 3.10; cf Rom 12.3, 6; Gal 2.9). In 1 Cor 15.10 and Gal 1.15f Paul connects the grace of God to his commission and work in respect of the Gentiles (cf Rom 1.5). AE was aware of the way Paul would use the phrase and therefore, not inappropriately, employs it here with reference to God's mercy towards the Gentiles. It is because Paul is the recipient of God's gift for the Gentiles that he dares evangelise them and speak with authority not only to the churches he has founded but also to those he has never known or visited.

The noun **plan** can be taken either passively or actively; and either God or Paul can be its implied subject. It is easier to see Paul as the implied subject if the word is given an active sense, 'my stewardship of the charisma given to me from God for you' (cf Barth; so also Grosheide; Houlden; Van Roon; Lincoln), it being implied that the stewardship was given to Paul by God; the word is used in a similar way in 1 Cor 9.17 and in 1 Cor 4.1 Paul describes himself as a **steward**, a related word in Greek. Yet in both Eph 1.10 and 3.9 God is the subject and, since the word is used consciously, there is much to be said for a consistent usage (cf Merklein). Moreover this section of the passage stresses God's use of Paul in the conversion of the Gentiles rather than his mission as his own activity. It is better then to take God as the subject of **plan** with either passive or active meaning. The two meanings are not so far apart as the difference between active (Schlier; Scott; Masson; Schnackenburg) and passive (Gnilka; Haupt; Gaugler) might suggest. If God administers or arranges to do something he can be expected to do it according to a plan. That God works to a plan is closely linked to the idea of foreordination (cf 1.4, 5, 9). Whether we accept the passive or active sense, **the grace** is epexegetical, 'God's arranging (arrangement) which consists in the (divine) charisma given (by him) to me for you'. The initiative lies with God who gives Paul his position *vis-à-vis* the Gentiles.The salvation of the Gentiles (**for you** picks up **on behalf of you** from v. 1) cannot be understood apart from Paul, and that does not mean apart from what he tells us about it but apart from his place within God's plan of salvation. This also means that the Gentiles, and in particular the readers, have their place within God's plan.

3. What follows is still explanatory of v. 2. A mystery has been made known to Paul **by revelation**. The lack of an article before the noun in Greek does not necessarily mean 'one particular revelation' as in Gal 2.2; Rom 16.25, but serves to identify the means through which Paul came to his knowledge (cf the phrase of Gal 1.12) or the basis for that knowledge (Lincoln). He had not been driven to the conclusion that Jews and Gentiles were in the same position before God either as a result of interpreting the OT or as a deduction from a democratic philosophy, or indeed any philosophy. It was not something he had been taught by other Christians, nor was it the product of his research for his Ph.D. at the University of Antioch or Damascus! He had come to this knowledge through a direct and personal communication from God. Already in Galatians (1.11f, 15f) Paul linked his preaching to the Gentiles to an act of revelation on God's part. It is assumed here (see v. 2) that AE's readers know of this revelation. We may compare what the righteous teacher says of himself, 1QpHab 7.4f; 1QH 2.13; 1QS 9.18–20; cf 4 Ezra 14.26, 45f (cf Mussner).

Revelation is mediated in different ways, sometimes through dreams and visions, sometimes through a new understanding of scripture as when it is allegorised (so Philo) or made to apply to a new situation as in the Qumran writings. Scripture itself is of course revelation. Revelation is not necessarily given in some outward experience, oral or visual, as in Mt 28.16–20 by the risen

Christ or as in the apocalypses through angels. 3.3 does not say when or how Paul received his revelation about the Gentiles.

It is generally held that Paul received the revelation about the acceptance of the Gentiles when he was converted or as a result of that conversion. As a prophet he could be inspired to receive new interpretations of the OT (cf v. 5), the veil of incomprehension covering it having been removed (2 Cor 3.12ff). However, v. 5 does not say that in other generations the sons of men did not look deeply enough into the OT to discern the revelation but that it had been withheld from them, though they had the OT. The knowledge given to Paul was then something new. Although it can be argued that Paul received divine revelations throughout his life (cf 2 Cor 12.1–10) the accounts in Acts of his conversion link that conversion, though in different ways, to his commission to take the gospel to the Gentiles. In Acts 9.15; 22.15 the commission is mediated through Ananias rather than given to Paul directly; in 26.12ff where Ananias is not mentioned Paul receives it directly at the time of his conversion; in Acts 22.21 it comes when he is praying in the temple. Moreover it is not always a commission to go only to Gentiles (Acts 9.15f) and Acts normally depicts his missionary activity in each city as commencing with the Jews. The implication of Gal 1.12ff is that the revelation was associated with Paul becoming a Christian. Yet this does not imply that Paul became aware of his special missionary task precisely at the moment of conversion. It may have taken time for the implications of his Damascus Road experience to come home to him; perhaps he only realised its full meaning while he was meditating on the experience during his time in Arabia (Gal 1.17). Though **made known** is a past tense this does not mean that the revelation was instantaneous, taking place at the moment of conversion, but that it began and ended prior to the time of the writing of Ephesians; the aorist could cover the period of time in which Paul thought out the full significance of his conversion. The verb is passive implying that God had given Paul his revelation. Whatever we conclude about the time when the revelation was given, it is important to note that AE accords Paul a special position in respect of it, for it was given to him alone; this is the implication of the use of **me** here and in v. 3. The emphasis on the first person continues in the passage, though the third appears temporarily in v. 5.

AE may be indebted for his knowledge of Paul's conversion to Galatians, or the tradition which it created; Col 1.24–8 reflects the same tradition.

What God revealed to Paul was **the mystery** (for the word see on 1.9). The use of mystery in connection with both **plan** and the Gentiles may go back to Paul (1 Cor 4.1; Rom 11.25). AE uses three words here, **revelation**, **made known**, **mystery**; all relate to revelation and often appear together in revelatory contexts; all three in Rom 16.25f, the first two in Gal 1.11f; the first and third in 1 Cor 2.7–10; 2 Th 2.6f; the second and third in Eph 1.9; 6.19. An associated set of ideas which are found together is hidden, revealed, proclaimed (1 Cor 2.6–8, 10–12, 13–16; Col 1.26–8; Tit 1.2f), and of course AE goes on to speak of proclamation in vv. 9f. In 1.9 the mystery is that of God's will which (1.10) in some way implies a comprehensiveness in God's intention. This comprehensiveness is also present here though cut down to the inclusion of the Gentiles in God's plan. The mystery is now described as **of Christ** (v. 4), though too much should not be made of this since Christ is mentioned in 1.9f.

The present passage expands what AE had earlier sketched more briefly about 'mystery' and the admission of Gentiles (1.9f; 2.11ff). In the earlier passages he had written of their admission but not of Paul's role in it (cf Percy, 350). Some who equate AE with Paul believe that he refers here to his earlier letters. This would imply the availability in all the communities to which Ephesians was sent of at least one of these letters, probably Galatians or Colossians. But could Paul have been sure that every community would know the content of at least one or other of these letters? If Galatians is supposed to have been known could it be described as 'brief'? It is then best to assume that, whether Paul was the author or not, v. 3 refers to the earlier parts of the present letter. It is difficult to see how AE, writing in Paul's name and obviously venerating him, could refer to his letters as written **in brief** (similar phrases in Heb 13.22; 1 Pet 5.12 refer to the letters in which they appear); even the sections about the admission of Gentiles in the various letters are all in all much larger than our section in Ephesians.

4. This verse connects to v. 3b (cf Gnilka; Schlier; Haupt; etc.) rather than v. 3a for there has been no previous reference to a special revelation to Paul. If AE's readers peruse carefully what he has written (v. 5 excludes any idea that AE has in mind the reading of the OT) they will know the content of the mystery, if not how it was revealed to Paul. There is almost an imperatival tone about **which when you read**. The reading would be aloud, as was normal in the ancient world, and would probably have been in the course of worship (Col 4.16; 1 Th 5.27; Rev 1.3). Westcott and Beare are wrong to think of private study of the letter. The reading of the letter in worship imparts to it a certain finality; it is not ephemeral (cf Ernst).

Since the letter contained no previous reference, apart from v. 3, to a special revelation to Paul it is appropriate here to speak of his **insight** in respect of what he has already written. **My** is not intended to suggest a contrast between Paul and someone else and it does not imply an unworthy boasting on his part, which might be the case if the insight were purely human. **Insight** is probably drawn from the Greek OT where, particularly in Daniel (1.4, 17; 9.13, 23; 10.1, 11; see both LXX and Theod) it is explicitly used of the understanding of dreams and visions and implicitly associated with revelations. Since the context here is one of revelation it should not be taken as referring to human insight but to an understanding given by God into his mystery (see also *T Reub* 6.4; *T Levi* 2.3; 18.7; Col 1.9; 2.2; 2 Tim 2.7; Ignatius, *Polyc* 1.3; 1QH 2.13; 12.13; cf Kuhn). Christian insight is of course never simple human insight for it takes place in a mind responsive to God and enlightened by his Spirit. The revelation Paul received has worked itself into his mind and become a part of him (cf Bouttier); **insight** is a suitable word to describe this process; in 2.11–22 it was expressed, not in the terms of a special revelation, but of what was believed in the church. It should also be noted, and this is important if Paul himself is the author, that the appeal is not to Paul as person or apostle but to divine revelation; there is no self-glorification on Paul's part.

Would AE if he is not Paul have used an apocalyptically nuanced phrase like **insight into** of himself? Would this not imply that he was placing himself among the apostles and prophets?

What mystery (for the word see on 1.9) is referred to here? Col 4.3 (cf 2.2) uses the same phrase, **the mystery of Christ**, yet if the mystery there is Christ that is not so here. Here it must be the same

137

as that of v. 3, the uniting of Gentile and Jewish Christians; as such it is a subsection of the greater mystery of the unification of all things in Christ (1.10). The uniting of Jew and Gentile can be described as the mystery of Christ because it is through him that it is attained, for both Jew and Gentile are now in the one body of Christ. Yet it is God who planned and accomplished the mystery. The mystery of Christ, while not identical with the mystery of God's will, is contained within it.

5. It is not until v. 6 that the content of the mystery is stated. Structurally v. 5 consists of two balancing statements, a negative and a positive, each possessing three items: a temporal datum, a verb denoting revelation, and the mention of recipients, or non-recipients, of the revelation.

The two halves of the verse are related by **as**; they indicate an absolute contrast between a past period of ignorance and a present one of knowledge, the past period being in effect that of the OT and the present that of the NT. But was there complete ignorance in the OT concerning God's plans for the Gentiles? It is not difficult to find passages which allow a place for them (Gen 12.1–3; 18.18; Isa 2.2–4; 11.10; 34.22; 49.6; 60.3; Jer 3.17; Jon 4; Zech 9.9f). Mare points out that some of these texts are understood in this way in the NT (Isa 42.6; 49.6 in Lk 2.32; Gen 12.3; 17.5; 28.14 in Gal 3.7f, 29). The NT also contains places where it is implied that the writers of the OT were not entirely ignorant in respect of God's intentions towards the Gentiles (Rom 1.2; 9.25f; 13.9ff; Gal 3.8; Acts 15.15ff; 17.11f; 1 Pet 1.10–12). In the light of this **as** could be given a comparative meaning, 'as clearly as'; God's purpose for the Gentiles was not understood as clearly in the OT as now after the death and resurrection of Christ (so Beck; Macpherson; Abbott; Foulkes). However, v. 3 suggested something new, not that Paul came to appreciate a truth which had lain hidden from the Jews though written in their scriptures. Were the latter the case, then v. 3 ought to have run '*the understanding of* the mystery was made known to me by revelation' and something similar would be expected here and in 3.9f. Since it is almost impossible to find OT passages to parallel 3.9f, those verses cannot refer to the imparting of a true understanding of already known passages. There are moreover no good grammatical or stylistic reasons for modifying the absolute nature of the contrast implied by **as**. This absolute nature is supported by 1.9 and is found in, or can be read into, other parts of the NT (Rom 16.25–7; Col 1.26; Gal 4.21–31; 1 Cor 2.7ff; Tit 1.2f; 2 Tim 1.9f). In the commission to the Twelve (Mt 28.16–20; Acts 1.8) to go into all the world the command is presented as something new and not as the unfolding of an existing though partly veiled secret. Eph 3.2ff stands under the general schema in relation to revelation of 'once hidden – now revealed' which appears to exclude OT revelation. There is both continuity and discontinuity between the testaments; our passage stresses the discontinuity, perhaps overstresses it, but it is corrected elsewhere by the importance given to the OT by AE when he quotes it. The non-recipients of the revelation were literally 'the sons of men', a frequent biblical idiom for **humanity** in general, or all Israel (Gen 11.5; Ψ 11.2; Joel 1.12; Jer 38.19; Dan 3.82; Mk 3.28). Its OT usage however gives no reason for seeing it in v. 5 as not including the prophets and patriarchs (so Jerome; Ellicott in attempts to avoid the implication of an absolute ignorance on the part of the OT). If it refers to all humanity then that includes all Israel. The passive **not made known** (implicit subject God) implies that human ignorance in this connection came from God and was not simply the result of human weakness. The time of their ignorance is expressed by **in other periods** (literally 'in other generations') (a temporal dative; the noun is used with temporal sense at 3.21; Acts 14.16; 15.21; Col 1.26; Ψ 48.12; 88.2; Lk 1.50; Exod 17.16).

Turning now to v. 5b the revelation is said to be made **to his holy apostles and prophets through the Spirit**. That the group is *now* the recipient of revelation implies that the prophets belong to the same period as the apostles, i.e. they are Christian prophets. A revelation restricted to the apostles and not to all believers does not indicate a later stage in church development; the revelation to a limited group was part of the tradition from the beginning (cf Mt 28.16–20, etc.); it is the revelation to all believers which is the new element.

What does **holy** mean? In view of the widespread use of the root in the NT in relation to God's activity in salvation it can hardly refer simply to the moral piety of the apostles and prophets. Probably its frequent association with **prophets** led to its use here so that it also applies to **apostles**. Applied to both apostles and prophets it may indicate they have a special position in God's plan of salvation, and this would be in line with 2.20 (Van Roon takes it as the equivalent of 'called'). Yet if the phrase is derived from 'holy prophets' the adjective was already losing much of its 'theological' meaning in that phrase. Nowhere in the NT is it used to distinguish Jewish or Christian prophets from those of other religions; it was tending rather to imply a position of dignity and importance (cf Ignatius, *Magn* 3.1, 'holy' presbyters). The description of the apostles as 'holy' has often been used in the argument against Pauline authorship. Would Paul have given such a position of dignity to himself? Also if Paul were the author he may have limited the term apostles (see on 1.1 and 2.20 for the term) to the Twelve, of which of course he was not a member, and so the adjective would not have applied to him. The phrase then need not be an insurmountable obstacle to his authorship. Yet it is more easily understood if he is not the author. In v. 3 he emphasised his own position as recipient of revelation; in line with this we might have expected him, if he were the author, to write here 'to us apostles and prophets'.

The final phrase (literally, 'in spirit') has been related in different ways to the other words (cf the same phrase at 2.22); it refers of course to the Holy Spirit and has been linked to (i) the verb, (ii) 'his holy apostles and prophets', (iii) 'prophets' alone. If (iii) is chosen it would be natural to restrict **his** to the apostles alone (Schnackenburg) yet the prophets belong to God as much as the apostles and since all prophecy is 'in the Spirit' their connection to the Spirit hardly needed to be stressed. Moreover in 2.20 the apostles and prophets together form a distinct group. There appears then no need to distinguish between them here by applying different phrases to them. (ii) would imply the existence of apostles and prophets who had no connection with the Spirit if those mentioned here need to be identified as recipients of the Spirit; nothing else in the letter suggests the existence of unspiritual apostles and prophets. (i) is probably then the best solution; in 5.18; 6.18 the phrase is also linked to the verb (Reynier). The revelation is **through the Spirit** (Adai).

Now must refer to a period in which apostles and prophets existed, but is this a period in the past or the one in which AE lives? In 2.20 the apostles and prophets are the foundation of the church and this suggests a group belonging to the past, or at least a group which would cease to exist once its original members were dead (see on 2.20). There seems no reason to draw any other conclusion here. When we look elsewhere in the NT we find a strong tradition that a revelation of the universal nature of the gospel was made to a group approximately equivalent to the apostles (cf Mt 28.16–20; Lk 24.47; Acts 1.8; Jn 20.21). This revelation belonged to the past in the period immediately after the resurrection. It is not possible to recover from the varying statements about it a form of words which may have been original. Indeed if there had been any clear form of words it is difficult to see why the church was at first so slow to respond to it and admit Gentile believers. Probably the suggestion that there was a revelation preceded its exact formulation so that it came to be expressed in different ways and slightly different groups were regarded as its recipients. The one significant variation in Eph 3.5 is the introduction of the prophets among the recipients. However, within the early church these were recipients of revelations (1 Cor 14.29–31) and this may account for their presence in v. 5; apostles when receiving revelations were in fact acting in the role of prophets (see also on 2.20 for the linking of prophets with apostles).

Finally we should note that 3.1–13 contains two traditions about the revelation to evangelise the Gentiles. In 3.3 AE retains that belonging to the Pauline school in which Paul is portrayed as its recipient; in 3.5 he has added another strand from the tradition of the wider church. Paul was apparently not aware of this wider strand when he wrote Gal 2.1–10; if he wrote Ephesians, when did he become aware of it? The traditions of 3.3 and 3.5 may not have been the only two traditions current, for in Acts 10.9ff Peter received a revelation to take the gospel to Cornelius, and in Antioch the step to go to the Gentiles seems to have been taken almost spontaneously (Acts 11.20f) and prior to Paul's arrival in that city. Theologically all AE needed to say was that some person or group had received a revelation about the admission of Gentile believers into the church to justify their presence there. This purpose was fulfilled once he had mentioned Paul in v. 3; however, having done this he must have realised that his readers,

141

or at least some of them, would have known of the tradition of a revelation to the Twelve and so he is forced to refer to it. Was it an afterthought? If so this would justify regarding vv. 3b–5 as parenthetical.

6. The content of the mystery is now disclosed. Jews and Gentiles meet in the church on equal terms. Since an understanding of this mystery was already assumed in 2.11ff, it is surprising that its formal disclosure only comes now (Ernst); the emphasis may then lie here not so much on its content as on the fact of its disclosure and on those to whom the disclosure was made. The content of the mystery is expressed through three terms which echo ideas found elsewhere in the letter: **heirs, body, promise**; of them the first and third also echo Jewish ideas. For **heirs** see 1.12, the Jewish Christians being the heirs with whom the Gentiles share; for **sharers in the promise** see 2.12 and its reversal in 2.13–17 (Mussner). In contrast to the other terms **members of the same body** introduces a clear Christian theme picking up the widespread use in the letter of **body** for the community; though there is a little evidence in Philo for regarding Israel as a living organism (*Spec Leg* 3.131; *de Virt* 103; *de Praem et Poen* 114, 125), there is nothing of the emphasis or interest that we find in the Pauline corpus; of the three adjectives it is the one most characteristic of the ideas in the letter. This is its first known appearance of this adjective in Greek literature (since we do not know all Greek literature it is wrong to speak of it as a neologism) but this provides no justification for regarding it with Schlier as the most important in the series. There is no need either to see with Barth and Hendriksen a progression of importance through the three terms; they are simply different ways of expressing the same thought. In each case the togetherness represented in Greek by the incorporation of the prefix 'with' in each of the three terms refers to the unification of Jews and Gentiles rather than to the relation of either to Christ. That believers are fellow heirs with one another derives ultimately from the fact that they are fellow heirs with Christ (Rom 8.17); that they belong to the same body follows from their being members of the body of Christ. In Christ too the 'promise' of God is fulfilled (2 Cor 1.20).

AE has Gentile believers in mind here and not, as Barth argues, Gentiles as such, for there is no reason to suppose he is making a universalist statement, or, what would necessarily follow, that all

Jews would be saved. These Gentile believers are fellow heirs with Jewish believers, not with all Jews, of the promised inheritance (see 1.14, 18 for its nature), fellow members of the body of Christ and fellow recipients of the promise of God. Together they form the new people of God, the 'third race'. **Promise** in the singular may refer either to the total of what is promised in the OT in relation to salvation or to the particular promise made to Abraham on which the whole position of Jews rested and which is seen in some parts of the NT to apply to Gentile Christians (Gal 3.29). There is no reason to restrict the promise to that of the Spirit and so find a Trinitarian reference: heirs of the Father, members of the body of Christ, sharers in the Spirit (so Lock).

Behind the togetherness of Gentile and Jewish believers in the one people of God lies God's activity in Christ; this is brought out in the final two phrases of the verse which relate to all that preceded in the verse. **In Christ Jesus** applies to all three adjectives and serves either to stress the idea of the fellowship of Jewish and Gentile believers as taking place in Christ or indicates the sphere of God's activity, Christ's death and resurrection by which they were brought together (2.14–17). **The gospel** can refer to either the content of what is preached or the act of preaching. The latter interpretation is to be preferred, since the unification of Jew and Gentile is not automatic but takes place as a response to preaching and vv. 7f goes on to stress the actual ministry of Paul (cf 1 Cor 4.15). If **the gospel** is taken to indicate its content we should have to take **in Christ Jesus** as denoting the spiritual sphere within which Jews and Gentiles are fellow heirs (cf Ernst).

If v. 6 supplies the content of the mystery of vv. 3f how does this mystery relate to that of 1.9f? Both refer to a unification or bringing together; 3.3–6 restricts this to human beings, Jewish and Gentile believers comprising its totality; in 1.9f all creation is gathered together to Christ. 3.3–6 therefore represents a partial fulfilment of 1.9f. Dibelius may be correct in viewing the two mysteries as identical, for that of 3.3–6 attains a cosmic dimension in 3.10. Unresolved is the identity of those to whom the revelation of 1.9f was made known, and when it was made known and how it was made known. AE tells us nothing about these matters. He clearly knows the mystery and we assume that he believes Paul knew it and perhaps also that the apostles and prophets knew it.

7. 3.2–6 treated the place of Paul, and others, in God's plan and the nature of the mystery which was disclosed. In v. 7 we begin to be told how Paul communicated what he had learnt to others. Vv. 8–12 continue the account of the communication of the revealed mystery; v. 7 is in effect a transition verse between the disclosure and the action taken in response to that disclosure. The apostles and prophets now drop from view and Paul alone occupies the centre stage; if he has a ministry to fulfil it is necessary both to say what it is and to describe how he accomplished it. The move from the content of the mystery to its proclamation is made through the reference to the gospel which in v. 6 probably referred to the activity of preaching rather than its content (cf Rom 10.14f). In fact, in so far as we know the story, Paul was the leading exponent of the gospel to the Gentiles, though the evidence of Acts (e.g. 10.44–8; 11.20f) suggests he was neither the first to preach it nor the only one to do so. If Acts is correct, Peter had evangelised Cornelius before Paul was brought to Antioch, and it cannot be assumed Barnabas ceased his missionary work with Gentiles after his split with Paul. The speedy growth of the early church shows that there must have been many Gentile areas which were evangelised by people whose names remain unknown. AE may not then know the whole story of the evangelisation of the Gentiles, but he is not so much concerned with Paul's historical place in it as with his theological position as the recipient of God's grace. In this he follows a line which Paul had originally put forward (e.g. Rom 1.1, 5; 1 Cor 1.1; Gal 1.1, 15f) and which was continued later by the Pastorals alongside their veneration for him (2 Tim 1.11; Tit 1.3).

Minister, used here to describe Paul's function, is not a word which would stress either his importance or personal renown. The root originally ranged widely in meaning from waiting at table to the action of communicating, including that of the impartation of heavenly knowledge, and this range of meaning would have been known to Greek readers. Because it does not refer narrowly only to humble service, like 'slave', it is seen by AE as a suitable term to describe Paul's ministry. The sense of the impartation of heavenly knowledge would be appropriate in v. 7 (see 2 Cor 3.7–9; 4.1, 5, 18 for a similar use in relation to Paul's ministry). Whether it would also have carried for Greek readers the sense of humble service (cf Mk 10.42–5; Lk 22.25–7) in its present context is debatable. It was brought into Christian thought to denote both Jesus' service to others (e.g. Mk 10.45) and their service to him (Mk 1.31; 15.41; Lk 8.3). Eventually among Christians it came to designate a particular group of people exercising a special function in the church. Before attaining this technical sense it was used, as here, of various people in the church and their different activities (Rom 16.1; 1 Cor 3.5; 12.5; 16.15; 2 Cor 8.4; 9.1, 12, 13; Phil 1.1; Col 1.7; 1 Th 3.2). Paul used the root to describe his own ministry (Rom 11.13; 15.25, 31; 2 Cor 3.3, 6; 4.1; 5.18; 6.3, 4; 8.19f; 11.8, 23; cf Col 1.23, 25) but in a general kind of way and not in relation to his ministry to the Gentiles alone; Rom 11.13 refers to that ministry and where Paul uses the root in connection with the collection for the church at Jerusalem he may also have it in mind. In Col 1.23, 25 it is attached specifically to the Gentile ministry and its use in relation to that ministry may have been common in the Pauline school of AE and A/Col. AE probably derived his usage from there rather than directly from Romans or 2 Corinthians (in Eph 4.12; 6.21 it does not relate to Paul). It continued in use in the Pauline schools to describe his activity (1 Tim 1.12–16). How much the flavour of humble service clung to it by this time is difficult to answer, but Gentiles coming freshly to it would hear it with such overtones. It is interesting that Paul does not say, or is not made to say, 'of which I became an apostle'; apart from 1.1 AE makes no reference to Paul as apostle and in this he may be following Paul's own lead (see Best 'Authority').

In accordance with the gift of the grace of God given me qualifies **minister** making absolutely clear that whatever Paul is in relation to the Gentiles he is by the gift of God's grace. Most of v. 2 is repeated here. When God gives he is not simply conferring a benefit; the gift entails also a particular duty. **Grace** means saving grace or the equipment for a particular task. Here as in v. 2 it means the latter: the grace which calls to and empowers the recipient for a duty. Paul (cf 1 Cor 15.10), or AE, does not clearly distinguish, as systematic theologians do, between saving grace and the grace which equips for a special function. Paul's conversion (saving grace) and his call to minister to Gentiles (the 'grace' of our verse and of 3.2; Rom 1.5; 15.15f; 1 Cor 3.10; Gal 1.15f) were not two distinct events in either his eyes or those of his school, for it was on the Damascus Road that he was saved through grace and received grace to be the minister to the Gentiles (cf v. 8). The inseparability of 'saving grace' and missionary activity should be true not only for Paul but for all Christians.

The **power** is that of God. Paul received the power appropriate to the ministry to which he was appointed. It is this power and not some inborn ability or talent which enables him to be the servant of the gospel. Whether such a clear distinction can be made in actual practice is another matter; it was Paul's nature to be zealous, whether prior to his conversion in respect of the Law or the persecution of Christians, or after in respect of the Gentiles. God uses people with different talents, if not characters, in different ways. It is difficult then to say that the energy with which Paul pursued his mission was simply and solely a matter of grace. Within Ephesians God's energy and power operate in relation to the resurrection and ascension of Christ (1.19f), the building up and sustenance of the church as his body (4.16), the pre-arrangement of affairs by his will (1.11), the transformation of believers (3.20). God's power is thus related to many issues and it would be wrong to restrict it here to one particular facet, e.g. the power of resurrection. In so far as power is stressed it serves to lead into v. 8 and Paul's proclamation to the Gentiles.

8. A new sentence begins here and continues to the end of v. 12. **This grace** points forward linking the two halves of the verse and the thought moves forward to the process of the proclaiming of the gospel. There are three named groups to whom it is offered: the Gentiles (v. 8), all people (v. 9), the powers (vv. 9f).

In v. 8a AE stresses the great contrast between Paul missioner to the Gentiles and Paul prior to his conversion: 'it was precisely to me *though* I was less than the least ...'. Paul places himself below any Christian whom any reader may care to name. Is Paul then excluded from the number of the saints? Although the statement differs here from the apparently similar 1 Cor 15.9, 'I am the least of the apostles', there is no reason to see the phrase as excluding Paul from the saints. Since AE has spoken of the apostles in v. 5 and his point could have been made as easily by comparing Paul to them, we may assume that he is not indebted here to 1 Cor 15.9 but is using a tradition current in the Pauline school deriving from Paul himself which contrasted his pre-Christian and Christian existence; 1 Cor 15.9 is one expression of this; 1 Tim 1.15 confirms that the tradition existed. The Pauline school did not soften but intensified the tradition. The tradition may also have influenced Ignatius, *Trall* 13.1. However, the contrast between pre-conversion failure and post-conversion success is a familiar feature of Christian hagiography (Bouwman). Our discussion has assumed Paul was not the author of Ephesians, but in the light of 1 Cor 15.9 there can be no possible psychological objection to his penning Eph 3.8. Whether Paul is the author or not, the phrase serves to emphasise his humility.

AE does not specify in what way Paul regarded himself as 'less than the least', perhaps he assumed his readers knew. Despite 1 Tim 1.15 there is no hint in the major Pauline letters of an excessive consciousness on his part of sin. He does not hesitate to put himself forward as someone to be imitated (1 Th 1.6; 1 Cor 4.16; 11.1; 2 Th 3.7), he never seems to allow that his advice to his readers might be prejudiced, and he never exercises any self-criticism. Probably AE assumes the same reason for what he writes about Paul as that underlying 1 Cor 15.9, Paul's pre-conversion persecution of Christians. The undisputed letters contain several references to this suggesting that sorrow at it was never far from his mind (1 Cor 15.9; Gal 1.13, 23; Phil 3.6; cf Acts 7.58; 9.1, 2). The total context of Ephesians may have strengthened the contrast between before and after conversion in that it relates to the Saul who persecuted *Jewish* Christians and the Paul who forced Jewish Christians to accept *Gentile* Christians as equals.

If v. 8a repeated briefly the thought of v. 7 in saying that Paul was given a gift in relation to the Gentiles, v. 8b goes further in referring to Paul's actual preaching to them.

When Paul uses the verb **to proclaim** he does not normally give it a direct object for in Christian parlance its object lies within itself. Where Paul does express a direct object it is the cognate noun (1 Cor 15.1; 2 Cor 11.7; Gal 1.11), Christ (Gal 1.16), the faith (Gal 1.23), the faith and love of others (1 Th 3.6), peace (Eph 2.17), and in an OT quotation 'good news' (Rom 10.15 = Isa 52.7). Here in 3.8, in accordance with AE's verbose style, the object is expressed through an unrelated noun: **the unimaginable riches**, a favourite of AE (1.7, 18; 2.7; 3.8, 16; see on 1.7), and a less usual adjective. The adjective is used of God's activity in the world (Job 5.9; 9.10; 34.24; Rom 11.33; cf 1 Clem 20.5); it is an extension of this usage that we find in Eph 3.8 (cf *Odes Sol* 12.6; *Prayer of Manasseh* 6; *Diog* 9.5) in that what is praised is God's mercy rather than his activity in creation. Implied in the word are both the wonder of God's activity and the inability of the human mind, even after revelation, to deduce and plumb the depths of God. The **riches** are those **of Christ**, which are either those which he supplies, if so they would be those detailed elsewhere in the letter, or those which consist in Christ himself (so 1.7, 18; 2.7; 3.16); in view of usage elsewhere in the epistle the second alternative is preferable.

9. Grace has been given Paul not only for preaching the riches of Christ (v. 8) but **to enlighten all**. Who are meant? Had AE been thinking only of the Gentiles he would have used the pronoun 'them'. Since the content of the mystery is the co-membership of Jews and Gentiles and these together form all humanity, it is better to give **all** its widest sense, 'all people'. If enlightenment is taken to include redemption (cf 2 Cor 4.6) is this then a universalist statement? It appears like one, but since the reading is uncertain, the word being omitted by some manuscripts, it would be wrong to press it. Moreover 'all' is not emphatic by position. In 1.18 where the same verb is used God was its subject; here it is Paul. In each case darkness symbolises the past state of unbelief, and light that of redemption. Those who have been enlightened are those who have been evangelised (v. 8; cf Heb 6.4; 10.32). Here however enlightenment lies closer to the imparting of knowledge, knowledge of God's plan. Gentile Christians needed to be evangelised and brought into the church; Jewish Christians were already in the church but needed enlightenment about God's plan just as much as Gentile Christians; this may be the reason for the change from the idea of evangelisation to that of enlightenment.

The content of what is brought to light or of the instruction given to all is **the plan of the mystery**. (For the word **plan** see 1.9; 3.2). It cannot refer here to Paul's stewardship, even if it does so in 3.2, but to the plan of God or the working out of that plan. It is the plan, of course, and not the mystery itself, in which all are instructed or on which light is thrown. That of course does not mean that the mystery is not revealed (cf v. 3). The mystery (for the word see on 1.9) is the same mystery as that of vv. 3f; v. 6 gives its content, viz., the common membership of Jews and Gentiles in the body of Christ.

The mystery has been **hidden** up to the 'now' of v. 10, **from the ages**. **From** could be taken either temporally (hidden during periods of time; so Gnilka; Barth; Mussner; Gaugler; Schnackenburg; Lincoln) or spatially (hidden away from personal beings; so Schlier; Dibelius; Steinmetz; Lindemann). The 'now' of v. 10 suggests a temporal contrast, implying a temporal understanding of the preposition. **Ages** is also a word having temporal and personal significance (see on vv. 2, 7). The plural provides no reason for rejecting the temporal meaning as we see from Lk 1.33; Rom 9.5; 11.36; Gal 1.5; Phil 4.20. Since, however, v. 10 refers to the heavenly powers perhaps the personal meaning should be adopted, the personal beings would then be the powers mentioned there. The two meanings are in fact not unrelated, for if the aeons are personal beings we must ask when was the plan hidden from them and if they are periods of time we must ask from whom the plan was hidden.

The God who has hidden the plan of the mystery is finally defined as the **God who made everything**. This is a little surprising since AE's interest, unlike that of Colossians, lies in the second creation rather than the first. How is the phrase to be accounted for? (a) It could be the use of a familiar liturgical phrase. The praise of God as the creator of all things was widespread in contemporary Judaism (e.g. Wisd 1.14; Ecclus 24.8; 3 Macc 2.3; Esth 4.17c: Jth 13.18; 1QH 1.13f; 16.8; 1QM 10.8f; *1 En* 9.5; 81.3; *Jub* 7.36) and was accepted into Christianity (Acts 14.15; Col 1.16; Rev 4.11; *Did* 10.3; 1 Clem 33.2–6; Hermas, *Mand* 1.1; *Sim* 5.5.2); AE would hardly have used this liturgical phrase without thought, for it is not the way he writes; he may add synonym to synonym but here we have the introduction of a fresh idea. (b) The divorce between creation and redemption became a common theme in some gnostic circles in the second century; Schlier therefore argues that AE introduced the reference to creation to ensure its link with redemption. Schlier's references are drawn from the second century and we cannot be certain that this tendency existed in the first (Barth; Bruce). But even granted it did, the phrase in v. 9 would be a roundabout way of countering it, and if AE had been concerned about such a possible divorce we should expect more evidence elsewhere in the letter. (c) More probable than any of these is the view that the phrase is intended to place the time when the plan was hidden as prior to creation; it was no afterthought but part of God's intention from the beginning. In that way it accords with AE's emphasis on God's foresight and predestination (1.4, 5, 12). Creation and redemption are in the final issue the result of the work of the one God; the presence of this idea does not necessarily imply a polemic against a proto-gnosticism or proto-Marcionism. The plan of God built into the first creation is now realised in the church, the second creation (Ernst).

10. God's final purpose in endowing Paul with grace is that the manifold wisdom of God may now be made known to the heavenly powers. This brings us back to the cosmic scope of 1.10. Our verse partially parallels v. 7, but now it is not Paul who is the proclaimer of the gospel but the church. Nothing in the preceding discussion from as far back as 2.11 has prepared us for this reference to the church or indeed for that to wisdom. But there is much to suggest that Paul and his school knew Jewish wisdom speculation and were aware of the opposition to humanity of the heavenly powers. Verse 10 depends on **to me this grace was given**: the proclamation to the Gentiles (v. 8) and the instruction of all in the plan of the mystery leads to the wisdom of God being made known through the church to the powers. It is God's plan to reconcile Jews and Gentiles in one body, the church, and so provide the powers with knowledge of his desire to win them (cf Lincoln).

The powers (for these see on 1.21) are those **in the heavenlies** (see Detached Notes: The Heavenlies, The Powers). As we saw earlier, the reference is to 'hostile' powers or angelic beings.

It is God's **wisdom** which is made known to the heavenly powers. We might have expected his grace, or the lordship of Christ as in Phil 2.9–11 (cf v. 11 here), or salvation to be revealed, but it is wisdom; this follows appropriately after the many terms denoting revelation in 3.2–13. In 1 Cor 1.18ff God's wisdom is related to the cross, and this relationship lies in the background here for the revelation which is disclosed is that of the reconciliation of Jews and Gentiles and the basis for this is the cross (2.14–22). Wisdom is not a simple concept capable of being expressed in a brief statement, but a complex idea with many aspects. AE will have been influenced in his understanding of it chiefly by the existing Jewish Wisdom literature reaching him, if he was not born a Jew, by way of early Christianity. Jewish thinking on wisdom had of course been affected by non-Jewish ideas and AE's understanding may also have been affected by contemporary non-Jewish, non-Christian ideas, for example those of gnosis. AE however says so little about wisdom (1.8, 17; 3.10) that it is difficult to discern outside influences. When wisdom is personified in the Wisdom literature it is presented as active; in 3.10 it is conceived as passive, for it does not make itself known to the heavenly powers but is made known (cf Gnilka); it is not the revealer but the revealed. As such it is described by the infrequent adjective **much-variegated**.

God's wisdom has now been **made known**; the past tense suggests a single action rather than a continuous process of slow revelation. When was wisdom made known? Because this is related to the church it must be since the church came into existence, and, since the church is the church of Jewish and Gentile Christians, it must be since the cross and resurrection of Christ. There is a time of hiddenness, the period prior to Christ or to his ascension, and then, 'now', a period of disclosure, the period of the apostles, prophets and Paul.

But how is God's wisdom made known to the powers through the church? Did Christ make it known when he ascended into the heavenlies, or, possibly, when he descended into Hades, as some interpretations of 1 Pet 3.19; 4.6 might suggest? Since believers are already in the heavenlies (2.6) the church must also be there; the church can thus be an appropriate vehicle for the disclosure of God's wisdom to the powers since they also are in the heavenlies. In addition the church has some continuity with Israel and wisdom has a special relationship with Israel (Ecclus 24.8, 23; Bar 3.22f). Finally wisdom has already been disclosed to the church (1.8, 17; 3.2ff; cf Roels). That good angels know what happens on earth is seen in passages like 1 Pet 1.12; Lk 15.7; it is then possible to conceive of the evil powers as also aware of the church; if they are involved in the warfare of 6.10ff this must be so.

The church is of course not here a particular local community, which might have been so if Ephesians had been written to a single congregation; it is the whole church, the body of Christ. Whereas vv. 8f spoke of Paul's missionary activity, v. 10 does not suggest any activity on the part of the church, for example, that it taught the powers. It is the very existence of the church, the church of Jews and Gentiles in which there is no division, that discloses the wisdom of God to them. This idea is close to that of Jn 17.21 where the world is saved when it sees believers are one. If the division between Jews and Gentiles was due to the activity of the powers its removal would speak to them.

What is the precise aspect of wisdom made known through the church to the powers? That will in part depend on how the powers are understood. If these in their control of the universe represent its 'meaninglessness' (Gnilka), then wisdom reveals to them, and of course to the universe, the divine meaning of the universe. If the powers are the influences which lie behind and order world history (Schlier), then wisdom reveals the divine purpose of history. If the powers represent the social, cultural and religious forces, the earthly institutions which control human lives, then these 'are given a unique chance by God: they are entitled to see in their midst the beginning of a new heaven and a new earth' (Barth). If the powers are the 'spiritual environment' in which people live and in which forces compete to control them, then we are assured that 'even such structures of power and authority as the secular state are capable of being brought into harmony with the love of God' (Caird). If the powers are primarily responsible for human religious errors, wisdom needs to be revealed to them so that their erroneous teaching may no longer affect people (Hugedé). If the powers are taken to be the rulers of 1 Cor 2.8 who crucified the Lord of glory, their great error is now brought home to them (Scott), but whether this results in their reconciliation or destruction is not made clear. If the powers are those which control the Gentiles, then by the formation of a church containing both Jews and Gentiles their stranglehold is broken; the existence of the church reveals to them their failure (Mussner). There is a reversal then of what would have been expected: it is not the stars or the heavenly powers which control human life but human life, represented as the church, which controls or will control the powers.

None of this makes clear whether, when the powers come to know the wisdom of God, this means they have been or will be saved. Will they have lost their ability to harm humanity? Within Jewish Wisdom literature those who know wisdom are those who are faithful to God. To learn wisdom is not to be supplied with a selection of interesting information; the powers do not then learn a little more about how the world works but are given a way of life; to know wisdom is to live in that way. The reconciliation of Jews and Gentiles in the church is a kind of pilot scheme for a much greater reconciliation in which the powers will in turn be embraced (cf Bruce). This suggests that when the wisdom of God, and note it is not human wisdom, is made known to the powers their response will be positive. Yet in 6.12 they are still hostile to the members of the church; in 1.22 Christ is their head to whom they are made subject, not someone with whom they are reconciled. On the other hand in 1.10 there is a summing up of all things in Christ, and the powers must be included among 'all things'. There are two inconsistencies here: (i) Can the powers still be active if they have been defeated in Christ's death, resurrection and ascension? This is an inconsistency which seems to belong to the fabric of NT Christianity, paralleling the idea of the Kingdom of God as both realised and yet to come. (ii) The second inconsistency arises out of the way God is conceived: does he overcome cosmic evil by destroying it or by winning it to himself in love (Col 1.20)?

We have seen above how various scholars have reinterpreted the powers and so understood v. 10. If the powers do not exist, they cannot be demythologised and to speak of the disclosure to them of God's wisdom is meaningless. Our passage began with the disclosure to Paul of the mystery; it ends with the winning of the cosmos, and so his mission is given a cosmic dimension (Sullivan). His position, which at the start seemed to be unique as the one who first brought salvation to the Gentiles, is now seen as unique because it relates to the salvation, or destruction, of the cosmos.

11. God is the subject of the verb **resolved** and also the real subject of **according to his ... intention**. We have already rejected a personal meaning for the aeons in v. 9, and it is highly probable that the words have the same sense here as there. Had personal beings been intended a pronoun would probably have been used 'according to their intention' (referring back to v. 10), or one or both of the words for the powers in v. 10 would have been repeated here. The Greek reads literally 'according to the intention of the aeons'. The aeons are periods of time inhabited by personal beings. The phrase 'of the aeons' is probably adjectival (a Semitism?) and equivalent to 'eternal' (Bouttier).

The verb in the subordinate clause is best understood to mean God **resolved**: 'according to the purpose ... which he made, resolved' (Ewald; Conzelmann; Barth; Schnackenburg). How much of what is referred to earlier in the passage is to be regarded as lying within God's purpose? Certainly v. 10. Yet is the grace given to Paul for his ministry not also to be included? What also about the period during which the plan or mystery was hidden? The structure of the sentence suggests we do not go back beyond v. 8 but also suggests that there is no need to limit God's intention to v. 10. If it was his purpose to make his wisdom known to the powers, he achieved this through the church and vv. 8, 9 show how his grace brought the church into being through Paul. It is impossible then to limit God's intention to v. 10; vv. 8, 9 must also be brought in. It is then easier to say that what they describe lay always in God's plan. This fits with the way we have taken the initial phrase of the verse. That in much Jewish teaching wisdom was regarded as eternal makes it easier to accept this. We should note the unique position that all this gives to Paul whom, unlike the apostles and prophets, AE brings into the centre of God's intention.

God made his purpose known 'in Christ Jesus our Lord', thus giving his purpose a christological orientation. The threefold title, Christ, Jesus, Lord, is found elsewhere in varying forms in the address (1.2) and final greetings (6.23f), at the beginning of the eulogy (1.3) and the renewal of prayer (1.17), and in the thanksgiving of 5.20. It is thus used at solemn and liturgical moments. Its use here is then deliberate and emphatic and not simply evidence of AE's prolixity. Christ is placed first with the definite article. This could be a deliberate messianic reference, for the divine intention included the history of the people from whom the Messiah came. It is through the Messiah that Jew and Gentile are united in one body and that wisdom is proclaimed even to the powers.

12. The Christ in whom God made his purpose known is *our* Lord and AE now returns from cosmic speculation to his readers (cf v. 1), using the first plural as at the end of v. 11, and not the second, because he and his readers, or Jews and Gentiles if that is the distinction, stand in the same relation to God's grace. The redemption and reconciliation of believers takes place through the same Christ as the one through whom God's purpose was made known to the aeons. The significance of redemption for believers is now spelt out.

Boldness, originally relating to behaviour towards others and indicating the democratic freedom to speak out an opinion, came in Jewish Greek to be used also of freedom to speak to God. While people may have an inherent or democratic right to address others and express their opinion, it is only through Christ that they gain the right to speak without fear to God. Without Christ they may shout rashly at him and go unheard but with Christ believers may speak boldly knowing that they will be heard. Believers have **access** to God (see on 2.18 for the word); the two nouns **boldness** and **access** have a single article and probably form a hendiadys, 'boldness to enter' (Bratcher and Nida). The idea comes in appropriately here because in v.14 the thought moves on to access to God in prayer. Believers may enter the door of prayer **with confidence** (only elsewhere in the NT in Paul, 2 Cor 1.15; 3.4; 8.22; 10.2; Phil 3.4), sure that they will receive an audience. Their confidence is increased because they are already in the heavenlies (2.6) and together form the temple in which God dwells (2.19–22). The positive reference to confidence is necessary since access of itself does not give confidence; the guilty prisoner is given access to the judge when brought before him but he wishes he was not there for he lacks confidence in the procedure. Christians however approach God without anxiety, not because of clear consciences or past good behaviour, but because of Christ. The theme of confident access to God appears regularly towards the end of the first century (Heb 4.16; 1 Pet 3.18; 1 Clem 2.3; 35.2). Within the Pauline writings access to God depends on faith, but faith is not however mentioned so regularly in the later writings. In Ephesians, in line with the undoubted Paulines, salvation comes through faith (2.8) resulting not only in an objective status giving access to God but also in an inner attitude, a bold and free approach.

It is possible that in v. 12 the faith is not that of believers but of Christ. Both usages appear in Paul, the latter being the more frequent.

13. In Greek **I beg** lacks an object and **lose heart** a subject; both must be supplied from the context. The three most probable solutions, all grammatically possible, would result in the following renderings: (i) I pray God that I may not lose heart in my trials (thus many of the Fathers, but not many modern commentators apart from Grosheide and Dibelius); (ii) I pray God that you may not lose heart because of my trials; (iii) I beg you not to lose heart because of my trials. When elsewhere Paul speaks of his sufferings he does not envisage the possibility of despair but rejoices in them (Rom 5.3; 2 Cor 12.10; Col 1.14); if Paul is not the author but someone is writing in his name that person would hardly present his hero as subject to despondency. The final clause of the verse is strongly positive in tone and would be considerably weakened if Paul is supposed to be in danger of despair. Paul's personal feelings do not surface elsewhere in the letter in distinction from most of his others; 6.21f is a possible exception but in it there is no suggestion of his losing heart. That counts against (i). Solution (ii) would entail the introduction of a different object for the main verb from that of the subject of the infinitive. (iii) is the most satisfactory and provides the smoothest transition to the final clause. The readers are in greater danger of losing heart than Paul. AE's readers know of Paul's imprisonment and they might be afraid that they would also be imprisoned or might believe that God was no longer using Paul as his minister (in 2 Corinthians Paul defends himself against such ideas). The readers are encouraged to believe that whatever befalls them should not lead to despair.

Paul's **tribulations** are his imprisonment. They are on behalf of his readers. His imprisonment is neither personal tragedy nor personal victory; it is the result of what he had done in making known the salvation of God for the Gentiles. The connection with his readers is made more precise in the final clause of the verse. Several places in the Pauline corpus relate his sufferings to the good of his converts; in these he depicts himself, or is depicted, as suffering representatively (2 Cor 1.6; 4.12; 12.15; Col 1.24; 2 Tim 2.10). Representative suffering and suffering for the benefit of others are familiar phenomena, for example, a parent for a child; both ideas were known and accepted in the ancient world. Paul and his fellow Christians belong together in the body of Christ; what affects one affects all; if one suffers all suffer (1 Cor 12.26); but also if one suffers others are strengthened in their faith, and some may indeed be converted (the blood of the martyrs is the seed of the church).

In 2 Cor 1.6 Paul's sufferings are for the encouragement and salvation of his readers, in 4.12 they bring life to them, and in 12.15 his life is spent on behalf of their lives. We might then have expected AE to write here 'which are for your strengthening' or even 'for your salvation'. Instead he refers to **glory**. This is a variant of the theme, for the 'life' in question is not physical or psychic life but eternal life, the life which is associated with glory (1.18; Col 1.27). In Rom 8.17f; 2 Cor 4.17 Paul connects his suffering to his own glory. All this suggests that the connection of his suffering with the glory of others is within the range of his thought, and does not require the supposition that AE is not Paul, though it naturally does not imply he is; if AE is not Paul all he has done is to take up a Pauline theme and develop it. The clause does not mean that the readers are to give glory to Paul or to boast about him, and AE is not setting Paul in the place of Christ as redeemer, for too much in the letter indicates the unique position he gives to Christ (1.3–11; 2.5f, 12–16; 5.2, 25f) for that to be true. We have now come full circle back to 3.1 (a kind of *inclusio*); we are therefore ready to move on to the next stage, the prayer of 3.14ff.

Throughout 3.1–13 Paul is given a unique position, for a mystery once revealed never needs to be revealed again. Can however the suffering of any Christian bring glory to other Christians? While Paul at times gives himself a position different from that of others in the church, he also recognises his equality with them; he terms them his brothers and with them is a member of the one body of Christ. Just as he refreshes them so they refresh him (Philem 20); in 1 Th 3.8 he says that he will live if they stand firm, and living does not mean merely going on existing but living in Christ. When the Philippians support him with money, it is their love flowing to him (Phil 4.15–17) and their prayers help in respect of his salvation (1.19). If this reciprocity is present in

Paul's own writings it is not clear that AE takes the same view. We cannot really know how AE would answer our initial question, but we may be reasonably sure that Paul would have said that when any Christian suffers in the ministry of Christ he may bring glory to others.

VII

INTERCESSION AND DOXOLOGY

(3.14–21)

[14] **For this reason I bow my knees to the Father,**
[15]   **from whom is named every (social) grouping**
        in heaven and on earth,
[16]   **that he may give you**
        in accordance with the riches of his glory
        to be strengthened mightily by means of the Spirit,
        directed towards the inner person,
[17]   **(and) Christ to dwell in your hearts through faith**
        – you are rooted and grounded in love –
[18]   **that you may have the ability with all the saints to grasp**
    what is the breadth and length and height and depth
[19]   **and to know the love of Christ**
        which surpasses knowledge,
    that you may be filled
        to attain to the total fullness of God.
[20] **Now to the one able to do infinitely beyond anything**
    which we ask or think
    in accordance with the power working in us,
[21]   **to him is the glory**
    in the church and in Christ Jesus
    unto all generations for ever and ever.
  Amen.

AE began 3.1 as if intending to launch into a prayer related to
what he had just been writing, and prayer would have followed
appropriately after the reference to the temple (2.21f, Eadie). For
some reason he drew back; more needed to be said before he
could move on from his discussion of the admission of Gentiles to
God's grace to offer his prayer; and so we had the parenthesis of

vv. 2–13. The reference in 3.1 is to Paul's sufferings on behalf of the Gentiles and 3.13 links back to this. The parenthesis explained his personal involvement as the one who had both received the revelation of the admission of the Gentiles (v. 3) and had been foremost in evangelising them. That gave him more than anyone else the right and the duty to pray for the Gentiles. In the parenthesis the cosmic nuance of salvation again came to the fore (vv. 9f) and this prepares for v. 15.

The prayer, addressed like most of those in the NT to God rather than Christ, provides a transition from the 'theology' of the first half of the letter to the 'paraenesis' of the second. After a solemn opening (vv. 14f) it becomes an intercession. In his earlier intercession (1.17ff) AE prayed that the readers should understand their salvation; now he concentrates rather on their personal experience so that they may be spiritually deepened and adequately prepared for the moral exhortations which are to follow. Above all, if they are to be truly God's temple, they need to be strengthened in love, and this is the main burden of the prayer. For AE merely to tell them what good behaviour is would not of itself ensure that they would follow his counsel and behave well.

Verses 14–19 form one long unwieldy sentence reminiscent of the language and style of the initial eulogy (1.3–14), yet that gives no reason to suppose that AE is employing a piece of preformed tradition. Vv. 14f tell us to whom the prayer is addressed. The content of the prayer follows in three successive clauses (vv. 16f; 18–19a; 19b), each beginning with **that** and each to some extent dependent on the preceding; the first two have several qualifications; the third is brief and forms the climax. The burden of the prayer is that God's strength should become that of the readers, mediated through the love of Christ in which they are already grounded. A doxology rounds off the prayer and it is terminated with a solemn 'Amen' (vv. 20f). The doxology consists of one sentence, and though comparatively brief it is stylistically similar to the eulogy; unlike the intercession it is in the first plural, tying together writer and readers. Its position makes it the conclusion to the doctrinal and devotional first half of the letter and it prepares for the change of tone in what is to follow.

An intercessionary prayer at this point in a Pauline letter is surprising; normally they follow the initial address, and they occupy the same position in most of the NT letters. However, letter writing by its nature does not follow strict rules. In 1 Th 3.11–13 Paul introduced a prayer into the middle of his letter, and doxologies appear in different parts of other letters.

14. After the link back to v. 1 with **for this reason** the move to prayer is expressed, not with a simple 'I pray', but with a more complex phrase in the Pauline manner (cf Rom 1.9; Phil 1.4; 1 Th 1.2), yet, unlike 1.16, it does not resemble any that Paul employs.

Jews normally stood when praying (Mt 6.5; Mk 11.25; Lk 18.11, 13; 1 Sam 1.26; 1 Kgs 8.14, 22; Josephus *Ant* 10.255; 12.98; *Tos Berak* 3.20; *m Ber* 5.1; *m Taan* 2.2) but kneeling and prostration (it is not always clear to which the words and phrases refer) were also known (1 Chron 29.20 LXX; Isa 45.23; Ps 95.6; Dan 6.11 Theod LXX, 'fell on his face'; *Prayer of Manasseh* 11); in 1 Kgs 8.54; 1 Esdr 8.73; 3 Macc 2.1 prostration where the forehead touches the ground is impossible because of the position of the hands. Kneeling is the approach to Baal in 1 Kgs 19.18 and may have been the regular posture in pagan worship, as in approaches to important people (2 Kgs 1.13; 1 Chron 29.20), perhaps implying submission including an appeal for help. Apart from Eph 3.14 it is only in OT quotations that kneeling is mentioned in the NT (Rom 11.4; 14.11; Phil 2.10). It is not known what the normal posture of worshippers in the early church was when praying. Mk 14.35; Lk 5.8; 22.41; Acts 7.60; 9.40; 20.36; 21.5 yield no certain answer but do not exclude the possibility of kneeling; Mt 26.39 implies prostration; the soldiers kneel in Mk 15.19 before Jesus but this is in mockery and not prayer. By the time of Origen there are references to the suitability of kneeling (*Hom Judges*, GCS 30, 475.16).

Whatever the contemporary normal posture in prayer, v. 14 refers to mental, not physical, kneeling. Since there is no word for prayer in v. 14, kneeling must have been instantly recognisable as indicating that a prayer was about to commence; had AE spoken of Paul as standing in the Jewish manner, his Gentile readers might have needed an explicit reference to prayer. Probably kneeling conveyed to them a greater sense of humbleness than would standing.

The prayer is addressed **to the Father**; only here and in 2.18 do we have the undefined 'Father'.

The Fatherhood of God has been variously understood here: (i) The scribes who added 'of our Lord Jesus Christ' clearly thought that the reference was to Christ alone; the rejection of the variant entails the rejection of this view. (ii) The reference may be to God as Father of believers; this is the most common understanding in the NT of God as Father, but the word play with v. 15 implies that God's Fatherhood here embraces some who are in heaven. (iii) Most probably the Fatherhood is conceived cosmically involving all sentient beings in heaven and on earth (v. 15; cf 4.6). This view (see notes on 4.6) was well known in the ancient world, God being often regarded as the progenitor of all living beings; when however the Bible wishes to express the idea of God as universal Father it speaks of him as creator and not progenitor. The description here of God as Father saves him from being seen as a remote deity to whom it would be impossible to pray.

15. As Father God is the one who gives names (see on 1.21). In biblical thought this does not imply that those he names take on his name. A name is a means of identification, but it is much more. In the creation story Adam is given a responsibility for what God has created and gives names to the animals. Name-giving is thus associated with creation and to possess a name implies existence (cf Ps 147.4; Isa 40.26; Eccles 6.10); the name is also associated with redemption for believers are baptised into the name of Christ and so come under his authority. V. 15 is then saying something more than that God puts names on people and things. It is the source of the naming that is stressed rather than action of naming.

What is named is *every* **social grouping**. The Greek word *patria* is related to the word *pater*, father. **Every** indicates a multiplicity. But a multiplicity of what? The Vulgate and Syriac translate the word as if it were an abstract noun meaning 'fatherhood' and those interpreters who follow them (e.g. Percy; Bruce) justify this on the grounds of the word play. We do not however need to see such a direct play on words. More importantly 'fatherhood' is not a recognised meaning of *patria*. In the LXX it always indicates a group of people with a common ancestor such as a family or tribe (Exod 12.3; Num 32.28; Jth 8.2; *T Dan* 1.2), but it is also often used in a wider way to denote a group linked by consanguinity with no implication of a common father, and even more widely of a social unit distinguishable from other social units (Ψ 21.28; 95.7; Ezek 20.32; Jth 8.18; Acts 3.25 in quoting Gen 22.18 substitutes it for 'the nations'). English translations frequently use 'family' but this is too limiting; '(social) grouping' is to be preferred as less exact. It should not be taken as if it indicated local congregations (Mitton; Goodspeed). The use of **every** implies more than two groupings are in view, and so excludes a reference merely to Jews and Gentiles or to one group on earth and one in heaven.

While it is easy to imagine different groupings on earth whether defined as nations, tribes, peoples which use a common language or inhabit an area with boundaries, it is more difficult to think of such groupings in heaven where there is neither physical consanguinity (cf Mk 12.25) nor limited geographical area. Yet in heaven there are rulers, powers, principalities, seraphim, cherubim, ophanim (*1 En* 71.6ff; 61.10) and the angels are arranged in groups with leaders (*1 En* 69.3), though this should not suggest the archangels as fathers (cf Jerome). There is no need to resort to thinking of the groups in heaven as those of dead believers or the church triumphant (so Hodge; Eadie quoting Bodius, i.e. Robert Boyd). Since no distinction is made in the earthly groupings between good and bad, it may be assumed none should be made in respect of those in heaven (*pace* Schnackenburg). Believers would be reassured when they realised that the powers were dependent on God (Houlden), and this may be why AE has not simply described God as the Father of every family in heaven and earth but has said that God named them, so setting him in a closer and authoritative relation to them.

Verse 15 builds up an impressive picture of the extent of God's authority and therefore of his power and so leads to, and fits with, the intercession which follows with its stress on his might and love.

16. AE now enters on the content of his intercession reusing many of the words and ideas of his earlier intercession, 1.17–19, with a similar tautological style as there and as in the Qumran writings (1QH 7.17, 19; 12.35; 1QM 10.5; cf Kuhn). God is the source of any strengthening in love that the readers are to receive and this because of his inexhaustible riches. The wealth of God's resources is there to sustain the readers in their daily lives.

Glory (for the word see on 1.6) in its biblical usage carries two flavours: radiance, power. The former predominated in the refrain of the eulogy (1.6, 12, 14), the latter is more appropriate here and was prepared for in 3.13. **To be strengthened mightily** (Lk 1.80; 2.40; 1 Cor 16.13) introduces again the theme of power. It is God who strengthens (cf Phil 4.13) just as it was he who was powerful to raise Christ from the dead (1.19f). Believers are not left to whistle up strength from within themselves in order to be able to do God's will (cf 6.10). The reason for their strengthening is not defined here but emerges in vv. 17b–19. It is necessary if the injunctions of the following paraenetic section of the letter are to be observed. The agency of strengthening is God's **Spirit**; the Spirit is regularly associated with power (1 Cor 2.4; 2 Cor 6.6f; Rom 1.4), an association deriving from OT *ruah*.

It is the **inner person** which is to be strengthened. The term 'inner person' appears also in 2 Cor 4.16; Rom 7.22. The concept appears to have been current in Hellenistic thought; it is difficult to see how any reflection on the nature of the person could avoid the concept, if not the precise phrase; in fact it goes back at least to Plato, *Rep* 9.589A, appears in Hellenistic Judaism (Philo, *Det Pot* 23; *Plant* 42; *Congressu* 97), in gnosis (*CH* 1.15; 9.5; 13.7; Irenaeus, 1.21.4f; Hippolytus, 5.7.35f; *Ep Pet Phil*, NHC VIII, 2 137.20–2), and then very frequently in the Fathers. The term by its nature suggests some form of dualism which in Greek thought would be basically that of spiritual/material, but there is no uniform presentation of it. As a current and indeed natural term to express the moral and spiritual side in people it was picked up by Paul who used it first in 2 Cor 4.16 and then in Rom 7.22. In 2 Cor 4.16 it is contrasted with the outer being, though the outer being is not there devalued as 'material', but is that part of Paul which suffers in his missionary labours; the inner person is apparently set in parallel with the heart as that which God renews daily. In Rom 7.22, where the antithetical 'outer person' is not mentioned, the inner person is paralleled with the **mind** and is almost equivalent to the personal pronoun. It is then the whole person viewed from one aspect, the aspect on which the Spirit may act. It is what people are 'deep down' within themselves (Houlden), yet it is not a purely psychological term for it involves the whole person. The inner person did not come into existence with baptism/conversion, but in Ephesians it finds its purpose and fulfilment in those who are redeemed (Rienecker). It is not the old person (4.22) but when worked on by the Spirit it approximates to the new person (4.24; cf 1 Pet 3.4). AE does not use it with precisely the same significance as Paul; having found it in the Pauline vocabulary he was able to adapt it to his own purposes since it lacked fixed technical meaning; equally if AE is Paul he was free to adapt its usage. That it is paralleled with 'heart' in v. 17 and that love, power and understanding feature in the intercession show that not much adaptation was necessary.

17. Since no particle links this verse to the preceding it is probably parallel to it, yet also clarifies it. The two verses express the same idea; v. 16 would have been more easily understood in the Hellenistic world; v. 17 is more Semitic (Hugedé). There is no temporal distinction between the two verses as if v. 16 were a necessary pre-condition of v. 17.

The verb translated **dwell** normally indicates a settling in or colonising tenancy which has a beginning and continues without interruption. The moment of settling in or colonising will have been that of conversion/baptism. Since then Christ has been the permanent tenant. In comparison to the corporate tenancy of 2.22 the tenancy is now individualised (Eadie). Corporate and individual aspects of the Christian life balance one another throughout the letter, the corporate reappearing in v. 18.

Paul had already argued that the Spirit of God dwelt in believers (Rom 8.9, 11; 1 Cor 3.16; cf 1 Cor 6.19); in the OT God's law is said to be written in the hearts of people (Jer 31.31–4) and his Spirit to be in them (Ezek 36.27). God also lives and walks among them (Exod 29.45; Lev 26.12). Wisd 1.4 implies the dwelling of wisdom in the wise. The Johannine literature expresses a thought parallel to Eph 2.17 with the word usually translated 'abide' (Jn 14.17; 15.4–6; 1 Jn 2.14; 3.17, 24; 4.12, 15f), though often there it is believers who dwell in God or Christ; in Paul of course believers are regularly said to be 'in Christ'. He does however sometimes speak of Christ as in believers (Rom 8.10; 2 Cor 4.10f; 13.3, 5; Gal 2.20; 4.19; cf Col 1.27). In Paul the experience of believers in respect of the Spirit and of Christ is very similar. It is not then surprising to find AE writing of Christ in the hearts of believers. God does not force the indwelling of Christ on believers; it takes place **through faith**. AE has already used this phrase at 2.8 (see there for the meaning) and 3.12. Faith which began at conversion/baptism continues throughout the whole of the Christian life. It denotes a relationship between people. Believers have faith in Christ; this relationship eliminates any idea of a Christ-mysticism where the personality of believers would be absorbed into that of Christ. Instead obedience always remains an essential part of the relationship; the Christ who enters does so, not merely as guest, but as Lord (Rienecker). Vv. 16f again contain the raw bricks which eventually led to Trinitarian doctrine. God gives through the Spirit and Christ indwells.

Verse 17b centres on two verbs **rooted and grounded**, and **in love** qualifies both participles. The whole clause should be taken as independent (Eadie) or parenthetical (Ewald). The tense of the verbs implies a condition which came into existence in the past and still continues; the verbs are not then part of the prayer, i.e. AE is not praying that the readers should be well founded in love, nor are they imperatival, 'be well founded in love'. Instead they state that believers have been and continue to be well founded in love. As empowered by the Spirit and indwelt by Christ they have been rooted and founded in love and therefore are able to grasp the nature of love, and so will be in a position to keep the injunctions of the later part of the letter.

The verbs present two distinct but allied images; one botanical, the other architectural; it is imprecise to refer to them as a mixed metaphor, as Ellicott points out. The first, rare in the NT (Col 2.7), is found in Jewish writing (Jer 12.2; Ecclus 24.12; 1QS 8.5; 11.8; 1QH 6.15f; 8.4–11) and is related to the image of planting (1 Cor 3.5–9). The second (see on 2.20) is found much more widely in the NT (Mt 7.25; Lk 6.48f; 1 Cor 3.10–12; Eph 2.20; Col 1.23; Heb 6.1; 1 Pet 5.10; 1QS 5.5) and is related to the image of building or edification (1 Cor 14.3–5; Eph 2.20–2; 4.12, 16, 29). Both images appear together in 1 Cor 3.9. AE has already told his readers that they form part of a building whose foundation is the apostles and prophets (2.20); here the foundation is love. But is it divine or human love? In favour of the former is the lack of reassurance which human love would provide; in v. 19 Christ's love is clearly in view; the salvation of believers issues from God's love and not human love; if human love is meant it might imply that love was a pre-condition of salvation; if a human quality was to be expressed 'faith', following on from the earlier part of the verse, would have been more appropriate. On the other hand if the reference is to God's love why do we not have **his love** as in 2.4 (Haupt)? **Love** is used more often of human (1.15; 4.2, 15, 16; 5.2) than of divine (1.4; 2.4; 3.19) love in Ephesians; statistics however prove nothing when the two possibilities exist; context must decide the meaning. Perhaps at times little distinguishes human from divine love if the former is the result of the presence of the latter in the believer (Rom 5.5). Yet if our analysis of the construction of the passage is correct it seems necessary to decide in favour of divine love.

18. After the brief parenthesis of v. 17b the intercession is resumed. Though empowered by the Spirit and indwelt by Christ the readers still lack something (Ewald) and, as we shall ultimately see, this is not gnosis but love. This verse assumes v. 16 and takes it further; though underpinned by love believers need a fuller understanding of that love. The readers need an ability to attain an objective, here that of comprehending something or grasping it for oneself. On the basis of Phil 3.12f **grasp** is sometimes given a mystical flavour (Dibelius), but that sense is not necessary here (Dupont). We must give it the wider sense of understanding; it then differs little from **to know** (v. 19). The object of knowing is love. If this is its ultimate objective the verb cannot denote a purely intellectual process and, since it is not love itself which is to be grasped but its extent, it cannot be taken existentially with Schlier. It is the same kind of knowledge as in 1.18; Col 1.27, a knowledge possible only because the Spirit has strengthened the readers and Christ indwells them (Lemmer). It is also a communal knowledge shared **with all the saints**, and this whether **saints** means only believers or includes also heavenly beings (Dahl; Houlden). Since we learn from other people, knowledge is generally communal; this is especially true of love whose nature can only be grasped through interaction with others. The true understanding of Christ's love is not then an individual experience but takes place in the community.

The final fourfold phrase is difficult; it is wrong to speak, as many commentators do, of four dimensions; there are only three spatial dimensions; here width and length are two measurements at right angles in the same plane, height and depth two measurements at right angles to that plane but in the same vertical dimension and therefore indicate only one dimension. The phrase of the commentators is then geometrically incorrect, a mistake which no educated Greek would have made. A single article governs the four nouns implying that they are to be taken as a unit and not interpreted separately; AE may be using a pre-existing formula. Since actual physical measurements cannot be in mind the phrase must be interpreted metaphorically. But what metaphor is involved? Eadie supplies a list and a brief discussion of the interpretations suggested prior to his time.

(a) In view of the dependence of the NT on the OT the latter seems the obvious place to begin the search. Ps 139.8–10 though using spatial imagery to express God's omnipresence employs none of the actual words; Amos 9.2f uses only **depth**; Job 11.7–9 speaks of the height of heaven, what is deeper than Hades, longer than earth and broader than the sea; Ecclus 1.3 has two of the words. In each case the words are not set alongside one another as in v. 18 but appear in separate phrases or clauses. Where we find four items in OT passages they relate to four areas, heaven, earth, sea, Sheol, and not to four measurements. Outside scripture but still within Palestinian Judaism we find the idea of measurement in different directions (*1 En* 60.11; 93.11–14; *2 Bar* 54.1–4) but the use is non-metaphorical.

(b) In the Hellenistic world several possibilities have been suggested. In some philosophical thought, in particular that of Stoicism (cf Dupont), the soul is thought to walk (metaphorically) in heaven and, by seeing and understanding its dimensions, to understand the greatness of God (Cicero, *Nat Deorum* I 53f; *Tusc* I 64, 69f; V 69; Plutarch, *Mor* 939A; Seneca, *Nat Quaest* 1.12f; *CH* 10.25; 11.20; *Asclep* 6; *Pistis Sophia* 133). Yet we never encounter the fourfold formula and classical writers would probably never have thought of four spatial dimensions. Apart from the references in *CH* which are very slight, all relate to human ability to know and not to revealed knowledge (cf Schnackenburg; Feuillet). The closest verbal parallel is found in a fourth-century magical papyrus, *PGM* IV 964–74, 979–85. Although this parallel has been noted by many recent commentators it has been most strongly advocated by Arnold. The papyrus contains the fourfold formula but links with the fourfold series two other nouns, 'light', 'dawn', which are not spatial, so that there is actually a sixfold formula and therefore no proper parallel. Since the terms of the formula could be applied to the measurements of a building it has been thought to refer to the heavenly city (Rev 21.16; cf Hermas, *Vis* 3.2.5; *b B. Bat* 75b; *Pesiq R* 143); this gives the formula too physical a sense and nothing in the context suggests a building is in mind. Schlier, working from the shape of the cross, argues for a reference to the cross as a world body, an idea taken up by later Christians (*Act Andr* 14; *Act Petri* 38; *Act Philip* 140; cf Irenaeus, 5.17.4). None of the solutions we have outlined is more than vaguely possible. Lacking then an indication of the contemporary use of the fourfold formula, it is better to see it as a typical piece of AE's hyperbole; AE uses four measurements to drive home the greatness of whatever the formula refers to.

To what then do the measurements refer? In line with the attempts to explain the formula it has been supposed it refers to wisdom (Van Roon; Feuillet), to the new Jerusalem and/or the heavenly inheritance (Dibelius; Conzelmann), the power of God (Arnold), the cross (Schlier), the body of Christ (Usami), God's plan of salvation or the mystery of salvation (Mussner; Percy; Schnackenburg), the redemptive activity of God (Beare). To be entirely rejected are the allegorical explanations of some of the Fathers (e.g. Athanasius, *De Incarnatione* 16 [the self-revealing of the Word is in every dimension: above, in creation; below, in the incarnation; in the depth, in Hades; in the breadth, throughout the world]; Augustine, *Doct Christ* 2.41; *In Joh* 118). It is difficult to argue for any of these from the immediate context which is that of love (v. 19), and with the majority of commentators we take this to be the reference. Paul had already moved in the direction of relating love to height and depth (Rom 8.39). The love will be that of Christ or of God. This love is without limits and ultimately immeasurable.

19. This verse is coordinate with v. 18 and to some extent parallel to it; both verses begin with verbs of 'knowing'. **To know** has much the same sense as **to grasp** in v. 18. Believers need to grasp the intensity with which Christ loves them ('the love of Christ' is not their love for him but his love for them as in 5.2, 25;

cf Romaniuk). This love goes so far beyond any ordinary scheme of measurement that it cannot be fully understood; it **surpasses knowledge**. AE neither depreciates knowledge here as if he were attacking an early form of gnosis nor compares love and knowledge; if he were doing the latter, knowledge would come off as badly as every other virtue with which love might be compared (cf 1 Cor 13); in a sense love and knowledge are incomparable since the knowledge is human and the love divine. Knowledge is of course necessary, otherwise revelation could not be appropriated (1.9; 3.3ff) nor love understood. Yet Christ's love can never be fully grasped either intellectually or existentially. Elsewhere and with various images Paul attempts to explain the extent of Christ's love and of God's: that love extends to sinners (Rom 5.6), overcomes all obstacles (Rom 8.35ff), constrains believers (2 Cor 5.14). AE has in mind here its effects on believers; when love rules their lives they are able to face up to the moral duties which AE is about to lay on them in the remainder of the letter.

AE's prayer has been steadily building up to the final intercession of v. 19b. Believers can only grasp the extent of Christ's love when they have been strengthened through the Spirit in their inner being, Christ has come to dwell in their hearts and they are underpinned by love. The interpretation of v. 19b is disputed.

The ultimate purpose of the prayer is the filling of believers; since there is no explicit statement saying with what they are to be filled this must be deduced from the context. The answer would be simple if we could translate the clause, 'that you may be filled with all the fullness of God' (AV, RSV, REB and many other translations), but this would rob a preposition of its true force, literally, 'that you may be filled *unto* all the fullness of God'. The word 'unto' suggests a movement towards all the fullness of God. We have translated the clause, **that you may be filled to attain the total fullness of God**. There is a goal which has not yet been attained (this is a prayer) and the goal is to be filled with what distinguishes God. This taken abstractly and apart from the context might be the full total of either his attributes or the spiritual gifts which he imparts to believers. The context from v. 17 has however been that of love. The nature of God is love; his greatest spiritual gift is love. Probably then we should understand

God as able to fill with that love (cf Belser; Spicq) which summarises his own being and to whose fullness AE's readers have not yet attained, but which in itself enables them to move towards their goal. This interpretation accords with 5.1 where believers are summoned to imitate God, again in a context of love. Their nature and God's should coincide but this can only happen when God fills them with his love.

20. The first and 'theological' section of the letter concludes, as Romans, with a doxology (cf Rom 11.26). The only possible response in the light of what has been said about God in 1.3–3.19 is to voice his praise. The doxology is probably not a separate item tacked on at the end of the intercession but should be regarded as a part of the prayer (Pokorný).

The doxology is a form appearing regularly in the NT but of uncertain origin. It was already in Pauline usage prior to Ephesians (Gal 1.5; Rom 11.36; Phil 4.20; Rom 16.25–7 may however be post-Pauline); its widespread use is seen in later parts of the NT (1 Tim 1.17; 2 Tim 4.18; Heb 13.21; Jude 24f; Rev 1.6; cf 1 Clem 20.12; 32.4; etc.). It consists of three elements: the name or title of the addressee, a statement of praise, a period of time. Its simplest form (Rom 11.36; *Did* 9.2, 3) is 'to God is (be) the glory for ever'. It is not clear if the accompanying 'amen' belongs to the form or represents an expected response from hearers. Each basic element may be extended.

The position of 3.20f as a doxology is unexceptional in coming at the end of the first half of the letter and at the end of the prayer. Each of its units has been extended beyond the basic form. These extensions because of their language, style and content mark it as AE's own construction (Masson): he has introduced into the form his main theme of the church and one of his favourite phrases 'in Christ'. V. 20 identifies the addressee, and this identification, perhaps because of its length, is renewed in v. 21. The 'praise' element is qualified with references to the church and Christ.

The addressee is unnamed but God is the nearest referent (v. 19) and so the doxology is offered to him; it cannot be Christ since he is referred to in v. 21. AE describes the addressee with his normal exuberance of language. God's power is the central element of the praise (Arnold).

We ask or think moves us to the plural from the first singular which has governed the passage since v. 14; intercession by its nature cannot be offered by those for whom it is made, but they can be embraced in praise; hence the plurals here. Humans can neither encompass and contain God by their thinking (cf Isa 55.8f) nor even imagine how all-embracing his care for them is. The greatness of his care is linked to his power, a theme which came to prominence in the first intercession (1.19), was renewed in the second (vv. 16–18), and occurs repeatedly throughout the letter. This power is already at work.

21. The length of the first element of the doxology forces AE into resuming the address: **to him**. The missing copula, as in 1.3, is indicative, for we have a statement of fact, rather than a wish or prayer. God already has glory and there is no need to pray for him to receive it.

The second element of the doxology is extended. Christ, when not the one to whom the doxology is addressed, often appears as the one through whom God is approached (Rom 16.27; 1 Pet 4.11; cf *Mart Polyc* 14.3), but here however glory is said to be 'in him' and then, surprisingly, the church is set in parallel with him.

In the phrase **in the church and in Christ Jesus**, **in** must be given the same meaning on each occasion. Since it can hardly have any other than a local significance with reference to the church, it must mean the same when applied to Christ. Such a local significance is found elsewhere with the phrase 'in Christ' (see Detached Note: In Christ). AE appears to have come close here to equating Christ and the church, yet elsewhere he clearly distinguishes between them: Christ is head and bridegroom; the church is his body and wife or bride. As for the positioning of the church before Christ, the same order appears in 4.4f. In v. 21 AE may be seeking a climactic effect. God's glory is both to be praised in the church and can be seen in the church, for the church is related to the fullness of Christ (1.23), and is his body and bride. In so far as the church is worthy, pure and immaculate, and this she is (5.27), she exhibits God's glory, and the powers learn from her. She is his dwelling-place in the Spirit (2.22; 1 Cor 3.16) and where he dwells, his glory dwells, as it did in the temple in Jerusalem. The church however has no human glory for, of and in herself, she is weak and sinful. God's glory is certainly to be found in Christ and may be ascribed to him (1 Cor 2.8; 2 Cor 3.18; 4.4; 8.23; Phil 4.19). It is neither the statement that God's glory is to be seen in the church nor that it is to be seen in Christ that is then exceptional, only their collocation. As for their collocation, Christ and the church are regularly related in the letter: 1.23, the church is the fullness of Christ; 2.21, Christ is its angle-stone; 4.15f, he is the head of his body which is the church; 5.22ff, he is the bridegroom (husband) of the church which is his bride (wife). It is their close relation which has led them to be put in parallel: 'The glory that belongs to the Head fills the Body; the glory that belongs to the Husband shines in his Wife, whose status is determined by his. Thus the glory that is seen in the Church is not its own glory but derives from Christ' (Best, *One Body*). Perhaps AE has been carried away by his own enthusiastic use of words beyond what is strictly logical.

The third element of the doxology is again unusually lengthy, thereby emphasising the everlasting significance of God's glory.

Amen appears regularly in the NT as the final word in doxologies and prayers (e.g. Mt 6.13; Rom 1.25; 9.5; 11.36; 15.33; 16.27). While it can also denote the response of a congregation affirming agreement with a prayer which has just been uttered, this is hardly its function here or indeed in many other NT passages. When a letter was read aloud in a Christian gathering, unless believers knew it well, they would not have known where to respond with their **Amen**. It is the author's way of affirming the importance of what he has just said, 'This is true', and so adding emphasis. Yet it may be that a skilful reader, realising the change of subject-matter which is just about to take place, would see it as an appropriate place to halt for a moment and draw breath, and in the brief interval the congregation would respond with their **Amen** to his.

VIII

PARAENESIS

(4.1–6.20)

At 4.1 the tenor of the letter changes; up to now it has been basically doctrinal though including extensive liturgical passages, but teaching about God and praise of him are now replaced with concern for behaviour, though since the type of behaviour required is closely related to the previous teaching that aspect continues to appear. There is also a significant change of style in that, 4.11–16 apart, the long convoluted sentences of the earlier chapters disappear and are replaced by a crisper approach consisting mainly of brief sentences. 4.2f is the hinge on which the change swings, for it introduces the need for the kind of conduct which would enhance the unity of a group. The changes at 4.1 are apparently similar to those at Rom 12.1; in both the summons to behaviour is followed first by a general but brief exhortation (Eph 4.2f; Rom 12.1f) and then by a reference to the church (Eph 4.4–16; Rom 12.3–8) before the detailed ethical instruction is given. Yet the balance is different, for the exhortation in Romans is relatively much briefer in respect of the length of the letter than that in Ephesians where it occupies half the letter. Romans is the only Pauline letter in which this clear-cut division is obvious. AE may have known Romans and sought to imitate it; alternatively, as a member of a Pauline school he may have known that Paul based instruction for behaviour on doctrine and developed a trend in his master's work which had become clearest in his last writing. If Paul is himself the writer he may simply be following a pattern which as time went by he found more and more useful. If Berger is correct in saying that secular letters did not contain paraenesis, Paul may have been responsible for introducing this type of discourse into the letter form; it is of course widely present in philosophical writings.

174

Behaviour is thus seen in Ephesians as both response to what God has done in Christ, and as the proper accompaniment to the praise of God, the two themes present in chaps. 1–3. Gentile Christians ought to be especially responsive since, as was argued in chaps. 2, 3, God has done so much for them. Yet doctrine to which behaviour is the response is not missing from the final three chapters (see 4.4–16; 4.32; 5.23–32) just as it is not wholly absent from chaps. 12–15 of Romans (see 12.3–8; 13.1–6; 14.9, 14, 17).

But why does AE after commencing his paraenesis (vv. 2f) break off from it with a discussion of the church (vv. 4–16)? Perhaps he realises he has not said enough about the nature of the church to provide a proper basis for the instruction of how Christians should live together; for the nature of the church is the theme of 4.4–16, even though the word church is not used. The virtues mentioned in vv. 2f are those appropriate to this theme and the need for 'one-ness' which they suggest is carried on in the repeated use of 'one' of vv. 4–6. Vv. 7–16 continue the theme in showing how diversity may be combined with unity, though unity precedes diversity. Discussion of unity had been already present in 2.11–22, but there it was the unity of Jewish and Gentile Christians; now it is the unity of all believers irrespective of racial or religious origin (cf Percy). Thus the inner condition of the church is discussed in relation to individuals as individuals within it; only after this is it proper to discuss in detail the behaviour of Christians towards one another (4.17–5.14). The inner unity and strength of the community enable believers to live with one another. 4.2–16 thus sets all that follows within a corporate frame of reference. Did AE see the danger of an excessive individualism, arising perhaps from an incipient gnosticism? Individualism however always characterises behaviour; it manifests itself in Romans in differing attitudes to food and days. Ephesians however is too general to enable us to tie down the danger of individualism to particular influences.

In 4.17–24 AE contrasts the present life of Gentile believers with their past pagan life. In 4.25–5.2 he picks on certain sins into which believers may fall and which would destroy community life, while avoiding them would build up that life. This is largely also the theme of 5.3–14 where the sins are set in the light of God's judgement (vv. 3–7), and the need of the community is brought out to confront those who sin so that they may reform themselves. In 5.15–21 warnings on conduct are again set together, now with a reminder of the help that may come from common worship. 5.21–6.9 discusses certain specific areas of behaviour pertaining to individual households rather than to the community as a whole. 6.10–20 indicates the personal devotional equipment that believers need if they are to live as AE sets out.

Throughout 4.1–6.20 a number of terms appear which are also found in the paraenetic sections of the later NT letters (1 Peter, Colossians, James), e.g. putting off/on, resisting, being subject to. Many, in particular Carrington and Selwyn, have attempted to argue from this to the existence of a primitive Christian catechism and to see it as related to baptism. Common topics are certainly present; in different areas the early Christian communities must have encountered the same general questions relating to behaviour, for example, the need to resist temptation and give up various sins. It is not then surprising that there should be common teaching, though it is not necessary that it should have been coordinated, or have existed in a common oral or written form, nor is it necessary to suppose that it preceded baptism; in the accounts of conversion in Acts baptism follows immediately on belief and there is no period of instruction. The paraenetic material in Ephesians is so general in nature and shared with so many other NT writings that it is difficult to discern any precise situation into which it might fit; it offers no help then in determining the date or destination of the letter. The material moreover betrays no interest in Christian behaviour in relation to the world outside the church nor of the effect of what was happening outside on the church; it is wholly concerned with what happens within the church; this is probably why AE chose to begin these chapters with a discussion of the nature of the church where the behaviour will take place.

IX

UNITY AND DIVERSITY

(4.1–16)

AE sets out here to treat the unity of the church and the manner in which it is both built up and preserved through the activity of its office-bearers and members. 4.4–6 shows unity as already existing and perfect, and 4.7–16 shows how it is to be continued and matured. 4.1–16 begins (4.2f) and ends (4.4–16) with explicit exhortation (Lemmer). More than once AE begins a subject, drops it and then picks it up again. Thus intercession begun at 1.16f is resumed at 3.14 and 3.13f picks up 3.1; 2.5 resumes 2.1. Here 4.2f is picked up again at 4.17ff. In view of the attention given to the final few verses of this section in today's church in relation to unity, it is surprising to find how rarely the earlier Fathers quote the passage. Vv. 4, 5 with their reference to one baptism were important in the discussions whether heretics should be rebaptised (see Synod of Carthage, September 256) and vv. 9, 10 in christology because of their references to what happened to Jesus after his death.

A

UNITY

(4.1–6)

[1] **I, the Lord's prisoner, exhort you therefore**
  to live worthy of the calling with which you were called,
[2]   **with all humility and gentleness,**
    with patience,
    paying attention to one another in love,
  working zealously to preserve the unity of the Spirit
    by means of the peace that binds.
[4] **One body and**
  one Spirit
    just as you were also called in one hope of your calling,
[5] **one Lord**
  one faith
  one baptism
[6] **one God and Father of all**
    who is over all
      and through all
      and in all.

4.1–6 contains three brief sections: v. 1 reminds us again that Paul is a prisoner and employs one of his favourite phrases for introducing ethical instruction; vv. 2, 3 set out in a general way how readers are to respond if the unity of the church is to be preserved; vv. 4–6 pick up the theme of unity, providing a series of declarations in each of which unity is stressed through the use of the word **one** and God's total government through the use of **all**.

Verses 4–6 are so tightly structured that they raise the question whether they, or some part of them, were pre-existing material. There can be little doubt that v. 6 could have existed as a liturgical unit since similar units are found elsewhere in early Christianity, in pre-Pauline Judaism and in the Gentile world. Most modern commentators accept v. 5 as tradition though not necessarily previously linked with v. 6; they hesitate however over v. 4. Supposing there was a formula involving all vv. 4–6, it would have run:

one body, one Spirit, one hope,
one Lord, one faith, one baptism,
one God and Father of all,
    who is over all and through all and in all.

Such a formulation has a clear structure containing seven (a favourite number in religion and magic) units with the final unit containing three (again another favourite number) units. AE requires to tie this formula into his argument; he has already associated hope and calling in 1.18 and so he writes v. 4b in order to create a link with v. 1, and, since the balance of the structure has now been disturbed, he adds 'and' between body and Spirit. **Body** is the only word in the whole formula which is important for him at this point in his argument. Vv. 5, 6 are not strictly relevant to what he is about to say, and it is difficult to see why they should have been introduced unless they already formed part of a statement known to his readers and therefore could not easily have been omitted.

It is impossible to determine the role such a formula would have played in the early church for very little is known about its life and worship. Baptism is too minor an element in the formula for us to be sure it was a baptismal hymn or confession or that it was used in catechetical instruction.

The statement is designed for internal Christian usage rather than to help non-believers to clarify the distinction between Christianity and their religions. In the light of its employment of **body** as indicating the body of Christ, the origin of the statement probably lay in the Pauline school. Though it contains the terms Lord, Spirit, God the Father it is not however to be taken as a deliberate Trinitarian formulation; this would be more likely if both Spirit and Lord had headed their triads and the order had been Father, Lord, Spirit. The existence of other elements between the terms also spoils any idea of a Trinitarian formulation. Yet even if our formula was not deliberately Trinitarian, it strongly influenced the language of later creeds, particularly those of the Eastern church.

1. A strong connection is made through **therefore** (cf Rom 12.1; 1 Th 4.1; Col 3.1) with the preceding three chapters, and not just with 3.14–21 as Ellicott suggests. AE has told his readers of their redemption in Christ with whom they have been raised and sit in the heavenlies so that although once Gentiles they now have equal place with Jews in the church, the body of Christ. Their behaviour, to which the remainder of the letter will be devoted, should correspond with their position. 4.1 thus governs all that follows; the 'good works' of 2.10 are now to be detailed.

I exhort you was an epistolary formula sometimes used by those in authority writing to others whom for diplomatic reasons they did not wish to order. It is thus weaker and more friendly than 'command', 'instruct' (cf Philem 8ff). Paul uses it regularly writing, for example, from the position of a parent (1 Th 2.7) and AE has adopted it from him. Prisoners can hardly order others. The meaning here lies in the area, 'beseech, exhort', yet also carrying latent or implicit authority which the explicit personal pronoun **I** serves to stress. Normally Paul associates 'brother' with the phrase (Rom 12.1; 15.32; 16.17; 1 Cor 16.15; 1 Th 4.10; 5.14) but this is a word which is lacking as an address in Ephesians. Its absence enhances the authority and diminishes the friendliness of the phrase.

Unlike most instances of the formula, its subject is here emphatically identified (only elsewhere at 2 Cor 10.1; Philem 9), **I, the prisoner of the Lord**. Prisoners do not normally exercise authority; but Paul had authority within the church, because of his connection with the Lord, and he was suffering for his readers' Lord (cf Hugedé); but AE is not attempting to win their sympathy by recalling his imprisonment (contrast Ign *Trall* 12.2).

The readers are summoned **to live** in a manner appropriate to their calling, as Paul himself does as a prisoner. Believers have not been called because they have lived worthily, but now that they have been called, **worthy** living should be their appropriate response. To live worthily is not just to live morally; there are two great commandments and worthy living relates as much to the first as to the second. The nature of worthy living is outlined first in 4.2f and then throughout the remaining paraenesis.

AE uses here both the verb 'to call' and its cognate noun as in 1.6, 19, 20; 2.4: **the calling with which you were called.** This helps to emphasise the fact of their calling by God who is the unspoken subject (cf 1 Th 2.12; Gal 1.6; 1 Cor 1.9; Rom 11.29). The Gentile readers are only where they are as believers and members of the people of God because God has acted. Their calling is not to a special position or function within the church (Rom 1.1; 1 Cor 1.1) but to being Christians (Rom 8.28, 30; 9.11, 24; 1 Cor 1.9; 1 Th 4.7; Eph 1.18) and is closely related to their election (1.4). They are reminded here of their entry into the Christian life through their conversion/baptism. Since Christians are not isolated, their calling is a calling to be with other Christians (Col 3.15; cf 1 Cor 1.2; Rom 1.7) and so it is again referred to when the discussion of the church is taken up in 4.4. AE does not enter into the philosophical question of the relation of calling to the freedom of those who are called, but his later stress on conduct shows that he does not regard the call as affecting freedom of action.

2. In vv. 2, 3 AE outlines in general terms the nature of worthy living in relation to life within the Christian community rather than within society as a whole. The structure consists of two prepositions **with** (two virtues), **with** (a third virtue), followed by two parallel participial clauses: **paying attention to one another ...** and **working zealously to preserve ...** The three qualities or virtues highlighted by AE in the prepositional phrases are the final three in a sequence of five in Col 3.12 (see also Mt 11.29 for two of them); they are probably therefore a part of the paraenetic tradition (cf Halter). Vv. 2f assume unity exists and exhort those who enjoy it to maintain it.

It is the relationship of members to one another that is above all important in what is to follow. AE emphasises his first two qualities through the use of **all** ('every kind of ...'), a favourite of his for this purpose (cf 1.8; 3.19; 4.19, 31; 5.3; 6.18).

The first virtue in the list would probably have surprised Gentile readers when as Christians they first encountered it. Normally the root carries in Greek the derogatory sense of servility; for example, in Epictetus 3.24.56 the word we have translated as

humility heads a list of qualities which cannot be commended. However the root, through its use in the LXX and Jewish Greek (Ψ 17.28; 33.19; 101.18; Prov 3.34), took on the meaning of non-assertiveness, and this is the more normal sense in the NT (Mt 11.29; Rom 12.16; 2 Cor 7.6; Phil 2.8;1 Pet 5.5; in Mt 23.12; Lk 14.11; 18.14 it has both senses) and is the meaning in our verse. Though often used to describe a proper relationship to God, in v. 2 the root is used of the relationship of Christians to one another. Nothing is more destructive of group unity than that some should assert either themselves or their particular point of view. The same concern for unity governs the use of **humility** in Phil 2.3 (see also 1QS 2.24f; 4.3; 5.3 though of course the Greek word is not used in these cases) and is continued in 1 Clem 16.1, 17; 30.3, 8. True humility ensures the absence of the envy which can corrupt corporate activity and Jesus is its prime example (Mk 10.45), though it would be wrong to imagine that AE is actually thinking here of Jesus' earthly example; when his humility is stressed in the Pauline corpus, it relates to his descent from heaven (2 Cor 8.9; Phil 2.5, 8). The belief that they are among the saved and elect has sometimes made some Christians arrogant in relation to those they consider not to be saved. Humility is not self-depreciation, nor the suppression of the feeling, 'I'm important'; it is regarding oneself as unimportant because in the end one is so in relation to the group; it leads to recognising the genuine Christian existence of others and their importance.

The second term, **gentleness**, in v. 2a is also joined with the first in Mt 11.29; Col 3.12. Like the first it was used in biblical Greek but, unlike it, had a good sense in non-biblical Greek and is commended by secular authors (e.g. Aristotle, *Nic Eth* 1125B, IV 5; M. Aurelius, 9.42). In the NT it is often depicted as the virtue with which to approach opponents and those who have strayed from the faith (1 Cor 4.21; 2 Cor 10.1; Gal 6.1; 2 Tim 2.25) and also the quality with which to treat those outside the church (Tit 3.2; 1 Pet 3.15). Though often rendered 'meekness' this is too passive a rendering for the present context; 'gentleness' suggests more adequately the manner with which other members of the church should be treated. A fruit of the Spirit (Gal 5.23) it is active in promoting unity and does not just seek to avoid trouble by ignoring what is wrong or taking things lying down. Such a gentleness towards others comes in part from an awareness of one's own sin.

The second prepositional phrase, v. 2b, contains only one quality, **patience**. The word was used in the LXX to describe God's merciful way with sinful humanity; he is patient and not easily angered (Exod 34.6; Num 14.18; Ψ 85.15; 102.8). This use reappears in the NT (Lk 15.7; Rom 2.4; 9.22; 1 Pet 3.20). Such a quality is necessary also within a community (cf 1 Th 5.14; 2 Tim 4.2); those who display it do not increase bitterness and its exercise should lead to the dissolution of existing tensions. It is an aspect of love (1 Cor 13.4) and a fruit of the Spirit (Gal 5.22), and God strengthens believers to practise it (Col 1.11).

Of the three virtues expressed here none is peculiarly Christian; the second and third are found in the contemporary secular society, and the first in Judaism.

In vv. 2b, 3 there is a change to participial clauses. Verse 2b with its implication of reciprocity, **one another**, makes it clear that AE is thinking primarily of behaviour within the community and not of that directed at those outside it. While the participle translated **paying attention to** could suggest an attitude of endurance, a resignation to suffering, or a willingness to tolerate what others are doing in order to avoid trouble, it indicates here the more dynamic attitude of love (it reappears in v. 16). Love is never passive but always active, looking to see where others may be helped. It is the primary virtue in relationships (1 Cor 13) and the basis of all behaviour (Rom 13.9, 10; Gal 5.14). No one ever finds it easy to see and allow for the point of view and the actions of others; within the community Christians do not escape this but have regularly to deal with what they regard as the faults of their fellow-Christians and for this love is essential.

3. The second participial clause, the fourth member of the general introductory exhortation, moves from the qualities of character which work for unity to a plea for its preservation; if unity needs to be preserved it must already exist; it does so in respect of Jewish and Gentile Christians (2.11–22) but the outlook here is wider and refers as much to Jewish–Jewish and Gentile–Gentile relations as to Jewish–Gentile relations. While parallel to the participial clause of v. 2b, v. 3 is also to some extent its result and a suitable climax to the phrases of v. 2 (Schlier;

Schnackenburg). Those who pay attention to one another in love will work zealously to preserve **unity**. Unity (only here in the NT and in 4.13; the word is found regularly in Ignatius, e.g. *Eph* 4.2; 5.1; 14.1; *Philad* 2.2; 3.2; 5.2), is something which Christians already possess; they are one body (4.4). They did not create their unity, though they can destroy it; the later parts of the paraenesis show how this can happen. Effort is necessary to maintain unity and believers must strive to this end with all zeal. **Working zealously** implies an active and vigorous effort (cf Gal 2.10; 2 Tim 2.15).

In v. 2 **love** gave believers the means of living harmoniously with one another; here unity is preserved **by means of the peace that binds**. Love (v. 2) may be the assumption for unity; peace is the cement of its working out in the church. Christ became the peace of the church in his death (2.14–18) and only because he is peace can there be peace between members and unity within the church. 2.14–18 revealed the two aspects of peace, between God and humanity and between one human being and another. It is the latter aspect which enters here but it is in tandem with the former and depends on it.

4. The style now changes abruptly. While a few commentators (Dibelius; Gaugler) have understood vv. 4–6 as imperatival ('there ought to be one body') and thus as continuing the exhortation, it is better to take vv. 4–6 as preparation for what is to follow in vv. 7–16 and as continuing the theme of unity which is already present. AE probably uses, as we have argued, an existing section of tradition and by using all of it, though it may not all be strictly relevant, he awakens echoes in the minds of his readers, echoes centring on **one** and therefore on unity. In style vv. 4–6 are an acclamation or declaration.

The first phrase **one body** recalls 2.16; Col 3.15; Rom 12.5, and there can be no doubt that AE understands it to refer to the church and not to the eucharistic or physical body of Christ. It suitably heads the list since what follows relates to the church and life within it. Normally when AE speaks of the body he makes a close reference, if not a direct one, to Christ, so that the body is identifiable as his (cf 1.23; 2.16; 4.12, 16; 5.23, 30); the absence of such a reference here probably arises from the use of tradition (Schnackenburg). But why *one* ('one' implies 'one only') body?

Ephesians is not a polemical writing contrasting the body of genuine believers with another of heretics claiming to be the only true body. Perhaps the emphasis on 'one' is in contrast with the variety within the body to which AE will go on (vv. 7–16; cf Rom 12.5; 1 Cor 12.12ff). The body is one over against this variety, yet this would be an unusual use of 'one'.

The body and the Spirit had been already connected in 1 Cor 12.13 and lie closely together in Eph 2.16, 18 (cf 2.22); the variety of gifts which exist in the body come from the Spirit (1 Cor 12–14). It is not then surprising to find here the Spirit associated with the body, though we should not think in anthropological terms of a spirit within a body, for the existence of charismatic gifts, though not expressly ascribed to the Spirit, appears in vv. 7–13.

In the clause **just as you were called in hope of your calling** AE has rewritten the original tradition (one body, one Spirit, one hope) in such a way as to connect the tradition to what preceded. AE's readers received their hope simultaneously with their call. They are not called to hope but as those who have been called given hope. Previously as Gentiles they had been without hope (2.12); now hope is a part of their inheritance (1.18). 'Hope' is not the feeling of hopefulness but is the content of their hope (*res sperata*).

5. The title **Lord** was applied to Jesus prior to Paul as its use in pre-Pauline material shows (Rom 10.9; Phil 2.11; 1 Cor 8.6; 12.3). Some of the statements where the term is used may have been confessional formulae associated with baptism. As there is no identification of 'Lord' here, the origin of our triad probably does not lie in a confessional statement intended for use by those becoming Christians, despite its reference to baptism. It is a statement for internal church use. It may be that we should see in it the church's acknowledgement that it has only one Lord over against other religions which may have many.

Faith has been understood here as the trust which believers have in Christ or as their personal faithfulness (e.g. Alford; Macpherson; Salmond; Hendriksen) but much more probably it denotes the content of their faith. It is true this is not the normal Pauline sense but he does give it this significance in Rom 1.5; 10.8; Gal 1.23; 3.23ff, and it becomes increasingly frequent in the later NT writings (Col 1.23; 2.7; 1 Tim 3.9; 4.1, 6). The content of the faith while in a sense invariant has always to be expressed in words and in relation to a particular context. Ephesians itself is an expression of the faith set in the context of ecclesiology. There is *one* faith, yet it has many verbal expressions.

The **one baptism** is obviously the Christian initiatory rite of water baptism and not Spirit baptism, though of course the two cannot be dissociated. The first two terms of v. 5 are linked to the third in so far as believers are baptised in, or into (the name of Christ) the Lord (Acts 8.16; 19.5) and confess their faith in him through a form of words containing the term **Lord** (e.g. Rom 10.9, 10). Baptism is also linked to the **Spirit** and the **body** (1 Cor 12.13), for believers become members of the body on being baptised and thereafter the Spirit dwells in them (1 Cor 3.16; Rom 8.9) and they participate in the gifts of the Spirit (1 Cor 12.7). As baptised they are now united with one another (1 Cor 12.12f; Gal 3.26ff). They now also have a **hope** which was not theirs as unconverted Gentiles. Why should the baptism be described as *one*? It can hardly be one in contrast with the washings of Qumran (cf Heb 6.2), the Mystery Religions, or gnosticism (Iren *adv Haer* 1.21.2); nor does 'one' mean 'once for all', i.e. that it is unrepeatable, a position occasionally adopted by paedo-baptists against anabaptists, for as an initiatory rite that is implicit; 'one' is not also an attempt to assert that believers are all baptised with the same baptism (Van Roon, Grosheide), and it does not refer to some all-inclusive act of Christ in his baptism and death. Probably AE uses it because it was already present in the formula; it may have served there to preserve the formula's symmetry. This is the only place in Ephesians where baptism is directly mentioned and it does not provide a sufficient basis for regarding the letter as, or as embodying, a baptismal tract, let alone for regarding vv. 4–6 as a baptismal confession.

6. This is the climax of the sequence, the **one God and Father**, who is the one God of one people (cf Josephus *Ant* 4.201). There can be little doubt that **one** is here intended to make a monotheistic assertion and such an assertion would have been important for Gentile Christians (cf Rom 3.30; 1 Cor 8.4–6; Gal 3.20; 1 Tim 2.5; Jas 2.19), though unnecessary for Jewish Christians whose basic text was Dt 6.4. It also came naturally to Jews to think of

God as Father, though this received a new emphasis and direction in the teaching of Jesus. Gentile Christians thus encountered God as Father from the beginning, yet since the idea was not entirely missing from Greek, in particular Stoic, thought, they were conditioned to accept it, even though they had previously understood it in a more pantheistic way. The association of God and Father is found regularly in the Pauline corpus (Rom 1.7; 15.6; 1 Cor 1.3; 2 Cor 1.2, 3; 11.31; Gal 1.3; Eph 1.3), with the words often linked by **and**.

In the teaching of Jesus God's Fatherhood sets him in relation to all humanity. Is that the meaning here? In the Pauline corpus God's Fatherhood is generally seen as relating Christ to believers. Normally this limitation arises from the context and we cannot conclude that for Paul God's Fatherhood does not extend to non-believers, if only in a potential manner. In the confessional formulae of 1 Cor 8.6 God is presented as Father in relation to all things. To what then does **of all** refer here? It can be either neuter or masculine. Whatever is decided it is probably correct to see a consistent gender throughout v. 6 (*pace* Iren *adv Haer* 2.2.6; 4.20.2). Favouring the masculine (Haupt; Dibelius; Gaugler; Schlier; Schnackenburg) is the general context relating to the unity of believers in the church and the immediately following **to each one of us** (v. 7) which can be regarded as individualising the preceding **all**. Favouring the neuter understanding (Robinson; Houlden; Gnilka; Barth; Lincoln; Lindemann) are: (i) the parallel Greek formulae which certainly relate to the cosmos and not to humanity (e.g. M. Aurelius 7.9); (ii) the relation in Jewish Hellenism of a cosmic fatherhood to God's role in creation (Philo, *Post Cain* 6; *Rer Div* 62; *Det Pot* 147; *Ebr* 147), though this is not viewed pantheistically as in Hellenism (cf Conzelmann); (iii) NT passages such as 1 Cor 8.6; Rom 11.36; Col 1.16; (iv) the cosmic use of **all** at other places in Ephesians (1.10, 22, 23; 3.9; 4.10); (v) the cosmic role of the church in Ephesians (cf 3.10). In the end it is probably better to give **all** a neuter meaning throughout with the sense, 'one creator God and Father who governs the cosmos, works through it and is present in it', but the sense might be 'one God and Father of humanity (or all Christians) who governs all, works through them all and is in them all' (presumably by means of his Spirit, Rom 8.9, 11; 1 Cor 3.15; 6.19; 2 Cor 6.16; Gal 3.5).

When we look back over vv. 4–6 we can see that there was a constant difficulty in determining the precise significance of the 'one' attached to each noun. Only in v. 6 can we be sure why it is used, as a rejection of multiplicity, yet it is hardly possible to see this meaning as intended throughout. It may be best to see the use of 'one' as no more than a rhetorical device to hold the sequence together. Examples of its use in this way can be found in ancient literature, e.g. Orphic Frag 168 lines 6f (see O. Kern *Orphicorum Fragmenta, Berlin*, 1922); Plut, *Mor* 329AB; 983C; *Thes* 24.1; M. Aurelius 7.9; *CH* 11.11; Epictetus, 3.24.10. Brief lists appear in Jewish literature, 2 *Bar* 48.24; Josephus, *c. Ap.* 2.193; *Ant* 4.200f. The use also appears in early Christian literature: 1 Clem 46.6; Ign *Magn* 7.1, 2; *Philad* 4; Hermas, *Sim* 9.17.4; 18.4. In 1 Clem 46.6 where we have successively God, Christ, Spirit, calling, we may suspect rather than dependence on Ephesians the existence of the list of Eph 4.4–6 in a variant form, thus confirming that it pre-existed Ephesians.

B

UNITY AND GROWTH OF THE CHURCH

(4.7–16)

7 Grace has been given to each one of us
    in accordance with the measure of the gift of Christ;
8   therefore it says:
        Ascending on high he led captives captive;
        he gave gifts to men.
9   And what significance has 'He ascended'
        unless he also descended into the lower regions,
            that is, the earth?
10   He who descended is himself also the one who ascended
            above all the heavens,
        so that he might fill all things.
11 And he gave some as apostles, others as prophets, others as
        evangelists, others as shepherds and teachers,
12   for the equipment of the saints,
        for their ministering activity,
        for the building up of the body of Christ,
13   until we all attain
          to the unity of faith and knowledge of the son of
            God,
          to a mature male,
          to the measure of the size of fullness of Christ,
14   that you may no longer be children,
        tossed by the waves,
        and blown about by every wind of teaching,
        by human trickery cunningly pointed towards the
          planning of error,
15   rather speaking truth in love
        let us grow in every respect unto him.
        who is the head, Christ,

16   **from whom the whole body.**
    fitted and held together
      through every ligament of supply,
       in a powerful manner,
       in the proportion of each individual member,
   makes its increase
     unto its own upbuilding in love.

At v.7 AE changes from the second person plural to the first, returning to the latter at v. 17. Vv. 7–16 are consequently a distinct unit and this is emphasised by the use of the same expression (but translated diffently: **each one of us; each individual**) in both v. 7 and v. 16 (an *inclusio*). The movement from the second to the first person is similar to that in 2.14–18; in each case AE wishes to identify Paul, or himself, with his readers (cf 2.3). With the use of the first person plural the direct paraenetic element appears to disappear, but it is implied throughout since the duties laid down for 'us' are obviously duties laid on the readers.

We move from the stress on unity (vv. 4–6) to diversity in vv. 7–10, but unity returns as the prevailing theme in vv. 11–16. A true unity will not be monolithic (Bouwman) but will contain variety within itself, as Paul had already stressed in 1 Cor 12.12–31; Rom 12.3–8. The unity in question is of course that of the church, though strangely the word church is not itself used in this paragraph. Underlying it is the image of the body of Christ, though this concept is not made explicit until v. 12. AE does not need to explain it, for he can presume the familiarity of his readers with it through its use by Paul.

One was the term echoing through vv. 4–6; v. 7 continues it with **each one** (cf v. 16) and in this way links together unity and diversity. But the **one** of v. 7 also introduces a new turn of thought in setting out the diversity as deriving from the variety of gifts among the members of the church. This variety is not that of natural talent, educational attainment or cultural variation, but has its source in Christ the giver of the gifts of vv. 7, 8, 11. Members do not bring with them the gifts which AE has in mind when they enter the church, but on entering receive them. These gifts are not given for self-promotion, but for the building up the church in unity. The giving of the gifts is supported in v. 8 with a quotation seemingly drawn from Ps 68.18 to which is added a midrashic-type interpretation (vv. 9f); as an exegetical excursus it enables the quotation to be applied to Christ. It might seem that vv. 8–10 could be omitted without disturbing the flow of the argument, but if they were v. 11 would jar with v. 7 in that, unlike the latter, it offers a limited range of gifts to a minority of believers. The gifts went unidentified in v. 7; v. 11 specifies them, not as functions to be exercised, but as 'officials' who are given to the church. This variation causes some problems. The function of these officials towards other believers is then expressed (v. 12) and also the goal for all to aim at, first positively (v.13) and then negatively (v. 14). All of vv. 12–16 depend on v. 11. The naming of the office-bearers indicates a distinction between them and ordinary members of the church, a distinction which later developed into that between clergy and laity, though in no way does AE demean or devalue the ordinary or lay members of the church. In a sense vv. 7–14 are descriptive; the direct paraenetic element reappears in vv. 15, 16 though it was latent throughout. Vv. 11–16 are one sentence and provide another example of AE's complex and unwieldy style in which prepositional phrases intermingle with subordinate clauses and participles.

The unity which belongs to the church has not come because it has harmonised itself to the norms of society, or subjected itself to the powers, or accepted false teaching, or undervalued its own diversity, but arises out of its position in relation to God and Christ (vv. 4–6); the church may have an organisation but it is not simply a social organisation; it is the body of Christ.

7. The move to the first person plural shows that Paul himself, or AE, is to be included within the process by which the whole church is built up into a unity. But is Paul included as Christian or apostle, AE as Christian or teacher?

Does the introduction of the first person plural mean that all believers are included or only those listed in v. 11? The main argument (cf Schlier; Mussner; Merklein) in favour of the restriction of v. 7 to specified leaders is the direct move from v. 7 to v. 11 with nothing intervening to suggest a change in respect of those in mind.

However, there are positive arguments in favour of taking v. 7 to refer to all believers, with the vast majority of commentators.

(i) Elsewhere charismatic gifts are given to all Christians and not office-bearers alone (Rom 12.6–8; 1 Cor 12.28–30; 1 Pet 4.10f). (ii) V. 7 differs strikingly from v. 11 in that in the former gifts are given to people, in the latter the gifts are the people. (iii) The paraenesis of the letter is addressed elsewhere to all believers except where it is made clear that limited groups are in mind (e.g. in 5.22–6.9); in particular 4.2, 3 apply to all believers. (iv) Vv. 13ff refer to all believers and this is a return to vv. 7–10. (v) The existence of ministry is not a major theme in Ephesians; for example, the readers are never instructed to obey ministers. Perhaps AE inserted v. 7 so that no one should be envious either of those named in v. 11 or of their roles.

Grace is used here in relation not to redemptive grace as in 2.5, 8 but to special graces, an extension of its use in 3.2, 7, 8 of Paul's ministry; Paul had already used this sense (Rom 12.6). Only those receiving redemptive grace receive charismatic graces. **Grace** by its nature is a gift and its given nature is stressed through the verb **has been given** whose subject is probably Christ since he is the giver in v. 8; in Rom 12.3ff and 1 Cor 12.28ff God is the giver; in 1 Cor 12.4–11 the Spirit is the giver; the position of Christ is thus emphasised here. The grace is given according to the **measure**. The word appears twice more in our passage (vv. 13, 16) but only twice elsewhere in Paul (Rom 12.3; 2 Cor 10.13), and has probably the sense 'full measure'. The giving is not random but in accordance with Christ's plan; he apportions gifts to believers. Graces are not given because of an existing degree of faith in believers; they are gifts, not the result of works (cf Origen; Chrysostom).

8. Though AE often quotes without giving any indication that he is doing so (e.g. 4.25; 5.31; 6.2f), his **therefore it says** here makes it clear that he is consciously citing. A number of questions at once raise themselves: From where does he cite? Why does he do so? What is the subject of **says**?

We commence with the last question. Paul uses this verb, or an equivalent, to introduce OT quotations; he normally specifies the subject: scripture in Rom 4.3; 9.17; 10.11; Gal 4.30; God in Rom 9.15; 2 Cor 6.16; David in Rom 4.6f; 11.9; Isaiah in Rom 10.16; 15.12; Hosea in Rom 11.25. Only 2 Cor 6.2 (cf Jas 4.6) has a simple **it says**; and Rom 15.10 **it is written**. At first sight 4.8 appears to be a quotation from Ps 68.18 but this is not so, for there is not only the major variation from 'receiving' to 'giving' but also minor variations. Such changes take place regularly when the NT quotes the OT; and passages originally referring to Yahweh are regularly applied as here to Christ. This problem about the quotation of Ps 68.18 is not unique. When James cites Amos 9.11f in Acts 15.15ff, he is presented as quoting it in its LXX form because only the LXX version supports his argument; the LXX form probably arose out of a mistranslation of the Hebrew; but which is scripture, MT or LXX? James, or the author of Acts, certainly regards what he cites as scripture as the introductory formula ('as it is written') shows.

The same change of meaning in the verb is present in the Targum of Ps 68. The targums were renderings into Aramaic enabling those who spoke Aramaic but not Hebrew to understand Synagogue readings.

The targum version of Ps 68.18 runs as follows,

You ascended the firmament, Prophet Moses; you took captivity captive;

you learned the words of the Law; you gave them as gifts to the sons of man.

Here Moses receives the Law and gives it to Israel; while 'sons of man' might indicate humanity as a whole it should probably be understood as referring to the Jews. It is clear v. 8 is no more a quotation of the targum than it is of the MT or the LXX; it differs from the targum in rejecting the references to Moses and the Law and in its second line it has only one action on the part of Christ ('giving') unlike the two of Moses. There is some evidence supporting the targumic understanding of the Psalm in other Jewish sources (*Midr Ps* 68 §11, 160a; *Exod* R 28.1; *Ab R Nathan* 2 (2a); cf SB III, 596–8). Philo in featuring Moses gives him almost mystical significance and his writings might have been known to Greek Jews in Asia Minor. Justin Martyr, *Trypho* 39.4; 87.6, knows the form of Ps 68.18 as found in Ephesians but shows no sign of knowing Ephesians. The targumic tradition may thus have been early and fairly widespread.

There seem to be two possibilities: AE, or a predecessor, either replaced Yahweh with Christ in the Hebrew or LXX of the Psalm and at the same time altered the verb, or replaced Moses with Christ in the thought of the targum, and at the same time removed the mention of Moses, the Law and the reception of the Law. The second seems more probable, since to suppose that two independent thinkers altered the verb in the Psalm in the same way at or about the same time and one replaced Yahweh with Christ and the other introduced Moses is hard to credit. The targumic tradition may have been known among some Jews in Asia Minor from which it was picked up either by Gentile Christians or, much more probably, by Jewish Christians, and adapted to suit their purposes. All this suggests it is better to conjecture that AE himself did not alter the text but used a tradition known to him and his readers.

We have now answered the first and third of our initial questions. The second remains. From what we have said, AE at any rate uses the citation (did he realise it derived from Ps 68?) in order to confirm his statement of v. 7 and not in anticipation of v. 11, for in the latter verse God (Christ) does not give gifts to people but gives people to the church. It is also possible AE used it because he could develop it in relation to Christ's ascension, which he does in vv. 9f. It may have had an existing interpretation which he feels he ought to correct and therefore writes vv. 9f.

Who are the captives whom Christ leads captive? Since AE probably did not derive v. 8 directly from Ps 68, the Psalm can provide no answer. AE himself provides no explicit clues and perhaps it is wrong even to pose the question. The introductory participle is almost certainly to be taken to denote an action simultaneous with the main verb so that the captives are brought up with Christ as he ascends and are not found at the completion of the ascent. If his descent involves his journey to Hades, then he will have brought the captives from there and they may well be the souls of the dead, or, more generally, Satan's captives; this is the opinion of most of the Fathers. If the ascent is taken to be that to the cross (so Oecumenius; Ambrosiaster) in the light of Col 2.14f the captives would be the powers. If the descent of v. 9 is to earth in the incarnation and the ascent that of the ascension, then in the light of 1.21f the captives will again be the powers. This solution goes back as far as Irenaeus who calls them the rebellious angels (*Epid* 83). Even if AE does not identify the captives he does identify in vv. 7, 11 the booty, i.e. what the captor in accordance with ancient custom distributes to his accompanying army. The booty is either charismatic gifts (v. 7) or church leaders (v. 11), or more probably both.

9. The **ascending** of the quotation is now picked up and developed and we appear to be led away from the main theme of Christ's gifts to the church; we return to it in v. 11.

Christ is the subject of **he ascended** and therefore also of **he descended**: the same person ascends and descends. The idea of Christ's ascension (see on 1.20 for references) is common in the NT. It completes his incarnation in a victorious manner. If he ascended into heaven to where did he descend and when did he do so?

The almost unanimous answer of the Fathers was that Christ descended into Hades after his death, e.g. Irenaeus, *Epid* 83; Origen, *Exod Hom*, GCS 29, 198.2; Tertullian, *adv Praxean* 30; Chrysostom, Jerome (Theod Mops and Ambrose *Ep* 76.10 appear to be the only exceptions). They take **the lower regions** as the lower regions of the earth as indicating a place lower than the earth. In his ascent from Hades Christ brought with him the souls of the dead or the devil, death, sin, the curse. This view has also the support of some modern interpreters, e.g. Selwyn; Beare; Robinson; Arnold; A. T. Hanson. The Fathers found support for their idea that Christ after his death and prior to his resurrection made a journey to the place of the dead in 1 Pet 3.19 (they also often took Rom 10.6–8 in this way). The idea eventually became embedded in the Apostles' Creed, though actual evidence for its acceptance only begins to appear in the middle of the second century (Justin, *Trypho* 72; *Gospel of Peter* 10 (41f)). This implies a three-layer picture of the cosmos (heaven, earth, Hades) as in Phil 2.10; this is at variance with the picture elsewhere in Ephesians of two layers (heaven, earth) with the evil powers not below the earth but above it; they are subdued in heaven and not in Hades (cf 1.10, 20f; 2.2; 6.10 and see Detached Note: The Heavenlies).

If the lower parts of the earth are not the underworld they must be earth itself: **he descended into the lower regions, that is, the earth**; the contrast would be with heaven, earth being below heaven. At this point those who adhere to the theory of an ascent from earth diverge over the time and nature of the descent. Is the reference to the incarnation or to Pentecost?

The case for the latter has been argued vigorously and clearly by G. B. Caird and more recently by W. H. Harris. According to this theory Christ is viewed as ascending to heaven after the resurrection, descending at Pentecost with his gifts, and then ascending once again to heaven. This view succeeds in incorporating vv. 9,10 into the argument of the letter and does not leave them as a parenthesis. The theory is attractive but has its weaknesses. Perhaps the greatest difficulty for the theory, apart from its complexity (would Gentile Christians have been able to appreciate it without further explanation?), is the normal Christian association of the Spirit with a descent at Pentecost.

If Christ's descent is not then to the underworld and is not linked to Pentecost, it must be the descent of the incarnation. It is true that the word used to say he descended is an unusual word to denote this (it is applied to the parousia in 1 Th 4.16; cf Jas 1.17; Rev 3.12; 21.2, 10), but the incarnation as event is not often described in Paul. Even if this is the obvious solution it is still puzzling why the descent should be mentioned at all. The descent may be mentioned in preparation for v. 11 since it was the earthly Jesus who gave the apostles to the church.

10. We continue with the idea of the ascent and descent of Christ though these are now mentioned in reverse order (a chiastic arrangement, Lemmer).

That God sent Christ into the world or gave him to it was already accepted Pauline doctrine (Gal 4.4; Rom 8.3, 32; cf Jn 3.16f; 1 Jn 4.9f), but God is not depicted here as initiating the coming of Christ; Christ himself is responsible for his descent (cf Phil 2.6–8) just as he is for his ascent. If Christ descended this necessarily implies his pre-existence. Christ's ascent is said here to be **above the heavens** (cf Heb 7.26) and not into the heavens (Acts 1.10), leaving the impression that AE conceived of him as passing through the heavens to something above and beyond them (see Detached Note: The Heavenlies for the varying ideas about heaven in the NT). The Hebrew word for heaven is a plural and this leads sometimes to the use of the plural in the NT where we would expect the singular; this cannot be the case here for the qualification **all the heavens** implies a multiplicity of heavenly regions. This multiplicity was already a part of Pauline thought (cf 2 Cor 12.2).

The chiastic arrangement of ascent and descent in vv. 9, 10ab sets off 10c by itself: **so that he might fill all things**. It supplies either the purpose of the ascent or, possibly, its consequence. We are led back to 1.20–3, and in particular to 1.23 where Christ was seen to fill the church and to be himself filled by God. Here Christ fills **all things** (cf 1.22) which can only mean the cosmos and not the church (*pace* Grotius; Beza). God's filling the universe (see on 1.23) was a concept acceptable to Jewish Hellenism (Jer 23.24; Wisd 1.7; Philo, *Leg Alleg* 3.4; *Post Cain* 30; *Somn* 2.220–1; *Conf Ling* 136). In addition Gewiess argues that God's transcendence, power and rule are also found associated with his filling all things in Philo, *Post Cain* 14; *Gigant* 47; *Mos* 2.238. Jer 23.24 speaks of God filling heaven and earth and Jer 23.25ff goes on to speak of his power. Power is also naturally associated with exaltation to a high position. The concept of Christ's presence in every part of the universe was developed in *Gos Thom* §77 = II, 2 46.23–8 and Pap Oxyr 1. AE differs here both from Judaism in that Christ and not God fills the universe and from his own statement in 1.23 where Christ fills the church. The former alteration is acceptable in the light of the way the NT transfers functions ascribed to God in the OT to Christ. The latter accords with the cosmic position AE attributes to Christ in 1.10 and with his rule over the hostile powers. Granted this understanding of v. 10c, how does it fit into the argument? It does not lead on naturally to v. 11, for Christ fills the universe with his presence and not his gifts or blessings. It may not be intended to fit in with the argument but be an aside by AE to provide a fitting conclusion to vv. 9f; it thus leaves him free to return to his main theme; people sometimes write in this kind of way.

11. Another of AE's long intricate sentences begins here and runs through to the end of v. 16. Vv. 9f were in effect a commentary on the first line of the quotation in v. 8 and vv. 11–16 are a commentary on its second. An emphatic word for **he** picks up the same word in v. 10a: the giver is the one of whom we have just been speaking. **He gave** picks up the use of the same verb in vv. 7f, retaining its normal sense of 'give' and not 'appoint' (*pace* Van Roon; Roberts; see on 1.22). The church does not create its own leaders; Christ, not God as in 1 Cor 12.28, does so (Schlatter).

The gifts are not gifts made to people but gifts of people, people who have a particular role to play in the church; it may be assumed however that the charisma appropriate to the role which each is to play will have been bestowed (Calvin). It is not suggested that every believer will be one of these people, a change of emphasis from v. 7, and a change already foreshadowed in 1 Cor 12.4–30; that passage began by enumerating the various charismata with which different members of the community might be endowed, but ended by enumerating identifiable leaders, apostles, prophets, teachers (1 Cor 12.28a); Paul apparently then ran out of 'titles' and continued by listing functions. Since none of the 'titles' is explained in 1 Corinthians, we may assume that Paul's readers were familiar with them. The same must be true of the titles mentioned in our verse in respect of AE and his readers. There is no need to cross-identify his titles with those in other parts of the NT (e.g. the bishops and deacons of Phil 1.1) or with those which the later church came to use. In the first century the situation in respect of ministry was fluid; it was only after AE's time that titles and the functions attached to them began to harden. This fluidity of ministry makes it impossible to use AE's titles to date his letter. The titles are not mutually exclusive; Paul is termed both apostle and teacher in 1 Tim 2.7 (cf Acts 15.35). Indeed AE does nothing to differentiate from one another the functions of those he lists. AE limits his list to five names, three of which were mentioned in 1 Cor 12.28.

If AE is Paul he would have classed himself among the apostles (cf 1.1) even though in 3.3 he sees some distinction between himself and the other apostles; he differed from them in that he had been called by the exalted Lord and not by the earthly Jesus as they were. If AE is not Paul doubtless he would have placed Paul in the same category; but where would he have placed himself? As evangelist, shepherd, teacher? It is impossible to say for, as we shall see, the roles are not clearly distinguishable.

In 1 Cor 12.28 as here the list is extended beyond apostles and prophets. Here the first additional category is that of the evangelist. We need to be careful not to read modern usages of this term back into Ephesians. It does not refer to: (i) the authors of the Gospels; it only obtained that sense later; the first evidence is found in Hippolytus, *De Antichristo* 56 and Tertullian, *Adv Praxean* 23; (ii) those who conduct missions in existing Christian countries; (iii) those who travel as missionaries taking the gospel into fresh areas, though Eusebius applies it to them (*HE* 1.13.4;

198

3.37.2; 5.10.2; etc.); in this sense evangelists have been regarded as successors to the apostles.

The NT mentions evangelists only twice elsewhere. In Acts 21.8 Philip whose work as a travelling missionary is recorded in Acts 8.4ff is described as one, yet in Acts 21.8 he is not a traveller but has an established home where his family live with him. In 2 Tim 4.5 Timothy is told to do the work of an evangelist and this appears to be equated with fulfilling his ministry and not be the title of an office. 1, 2 Timothy show what Timothy was expected to do; he is to remain at Ephesus (1 Tim 1.3) and exercise a ministry among established Christians; 2 Tim 4.2 sums up his ministry and confines it to one within the church. This is in line with the use of the word in Eph 4.11, for 4.12 shows that the ministry of those listed in 4.11 is directed towards believers. The NT use of the word then provides no evidence that it relates to a ministry outside the church. There is some confirmatory evidence that for a while the word continued to be applied to 'ministers' working within the church; 'readers' who did much more than read scripture aloud in services of worship were sometimes termed 'evangelists'. This conclusion that part of the ministry of evangelists concerns life inside the community as well as, possibly, recruitment to it accords with what follows in v. 12 where the ministry of all five named officials is directed towards the community. Of course it would also be wrong to exclude evangelists from work directed towards unbelievers; as preachers they go both to the unconverted and the converted (Belser). Paul the apostle exercised that same dual role and in that sense evangelists might be regarded as successors to the apostles.

The use of a single article links the final two names in the list, **shepherds and teachers**. Are there here two groups of people each fulfilling a separate and distinct role, or one group of people exercising two roles? This question can only be answered after the two roles have been identified.

Teachers are listed after apostles and prophets in 1 Cor 12.28 (cf 14.26) and their work appears among the charismata of Rom 12.7. Not everyone would possess the charisma of teaching; the existence of 'specialist' teachers is confirmed by Gal 6.6; Jas 3.1; *Barn* 1.8; 4.9; Hermas, *Sim* 9.15.4. Teaching is set out as an important part of the work of Timothy and Titus (e.g. 1 Tim 4.6,

11, 13, 16; Tit 2.1, 7). Teachers will have both transmitted and interpreted tradition from the OT and earlier Christians (cf Rom 6.17; 1 Cor 4.17; Col 2.7; 2 Th 2.15) and drawn new lessons from it for fresh situations. Their task however will have gone beyond the imparting of information and the opening up of new ways of thought and have included exhortation to live by what they taught. Gentiles will have had much to learn when they became Christians; in 4.20 AE writes of 'learning' Christ. Apart from designated teachers all Christians were also expected to be active in teaching (Heb 5.12; Col 3.16).

This seems relatively clear but the same cannot be said of **shepherds**. It is best to translate this as 'shepherds', so retaining the original underlying image and avoiding all the overtones in the modern use of 'pastor'. The shepherd image probably entered Jewish thought from its use in the Near East of rulers who led their people, and then was adopted by Christians. It was an obvious metaphor easily understood by AE's Gentile readers. In the OT it was applied to God (Gen 49.24; Ps 23.1; 80.1; Isa 40.11) denoting his care and protection of his people (cf 1 Sam 17.34ff) and in the NT transferred to Christ (1 Pet 2.25; Heb 13.20; Jn 10.1–10; Mk 6.34; 14.27: Mt 25.32). It was applied in the OT to the leaders of Israel (2 Sam 5.2; Ps 78.71; Jer 2.8; 3.15; Ezek 34.2), and in the NT to the leaders of the church (Jn 21.16; Acts 20.28; 1 Pet 5.2), with the church itself being described as a flock of sheep (Jn 10.2ff; 21.16; Acts 20.28; 1 Pet 5.2; cf Jer 23.2f; 50.6, 17). Eph 4.11 is the only NT passage where the noun is used of leaders. The image is vague; its OT and pre-OT usage would suggest that primary emphasis would lie on shepherds as those who led (the shepherd in the East did not drive his flock but led it), provided for and protected those in their care. Yet to carry out these duties would not shepherds in the church have had to preach and teach, i.e. to act similarly to evangelists and teachers? If it is necessary to differentiate between these groups, it is probably right to stress in the case of shepherds either their leadership or general oversight (Acts 20.28; 1 Pet 5.2; yet Jn 21.16 hardly relates to leadership or oversight). But it may be wrong to attempt to draw rigid distinctions between evangelists, shepherds and teachers; in the modern church every priest or minister exercises all three roles. Rather we should see evangelising, shepherding and teaching as three essential ministerial functions. Some distinction exists between evangelising on the one hand and shepherding and teaching on the other in that the latter two functions are exercised entirely within the community, but the other both inside and outside it.

Those holding office as evangelists, teachers and shepherds are clearly distinct from believers in general and are therefore in the nature of permanent 'officials'. By introducing 'officials' AE may be said to have hastened the division between clergy and laity, have begun the sacralisation of the ministry and have suggested that ministry of a permanent and non-spontaneous nature was necessary. We should note finally that AE offers no argument for the existence of ministry, implying that this was not an issue within the communities to which he was writing.

12. The purpose of Christ's gift of office-bearers to the church is now expressed through three prepositional phrases whose surface meanings are on the whole clear but whose interrelationship is difficult. We examine first the surface meanings of each phrase.

In v. 12 we have the only NT use of the noun we have translated **equipment**, although it could mean restoration, reconciliation or training, discipline. Restoration, if understood in the sense 'repair', is found in relation to the verb in Mt 4.21; Mk 1.19; 2 Cor 13.11; Gal 6.1; 1 Pet 5.10, but this meaning hardly fits the context of v. 12. The meaning training, discipline if accepted would relate the noun only to the last 'official' listed in v. 11 and not the others. **Equipment** is therefore preferable but it requires an object; people are furnished or prepared for some purpose; this purpose could be found in v. 12b if it relates to an activity of the saints for which church leaders are to prepare or equip them.

The phrase in v. 12b either means 'for the work of the ministry' (cf. 2 Tim 4.5: 'Do the work of an evangelist, fulfil your ministry') or, as we have translated it: **for their ministering activity**. 'Work' needs to be taken actively as in 1 Cor 15.58; Phil 2.30; 1 Th 1.3; 2 Tim 4.5, or given the related sense of 'what has been done' as in 1 Cor 3.13–15; 9.1 (cf Rom 14.20); it describes an ongoing activity seen in service. 'Ministry' (see on 3.7 for the word 'minister') normally has some word or phrase qualifying it and indicating the nature of the service or else this can be determined from the context (e.g. Acts 6.1, 4; Rom 11.13; 15.31; 1 Cor 4.1). The qualification may be found here in v. 12c (a ministry which works towards the building up of the church). Only at Rom 12.7; 1 Cor 12.5 does 'ministry' lack a defining qualification and in both those passages, as here, the context is charismatic (v. 7). The root is often used by Paul of his preaching ministry (cf Schnackenburg) both within and outwith the church (e.g. 2 Cor 3.6–8; 4.1; 5.18) and this would correspond to the work of the evangelist (v. 11); yet there is no reason to restrict preaching to church officials. More generally it is wrong to tie the meaning down to only one of the ministries of v. 11. The term certainly does not have here the 'official' sense which 'deacon' had later in the church. It can have a quite general sense (Heb 1.14; 2 Tim 4.11; Mk 10.43; cf Mk 10.45 for the verb). The absence of the article suggests the noun here is to be understood as equivalent to a verb (Haupt), i.e. as referring to the activity of ministering. Whether the word is applied here to the work of the office-bearers or to that of believers as a whole, in the light of its use by Jesus (Mk 9.33–6; 10.42–5) and the early church, it gives no support to a claim to self-importance.

The two concepts of v. 12c have already appeared in the letter: (i) **building** in 2.20–2; the word is used here again in the sense of the process of constructing and not of a finished construction, but the metaphor has another connotation, educational rather than physical; (ii) **body of Christ** in 1.23; 3.6; 4.4. If 'building' is given its more physical sense it might imply the addition of new members to the community, though this does not necessarily follow as 2.20–2 shows, but if it has its more educational sense it would refer to the maturing of the community as in 2 Cor 10.8; 1 Cor 14.3, 12, 26. That the latter conclusion is correct is seen by the reference in 4.16 to growth in love. The metaphor is then used here with an ethical or educational sense. The mixing of the building and growth metaphors (the latter implicit in **body**) was already present in 2.21 and reappears in v. 16. The inspiration for 4.12, 16 lay in passages like 1 Cor 14.1–19, 26 (cf Rom 14.19; 15.2; 1 Cor 8.1; 10.23) where believers use their different charismata to build up other believers. The background to this is again Jewish (cf Isa 49.17; Jer 1.10; 18.9; 24.6; 31(38).28; 42(49).10; 45.4(51.34); Ψ 27.5; Ecclus 49.7). If many of the OT passages envisage God as the builder, it is again he who builds in 1 Cor 14.1ff, but through the charismatic gifts he has given to church members. The appropriation here of the idea of 1 Cor 14 was made easier because sometimes in the former the object of the building is expressly identified as the church (1 Cor 14.4, 5, 12), that is the body of Christ. The context of 4.12, 16 is again the giving of charismata to believers. If the process of upbuilding is described here then v. 13 gives its result. AE says nothing directly about how the building up of the community is to be carried out; 1 Corinthians implied that it was through the charismatic gifts of all the community. Here it must be through the variety of gifts of administration, healing, prophecy which ordinary members possess. It is certainly not a purely instructional building up in the details of the true faith, for love is involved (v. 16). It will be a mutual building up (5.19; cf 1 Th 5.11).

If the three phrases can be explained in these ways how are they to be related to one another within the total paraenetic context? The punctuation of the English translations reflects only the opinion of editors, for the Greek text was punctuated sparingly, if at all. 4.11 refers to the limited group of officials; v. 13 with its first person plural draws in all believers; v. 12a refers to the officials of v. 11; at the beginning or end of v. 12bc or within it we must then move from the limited group to all believers; but where? If we take the three phrases as parallel then the change comes at the beginning of v. 13, a view held at least as early as Chrysostom. If 12a, 12b, 12c are parallel then it is surprising that v. 12b, the most general of the phrases, does not come first with 12a and 12c developing it; Grotius, recognising this, transposed their order! In English the three phrases begin with the same preposition **for**, but in Greek the first begins *pros* and the second and third *eis*. Meyer, noting this variation, sees the former as denoting the primary purpose and the latter secondary purposes (he gave leaders for the work of ministry and for building up the body of Christ; his main object being to perfect the saints); if this were so the ultimate purpose should be put last; Meyer's solution also makes difficult the transition to the first plural of v. 13. If all three phrases of v. 12 refer to the activity of the ministers then it might be possible to relate 12a to the teachers and 12b to the evangelists, yet there is no apparent justification for relating 12c to the shepherds; in fact the activity of 12c is an activity of the whole church in v. 16 (apostles and prophets may be ignored in this connection as their ministry belongs to the past). No reason exists then to associate the phrases of v. 12 with different ministries. This apart, the most probable meaning of 12a did not relate it to teaching but to preparing and equipping the saints. But preparation and equipment are always for some purpose; 12bc can give this. 12b itself requires something to explain it; 12c fulfils this function; 12c is then not strictly parallel to 12b but amplifies it. The change in preposition between 12a and 12bc confirms that the movement from the discussion of the work of the ministers (v. 11) to that of the whole church takes place between 12a and 12bc. The change in preposition also militates against taking 12a and 12b together (so Beare following Goodspeed, 'in order to fit his people for the work of service'). Office-bearers then exist to prepare other believers for their service to the whole community; they have an enabling function; the clergy exist to serve the laity (cf Haupt).

This view is contested by Gordon who takes all of v. 12 to be the duty of the officials. He argues in support that a clear distinction is drawn between the ministry and the laity not only in 4.11f but throughout the NT and has no difficulty in pointing to a number of places where the ministry has a special position, e.g. Acts 6.4; 13.2–5; 1 Tim 3.2; 2 Tim 4.1–5; 1 Tim 5.17; Jas 3.1. This is not in dispute. What he fails to do is to consider whether there are passages showing non-ministers fulfilling what he would term ministerial functions; there are many, e.g. Eph 5.19; Rom 15.14; 1 Cor 14.26; Phil 1.15; Col 3.16; 1 Th 5.11; in every case the church is being built up.

The building up of the body of Christ is not then to be left to the ministry but is the responsibility of all believers. Yet the beginning of the clerical-lay division may be said to appear here. It is absent from v. 7 and 1 Cor 12.4ff; Rom 12.4ff, and essentially it conflicts with the image of the body of Christ where all members have their special functions. The clerical-lay division is of course found in other parts of the NT, e.g. Heb 13.24, even if at the same time the NT lays strong emphasis on all believers as possessing a ministerial function.

13. The purpose of Christ's gift of ministers to the church (v. 11) to prepare all its members (v. 12a) to serve (v. 12bc) is now made clear in three prepositional phrases (**to the unity of faith**; **to a mature male**; **to the measure of** ...) which together with v. 14 probably depend on **he gave** (v. ii); the argument flows evenly. The three prepositional phrases do not depend on one another but are in parallel.

The goal is presented as the end of a journey; it has not yet been attained. The goal is first defined as unity. This unity is probably that which belongs to, or comes from, a common faith and knowledge.

The very brevity of the second phrase makes it difficult to understand despite its use of two common words. Is AE referring to the manhood of individual believers, of Christ or of the church? The main drive in our context is corporate, relating to the building up of the church (vv. 12, 16). The individualistic interpretation is then unsatisfactory; any other must lie in the area of corporate understanding. Could the 'man' be Christ? Schlier provides a considerable number of references to the use of the term 'man' for the heavenly saviour and in some of these we actually have the phrase, 'perfect (mature) man'. The parallel of 2.15, 'one new human being' might suggest a simple equation of the phrase with the church but it is not certain that the phrase of 2.15 refers to the church. There is no easy solution to these difficulties. Even if no easy solution is possible a corporate solution accords better with the context, and with very great hesitation we must accept this and view the 'man' as the corporate Christ (he is thus referred to in all three phrases) who is the church.

The third phrase, while introducing Christ, does not make him the explicit goal to be attained. The *pleroma* (see on 1.23 for the word) of Christ can either be that which fills him or that which he fills. In 1.23 he was seen as filled by God and as filling the church; since here we have no suggestion of what might fill him the phrase is better taken as denoting what he fills, and, as in 1.23, what he fills will be the church, and not 'all things' as in 4.10. The goal to be attained is then the measure, probably as in v. 7 the full measure, of the maturity or stature of what Christ fills.

The three prepositional phrases may appear to provide three distinct goals but there can only be one goal; they must therefore be seen as drawing out different aspects of that one goal. How then do they relate to one another? Each phrase in v. 13 incorporates a reference to Christ involving an understanding of him and a relation to him. The church also is involved as the body of which he is head and as that which understands him and is to attain maturity through its relation to him. It is towards this goal that the ministry is to work by drawing in all members of the church so that they also take their place in working towards the goal. Since nothing is said about the missionary activity of ministers or believers in general, the goal must be an inward maturity and not an outward growth in numbers (Gnilka).

14. This is the third successive verse depending on v. 11 (Gnilka; Schlier and most commentators). Unlike v. 13 it is cast negatively. The ministry was given not only to enable the church to grow but also so that it would be able to resist any forces that might corrupt or destroy it. Ministers themselves are not the direct agents in this resistance; all believers are summoned to the task; should any fail, unity may become chaos. The structure of v. 14 is by no means simple and there are many ways of relating the various phrases to one another, but the main thought is clear; that however is not to say that whatever AE is attacking can be identified with any certainty. The language is imprecise and, in keeping with AE's normal style, plerophoric (Schlier), with AE using a series of images: children, a storm at sea, dice playing.

AE describes the Christian condition as immature rather than sinful (Grosheide); it may be for this reason that he uses the first plural and includes himself! Children tend to be volatile in their beliefs, and the readers might turn out to be unstable, foolish and incapable of understanding the truth, in contrast with the reference to knowledge in v. 13. The plural **children** is probably individualistic in orientation contrasting with the togetherness that ought to exist among believers. Childish individualism drives people apart and shatters unity.

AE now changes his metaphor, introducing the sea and its storms. The dangers of sea travel were sometimes used in the OT to depict life apart from God (Ps 107.23–7; Isa 57.20f), and sea travel was widely recognised in the ancient world as dangerous. The winds are those of false teaching. AE probably refers here to the variety of teaching within the church rather than false philosophies and theologies entering it from outside. The remainder of the letter is devoted to ethical instruction; this suggests that the false teaching may be about behaviour. The plural **every wind** suggests he did not have one particular false teaching or vice in mind. Writing to a number of churches he might not be sure what were the perversions in each.

AE's third metaphor is drawn from dice playing. Though games with dice may not of themselves be dishonest, in the ancient world they were often associated with dishonesty and deception and dice playing became a synonym for trickery. The total effect of these nouns (translated **trickery, cunningly pointed, planning, error**) is to stress the unscrupulous nature of certain undefined people who may be leading believers astray. The deceptive trickery is not attributed here to the devil but is regarded as human; literally, 'of men'; the plural is vague and again gives the impression with much else in the verse that the readers are assailed by a variety of false teachings. True teaching, especially that of Paul, is not of human but divine origin.

15. This verse contrasts with and is parallel to v. 14; that verse was negative in tone; this is positive. It makes explicit the idea of growth which was already implicit in passages like 2.20–2 and present in **until we all attain** of v. 13 with its implication of movement towards maturity.

The meaning of **speaking truth** is not simply that believers are never to tell lies but always speak the truth, though this is what is said in 4.25. In the context of v. 14, where believers are warned against those who would lead them astray in respect of doctrine or ethics or both, truth should be understood as the truth of the gospel. The truth is the gospel (see on 1.13; 4.21; 6.14; cf Gal 2.5, 14; 5.7; Rom 1.18; Col 1.5; 2 Tim 2.15). The true speaking of the gospel corrects error. Believers console, strengthen and correct one another through the gospel and so build up their communities. They can do this **in love** because their lives are founded on and built up by love (3.17).

When believers speak the gospel to one another the body is built up, or grows. Growth is into Christ, basically the same idea as v. 13c, and is of the church as a whole and not primarily of its members as individuals. The metaphor of growth suggests that here the head (see on 1.22) is regarded as the source of growth in so far as it is identified with Christ. Christ, v. 16, supplies the body with what it requires to grow. But how can the body grow into

Christ who is its head? The thought is probably parallel to that of 2.20–2; there the building grows into a temple even though the final coping-stone is regarded as already in position. Here the church both grows into Christ, which means more than that it becomes like Christ, and grows from what he supplies to it; it is true that the picture may not accord with either contemporary or modern physiological theories, but have we any right to expect it to do so (see on v. 16)?

16. This verse concludes the long sentence which began at v. 11. The general sense is clear though many details are not (Chrysostom describes it as obscure). The church is to grow from Christ its head and will grow in love. Growth has been the hidden agenda from v. 11. Much of the verse's obscurity arises out of its use of medical words. Modern physiology and anatomy have a different view of the human body and use terms differently from the ancient world; ancient ideas have to be translated into modern terms and none may correspond exactly.

From whom refers back to Christ (v. 15); whatever is described in v. 16 connects with Christ. Our verse stresses the togetherness of those in the **body**, but it is not stressing the growth together of laity and ministers guided by the latter. The church is more than the passive object of ministerial activity (Dahl). Each individual has an important contribution to make if unity is to be maintained and growth to take place. The phrase **fitted and held together** which qualifies **body** brings out the way in which the togetherness of the body is sustained. The present participles indicate that the togetherness requires continual achievement.

Ligament is probably a medical term whose exact significance is unclear, the accompanying word **every** makes it in effect a plural. It represents whatever (i) holds the body together (cf Col 2.19 (ii) enables nourishment to pass from one part to another, (iii) the whole to be controlled by the head. The translation 'joints' is inadequate since joints exist to make articulation possible. It is better to think in terms of ligaments, arteries and nerves, though no one of these by itself is correct since ligaments enable the body to act as a unit but do not convey nourishment and energy from one part to another, nerves convey not nourishment but information and arteries have no function in holding the body together. Even if we knew what part of the body AE had in mind, there may be no exact modern equivalent and efforts to determine this are probably wasted. **Ligaments** has been chosen in the translation for lack of a better word. V. 16 treats of the contribution of all members of the church to its upbuilding and we should not see the clerical–lay division as present. The word translated **supply** is found in Phil 1.19 and its cognate verb in 2 Cor 9.10; Gal 3.5; Col 2.19; 2 Pet 1.5, 11; its meaning lies in the area 'help, supply, nourish, provide'. In our context it means that something is supplied to the body, or that the body is helped or nourished by Christ the head. Whatever it is, the **ligaments** transmit it; the final words of the verse suggest that it is **love**.

There seems to be a break in the verse at this point as the emphasis on individual contributions is picked up in a new way with wording recalling v. 7. Each member has a proportional contribution to offer and makes it towards the growth of the body as a whole and not specifically towards the individuals within it. Least of all is it suggested that the office-bearers alone grow, or alone contribute to or create the growth of the body, though of course they have their role in equipping members to work towards growth. In the light of the final and emphatic reference to love, this growth should be understood as one of quality and not quantity. This accords with the stress in the earlier parts of vv. 11–16 on maturity rather than numbers. It is not that growth comes from within the body through some inner power, but it comes from Christ its head *via* (in part) ministers (v. 11). The physiology may be incorrect, but AE has been forced into it by his choice of metaphor. In the final phrase the metaphor in fact changes to that of upbuilding and AE employs again the language he had used in v. 12 with the same meaning of **upbuilding**. Though it is not the body's own power which creates growth but Christ, the body through its members has a part to play in that growth; at least if it does not assist but remains quiescent, it will prevent it. Growth is not in knowledge, still less in numbers, but in love. The association of love with charismatic gifts goes back to 1 Cor 12–14. The final position of **in love** in this long sentence makes it emphatic. In the light of the sentence's content the object of believers' love will not be Christ or God but one another; such a love of course has its source in Christ. Love coming from Christ is the cement fitting and holding together the members, and all members without exception have their part to play in this. AE has provided here the picture not of a static church, but of one which is growing and maturing (an organism either grows or dies away, Gnilka). It is moving towards its goal (v. 13) and is enabled to do so through the love and power of its saviour and head, Christ.

X

OLD INTO NEW

(4.17–24)

[17] This I go on to say and insist in the Lord
   that you live no longer as the pagans live
   in the worthlessness of your minds,
[18]   as those
      blind in understanding
      excluded from the life of God
         because of their inherent ignorance,
         because of the hardness of their hearts,
[19]   who being insensitive
         gave themselves over to undisciplined behaviour,
         working itself out in every kind of impurity,
         with covetousness.
[20] But you have not learned Christ to that effect,
[21]   assuming [as we can] that you heard him
         and were taught in him,
      because the truth is in Jesus,
[22]   that you were to put off the old person
      of your earlier way of life,
      which was being corrupted through deceitful desires,
[23]   but to be renewed in the spirit of your minds,
[24]   and to put on the new person
      which has been created in God's likeness
      in true righteousness and holiness.

The paraenetic half of the letter, which appeared to commence with 4.1–3 but turned into a discussion of the unity and diversity of believers, is now resumed and continued without interruption to the end. What was said about behaviour in 4.2f related to conduct within the community, but now when AE returns to the

211

paraenesis this element temporarily disappears to reappear at 4.25; this renders difficult the connection with vv. 7–16; it may lie in the movement of thought from believers as no longer babes but as growing up and so requiring more instruction in behaviour (vv. 20f; cf Jerome), or, more probably, 4.17–24 may be a necessary preparation for the detailing of instruction about conduct which follows in 4.25ff. The paraenesis implicit in 4.17–24 is not unrelated to the first half of the letter since it focuses on the former Gentile attitudes of believers whose new (theological) position in the people of God had been explored in 2.11–22; 3.2–13.

As AE sees it, the peril facing Gentile believers is neither persecution brought on by their new attitude to paganism nor the influence of heretical intellectual ideas but a relapse into their former pre-Christian ways, which are the ways of the world around them. This could happen if believers forsook their faith or introduced their pre-Christian attitudes into the church. In expressing both the negative and positive aspects of the Christian way of life he uses traditional paraenetical material, mostly drawn from Judaism, but material which was not out of accord with the teaching of many pagan moral philosophers. From the beginning the church had instructed its members in how to live and, since Christianity came out of a Jewish cradle, much of what was taught was similar to Jewish instruction; this may not have been needed for the first converts from Judaism but was very necessary when the majority of those entering the church came from the Gentile world.

One way of describing the new Christian life contrasts it with pagan ways, and this is how AE begins (vv. 17–19) before turning in later sections to more direct and detailed instruction. In 4.17–24 the thought moves twice from the negative to the positive. In vv. 17–19, after the general introduction of v. 17a, AE draws a picture of the heathen world which depends in part on previous Jewish thinking (e.g. Wisd 14.22–31; *Ep Arist* 152; Philo, *Vita Cont* 40–7). He then identifies the new element that has entered the lives of his readers (vv. 20–1) and concludes in vv. 22–4, where there is an antithetical *parallelismus membrorum* (Roberts), by contrasting their previous nature with their present; a new way of behaviour necessitates a new being from which it may proceed. Membership of the community involves a personal reorientation.

17. **This** points forward and not backward (cf 3.8; 5.5; 1 Cor 7.29; 1 Th 4.15).

The double phrase **I go on to say and insist** is impressive, solemn and wholly in AE's manner, though there are parallels in Paul (1 Th 2.12) and in secular Greek. The verb **insist** should not be joined too closely to **in the Lord** (see 1 Th 4.1; 2 Th 3.12 for their combination) as if AE were affirming on oath the truth of what he is saying. **In the Lord** qualifies both verbs because AE is writing to fellow-Christians; it reminds them of the bond between Paul and their Lord and therefore of that between their Lord and themselves; both AE and his readers are members of the body of Christ and he is seeking to build them up in the faith (4.12f). The phrase may also serve to remind them of the authority of their Lord over them.

Their behaviour is no longer to be as it once was. The manner of their new life, expressed positively in 4.2f, is now put negatively: they are no longer to live as 'the nations', a word whose meaning always needs to be determined from its context. It was used by the Jews to distinguish themselves from non-Jews in terms of religion, race and culture. This usage passed into early Christianity and is found in 3.1, 6, 8. These, not Jews by race or religious conversion, have been able to become members of the church on equal terms with Jewish Christians. Jews regarded the moral standards of Gentiles in general as debased and the first Christians, all Jews by birth, continued to think in this way and so applied the word to those who were neither Christians nor Jews, even though within the church the Jewish–non-Jewish distinction was disappearing. Consequently there is no single English word which can be used on every occasion to translate the term; the context must determine the rendering. In v. 17 the sense will be **pagans** or 'heathen' since stress is being laid on the non-Jewish nature of the culture from which the readers have been converted. AE now briefly describes that culture; the sins with which he categorises it are largely the same as those Jews used of Gentile culture (Wisd 12–15; 18.10–19; *Ep Arist* 132–8, 140, 277; *Sib Or* 3.8–45, 220–35; *Jub* 22.16–18; *T Naph* 3.3). Jewish writers regularly summoned their fellow Jews not to live like Gentiles (Lev 20.23; Dt 18.9).

The first characteristic of the culture which the readers had left is expressed as an attitude of mind. 'Mind' does not denote 'the mind or the intellect as a special faculty, but the knowing, understanding and judging which belong to man as man and determine what attitude he adopts' (Bultmann). AE is not then describing a defect in the ability of his readers to reason but their 'mind-set', the total person viewed under the aspect of thinking. The mind, as AE views it, can be renewed (Rom 12.2) so that the old mind of unbelievers becomes a new mind in believers (cf 4.22, 24). A close connection exists then between mind and activity. The pre-Christian pagan mind is characterised here by **worthlessness**. The Christian understanding and use of this word is determined by the LXX. Idols are worthless (Acts 14.15) and therefore all non-Jewish and non-Christian worship is worthless as unable to bring its worshippers to God. Non-Christian Gentiles have already been described as not knowing God (2.12). **Worthlessness** is not however applied to idolatry alone but to the whole of pagan life (1 Pet 1.18; cf Jas 1.26; Rom 8.20), since for Jews and Christians an attitude to religion will ultimately work itself out in depraved behaviour (Jer 2.5; Isa 28.29; 30.15; 33.11; Rom 1.21ff; cf 1QS 5.19). Even the ways of those who are accounted learned in pagan society may be described with this word (1 Cor 3.20, quoting Ψ 93.11). Heathen culture being then devoid of real value, its religions will be also. This of course would not have been the verdict of those in it. The worthlessness does not lie in the world as such, for all that God made is good (Theophylact), but in the minds of those who live in it. The accusation of worthlessness was widely used in Jewish and Christian apologetic, even beyond the NT period, e.g. *Barn* 4.10; 20.2; 1 Clem 7.2; 9.1; in *Did* 5.2 it is one among a list of vices; in Ephesians and mostly elsewhere it describes a total attitude. The next two verses spell out more fully where the worthlessness of the mind may lead.

18. AE now gives his picture of heathen life; in doing so he employs many of the words and ideas of Rom 1.18ff, though with such variations as to suggest that that passage is not being used directly; doubtless its theme remained a part of the Pauline tradition. It is a bleak picture and accords with a great part of Judaism's view of non-Judaism, though Judaism could also see non-Judaism in a softer light. It is natural for AE to draw attention to the darker aspect since he wishes to warn his readers against relapsing into it.

The Gentile world out of which the readers were converted remained in a state of blindness. Earlier AE had described believers as those who saw (1.18). The metaphor of sight, or lack of it, was used regularly by Jews of the spiritual as well as the mental condition of Gentiles: Jews see, others are blind; Jews are a light to blind Gentiles (Ps 135.16; Isa 42.6f; 49.6; 1QSb 4.27; Wisd 18.4); the non-Jewish world is one of darkness. In fairness it must be said that Jews also described fellow Jews as blind (*T Reub* 3.8; *T Dan* 2.4; *T Gad* 6.2; *T Levi* 14.11; 1QS 3.3; cf Mt 15.14; 23.16, 24; Rom 2.19). Christians took over the metaphor from Jews (Acts 26.18; Col 1.13; 1 Pet 2.9; Jn 8.12; Eph 5.11; 1 Th 5.4). It was also used widely in the ancient world, though generally in respect of mental rather than spiritual blindness; AE's readers would therefore have easily grasped its significance.

The reference to being **excluded from the life of God** is strange; we would expect something like 'alienated from God' or 'excluded from salvation'. The life of God is presumably not God's own life but the life he gives, and since God gives physical life to both pagans and believers AE will be thinking of eternal life. Life and light are associated in biblical thought; the Gospel of John exploits their connection (e.g. 1.4; 8.12) but it runs back into the OT (e.g. Ps 36.9). The two are also linked in gnostic thought (e.g. *CH* 1.9, 12). There is thus a natural movement, easily grasped by Gentile readers, from the blindness of the first clause to the loss of life implied in the second; the heathen are of course 'dead' in sin (2.1); life and death are opposites. In writing of exclusion from the life of God AE is not thinking of some kind of alienation which psychiatrists could cure. What is required is not psychological treatment but something wholly new, a new being (v. 24).

If the two passive participles, blinded in understanding and excluded from the life of God, allowed pagans to think their condition was not their own fault, being the result of the action of God or an evil power, the two prepositional phrases bring out their responsibility. They are blind and excluded because of their ignorance and the hardness of their hearts. Their **ignorance** cannot be offered as an excuse (as it may be in Lk 23.34; Acts 3.17; 17.30; *T Zeb* 1.5; Epictetus, 1.26.5–7) for it does not arise out of a lack of information about the world or morality. It is an ignorance both about God, though not an intellectual deficiency since the devils can believe God exists but do not come to true enlightenment (Jas 2.19), and about their own true nature as people. This ignorance has no higher and lower levels; all have it to the same degree; neither learning nor experience can modify or remove it (Rom 1.21f; Wisd 13.1, 7–9); it is not a passing or temporary ignorance, nor is it one among a list of possible vices. In Jewish thought, which again has modelled what AE writes, ignorance, sin and unbelief are closely linked (*T Gad* 5.7; 1QH 1.22f; 4.7; Wisd 14.22; 1 Th 4.5) and ignorance is also linked to idolatry (Philo, *Decal* 8; *Spec Leg* 1.15).

The second prepositional phrase, parallel to the first and not (as Schlier) its interpretation, expresses the same thought in another way as a hardening of the heart.

The metaphor of 'the hardening of the heart' (the heart is the centre of personality, see on 1.18) is found elsewhere in the NT (Mk 3.5; 6.52; 8.17; Jn 12.40) where, unlike here, it is used to describe the condition of Jews (cf Rom 9.18; 11.7, 25). Jews used the image of hardness or stubbornness, usually in relation to the heart, to describe the condition of non-Jews (Exod 4.21; 7.3; 9.12; Jer 19.15). Gnostics also used the image (*Ap John* II, 1 30.7–11; *Testim Truth* IX, 3 32.5–8).

19. AE now spells out the nature of the pagan world in a new way.

The consciences of Gentiles do not stab them when they do wrong for they are insensitive in distinguishing what is morally good from what is evil. The thought is similar to that of 2.1 where Gentiles were regarded as dead. No outside power (God or Satan?) has inflicted their condition on them; they gave themselves up to it.

Insensitive to the distinctions required by true morality, unbelievers gave themselves up to sin; this is now described with three nouns whose precise meaning is difficult to tie down because each is used both in a wide sense, embracing a range of sins, and in a more restricted way of particular sins: **undisciplined**

behaviour, impurity, covetousness. The relation of the final noun to the preceding two is also difficult. **Undisciplined behaviour** appears regularly in vice catalogues (Mk 7.22; Rom 13.13; 2 Cor 12.21; Gal 5.19; 1 Pet 4.3; Wisd 14.26; *T Jud* 23.1; *T Levi* 17.11; Hermas, *Sim* 9.15.3) but it is also used with a more general significance (2 Pet 2.2, 18; Jude 4; Hermas, *Vis* 2.2.2; 3.7.2; *Mand* 12.4.6; Philo, *Vita Mos* 1.305; 3 Macc 2.26). In the catalogues it is normally found in the area where sexual sins are listed (Mk 7.22 is an exception; in *T Jud* 23.1 it is linked with idolatry) and this may still be its import when used more generally (e.g. Josephus *Ant* 8.318; 20.112) with it indicating sexual sin of many kinds; since however there are also clear instances where undisciplined behaviour without an explicit sexual connection is indicated (Jos *Ant* 4.151; 8.252), it is probably best understood as undisciplined behaviour especially, though not exclusively, of a sexual nature.

Impurity also appears in vice catalogues (2 Cor 12.21; Gal 5.19; Col 3.5; Prov 6.16; Eph 5.3), sometimes in proximity to the previous word (2 Cor 12.21; Gal 5.19); it is rare in classical Greek; in Leviticus (see especially ch. 15) it refers regularly to ritual uncleanness. Apart from this restricted use, in some of its scriptural occurrences its connotation appears to be sexual (especially Gal 5.19; Col 3.5) and this is also true when it appears by itself (1 Th 4.7; *T Jud* 14.5; *Barn* 10.8,18), though the reference may be more general (1 Th 2.3; Prov 6.16; Wisd 2.16; 3 Macc 2.17; *T Levi* 15.1). The phenomenon in which general moral terms are given a sexual orientation ('she is an immoral woman') appears in many cultures. There is nothing in the use of our two nouns to indicate a sexual orientation here. There is a suggestion of a general meaning in respect of the second, **every kind of impurity**, though it could be 'every kind of sexual deviation'.

Like the two other terms, **covetousness** appears in vice lists (Mk 7.22; Rom 1.29; 1 Clem 35.5; *Barn* 20.1; *Did* 5.1; Polyc *Phil* 2.2; Hermas, *Mand* 6.2.5; 8.5; *CH* 13.7) and is found separately (Lk 12.15; 2 Cor 9.5; Eph 5.3; Col 3.5; 1 Th 2.5; 2 Pet 2.3, 14; cf 1 Cor 5.10f; 6.10; Eph 5.5). It is never a general term like the others but may indeed be given a wider reference ('a morbid lust of acquisition', Eadie on 5.3), indicating a desire for more than a fair share of whatever is at issue, e.g. wealth, possessions. Its rejection runs back to the Decalogue and it continued to be rebuked not only in Judaism (e.g. Philo, *Spec Leg* 4.5; *Vita Mos* 2.186; CD 4.17; 1QS 4.9ff) but equally, if not more so, in the Hellenistic world (e.g. Dio Chrys *Or* 17) where sexual sin was by no means so widely condemned. 1 Tim 6.10 was probably formulated under Hellenistic influence. Jewish and Christian thought often linked sexual sin with greed (CD 8.5; *T Levi* 14.5f; *T Jud* 17.1f; 18.2; *T Dan* 5.5–7) and also greed with idolatry (*T Jud* 19.1; Col 3.5; Eph 5.3; Polyc *Phil* 11.2); the latter connection underlies the words of Jesus about God and mammon (Mt 6.24; Lk 16.13) but is probably not present in v. 19; AE's readers would take **covetousness** in the simple sense of greed.

AE paints here a very dark picture of the Gentile world. Questions immediately arise: From where did he derive his material? Why did he draw so dark a picture? Was he fair to the Gentile world? As to the first question almost all he says can be traced back through Christianity to Judaism; it is found also in all strands of early Christianity (cf Mk 8.38; Acts 2.40; Rom 1.18–32; 1 Th 4.3–7; Tit 3.3; 1 Pet 4.3–4; *Did* 3.1–6; *Barn* 20). It must be allowed however that Judaism has kinder things to say; Josephus, *Vita* 12, for example, compares Pharisees and Stoics with no intention of denigrating either. That AE has taken over a traditional view suggests that his picture of the secular world was not derived from actual observation, and as we go on we shall find much to confirm this.

The answer to the second question is more complex. Moralists tend to overstress the dark side of any society they attack. Small groups seeking to distinguish themselves from their prevailing culture do the same; this has been particularly true of small religious groups. AE, needing to draw a sharp line between how his readers once lived and how they ought to live in order to encourage them to live in the new way, overemphasises their past behaviour. Since converts regularly overplay the distinction between their past and new life his readers might not have noticed a discrepancy between what he says and what they know of the outside world.

As for the third question, it is possible to find non-Jewish and non-Christian pessimistic descriptions of contemporary culture (e.g. Heraclitus, *Epistula* 7). The satirists (e.g. Juvenal) concentrate on and pick out incidents from the dark side of society; they would not have been read if what they said was wholly untrue; like tabloid newspapers they highlighted what was obviously false in society and ignored what was good. On the other hand the fact that attention was paid to them implies that there were those who rejected the moral positions they satirised and accepted a different view. Thus AE's absolute picture of total darkness cannot be true. There is much else which shows that in fact it was prejudiced. When discussing 4.2 we saw that gentleness and patience were highly regarded by Greek and other thinkers. In 4.24 AE uses a word pair, **righteousness** and **holiness**, to characterise Christian behaviour which pagan moralists and philosophers also used. The Stoics commended prudence, justice, courage and temperance as virtues and attacked immoderate desire for pleasure, including sexual indulgence (e.g. Plutarch, *Mor* 441A; Seneca, *Ep* 9.3ff; 75.7ff; Epictetus, 2.18.15, 19; 3.7.21; 4.1.122; M. Aurelius 9.42) and anger (see on 4.26f, 31). Virgil's *Fourth Eclogue* indicates an aspiration for better things. The existence of catalogues of vices and virtues shows condemnation of various sins and approval of various virtues. The qualities demanded of Christian leaders in the Pastorals are little different from those for good leaders in society as a whole. Musonius Rufus writes of people having an innate inclination towards virtue (Frag 2, Hense, 7.7f). In Frag 8 (Hense 34.16–35.6) he provides a not unfavourable picture of society. This is not simply a philosopher trying to put a good gloss on his world; the same is found or implied in inscriptions which represent popular non-philosophical belief, e.g. Barton and Horsley, CIL 8.11824. Part of the problem arises from the concentration by early, and later, Christian moralists on sexual sin and other undisciplined behaviour. There were however areas where there was much to commend in the ancient world. Paul writes highly of Roman justice (Rom 13.1–7) from which he himself on a number of occasions benefited (e.g. Acts 16.35ff; 18.12ff; 21.31ff; 25.8ff). The sins of the nations criticised by Amos are what we would describe as social or political sins. What AE writes then represents a limited and unbalanced view of the nature of Gentile culture. Surprisingly he does not mention idolatry (contrast 1 Th 1.9f). The sins of society as a whole do not come into view; thus slavery is not condemned in the NT, nor the degradation of women. When we turn away from the restricted area of the Mediterranean we find societies in other areas, e.g. China, India, who venerate the golden rule and place a high value on honesty and truthfulness; not all are hotbeds of sexual immorality; monogamy is revered in many cultures. Finally, should it be said that while these cultures and societies may have high ideals they were not lived up to, no one who has read the history of Christianity would dare to suggest that Christians have lived up to their ideals. To sum up, AE's description of the pagan world must be classified as governed more by theology than by observation. It would presumably have prevented him entering into inter-faith dialogue with any other group than Jews.

What did AE's converts from the pagan world think of his description of it? Did they nod their heads in agreement or did they mutter 'He's got it all wrong'? If the latter, did it shake their confidence in the other things he wrote?

20. The basis of the readers' lives has been changed. They are then no longer to live as they once did as pagans. The abrupt beginning of v. 20 serves to stress the contrast between Christian and non-Christian existence (cf Macpherson). AE does not detail now the new Christian way of living (this begins at v. 25) but supplies the reason for the change.

You have ... learned Christ is an unusual phrase. It is unusual because a person is said to be learnt; normally subjects are learnt ('You have not learnt the Torah'). The unexpected use of Christ as the direct object of the verb would surely have shocked readers into looking for a deeper meaning than simply understanding Christ as the subject of instruction, though certainly since their conversion they will have learnt about him and his teaching. Learning Christ must also mean more than being taught about christology, though naturally since becoming Christians readers will have learnt about this. If 'learning Christ' meant learning about his teaching or person, v. 21a would have been differently expressed. More information about him would never have changed their way of life. Dibelius has attributed a 'mystical' significance to the phrase (to learn Christ is to grow in fellowship with him), pointing to *Odes Sol* 7.3ff: 'receive him', 'put him on', 'learn him'. The phrase is probably best understood with the help of Colossians where in 2.6f the readers are said to have received

Christ and to live in him and to have been taught, and in 1.6f to have heard and recognised the grace of God in truth. AE may also have been influenced by phrases like 'to know Christ' (Phil 3.10), 'to proclaim Christ' (Gal 1.16; Phil 1.17f; Col 1.28), 'to preach Christ' (1 Cor 1.23; 15.12; 2 Cor 4.5), where in every case something more than the passing on of information about Christ is intended. As Zerwick comments, to learn Christ is a good summary of what it means to be a Christian.

21. What learning Christ (v. 20) entails is now further explained with two verbs **heard** and **taught**. The first, because of the way it is used, would have been almost equally as startling as v. 20. The readers learnt Christ (v. 20); they heard Christ (v. 21). The present phrase may represent the idea that Christ himself is heard in those who proclaim him (2 Cor 13.3; Lk 10.16a; cf Barth). This becomes more likely if we take into account the Christian belief that Christ is risen and alive (Lindemann).

The two verbs of hearing and being taught may refer to the same event of becoming a Christian looked at from distinct angles. Acceptance of Christ implies not only some relation to him but also acceptance of some understanding of who he is and what he has done, i.e. the acceptance of some body, however slender, of doctrine.

What does it mean to say that they **were taught in him**? The great majority of commentators take the phrase as an instance of the 'in Christ' formula and explain it in various ways, e.g. Christ as the atmosphere in which the teaching was given, or 'those who are in Christ', are taught; Zerwick carries the 'in Christ' interpretation too far when he equates it with 'in the church'. The clue to a more adequate interpretation lies in following the sense of 'in the Lord' in v. 17. AE speaks with authority to his readers because both he and they are linked in the Lord. The readers and those who taught them were also linked in the Lord and so their teaching was 'in Christ' and as with the previous two verbs the reference to Christ may be taken pregnantly in the sense of being taught Christ in such a way that their relationship to him was deepened. This interpretation would be strengthened if the verb is taken as a divine passive, 'you were taught by God in Christ'; the teaching would then be a part of the way in which God acts graciously towards them (e.g. 1.4, 6; 4.32).

The final clause raises two problems: (a) What is the subject of the verb? (b) What is the significance of the use of the name Jesus? (a) It is preferable to translate 'the truth is in Jesus' rather than 'there is truth in Jesus'. Truth, which must always be truth about something, is here almost equivalent to the gospel (see on 1.13; cf Rom 2.8; 2 Cor 13.8; Col 1.5).

(b) **Jesus** cannot be passed over as a stylistic variation (Lincoln) – AE has gone out of his way to introduce the name. The name Jesus appears rarely in the Pauline corpus (Rom 3.26; 8.11; 1 Cor 12.3; 2 Cor 4.5, 10, 11, 14; 11.4; Gal 6.17; Phil 2.10; 1 Th 1.10; 4.14). Its presence here excludes any idea that the instruction is solely about the exalted Christ (e.g. that he intercedes in heaven for believers). At the other extreme, as it were, it is probably not intended to indicate that the instruction is based on the life and teaching of the historical Jesus; when the letter moves on to detailed moral instruction there is, in accordance with the normal trend in the Pauline corpus, no attempt to relate this to the earthly Jesus. Yet the use of **Jesus** suggests the historical person. By the time of the writing of Ephesians, assuming Paul is not the author, both the Gospel of Mark and the double tradition existed; there must by this time then have been some instruction about Jesus' life and teaching (cf Schnackenburg). In v. 24 believers are told to put on the new person; some concreteness to what this means may be supplied here by the reference to Jesus, just as appears to take place through the use of the name in 2 Cor 4.10, 11; Gal 6.17. It is not some ideal Christ who is the pattern but the incarnate Jesus; the name may then imply that the tradition which is taught stretches back to the earthly figure and is founded on him (Larsson). The name Jesus may be more appropriate to ethical instruction than Christ with its christological implications (Halter).

22. Vv. 2–4 contains three infinitives: **to put off, to be renewed, to put on.** Despite its difficulties the easiest solution is to take the three infinitives as dependent on **you were taught** (v. 21a) with **you** as resuming the subject after the parenthesis of v. 21b. If then the infinitives depend on the verb, an imperatival sense is to be favoured (cf Salmond; Schnackenburg; Lincoln) because of the continuing context of ethical instruction and the nature of what is being taught: **you were taught … that you were to …**.

If then the infinitives are given an imperatival sense it follows necessarily that they refer to the future and not the past; the putting off/on of the old/new person cannot refer simply to baptism, though from early times this connection has been made (Chrysostom; Theod Mops, *Gos Phil* II, 3 75.22–4); whatever the action is, it lies in the future. The metaphor of the putting on and off of clothing is central to vv. 22–4; it is an obvious metaphor for people manifest their character by the way they dress.

The metaphor was well known in the ancient world (e.g. Plato, *Rep* 457A; Euripides, *Iph Taur* 602; Dion Hal, *Ant Rom* ix 5; Libanius, *Ep* 968), in particular in religious writing (Apuleius, *Metamorphoses*, xi. 24; *Acts Thomas* 36, 66, *CH* 7.2), in the OT (e.g. Job 29.14; 35.26; Ps 132.9; Isa 59.17; 61.10) and in Judaism (e.g. Ecclus 45.8; Philo, *Fuga* 110; *Ebr* 86; *T Levi* 8.2; *Asc Isa* 7.22; 9.1; *1 En* 62.14–16; 1QS 4.8). In view of this widespread usage there is no need to resort to gnosis or the Mysteries to find the source of AE's use of the metaphor. Gnosis and the Mysteries indeed contain no proper parallel to his use. In the NT, apart from our present passage and Col 3.8–12, the metaphor is used, probably in catechesis, of the putting on and off of various vices and virtues (Rom 13.12; 1 Pet 2.1; Heb 12.1; Jas 1.21; 1 Th 5.5; Eph 6.11; cf 1 Clem 13.1; 57.2) and of the nature of existence after death (1 Cor 15.53f; 2 Cor 5.2–4). In Rom 13.14; Gal 3.27; Eph 4.22–4; Col 3.9f what is put on and off is described in personal terms.

By the time AE came to write, the metaphor was well established in Christian circles and had already been applied to the putting on and off of 'persons'; this appears first in Paul in respect of the putting on of Christ (Rom 13.14; Gal 3.27; cf *Gos Mary* BG 8502.1 18.16) prior to being used of the old and new persons in Col 3.9f; Eph 4.22, 24 (cf 'the body of flesh', Col 2.11). There is then no need to look for parallels in the non-Christian world which might have influenced AE. In Gal 3.27; Col 2.11f the metaphor is connected to baptism; is this relation present here? Certainly that relation is absent from its secular and OT usage and on those occasions in the NT when it refers to the afterlife; it is difficult also to find that relation when it is used of the putting on and off of virtues and vices and of armour. The metaphor has then no automatic connection to baptism and each occurrence must be

223

examined individually to see if it is present. In 4.22–4 the connection may be supported by 'old person' which recalls Rom 6.6 where the context is baptismal and by the parallel passage Col 3.8–12. There are however some significant differences between Colossians and Ephesians and it is impossible to call in Col 3.8–12 to determine the meaning of Eph 4.22–4.

If the putting on and off in Eph 4.22–4 referred to something that had happened in baptism, v. 24 would have followed directly on v. 22 (Haupt). It may of course be true that there had been teaching (v. 21) in the past about putting off and on, given probably at the time of baptism and conversion. There are also difficulties in the presentation of Colossians where in 3.8 believers are told to put off various vices and in 3.12 to put on various virtues; in 3.9 they are told they have put off the old person and in 3.10 have put on the new. But it is the vices which make the old person old and the virtues which make the new new. The putting off of the old and the putting on of the new must then be a gradual process which takes place by a renewal; v. 23 enables AE to avoid the ontological difficulties of Colossians and concentrate his attention on the actual ethical procedure.

In view of the way AE has coupled the old and new persons, we must leave the discussion of the nature of the old person until we can consider the two together at v. 24. Here in v. 22 we have two qualifying phrases **of your earlier way of life** and **which was being corrupted through deceitful desires**. Even if the metaphor has been drawn from the catechetical tradition it may not be fully understood by all AE's readers and requires some amplification. The first phrase connects the old person to his or her pre-Christian way of life. The former way of life has already been described in vv. 17–19 (cf 2.1f) and much more about it can be inferred from the remainder of the letter in so far as certain behaviour is no longer regarded as appropriate for believers. The second phrase depicts the old person as in a process of corruption through the desires of the flesh. The present tense implies a continuing process and therefore 'oldness' is not an inherited defect but something believers create for themselves. Since in 2.1 believers in their pre-Christian state were regarded as dead in sin there may be an inconsistency here, perhaps arising through AE's use of diverse strands of tradition; at this stage of Christianity not everything had been fully thought through. If 2.1 presented a realised eschato-logical death, 4.22 presents an eschatological death realising itself. The corruption spoken of here is not of course a destroy-ing of the old person but indicates instead the old person's increasing character. This inevitably leads to complete corruption in death, not merely physical but eternal death. The corruption takes place through **deceitful desires**. Wrong **desires** are seductive (cf Rom 7.11), but in the end they only deceive and fail to provide what they promise as Adam and Eve found in Eden (Gen 3.1ff; cf Van Roon). In 2.3 desires were seen as sinful and connected to the flesh; as such they cannot do other than bring corruption and ultimate destruction.

23. We now move from the negative to the positive (logically, of course, putting off precedes putting on) and the clothing metaphor is temporarily dropped to be taken up again in v. 24. Although v. 23 intervenes between the putting off of the old person (v. 22) and the putting on of the new (v. 24), it is not to be taken as suggesting a time interval between the two as if the old was put off, renewal took place and then the new was put on.

Renewal is an ambiguous term; it may refer to the restoration of a previous condition (cf Esth 3.13b; 1 Macc 12.10; 14.18, 22), but in Hellenistic Greek the preposition added to the verbs, represented in English by our *re-* in *renewal*, often served only to intensify the meaning of the verbal stem. It is unlikely that restoration is intended here, for nowhere else does AE depict the restoration of the Gentiles to a condition they once enjoyed and lost.

What is the role of the **spirit** in renewal? It has been interpreted as either the Holy Spirit, and taken as an instrumental dative (Origen; Theophylact; Oecumenius), or the human spirit as the sphere in which renewal takes place. Favouring a reference to the Holy Spirit are: (a) A power to bring about renewal is required and this would be the Holy Spirit (cf Tit 3.5); but the infinitive could be a divine passive and God be the one who renews. (b) Since the background to the metaphor of putting off and on may be baptism and the Spirit is given to believers at baptism (e.g. 1 Cor 12.13; Acts 2.38) a reference to the Holy Spirit is appro-priate; yet it is by no means certain that AE sees baptism as the background to the metaphor in 4.22–4. Favouring a reference to the human spirit are: (a) 'The spirit of your mind' is wholly in keeping with AE's style of using approximate synonyms with one in the genitive. (b) If the divine Spirit were intended the genitive **of your minds** is surprising. Probably then the reference is to the human spirit.

24. Just as the putting off of the old person was qualified with two phrases, so also is the putting on of the new (for the metaphor see on v. 22). The first of these indicates that **the new person** has **been created**; God is the real subject of this participle; the past tense denotes the moment of baptism/conversion. God who once created in Eden (Gen 1.27) creates again what has been spoiled by sin (4.17–19). Literally the Greek says that the new man has been created according to God. This could indicate (cf 2 Cor 7.9–11) the manner of creation, 'created in the way God creates' (cf Ewald), but that does not say anything of significance; God can hardly create in any other than in a Godlike manner. More probably the idea here is similar to that of Col 3.10 (and of Gen 1.26f) with the preposition signifying **in God's likeness** (cf 1 Pet 1.15; Heb 8.5).

In the light of the frequent usage of **righteousness** and **holiness** as a word pair it is not surprising to find them associated in the NT (Lk 1.75; 2 Th 2.10; Tit 1.8; Rev 16.5) and in early Christianity (1 Clem 14.1; 45.3; 2 Clem 6.9; 15.3). Their significance would have been easily grasped by Gentile Christians. AE will have known them as a word pair describing personal piety in accordance with God's will. Because they formed an ethical word pair it is pointless to enquire whether Paul could have used **righteousness** of human behaviour (2 Cor 6.7; 9.10; Phil 1.7; 4.8 imply he could); AE also gives the root an ethical connotation in Eph 5.9; 6.14. Their existence as a word pair also means AE neither selected them from a list of possible virtues in order to highlight them, nor attempted to distinguish between them as specifying conduct towards God and towards other human beings. Yet it is legitimate to ask why AE chose this word pair and neither the list of virtues of Col 3.12, which are apparently more Christian, nor 'love', which would sum up Christian conduct more adequately. The use of love in the two great commandments (Mk 12.29–31) shows that it covers all human activity and in Paul it is the supreme virtue (1 Cor 13.13). AE himself employs it frequently. Perhaps it was the secular usage of the word pair which led AE to prefer it here; if so it gives an interesting insight into his approach to his readers; he will use terms they already know so that they can grasp his meaning. The words moreover are sufficiently general for his audience to read into them their own Christian ideal of behaviour. By connecting the word pair directly to the new Christian existence, AE has given a more ethical slant to the new person than does A/Col and this enables him to move directly into his detailed paraenesis (4.25–6.20). The last Greek word of v. 24 is literally 'of truth', just as the last Greek word of v. 22 is 'of deceit'. It is possible to read deep meaning into the word for the gospel is truth (cf 1.13; 4.21; Col 1.5), and righteousness and holiness are founded on the gospel, but it is easier to take it as an adjectival qualification of the other two nouns. The contrast 'deceit/truth' may reflect the same contrast as found in Qumran (e.g. 1QS 4.2–11); 'truth' would then be a genitive of the subject: the righteousness and holiness which truth produces; this however gives too much prominence to truth as an agency and it is doubtful if the contrast would have been easily appreciated in this way by Greek readers.

For the literal expression 'the new man' we have chosen **person** as best representing the non-male use of 'man'. Yet the real problem does not lie in the choice of a suitable English word but in understanding how a 'person' can be put off or put on; *Acts Philip* 8 speaks of putting off the mind of the old man.

Paul, assuming he did not write Ephesians and Colossians, never used the phrase **new person**, but he does speak of the crucifixion of the old person with Christ (Rom 6.6) in a context of baptism and of the dissociation of Christian existence from sin. Gal 5.24 suggests a relation between the old person and the flesh (cf 1 Cor 3.3). If the putting off of the old person is not a single instantaneous action it resembles daily dying (1 Cor 15.31; 2 Cor 4.10–12) and repentance (Rom 2.4; 2 Cor 7.9f; 12.21; for Paul repentance is part of Christian living and not simply a prerequisite for conversion). Paul may have envisaged a similar contrast to that of old and new persons when he wrote of an outer and inner being (2 Cor 4.16; Rom 7.22; cf Eph 3.16; 1 Pet 3.4). If however Paul does not speak directly of the new person nor apply the clothing metaphor to the putting off of the old, he does write of the putting on of Christ; in Gal 3.27 this is related to baptism; in Rom 13.14 this relation cannot be present because we have an imperative addressed to those who are already Christians. Paul also writes of Christians as those made anew (2 Cor 5.17; Gal 6.15) and in this way introduces both the concept of newness and, through the idea of creation, the original Adam; this raises the possibility of either the identification of the old person with Adam and the new with Christ or their paralleling with Adam and Christ, an interpretation which may gain support from Paul's contrast of the first and second Adam in 1 Cor 15.45ff, where he indeed introduces the idea of the putting off of mortality and the putting on of immortality (15.53f). J. R. Díaz suggests a parallel to the putting off and on in God's stripping Adam of his pre-fall glorious clothing, but this seems too far-fetched for AE's readers to have grasped.

If we move to a more modern idiom and try to express what the old and new persons mean we might speak of an old mind-set and a new mind-set or an old lifestyle and a new lifestyle.

AE has now set out the basis of his ethical position; believers are new people called to live in righteousness and holiness. In 4.25ff he spells this out in practical terms in respect of their relation to one another.

XI

BEHAVE SO AS TO PRESERVE UNITY

(4.25–5.2)

25 Putting off lying
   everyone should speak the truth to neighbours
   for we are members one of another.
26 If angry do not sin,
   do not let the sun go down while you are still irritated
27   nor give an opening to the devil.
28 Let the thief thieve no longer
   but rather labour working honestly with his own hands
      for the (common) good
   so that he may have (something) to share with the needy.
29 Do not allow evil speech to emerge from your mouth
   but only whatever is good
   so as to build up where there is need
      in order to bring a blessing to those who hear.
30 And do not pain the Holy Spirit of God
   in whom you were sealed for the day of deliverance.
31 Let all bitterness and wrath and anger and shouting and
      denunciation be put away from you
   with all malice.
32 But be good to one another, compassionate, forgiving each
      other
   even as God has forgiven you in Christ.
5.1 Be then imitators of God as (his) beloved children
2 and behave lovingly,
      even as Christ loved us
      and gave himself on our behalf
         a sweet-smelling offering and sacrifice to God.

AE now begins to describe how the new person ought to differ from the old and what being a new person entails, and does this in the context of the need to maintain the unity of the community. He has explained the theology of unity; now he comes to its practice. The major imperatives were given in 4.2f, 22–4; now minor imperatival statements fill in the detail. Here and in succeeding paragraphs AE has taken over ethical material originating in Judaism, if not in the secular world, and christianised it, usually through the motivation he offers. His exhortations relate to life within the community (cf 4.2), as is immediately made explicit in 4.25b, and not to the behaviour of Christians towards non-Christians.

Accepting v. 25 as the beginning of the pericope it should probably be seen as continuing to 5.2 (cf Schnackenburg) rather than ending at 4.32.

4.25–5.2 commences with four brief exhortations on lying (25), anger (26f), theft (28) and impure speech (29). Though lying and anger are associated in *T Dan* (see on v. 27) there is no reason to suppose that the order in which AE offers these four exhortations was traditional or that he is expanding a brief vice list which contained these four themes. Lying may come first because of the immediately preceding reference to 'truth' (4.24). Each of the four exhortations is balanced with a reason for avoiding it, a movement from the negative to the positive as in 4.17–24, from the old person to the new. These four exhortations are followed by a more general warning (v. 30) to readers lest they offend against the Christian position they adopted when they first believed. Two brief associated summaries follow, the first (v. 31), negative, a list of the ways in which anger expresses itself, the second (v. 32a) a brief list of virtues; again a reason is attached in v. 32b. The paragraph concludes with two positive exhortations (5.1, 2a), the first being closely linked in content to 4.32, and the two are reinforced with a reminder of what Christ has done for the readers (5.32b).

25. This first injunction picks up the references to truth and falsehood in vv. 21, 22, 24 and is introduced with the participle of the verb AE used in v. 22. **Putting off** is not to be taken with the sense 'once for all' as if lying were put off once for all in conversion/baptism. It is impossible to speak the truth until lies have been given up; the sense may then be 'once you have put aside the lie, speak the truth'. The verb has an established place in introducing catechetical instruction (1 Pet 2.1f; Jas 1.21; Rom 13.12; Selwyn).

Putting off lying is literally 'put off the lie' but 'the lie' is the neither 'the lie' as if implying a false attitude to life (Murray; Rienecker) nor does it imply that AE considered Gentile culture to be a 'lie' or every Gentile statement as false; it refers to the practice or habit of lying and here as in the following verses the reference is to particular sins. The stress on speaking the truth and the avoidance of falsehood goes back to the Decalogue (cf Mk 10.19; Mt 5.33) and is continually emphasised in later Judaism, Prov 4.24; 6.19; *T Reub* 3.9; *T Issach* 7.4; *T Dan* 1.3; 2.1, 4; 5.1; 6.2; 1QS 10.22; the same stress is of course also found among the pagan moralists, e.g. M. Aurelius 9.1. Despite the way in which he concentrates on sins which would destroy community life, AE does not go as far as Ps 101.7 in suggesting the exclusion from the community of those who lie.

AE reinforces his demand for truthfulness by quoting Zech 8.16, 'let every one speak the truth to his neighbour', which had been already used for a similar purpose in *T Dan* 5.2 and AE may well then have taken it from traditional catechetical instruction rather than directly from the OT. What did his readers make of the term 'neighbour'? In Zech 8.16 the neighbour is another Israelite; here it appears to be another Christian, for in the final clause of the verse AE employs the conception of the church as a body, and thus gives the injunction a Christian motivation.

When AE earlier used the conception of the body he had stressed the body as the body of Christ with Christ as its head; he thus laid emphasis on the relationship of believers to their head (1.23; 2.16; 4.7–16) and not as here on their relationship to one another, though 2.16 does relate the group of Jewish to the group of Gentile believers. The relationship of believers to one another within the body had been one of Paul's emphases in his use of the phrase 'body of Christ' (1 Cor 12.12ff; Rom 12.3ff). AE has returned to this original emphasis, an emphasis corresponding to the metaphor's use in the Greco-Roman world (see Detached Note: The Body of Christ).

If AE has interpreted neighbour in Zech 8.16 as 'fellow believer', has he failed to grasp the Christian meaning of the word? Jesus redefined the Jewish concept of neighbour to mean anyone and everyone (Lk 10.29–37). Jerome (cf Irenaeus, 4.37.4; Mitton; Houlden) is one of the few commentators to note this redefinition but after noting it he makes nothing of it and goes on to take v. 25c as referring to the church. Grotius, followed by Macpherson, takes v. 25c to refer to human society in general and not the church, and so is able to take neighbour in the sense Jesus gave it. Isolated from the letter and taken against the background of the contemporary world this could be the meaning; it would accord with the Stoic idea that all people were members one of another; it is also true that all human society depends on people speaking the truth to one another. If, however, we take v. 25c to refer to the church, as it surely does, does this mean that the speaking of truth by Christians is to be restricted to fellow Christians? If the point had been put directly to AE he would almost certainly have denied any such restriction, yet the restriction is implicitly present. Fairly rapidly within early Christianity the emphasis was placed on loving fellow Christians (Rom 12.10; 1 Th 4.9; Heb 13.1; 1 Pet 1.22; 2.17; John 13.34f; 15.12, 17; 1 Jn 3.11, 23; 4.11). We still find love to all in Paul (Rom 13.8–10; Gal 5.14; 1 Th 3.12; Gal 6.10; in the latter two instances the restricted idea is also present), but it is hard to trace it in the NT after Paul other than in the Synoptic tradition of the teaching of Jesus. Reciprocal love is also found in *T Sim* 4.7; *T Jos* 17.2–8; *Jub* 20.2; 36.4, 8; *Gos Thom* II, 2 (log 25) 38.10–12; *Treat Seth* VII, 2 62.19–21. It is fair to note that in *T Issach* 7.6; *T Gad* 4.7 love is to be offered to all and that in the case of at least one minor cult in Philadelphia (see Barton and Horsley) members are instructed not to practise deceit against any man or woman.

26. This forms with v. 27 a unit. The latter by itself, though a true and necessary injunction, requires some context to which it can apply; it is tied in here by **nor** (Ewald; Abbott). V. 26a is drawn from Ψ 4.5. The LXX does not render exactly the MT but this would not have concerned AE who may not have known the MT, and who, if he did, for the sake of his readers had to use the LXX. In fact he gives no positive evidence that he is aware that he is using the OT. Ps 4.2 already referred to lying and in *T Dan* 1.3; 2.1; 3.5f; 4.6f; 5.1; 6.8 lying and anger are associated.

Probably they were then linked in Jewish ethical tradition and from it entered Christian teaching joined together. Later, v. 26b was taken to be a saying of Jesus.

At first sight the translation of v. 26a appears to be 'be angry and do not sin'; such a rendering might suggest Christians were required to be angry. This need not however be so if the first imperative is taken as concessive or conditional (cf Jn 2.19; 2 Cor 12.16); the meaning is then, 'If you are angry do not sin', 'when angry do not sin'.

Anger leads easily to the loss of a sense of judgement and so to sin and can appear in different ways, from the passionate outburst to the sullen bearing of grudges. The question whether righteous anger is possible goes back as far as Origen. It is unlikely that AE has in mind here anger on behalf of those who are suffering at the hands of others, but the passion aroused in those who believe they themselves have been injured. This is also true of the rejection of anger in the Wisdom literature (e.g. Prov 15.1, 18; 22.24; 29.8, 11, 22; Eccles 7.9; Ecclus 1.22; 27.30; cf 1 Tim 2.8; Tit 1.7). In these cases action should be left to God (Rom 12.19).

Yet since anger does occur in groups of people and destroys their relationship, AE sees the need to put some limitation on it (v. 26b). His approach is thus practical rather than theoretical, and his limitation one of time. 'The day of anger should be the day of reconciliation' (Eadie). Twice in the OT the sunset limitation is introduced as a provision of mercy (Deut 24.15, 23) to prevent hardship. The same provision with a closer relation to anger is also found in CD 9.2–8; 7.2f; 1QS 5.26–6.1. Plutarch, *Mor* 488BC, mentions it in relation to the Pythagoreans. 4.26b may then be a proverbial saying.

27. AE now offers an additional reason for the rejection of anger. Anger gives an opportunity for **the devil** to intervene. A few commentators (e.g. Erasmus; Ewald) have given the word a human reference, 'the slanderer'; while this is a legitimate meaning of the word it is contrary to its normal NT usage, and nothing in the context suggests it. Here in v. 27 the sin has already occurred in the anger of the believer before the devil is mentioned. He has not caused the anger, but as God's opponent can be counted on to stir the pot and use it to disturb the relation of believers with those with whom they are angry, who might then themselves respond angrily. Although the devil is associated with lying and anger in *T Dan* 5.1f (cf Hermas, *Mand* 5.1.3), it is not necessary to see this passage, or the tradition which it represents, as directly leading to his introduction here.

28. This verse continues the pattern of a negative statement followed by a positive in relation to community conduct.

The area of conduct treated here changes abruptly and is in the singular unlike the preceding and following injunctions.

While it is probable that lying and anger were connected in some Jewish paraenesis (see on v. 26) theft was not linked with them. Theft was, however, recognised in Judaism from the time of the Decalogue as a major sin (Isa 1.23; Jer 7.9; Lev 19.11; *Ps-Phoc* 153ff; cf SB I, 810–13), and was repudiated in the main streams of Greco-Roman culture; Epictetus, 3.8.10ff, deplores the view he attributes to Epicurus that it is not stealing itself which is wrong but being found out (cf Xenophon, *Anab* 7.6.41; Plato, *Rep* I 344b; Heroditus I 186.3)!

Those who have been stealing are bidden to work. Jews valued work highly as a normal human activity (Exod 20.9; Ps 104.23; Prov 6.6; 28.19; Ecclus 7.15; *T Issach* 5.3; Josephus *c. Ap.* 2.291); the idle rich were denounced (cf Amos 6.4–6). Jesus had a trade, and teachers of the Law were generally expected to support themselves (*m Abot* 2.2). Work was also highly valued in the Greco-Roman world (Epict 1.16.16f; 3.26.27f; 8.26.2f; Dio *Orat* 7.112f; 123f). AE's words in v. 28 are very similar to Paul's in 1 Cor 4.12.

Our verse provides no 'theology' of work. Its purpose has been viewed in many different ways. Here only the case of reformed thieves is considered: they should work so that they may not be a burden on the community (cf 2 Th 3.6ff). The connection here is similar to the Jewish link between work and almsgiving (Agnell; cf *T Issach* 5.3; 7 5; *T Zeb* 6.5f; *Ps-Phoc* 22ff).

While the total meaning is clear, the good of the community, the phrase may have been deliberately chosen to draw out the difference in moral value between what the thief could do now and what he has been doing, and should be taken adverbially, **working honestly**.

29. While v. 29 is not directly connected to v. 28 it is structurally similar: each begins with a negative statement, moves to a positive and ends with a final clause; they also share two major concepts, **good** and **need**. Judaism was certainly aware of the power of speech to do good or evil (Prov 10.31f; 12.17–19; 15.2, 23; Ecclus 5.10–14; 18.15–17; 21.25f; 1QS 7.9; CD 10.17f; *T Issach* 4.14, 17; *b Shab* 30b). The most detailed NT reference to speech is Jas 3.6ff (cf Mt 12.33–7). In v. 29 it is the power of speech to do evil which is introduced first, and this with a rather imprecise word. It must, given the general sense of **evil**, indicate a sin on the same level as lying and stealing (Robinson); evil speech not only harms the one who utters it but harms the community in which it is spoken (Barry); in contrast with what builds up, it destroys (Gnilka) and corrupts its community; it is then a metaphorical parallel to its use in describing decaying vegetable matter and fish. Yet it still leaves open wide possibilities; since v. 25 dealt with lying it may refer to abusive gossip, obscenity, pornography, heresy (cf 2 Tim 2.14), cynicism, sarcasm, or the attribution of evil motives to those who do good; a list open to indefinite expansion.

The mouths of believers should only utter (the main verb must be understood again in v. 29b) good speech which would serve to build up those who hear it. Though the main sense is clear this is not true of all the details, in particular the qualification **where there is need**. The word translated **need** should probably, but by no means certainly, be given the sense 'need' or 'opportunity': the building up of another takes place when there is a need for it and/or the opportunity opens for doing so (cf NRSV, REB, NJB). Believers build up one another in worship through what they say or sing (5.19; 1 Cor 14.3–5, 12, 26) or more generally in day-to-day living (Rom 14.19) where their words may mediate grace (v. 29c). **To bring a blessing** may be used in a general way of doing a good turn to someone (Eadie and Harless give classical references) but in the light of the Christian use of 'grace' it is preferable to restrict it to speech conferring spiritual benefit (cf Lk 4.22; Eccles 10.12). If it refers to spiritual benefit this is not to be taken in any narrow sense of spiritual; it will include words of comfort spoken in a time of sorrow, of encouragement in a time of doubt, of good counsel in a time of uncertainty as to action. In these and other ways the words of any believer can convey grace to hearers. Such helping speech is confined neither to corporate worship nor to the lips of religious officials, though this restriction may be present in 4.12.

30. This verse differs both structurally and in content from the injunctions of vv. 25–9; it contains only a negative injunction with no balancing positive; the motive for action appears in a relative clause and lacks the social aspect. It resembles v. 27 in being a general exhortation and moves the motivation from concern for the good of the community to a deeper level (cf 1 Th 4.8), though of course the Spirit is always the Spirit which is present in the community (1 Cor 3.16) and is generally related to behaviour (e.g. Gal 5.16, 25); at the deeper level it can be applied to all Christian behaviour. Before examining where the verse fits into its context we need to enquire after its content.

Fee sees dependence here on Isa 63.10. At first sight this seems justified but the resemblance relates to content in respect of the Hebrew text; verbal agreement with the LXX is much less pronounced.

AE employs an unusually full term for the Spirit; 'Spirit of God' and 'Holy Spirit' are normal; here they are combined (cf 1 Th 4.8). Similar references to the Spirit are found in Judaism (*T Issach* 4.40; *T Dan* 4.5), and the idea reappears in Hermas, *Mand* 10.2.1ff; 3.2ff.

The Holy Spirit sealed and authenticated believers at their conversion/baptism. Sealing is not exclusively connected with baptism (see on 1.13); it refers to the beginning of the Christian life as 'deliverance' does to its end (Stott). Believers now belong to God and this up to the time of, or with a view to, **the day of deliverance** (see on 1.7 for the word). The phrase is unique. The 'day' as indicating a future significant event appears in phrases like 'the day of the Lord' (1 Th 5.2; 2 Th 2.2; 1 Cor 1.8; 5.5; 2 Cor 1.14) which derives from the OT 'day of Yahweh', 'day of Christ' (Phil 1.6, 10; 2.16), and 'day of judgement and wrath' (Rom 2.5). The day of judgement is also a day of salvation (Rom 2.5, 7; 13.11f; Phil 1.6, 10; 2.16) and it is salvation and not judgement which is featured in v. 30. Our verse appears in a paraenetic passage counselling future good Christian conduct and containing a reference to the Holy Spirit in regard to whom the future cannot be eliminated (1.13f). A time is coming when believers will enjoy a fuller life. It cannot be denied that the letter contains an unresolved eschatological tension; to insist that the deliverance is fully accomplished is to ignore one side of this tension.

How does this verse fit into its context? It could be taken in isolation; since at least the time of Tertullian (*Ad martyras* 1.53) preachers and writers have detached it from its context and applied it to whatever sin they were attacking; this seems a weak solution. V. 30, like v. 27, expresses a different type of motivation for Christian conduct; it does not speak directly of doing harm to the community. It sets the activity of believers in relation to God; if vv. 25–9 run along the lines of the second table of the Decalogue, v. 30 corresponds to the first.

31. This verse is negative; v. 32a is positive; v. 32b gives a motivation. The pattern of vv. 25–8 is thus followed (Lincoln), yet vv. 31, 32a differ greatly from the negative and positive portions of the earlier verses in that they do not treat individual vices separately but several vices and virtues at the same time; the resemblance may then be purely chance. AE has been issuing a number of warning exhortations to his readers and it is good psychology to move from negative to positive and add a motivation. Since the positive exhortation of v. 32 relates to behaviour within the community ('one another') the negative exhortation of v. 31 will do the same, and so harmonise with the remainder of the paragraph.

Verse 31 commences with a pentad of substantives, all related to the theme of anger, and ends with a more generalised word for vice. What is the origin of these six vices? A list in Col 3.8 has four of them. This may suggest that the impulse to describe anger using a number of terms derives from Col 3.8 or from the Pauline school to which AE and A/Col belonged; however the description of anger using a succession of terms is also found in Stoicism (Chrysippus, *frag* 395, cf 394, 396f, v. Arnim III 96.3ff; Seneca, *De ira* 1.4; cf Philo, *Ebr* 223). For his list AE may then be directly or indirectly indebted to Stoicism; in v. 24 he defined virtue in Hellenistic terms; perhaps he deliberately chose terms known at least to the better educated of his readers.

The first term, **bitterness**, is not in Col 3.8 but is in the lists of Chrysippus and Philo. An infrequent term in the NT (Acts 8.23; Rom 3.14; Heb 12.15) its use apart from v. 31 derives from the LXX. The root is sometimes used with physical significance (Jas 3.11; Rev 8.11; 10.9, 10) but also in relation to vice (Jas 3.14; Col 3.19) and twice of Peter's repentance after denying Jesus

(Mt 26.75; Lk 22.62). In our verse it indicates that underlying feeling of bitterness and resentment from which anger springs.

The second and third terms are normal words for anger; they were distinguished by some of the moralists in their discussions of anger (Chrysippus, *frag* 395; Diog. Laertes 7.113f; Seneca, *De ira* 2.36) but were often used as synonyms (Rom 2.8; Rev 14.10; Ecclus 48.10; 1 Clem 50.4). Both terms are applied to divine anger (Jn 3.36; Rom 1.18; Eph 5.6; Rev 19.5; Rev 14.10, 19; 15.1, 7) and to human (Mk 3.5; 1 Tim 2.8; Jas 1.19f; Lk 4.28; Acts 19.28; 2 Cor 12.20; Gal 5.20). It is therefore difficult to argue that AE saw them as greatly different. If the words require to be distinguished in meaning, **wrath** indicates the passionate outburst, **anger** the inward seething. Together they display AE's condemnation of all forms of anger whether smouldering or passionate.

If the first noun suggested the inner feeling resulting in the anger of the second and third, the fourth and fifth relate to the outward manifestation of anger. Angry people often shout loudly. The fifth term is shared with Col 3.8, and may describe speech directed against God (Mk 14.64; Lk 5.21; Acts 6.11) or against humans (Mk 7.22; 1 Cor 10.30; 1 Tim 6.4; 2 Tim 3.2; Tit 3.2). The general tenor of the paragraph implies AE has primarily a sin against other church members in mind. Angry people shout loudly at and revile the objects of their wrath. There is thus a steady movement from the inner bitter disposition to denunciatory speech.

The interpretation of the five terms as a developing sequence (the same idea is expressed quite differently in *T Dan* 4.2–4) goes back at least to Chrysostom and describes what may happen in a quarrel (Murray). Only the elimination of bitterness can ensure the absence of the other vices. Because of the steady progression and concentration on only one vice it is doubtful if the five nouns can be properly classified as a vice catalogue (see on 5.3 for this 'form') since the catalogues normally list a variety of sins. Anger, then, with all its ramifications is to be put away by readers.

The final phrase of the verse summarises, broadens and concludes the discussion. **Malice** is a general word for wickedness but there are other such general words; AE has probably selected it because it can also have a more restricted meaning as its use alongside other words shows (Rom 1.29f; 1 Cor 5.8; Col 3.8; Tit 3.3; Jas 1.21; 1 Pet 2.1). In its present context we should take it as continuing the theme of the destructive power originating in bitterness and developing into anger.

AE warned against anger in 4.26f; why has he returned to the theme? He does not return to any of the other sins of vv. 25–9.

32. After v. 31 this verse returns to the pattern of vv. 25–30 with believers as the subjects of the imperatives. Unlike v. 31 it is positive in tone.

The Greek word *chrestos* translated **good** was in common non-Jewish and non-Christian use to describe a good person. Basically a term of relationship it is used in the LXX and the NT to describe: (i) God's goodness to humans (Lk 6.35; Rom 2.4; 1 Pet 2.3; for the noun, see Rom 11.22; Tit 3.4); this use is comparatively infrequent in non-Jewish Greek; (ii), as here, of the goodness of people to one another (2 Cor 6.6; Gal 5.22). Since the verse goes on to relate human to divine conduct its use is appropriate here. It is unlikely that there is any play, as in 1 Pet 2.3 which draws on Ps 34.8, on the similarity of the word to Christ. **Compassionate**, like many terms relating to the emotions, betrays its physiological origin in its structure: good in the inward parts. A term used by secular writers, though not in the LXX, it is applied in extra-biblical Jewish texts (*T Sim* 4.4; *T Zeb* 5.1; 8.1; 9.7; *Prayer of Manasseh* 7) to both God and humans. In *T Zeb* 5.1; 8.1; *T Benj* 4.2 it is used of the true attitude to everyone in contrast to that towards neighbours, i.e. other Jews; AE uses it of an attitude to other Christians and not to everyone. It appears in the NT at 1 Pet 3.8 and in later Christian usage (Polyc *Phil* 5.2; 6.1; 1 Clem 14.3). The third element in the sequence is expressed (cf Col 3.13) through a present participle, **forgiving each other**, suggesting an unlimited succession of acts of forgiveness (cf Mt 18.21f). Good and compassionate people will forgive others and so the vices like anger which would destroy the community (v. 31) are themselves destroyed. The verb, though not originally meaning 'to forgive', gained this sense, presumably through its relation to 'grace'; it is not used with this sense in the LXX but is in Josephus *Ant* 6.144; Lk 7.42f; 2 Cor 2.7, 10; 12.13; Col 2.13; 3.13 (it retains its older sense in Lk 7.21; Acts 3.14; 25.11, 16; etc.).

A motive is now introduced: God has forgiven believers. The past tense suggests the moment of forgiveness as that of conversion/baptism, though it could possibly have been that of the death of Christ. Christ enters the picture in Ephesians because God has forgiven **in Christ**. **Even as** is certainly causal (forgive because God has forgiven you; God's action in Christ is the basis of Christian behaviour). Christ is introduced here as in 2 Cor 5.19; God's forgiveness is linked to what has happened in Christ (cf 1.7). The two adjectives in v. 32a were qualities which could apply both to God and humans; now human behaviour is directly linked to divine. The parable of the unforgiving servant (Mt 18.23–35) teaches that those who have experienced forgiveness should themselves forgive; equally in Jn 13.34; 1 Jn 4.11, 19 (cf *T Zeb* 7.2) to be loved by God should lead the one loved to love. The basis of Christian action lies in what God has done for Christians. There is however a distinction here in respect of human and divine forgiveness from that in the Lord's Prayer (Mt 6.12, 14; Lk 11.4; cf Mk 11.25; *T Zeb* 8.1) where human forgiveness precedes divine forgiveness, even if it is not a pre-requisite of the latter. Goodness, compassion and a forgiving spirit are essential for those living in community (cf 1QS 2.24f).

5.1. The idea of 4.32b, forgive as God forgives, is now widened here into imitation of God and in v. 2 to 'love'. Naturally a widening to imitation can only be partial for it is impossible to imitate God in everything. Since human beings are part of his creation they can create neither him nor one another. It is only in 5.1 that the NT speaks explicitly of the imitation of God but the theme appears in early post-Ephesian literature (Ign *Eph* 1.1; *Trall* 1.2; *Diogn* 10.4–6; Iren 3.20.2).

Certain factors operated against the appearance among Jews of the idea of the imitation of God: the initial sin of Adam and Eve as the desire to be like God, the existence of human sin, the second commandment forbidding the making of any likeness to God, the Hellenistic usage of imitation in relation to sculpture. Indeed the thought of the imitation of the invisible God is paradoxical. As a result it was only towards the end of the first century that the idea began to appear in Palestinian Judaism (Abba Schaul in *Midrash Siphre* on Lev 19.2; *Tg Jer* I, Lev 22.28). None of this hindered the acceptance of similarity to God in the age to come (cf 1 Jn 3.2). It is sometimes suggested that equivalent ideas to the imitation of God are to be found in the OT, ideas such as following Yahweh, walking in his ways; these ideas however involve obedience. The very centrality of human obedience in the OT may itself have been another factor hindering the concept of imitation from entering Judaism. Lev 19.2 may seem to provide a parallel to imitation with its implication that Jews should exhibit the same holiness as God, and this is certainly how that passage is understood in 1 Pet 1.15f, but in Leviticus the relation is causal rather than comparative. 1 Pet 1.15f (cf Lk 6.36f; Mt 5.44–8; Jn 17.11, 21; Col 3.13, if Lord means God; 1 Jn 4.11) takes it comparatively, showing the idea had entered early Christianity, though Eph 5.1 is its only explicit statement. Paul writes of imitating Christ (1 Cor 11.1; 1 Th 1.6) and instructs his converts to imitate himself (1 Cor 4.16; 11.1; 1 Th 1.6; 2 Th 3.7, 9; Phil 3.17; cf Gal 4.12) and other Christians (1 Th 1.6; 2.14; 2 Th 3.7–9). We should not then be surprised to find AE speaking of the imitation of God; in doing so he goes beyond Paul, being more open to Hellenistic thought (Ernst).

If comparison was absent in 4.32b and perhaps also in 5.2 it is clearly present in 5.1; if so, what features of God's activities are believers to imitate? The context, 4.32 and 5.2 suggests the readiness to forgive and love, love being a generalisation of forgiveness. Philo's statement in *Spec Leg* 4.73 appears similar. In 5.1 believers are described as God's **beloved children** (cf 1.5); 'beloved' is used both of groups of Christians and of individual Christians (Rom 1.7; 11.28; 1 Tim 6.2; Rom 16.5, 8; Eph 6.21), and of Christ (Mk 1.11; 9.7). What is the significance of this address? Are believers to imitate God because they are his children (Bouwman) or in the way children should imitate a parent (Chrysostom) or are both ideas present (Salmond)? As we have seen, the imitation theme was used in the ancient world in respect of fathers and sons (cf 1 Cor 4.14, 16); is this why AE introduces children here? Unlike Mt 5.48 our passage lacks an explicit reference to God as Father. Yet believers as God's children is an important theme of Pauline theology (Rom 8.14–21; Gal 3.26; 4.6f; Phil 2.15) and appears in Eph 1.5. Probably then it was the theme of filial imitation which led to the present description of believers as children, yet it would be hazardous to go further and regard this as implying obedience or any kind of obligation. Action comparable to God's action in forgiving and loving is the primary emphasis.

Imitation of God seems somewhat more arid than imitation of Christ, particularly when the latter is understood as 'living like Jesus'. But imitation of Jesus as seen by Paul is not imitation of the day-to-day life of the historical Jesus; it relates rather to his incarnation and death (Phil 2.5–11; 2 Cor 8.9; Rom 15.3, 7). It may be this which enables AE to move directly from imitation of God to loving like Christ (v. 2), a movement perhaps also inspired in part by the depiction of Jesus as the image of God in the Colossian hymn (1.15), a hymn probably known in the Pauline school. It is through Christ that God's love and forgiveness are known and it is essentially in these that imitation should take place.

2. Since they are children whom God loves (v. 1) love should characterise the behaviour of believers. While AE's reference to love might be thought to come from Col 3.14 it is so much the essential characteristic of Christian existence (cf 3.14–19) that its introduction here is perfectly natural and there is no need to identify a precise verse in Colossians from which it may have been drawn. Love builds up the body of Christ (4.15f) and the preceding context suggests AE has the Christian community continually in mind. The nature of love is spelt out as little here as in Mk 12.31 (contrast 1 Cor 13.1ff), though a partial description lies in the positive statements of 4.25ff. No direct connection was made in v. 1 between God's love and that of believers; the latter is now linked to the love of Christ. His love is the supreme motivation of human love (cf 1 Jn 3.16). As in 4.32 **even as** may be either causal (Christ's love as motivation) or comparative (Christ's love as example) or a mixture of both. As in 4.32, it is difficult to take it as purely comparative for Christ's love, or God's love in Christ, is unique in that Christ gave himself for all. Our love cannot lead us to act soteriologically as he did, though in a willingness to forget ourselves and put others first it can be said to resemble his love.

In v. 2b action is ascribed to Christ. Normally it is God who is said to love people and either he or a human agent to hand Christ over to death (Rom 8.32). Here, as in 5.25; Gal 2.20, Christ is the real subject, the verbs are active and in each case the past tense refers to the historical Christ. Here it is believers whom he loves, in 5.25 the church and in Gal 2.20 Paul. This strongly suggests the use of an accepted form (the idea goes back at least to von Soden). Within the Pauline school, or at least that part of it to which AE belonged, what Paul said in particular of himself (Gal 2.20) has been generalised so that all believers are set on his level, not that Paul would have wished to imply that he was the unique object of Christ's redemptive activity. If then this is a formula in use within the Pauline school, the acceptance of the first plural reading as against the second plural of some manuscripts is made easier. As a formula it may have been originally connected to baptism (cf 5.25; Tit 2.13) with its inspiration coming from Isaiah 53. Christ loved us 'and so', or 'in that he', gave himself up. Christ's love is actualised in his self-surrender (Aquinas, depending on Gregory the Great). AE's readers would at once see a reference to Christ's death and this did not need to be explicitly stated. That this death was for the benefit of others was a pre-Pauline belief (Rom 3.24f; 4.25a; 5.6–8; 8.32; Gal 1.4; 1 Cor 15.3–5) which Paul continued to hold (e.g. 1 Th 5.10; Rom 14.15; 1 Cor 8.11; 2 Cor 5.14f; and Gal 2.20, if this is not to be placed in the pre-Pauline material); it is also found in Christian literature preceding or contemporary with Ephesians, if Ephesians is non-Pauline (e.g. Mk 10.45; 1 Jn 2.2; 4.10; 1 Pet 3.18). Gentile Christians would have been able to grasp something of the significance of such a death, for dying so that a city or state might benefit and dying as atoning sacrifice were well-known ideas in the ancient world. AE does not provide us here or elsewhere with sufficient information to enable the placing of his view of the benefits of Christ's death in terms of later developed soteriology, e.g. whether Christ died representatively, as a substitute, as liberating ransom, or as atoning sacrifice. Nor can we trace back from his brief reference a clear path to the origin of the idea in Isaiah, in the Maccabean martyrs or in some other source. Lacking information about AE's views it is unwise to speculate. It was not his intention here to express a soteriological theory but to remind his readers of Christ's death as one from which they have benefited so that they themselves will live lovingly. The nature of the benefit they receive from Christ's life, death and resurrection is spelt out in other parts of the letter: their sins are forgiven (1.7), they are adopted as God's children (1.5), they have been raised with Christ and sit with him in the heavenlies (2.5f), they belong to his body (4.7ff), they are new people (4.24).

The final words of the verse, which are not part of the formula, are intended to drive home the need to love, but do they not imply an understanding of Christ's death as sacrificial? **Offering** is not a word strongly associated with the sacrificial system; it is not found in the LXX translation of Leviticus (though Aq and Th have it at 1.2); it is frequent only in Ecclesiasticus. **Sacrifice** is a very general word. The two words are associated in Ψ 39.7, which is quoted in Ecclus 34.19; Heb 10.5, and with other sacrificial terms in Dan 3.38 (LXX and Th). In view of their linkage in Ψ 39.7 and its Christian usage (Heb 10.5) the Psalm is probably AE's source, though not necessarily directly. Neither noun can be given a precise equivalent in the sacrificial system and they are probably a hendiadys (Lincoln) for the whole system. Atoning offerings would thus be included but they would not be at the top of AE's mind. When we recollect also the way in which sacrifice is spiritualised in the OT (Hos 6.6; Isa 1.11–15; Mic 6.6–8; Ps 50.13f, 23; 51.17; 141.2; cf 1QS 9.4f; 10.8, 14) and then in the NT (Rom 12.1; 15.17; Phil 2.17; 4.18; Heb 13.15f) it seems probable that in our verse it refers only to Christ's self-sacrifice. This should drive AE's readers to love. That this was how the words were understood in the early church can be seen from their application to martyrs in Ign *Rom* 4.2; *Mart Polyc* 14.1, 2. That it is also AE's view is shown by the closing words of the verse which do not stress the benefits of Christ's death for his readers but the acceptability of Christ's action to God.

The final phrase (literally 'as an odour of fragrance') is frequent in the OT; though originally understood physically as if God was pleased with the smell rising from sacrifices (Gen 8.21; Exod 29.18; Lev 2.9; etc.) it, like sacrifice, was spiritualised (Ezek 20.41; Dan 4.37a LXX; *T Levi* 3.6; Phil 4.18; cf *Barn* 2.10) and applied to life and action which was pleasing to God.

The motivation to conduct provided here and in 4.32 is not just an additional motivation comparable with those in 4.25–31 but is the basic motivation in a Christian ethic in a way those of 4.25–31 are not (cf Halter). They were peripheral; this is central.

XII

FROM LUST TO LIGHT

(5.3–14)

3 But sexual misconduct and every kind of impurity or greed
   should not even be named among you,
        as befits those who are holy,
4   and no obscene act and no foolish or smutty talk,
            which are not fitting,
        but rather thanksgiving.
5   For certainly know this,
            that no one who is unchaste or impure or covetous,
                that is an idolator,
            has an inheritance in the kingdom of Christ and of God.
6 Let no one deceive you with specious arguments,
        for because of these (sins) the wrath of God comes upon
            disobedient people.
7   Do not then participate in their sins.
8 For once you were darkness but now light in the Lord;
        behave as children of light
9   (for light's fruit is in all goodness and uprightness and
            truth)
10   finding out what is pleasing to the Lord,
11   and have no share in the unfruitful works of darkness,
        but rather reprove,
12   for it is shameful even to speak of what they have done in
            secret,
13   but all that is reproved by the light is revealed,
14   for everything that is revealed is light;
        therefore it (he) says
            Awake, O sleeper
            and rise up from the dead,
            and Christ shall shine for you.

Having dealt with a number of miscellaneous sins in 4.25–5.2, where he ends with a strong Christian motivation, AE now concentrates on two main but related themes: negatively the avoidance of certain sins, predominantly of a sexual nature, and positively the need to live as children of light. This paragraph differs from the preceding in that the sins discussed in it are not criticised because of the harm they may do to other members of the community and are not connected to the pattern of God's love in Christ; instead they are set in the light of the relationship of believers to God. Since neither sexual sin nor greed necessarily involves other members of the community, they need to be given a different setting and motivation.

In addition to his use of material similar to that in Col 3.5–7, AE employs a number of traditional terms and concepts (**kingdom, inheritance, wrath of God**, the contrasts of **light** and **darkness**, hidden and made known), and concludes in v. 14 with a verse from a hymn or song.

3. Vv. 3, 4 are probably to be taken as one sentence with the nouns of v. 4 depending on the verb of v. 3. AE's reference to love in v. 2 may have reminded him of the amount of illicit love in the world which members of the community have left and which may still attract them. He moves also from the theme of self-sacrifice in 5.2 to the danger of self-indulgence (Stott).

The series of three nouns in this verse together with another three in v. 4 and the cognate adjectives of those of v. 3 in v. 5 and the series of three virtues in v. 9 are sometimes said to imply that AE here draws on some of the catalogues of vices and virtues current in the ancient world. For lists of vices see Mk 7.21f; Rom 1.29–31; 13.12; 1 Cor 5.10f; 6.9f; 2 Cor 12.20; Gal 5.19–21 and of virtues 2 Cor 6.6f; Gal 5.22f; Phil 4.8. There is no evidence for the existence of basic lists of vices and virtues from which selections were made to create the existing NT lists.

Two of the three vices named in 4.19 are now repeated (**impurity, greed**) and the third replaced with **sexual misconduct**, thereby bringing out the sexual connotation of **impurity**. A similar triad is found in CD 4.17f with 'defilement of the sanctuary' replacing one of the two references to sexual sin. The word translated **sexual misconduct** has a wide range of meanings in relation to sexual behaviour including fornication, adultery, homosexuality, prostitution, incest; 'fornication' is therefore too narrow a translation. The context normally indicates its precise significance and since this gives no help here we must take it as referring to all types of sexual misconduct as viewed from a Judaeo-Christian perspective and not a Hellenistic. Jews indeed believed that Gentiles were not pure in relation to sex (*m AZ* 2.1), but not all Hellenistic counsel in respect of sexual behaviour was libertine. In one Philadelphian cult (see Barton and Horsley) male members of the group are denied sexual relations with married women, both slave and free, other than their own wives; they are also denied sexual relations with boys and virgin girls. Married women were treated more strictly than men and not permitted sexual relations with anyone other than their husbands. Men were not generally forbidden recourse to prostitutes; Musonius Rufus is an exception (Frag 12, Hense, 64.5–12). Even though Jews were scornful of Gentile sexual behaviour, their own literature contains so many rebukes about it in relation to themselves that they could not legitimately adopt a holier-than-thou attitude. Various sexual sins are rejected not only in the OT but in later writing (e.g. Ecclus 23.16–27; *T Sim* 5.3; *T Levi* 14.5; *T Jud* 14.2ff; CD 4.17, 20; 1QS 4.9ff; Philo, *Spec Leg* 3.51). **Sexual misconduct** appears regularly in the NT vice lists (Mk 7.21; Gal 5.19; Col 3.5); Paul continually inveighed against it (Rom 1.26ff; 1 Cor 5.1; 6.13ff; 7.2; 10.8; 2 Cor 12.21; Gal 5.19; 1 Th 4.3).

AE has in mind the broadest possible spectrum of sexual misconduct (Lev 18.6–30 contains a long list of sexual impurities). In view of this sexual 'atmosphere' the introduction (as in 4.19) of the third term, **greed**, seems surprising (for its meaning and associations see 4.19). It is set alongside the other two terms disjunctively, indicating it is not a sin of the same type; in v. 5 it is connected to idolatry. Greed and sexual misconduct are found together (cf *T Levi* 14.6; *T Jud* 18.2; 1QS 4.9–11; CD 4.17f as well as in various vice lists). It may be because AE regarded avarice as a sin which can be the source of other sins, the love of money being the root of all evil (1 Tim 6.10), that he concentrates on it here. This sentiment was widely accepted in the ancient world and entered Judaism and Christianity (Philo, *Spec Leg* 4.65; *Decal* 173; *Mos* 2.186; *Ps-Phoc* 42; Polycarp, *Phil* 4.1). In AE's eyes greed may not then have been one of the 'grosser' sins but one out of which others grew.

None of the three sins should **even be even named among you**; with this AE drives home his point even more strongly that they are not to be committed (cf Ps-Isocrates, *To Demonicus* 15). Compare the OT passages which say false gods should not be named (Exod 23.13; Hos 2.17; Zech 13.2). 'Words are roads to deeds' (Chrysostom).

AE now supplies a reason for not mentioning or committing these sins **as befits those who are holy**, a reason repeated in v. 4 in different words. The sentiment is taken from Stoic thought where it was used of conduct appropriate to various types of people in differing situations. Appearing only in the later parts of the NT (1 Tim 2.10; Tit 2.1; cf *Barn* 4.9), it would be familiar to Greek readers. Here the stress is not on membership of a group, 'the saints', but on a type of conduct which can be described as 'holy' (Belser; Schnackenburg; Lincoln); in Stoicism the stress is on conduct which is in accordance with nature. Sexual sin, impurity and greed do not accord with holiness (cf 1 Th 4.3–7).

4. The first three nouns of this verse (**obscene act, foolish talk, smutty talk**) continue the dependence on the verb of v. 3. It is true that the second and third in referring to forms of speech do not apply to activities in the same way as the nouns of v. 3 but the first noun is similar to those of v. 3 and 'speaking' is not far removed from 'naming'.

The three vices of v. 4 are *hapax legomena* in the NT and, do not occur regularly outside it in vice catalogues. The first strictly refers to shameful behaviour, but in the light of the following two words referring to speech many commentators (e.g. Gnilka; Barth; Lincoln) understand it of shameful speech; the following nouns would then be taken as illustrations of such speech. However, there is a word for shameful speech which is found in Col 3.8; AE must have known it and, since he has not used it, it seems unlikely that he had intended here a reference to speech. Whether the noun refers to speech or behaviour, it is a general word indicating various forms of obscene action or speech. **Foolish talk**, strictly 'the language of fools', does not refer to the way those of low intelligence or lack of education speak. Foolish talk is probably impious speech. At Qumran it was subject to discipline (1QS 7.9, 14f). In 1QS 10.21–3 it is set in the context of other verbal sins and, as here, contrasted with thankfulness. As in Qumran, however, it is the effect of such talk on the community and not on the outside world which is at issue. The final term, **smutty talk,** has no necessary connection with speech and probably takes on this aspect from its present context and might be translated 'suggestive language' or 'smutty talk', perhaps including humour with *double entendre*. To some extent the two sins of speech here spell out the more general reference of 4.29. The condemnation of sins of the tongue is a popular ethical theme (e.g. Ecclus 28.13ff; Jas 3.1ff).

The verse ends positively: if people are to talk in the community then what they say should not be obscene, smutty or impious but full of thankfulness. This provides a good contrast to what has preceded. The thanksgiving will be offered to God and this gives a subtle twist to the discussion. Since 4.25 the dangers which might destroy community life have been in the forefront and have provided the motivation away from sin and towards goodness. Now God is introduced and, as we shall see, he becomes increasingly a felt presence in vv. 5ff. Not sexual lust and covetousness, but thanksgiving is the fitting response to God's goodness and is basic to Christian existence.

5. The triad of vices of v. 3 is now repeated by naming the persons who commit or embody them rather than the vices themselves, and a threat is added as motivation. Possibly AE chose to name people rather than sins because he was concerned, not about occasional lapses in conduct, but about those who habitually indulged in illicit sex and greed.

A reference to idolatry is added. Does this reference apply only to the final member of the triad or to all of it? Jewish tradition relates sexual lust and idolatry (e.g. Israel going awhoring after other gods, cf Rev 2.20); sexual sin and covetousness are often explicitly connected (Wisd 14.12; *T Reub* 4.6; *T Jud* 23.1; *T Benj* 10.10); sexual sin and idolatry would be linked in the minds of AE's readers through ritual prostitution. There is however also a connection in Jewish tradition between covetousness and idolatry (*T Jud* 19.1). It is also easier to see money and possessions as idols (cf Mt 6.24; Lk 16.13) since these are 'things'. It is best then to associate idolatry only with covetousness.

The three types of sinners mentioned here have and can have (Ellicott) **no inheritance in the kingdom**, a warning which may have been part of catechetical instruction (so Dahl; cf Gal 5.19–21; 1 Cor 6.9f).

The kingdom of God is a frequent NT phrase but **the kingdom of Christ** is not, being found only in later writings (2 Tim 4.1, 18; 2 Pet 1.11); Col 1.13 uses an approximately similar phrase 'the kingdom of God's son', and this may suggest that the idea of a kingdom associated with Christ was a concept of the Pauline school. The source of the idea perhaps lay in Paul himself, for in 1 Cor 15.24 he writes of Christ handing over a kingdom to God. Whether that is so or not, the total phrase 'the kingdom of (the) Christ and of God' is unique; its nearest equivalent is Rev 11.15 though, as we have seen, the beginnings of the idea may be present in 1 Cor 15.24. The kingdom of Christ is not of course the church.

It would seem that some of those who have been chosen in Christ, foreordained for adoption and now sit with Christ in the heavenlies may at some point in the future be excluded from the heavenlies and lose their election and adoption. AE's realised eschatology has thus created a real difficulty for him, and thereby caused problems for future systematic theologians and for exegetes who come to him with fixed theological positions into which he must be made to fit.

6. The threat of v. 5 is now repeated in a different way; v. 5 suggested possible failure to reach a hoped for goal, v. 6 asserts God's positive reaction to those who have allowed themselves to be deceived into false action or belief. But who are those who might deceive the readers? AE calls them **disobedient people** ('sons of disobedience'), employing the same phrase as in 2.2 (see there for its form); in 2.2 he applied it to Gentiles who were outside the church and subject to the powers of evil; these would certainly experience the wrath of God. Has AE the same people in mind here? **Disobedient people** is a general phrase and not a fixed term for Gentiles; it can therefore be applied in different ways as the occasion demands. 5.6–14 contains no clear missionary overtones and v. 6 is as easily explained on the supposition that the community is being perverted by some within it as by those outside. If its background is baptismal catechetical material, as many believe, it is difficult to see how its corrupters would be non-Christians. Above all, the threat of v. 6 would be irrelevant if addressed to outsiders for they would never hear it. So with Gnilka, Barth, Halter, we assume that it is insiders who are disobedient and who endanger the life of the community. In the early second century groups appeared claiming to be Christian but whose claim the contemporary 'orthodox' church denied. Already in the NT we find traces of these groups either within the church or on its fringes; the groups are variously labelled gnostics, semi-gnostics, proto-gnostics, antinomians, libertines, rigorists, ascetics, Judaisers. We do not have enough information to identify the arguments which were being advanced and which alarmed AE. Necessarily what he writes is very general since he is not addressing a specific situation in one church but is writing to a number of churches. Whatever the **arguments** being used, AE describes them as **specious** which here does not signify 'meaningless' but 'erroneous'. **Specious arguments** may be a biblical phrase (Exod 5.9; Deut 32.47; cf *T Naph* 3.1; *Did* 2.5; Josephus *c. Ap.* 2.225; *Diog* 8.2) but it would be one easily understood by Gentiles in relation to deceptive arguments which for a time sound good but do not stand up to thorough examination. Those who use them or accept them when others use them are subject to the wrath of God. The threat of v. 5 which implied exclusion is now expressed positively as implying punishment. That they are subject to God's wrath accords with the application of the same description **disobedient people** to them as to Gentiles (2.2).

God's **wrath** (see on 2.3) may be thought of as active either now or in the eschatological future. Both aspects appear elsewhere in the NT and in contemporary and earlier Jewish literature. God's present wrathful activity is seen in Num 12.9; 4 Kgdms 1.18d; 22.13; 2 Chron 19.2; Jn 3.36; Rom 1.18ff; 3.5; 13.4f; 1 Th 2.16; and his future in Lk 21.23; Rom 2.5; 5.9; 9.22; 1 Th 1.10; 5.9; Eph 2.3; 1QS 2.15; 1QM 4.4f; 6.3; context alone can decide which significance is intended. The possibility of a future reference here is not eliminated by the present tense of **comes**, for this verb when used in the present often has a future reference (cf Mt 17.11; Lk 23.29; Jn 5.28; 9.4; 16.2, 4; 1 Th 5.2; Heb 8.8). It would be wrong to deny that AE sees disobedient people as already suffering God's wrath, for the darkening of their minds and hardening of their hearts (4.17–19) are a present reality. Yet Paul could hold both to the present and future wrath of God and so 4.17–19 does not permit us to deny the same possibility for AE. On the whole, however, the thought of God's present wrath suits the letter's realised eschatological position and does not conflict with the context. Possibly AE has both present and future aspects in mind here (cf Abbott; Schnackenburg).

7. If the readers are not to be deceived by the specious arguments of disobedient people they should not associate with them. Believers are not to accept their views or participate with them in sexual sin, impurity and greed; it can be assumed that those who offer specious arguments which permit these vices indulge in them.

8. This is one of those verses to which pre-twentieth-century commentators gave relatively little attention but which now receives much more because the religious historical movement brought out the importance of the light–darkness contrast in gnostic and related literature and then the discoveries at Qumran showed that it was also important in contemporary Judaism; it is this latter background which most writers today stress in relation to the verse.

The contrast of light and darkness was a widespread metaphor and represents two spheres of human existence. It was, as we have seen, present in 4.18; it is frequent in the OT though there as in 4.18 only one side of the metaphor may at times be expressed (Ps 27.1; 49.19; Isa 5.30; 9.2; 42.6, 16; 47.5; 49.6; 51.4; 59.9; 60.1f) and in the NT, which often picks up OT usage (Mt 4.16 = Isa 9.2; Mt 5.14–16; Mk 4.21; Lk 2.32 = Isa 42.6 and 49.6; Lk 11.33; Jn 1.4–9; 3.19–21; 8.12; 9.5; 12.35f, 46; Acts 13.47 = Isa 49.6; Acts 26.23; Rom 13.12f; 2 Cor 4.6; 6.14; Phil 2.15; Col 1.12f; 1 Th 5.5; 1 Pet 2.9; 1 Jn 1.5; 2.8). In addition to the OT the NT writers were influenced by contemporary Judaism (1QS 3.20f, 24f; *T Levi* 14.4; 19.1; *T Gad* 5.7); it offered phrases very similar to **children of light** (1QS 1.9; 2.16; 3.13, 24f; 1QM 1.1, 3) and its opposite 'children, sons of darkness' (1QS 1.10; 1QM 1.7; etc.). Granted the indebtedness of the NT for the light–darkness contrast to Judaism and the OT, the contrast also appeared regularly in Greek literature; it would thus have been easily appreciated by AE's readers. Yet since it is found in all strands of early Christianity, there is no reason to seek here a NT source outside Judaism; in any case by the time of Ephesians it was an established Christian contrast in relation to thought and behaviour and may have been used in the catechetical instruction of new believers. It would not then have been unfamiliar to AE's readers.

While **children of light** can be paralleled, the bald statement **Once you were darkness; now you are light** apparently can not. For AE to say that his readers were once darkness goes much further than saying that their minds were once darkened (4.18). The clause expresses something other than implying that they once belonged to a 'dark' culture which has been changed to one of light, for it is not culture which has been changed but the individuals who once belonged to it. To say people are light may mean either that they provide light for others as lights shining in a dark world (cf Mt 5.14–16; Rom 2.19) or that they provide light for themselves; it is the latter which is being stressed here, since it is difficult to see how anyone can provide darkness for others and because the whole emphasis of the passage lies on the behaviour of believers; as light, believers are enlightened people; they have light within themselves to guide them in their conduct. It would be wrong to deny that as enlightened people believers do not provide light to others but this is not what is stressed here. Once, as unbelievers, they had no light and were blind; now they have light and can see. Once darkness characterised their existence, now light does. If they are light from where does that light come? AE says nothing about this explicitly but **in the Lord** (see Detached Note: In Christ; the phrase is not attached here to the verb) suggests that AE is aware of the early Christian view of the Lord as the light of the world. Through their relationship with the Lord believers have received light, being enlightened in their understanding (1.17f).

The phrase 'children of light' probably entered Christianity from contemporary Judaism but is not unGreek and AE's Gentile readers would therefore have understood it. Our discussion at 2.2, 3 showed that 'sons of, children of' was used in two different ways: 'sons of disobedience' (2.2) are disobedient people but 'children of wrath' (2.3) are not angry people but people subject to the wrath of God. In 5.8 'children of light' will follow the pattern of 2.2 and mean 'enlightened people'. Having light within themselves they are able to behave as enlightened people and discern (v. 10) God's will (for the connection of 'sons of' with behaviour see 1QS 1.8f; 2.16f). Once in darkness they could only stumble, now they know what God wills and can and ought to carry it out. Once they were 'old' people, now they are 'new' people (4.22–4) who have learned Christ (4.20) and been created anew in righteousness and holiness (4.24). As in 4.22–4 the contrast is absolute; there is no in-between position, partly old person, partly new, and there is no twilight; it is either light or darkness. In one respect there is a difference here from the earlier reference to darkness (4.18); there it was connected with ignorance, here with immorality. Finally we should note that in v. 8 we move from a statement of the nature of Christian existence (v. 8a) to a call to live in accordance with it (v. 8b), the move common in NT thought from indicative to imperative.

9. This verse indicates how enlightened people should live and is parenthetical (the second person plural of v. 8 is continued in v. 10). The result of their being light will be **goodness**, **uprightness** and **truth**. Paul had already applied the metaphor of fruitfulness to conduct (Rom 6.22; Gal 5.22; Phil 1.11; cf Jas 3.18), a connection also found in the teaching of Jesus (Mt 7.16–20; 12.33–5; Lk 6.43f; 13.7) and before him in that of John the Baptist (Mt 3.10; Lk 3.8f). The metaphor was in fact used even more widely (*Odes Sol* 8.2; 11.1, 23). In 1QS 10.8, 22; 1QH 1.28 (cf Heb 13.15) it is related to worship and in Gen 30.2; Lk 1.42 to the children of a marriage. It is thus very adaptable. **Fruit** here is applied in the singular (cf Gal 5.22) to good conduct; the singular suggests that the good fruit has a unitary aspect which unfruitful or evil actions lack. The contrast between good and bad fruit in Ephesians is not strictly that between fruit which comes from good or bad trees, as in the Gospels, but between fruit coming from the same tree before and after conversion/ baptism.

The contrast in the fruit is linked directly to the contrast between light and darkness. The **light** has produced **fruit**. While it is true that plants die if deprived of light, and this may be the underlying connection, we should be careful not to introduce modern botanical theory to explain the text. Light is a good quality in contrast to darkness and therefore is to be associated with good results.

A triad of nouns, in AE's customary manner (see on 5.3), identifies the fruit. **Goodness** has not been found in non-biblical Greek though its root and cognates are widely used. In scripture it appears in 2 Chron 24.16; Ψ 51.5; 2 Esdras 19.25, 35; Rom 15.14; Gal 5.22 (another connection of this passage with ours); Eph 5.9; 2 Th 1.11. It is difficult to derive from these instances any meaning more precise than 'goodness'. 'Righteousness', a favourite Pauline term, is not used here in relation to saving righteousness but with ethical significance. Like **goodness** it is a somewhat general word (see on 4.24), and **uprightness**, living in accordance with a divine norm or God's will, seems an appropriate translation. In Rom 5.7 Paul ranks goodness above uprightness but AE sets them on a level; Jerome and others used this equivalence to launch attacks on Marcion; in Phil 1.11 (cf Rom 14.17) Paul rates uprightness more highly. AE has already used **truth** several times. In 4.25 it is the opposite of what is untrue, but this would impose too narrow a meaning here; 1.13 relates it to the gospel, though it is generally used of human behaviour. In 5.9 it is set in parallel with goodness and uprightness and is not used as in 4.24 to qualify other nouns. The meaning probably lies in the area either of faithfulness, loyalty, sincerity, or of that which exhibits within itself nothing that is false or hypocritical; it does not mean being true to oneself or one's conscience, for both may be false; it might however mean being true to the new person (4.24). The virtues of our verse are sometimes found associated in Qumran (1QS 1.5; 4.2f, 24; 5.4; 8.2) but not in the NT virtue catalogues. As we have explained them, 5.9 does not contain three separate and distinct virtues which might appear in a catalogue, but three different ways of stating the nature of virtuous living. Not a virtue catalogue, they are also not the opposite of the three vices of 5.3, 5, nor can they be differentiated as obligations to self, others, or God (cf Westcott). Each stands for the whole range of Christian virtue revealing different aspects of it. Triads depicting the nature of a life in accordance with God's will are found in Mic 6.8;2 Chron 31.20 (not in LXX); Jer 4.2; Ψ 44.5. None coincides exactly with that of 5.9 and it would be wrong to think of AE as deliberately copying one of these OT verses or as modelling himself on them. Rather, as we have seen (5.3), he thinks in terms of triads and the three qualities he has chosen would have been easily understood by Gentile readers. The omission of love is interesting; would readers have taken this of sexual or other love unless it had been explained with a reference to Christ?

10. After the parenthesis of v. 9 the main theme is now resumed. As enlightened people, believers need to behave in a way which pleases their Lord so that their lives will bear the fruit of goodness, uprightness and truth. The verb 'to find out' is a favourite Pauline term which he applies to God's scrutinising and approving human beings (Rom 16.10; 1 Cor 11.19; 2 Cor 13.5ff; 1 Th 4.4; cf 1 Cor 9.27) and, as here, to believers determining how they should behave (Rom 2.18; 12.2; Gal 6.4; Phil 1.10; 1 Th 5.21); it was used in this latter way also by the Stoics (Epictetus 1.20.7; 2.23.6, 8; 4.5.16; 4.6.13; 4.7.40). If AE is not Paul then as a member of a Pauline school he has picked up the term, yet there is no dependence on any particular Pauline text; it follows here naturally on the reference to truth in v. 9 (Hugedé). When human beings are the subject more is intended than the intellectual reasoning out of conduct which pleases the Lord, i.e. Christ. What is reasoned out needs to be put to the test, and so the verb carries the sense of testing as well as of discerning (cf Roels); what pleases the Lord is the practice of what has been determined.

If decisions are to be made about conduct, criteria are needed on which to base them. Only one is stated here: whatever pleases the Lord. Paul has the same criterion in Rom 12.2 where he uses the same verb in relation to God's will (cf Phil 1.10); in 1 Th 5.21 the sense is more restricted since it relates to discerning truth in prophetic activity; when AE again introduces a similar criterion in 5.17 he connects it directly to God's will. To set up as the criterion what pleases the Lord is biblical (Gen 5.22, 24; 6.9; Wisd 4.10; Ecclus 44.16; Rom 12.1; 14.18; 2 Cor 5.9; Phil 4.18; Col 3.20; Heb 13.21; cf *T Dan* 1.3), but it is vague and affords little help in making practical decisions. It seems to leave believers on their own. More help is needed, especially for those moving out of a pagan environment and even for those who have been converts for some time but who still live surrounded by a pagan culture, yet the greater the degree of detailed help in relation to the multitude of different situations that may arise, the greater the approach to a legalistic religion. On the criteria provided by AE, by the NT generally and by the church in succeeding centuries see Essay: Moral Teaching.

11. From his initial premise that his readers are light in the Lord (v. 8), AE now draws two conclusions, first a negative (v. 11a) and then a positive (v. 11b).

In v. 11a AE plays on ideas already in the context: darkness, fruitfulness. There is no reason to see in these **works of darkness** a reference to the Mysteries (cf Ambrosiaster ad v. 8). **Unfruitful** is found only in the later parts of the NT (Mk 4.19, assuming the interpretation of the parable of vv. 3–8 was added to the original parable; Tit 3.14; 2 Pet 1.8; Jude 12) and is used in a derogatory sense. Believers are not to take part in unfruitful and sinful activities. If they do, they will not be acting alone but taking part with others: **have no share**. But who are these other people? There is nothing in v. 11a which would enable us to distinguish between believers who had sinned as in vv. 3–5 (other parts of the NT show that believers did sin in the ways described there) and unbelievers, and therefore nothing to suggest that only the latter are intended here.

An emphatic **but rather** introducing v. 11b indicates an important new stage in the discussion: not only are believers to avoid wrong conduct; they are to confront it when they see it in others; instead of participating in works of darkness they are to take positive steps against such works or against those who perpetrate them. The object of **reprove** is undefined; v. 11a would suggest a reference to the works of darkness, v. 12 to those who perform them. The word translated **reprove** has a wide range of meaning. Many commentators and translations choose the meaning 'expose, reveal'; in this case the object of the verb would be the works of darkness; believers in some way, by word or example, expose to those who perform works of darkness the true nature of their actions as works of darkness. This 'disclosure' interpretation seems to fit the flow of the argument with its emphasis on light yet it would anticipate the later verb **is revealed** in v. 13, deprive our verb of its peculiar significance and define the object of the verb as the works of darkness, which is by no means certain.

257

Engberg-Pedersen suggests 'confrontation' as offering the true sense of the verb: confronting people or their thoughts, words or actions with the aim of showing them to be, in some determinate sense, at fault. This understanding approximates to two of the meanings often given to the verb, 'convict, convince' and 'reprove, rebuke'; both of these involve confrontation and it is difficult to draw a precise line between them. That church members should rebuke, correct or reprove other members is seen as a Christian duty in a number of passages (1 Tim 5.20; Jas 5.19f; in Tit 1.9, 13 the references relate to the correction of belief rather than behaviour); it is in particular a duty laid on pastors (2 Tim 4.2; Tit 2.15); in Mt 18.15–17 where a more formal procedure for correction is set out it is as in Eph 5.11 a duty laid on all believers. The correction of the faults of one member by others within a closely knit community is a normal communal activity as evidence from Qumran shows (1QS 5.23–6.1; 9.17; CD 7.2f; 9.6–8; 20.4; cf *T Gad* 6.3, 6; *T Jos* 6.6); *Did* 15.3 says such rebuking should not be done angrily but in peace. The idea of reproval within the community runs back into the OT (Lev 19.17; Prov 9.7f; 10.10; Ecclus 19.13ff).

12. While the translation of this verse is apparently straightforward, it is difficult to link it in with what precedes and follows. It could be related easily to v. 11 if it could be taken concessively ('rebuke even though it is shameful to speak about . . .'), or if it is understood parenthetically, 'for it is shameful even to speak about what they have done in secret' (Bratcher and Nida; **for** introduces a parenthesis in v. 9). On the whole it is probably better to understand it in the latter way. Works of darkness cannot be left unreproved but to rebuke them publicly means admitting their existence within the community, where they ought never to be. It is therefore shameful even to have to acknowledge their existence. The idea that some deeds may be too shameful to mention is also found in non-Christian moralists (Philo, *Opif Mundi* 80; Epictetus 4.9.5; 1.6.20; 3.26.8; 4.1.177; cf Demosthenes, *Cononos* 1262.17).

Since v. 8 a contrast has been drawn between light and darkness; now a new but not unrelated contrast is introduced, that between secret and revealed (Bouttier). This contrast appears elsewhere in the NT (Mk 4.22; Lk 12.2; Jn 18.20; Rom 2.16;

1 Cor 4.5; 14.25). There will be a revelation (v. 13) of what has been done secretly. Vice fears revelation by light (cf Rom 13.13). Loyal members of the community should rebuke those who have gone astray (v. 11b) and drag their sins into the open, sins which it is shameful to mention, especially in a Christian community.

13. This is yet another verse difficult to fit into the flow of the argument, a difficulty realised from the time of the earliest patristic commentators (for their various solutions and all those later ones suggested prior to his time, see Ewald). The verse is linked to v. 11b through the verb **is reproved** and to the idea of secrecy in v. 12 through the verb **is revealed**. Whatever believers reprove or rebuke is made visible or revealed as wrong because believers are themselves light (v. 8).

14. While the clause itself appears easy to translate ('for everything that is revealed is light'), it is again difficult to understand and fit into the argument. In consequence translations have not been literal as a selection from the most recent will show: 'for everything that is clearly revealed becomes light' (GNB), 'for it is light that makes everything visible' (NIV), 'and anything illuminated is itself a light' (NJB), 'and whatever is exposed to the light itself becomes light' (REB), 'for everything that becomes visible is light' (NRSV). Some earlier translations like the AV solved the difficulty by taking the verb in an active sense 'for whatsoever doth make manifest is light'; evidence, however, for this form of the verb with an active sense is missing. The literal translation seems to be a truism: 'everything that is brought to light is light'; such a truism would not be out of accord with AE's general style; yet in fact it is not a truism; the devil when revealed is not, and does not become, light. As the variety of translations shows, it is necessary in some way to paraphrase the clause to accommodate it to the argument. On our understanding this has run 'Believers are light; some in the community have sinned; believers reprove them and so bring light to bear on their faults; when their faults [note the continual way in which we move in the paragraph between sins and sinners] are reproved they are revealed and every sin that is revealed is no longer sin and the one who has committed it is light, i.e. restored to his proper nature as light.' The purpose of bringing sins or persons to the light is not the negative desire to expose, but the positive wish to reform.

All of this is now confirmed in the second half of the verse with a quotation introduced with the same formula as at 4.8. In Jas 4.6 it introduces scripture. While the possibility cannot be excluded, it is unlikely that AE thought he was citing scripture here. It is, however, certain that he wished his readers to realise he was using a quotation which he and they regarded as in some way authoritative. The use of a quotation is confirmed by the change from the second plural of vv. 3ff to the singular and by the return to the plural in v. 15.

Accepting it as a quotation, from where does it come? Various suggestions have been made. (a) Since it not a direct quotation of any one particular OT text it may be an amalgam of a number, a position often argued in respect of 1 Cor 2.9. Older commentators spent a lot of time and ingenuity attempting to discover suitable passages; Isa 60.1; 26.19; 9.27 are normally suggested. (b) A Jewish apocryphal source; it does not however appear in any known to us, yet since much of the relevant material is no longer extant, this possibility cannot be eliminated. (c) A lost saying of Jesus; again this cannot be disproved; however style and content together with the use of the term 'Christ' make this improbable. (d) An early Christian hymn; this seems to have been first suggested by Severian; it becomes probable once we observe that the quotation 'has a certain "lilt" about it, and a parallelism comparable to that of Hebrew poetry' (Moule); if this is correct it may either have formed the whole hymn or, more probably, been part of a hymn (Clem Alex, *Protrepticus* 9.84.2, continues it with a second verse; there is no proof that this belonged to the original). Some justification for the resemblance of the introductory formula to that used in respect of scripture might then exist on the supposition that it was a 'spiritual' hymn (v. 19) spoken by a Spirit-inspired prophet. In form the first two lines are imperatival clauses with their verbs at the beginning in Semitic fashion; the third line is a promise. Those who obey the imperatives will receive the promise. The verse suitably rounds off the discussion which began at v. 8. Though believers are light, some of them seem still to be darkness and Christ needs to shine on them through the words of those believers who have not fallen back into darkness. The concept of light then both begins and ends vv. 8–14.

We turn now to examine the individual lines of the hymn, recognising that their meaning in the present context may not be the same as their original meaning. Sleep is a widely used metaphor, often as a euphemism for death. Paul adopted this usage either from Judaism (e.g. Isa 43.17 LXX; 1 Kgs 2.10; 11.43) or from the ancient world generally and employed it in 1 Th 5.13; 1 Cor 7.39; 11.30; 15.6, 18, 20, 51. Since line ii of the hymn directly refers to death, this may be thought to be the understanding of sleep in line i. Yet can those who are Christians and have therefore risen with Christ (2.6) be envisaged as still dead? Sleep may then be used metaphorically in another way as often in gnosis (e.g. *Ap John* II, 1 31.5ff) and elsewhere to indicate a lack of alertness, an ignorance of the true nature of a situation, a failure to understand what is going on (cf Rom 12.11–14; 1 Th 5.6f); this would be appropriate here since in v. 11 the readers were warned to avoid the unfruitful works of darkness. They are to arouse themselves from sin, the sin in which they lived before they believed and into which they have fallen back. It is however difficult to see this meaning as continued in line ii which clearly refers to rising from the dead. Believers prior to becoming Christians were dead in sin (2.1, 5). Though they may have reverted to their pre-Christian sinful ways they are hardly regarded as again dead and put back into the category of unbelievers. There are other possibilities: (a) Line i could be taken in the sense of arousal from the sleep of sin (cf v. 11) and so understood might fit into AE's purpose; he then went on to quote the whole verse because line iii also served to round off his argument about light, and because the whole verse was known to his readers he could not omit line ii. (b) AE understood line ii metaphorically, 'Arise from your sleep (= death) in sin'. (c) In 4.24 AE told Christians to put on the new person, something they had already done when they first believed but which they needed to continue to do. May he not then be applying here as in 4.24 the language of conversion to believers? If they have failed and have produced the unfruitful works of darkness, they should recover the position from which they began. Whichever solution is accepted, and whatever the original meaning of the verse, the 'coming to life' or 'awakening' should not be interpreted within the context gnostically as the attainment of a true understanding of the self; it has to do with a knowledge of sin.

Line iii firms up the connection of the verse with its context. When the sleeper awakens, when the dead rise, the light who is Christ shines to give them light. Christ as light is an idea found widely in the NT (e.g. Jn 1.4, 9; 8.12; 9.5; 12.46; Lk 1.78f; 2 Cor 4.6). When Christ shines again on the believers they again become light (v. 8).

If that is the interpretation of the hymn in its context, how was it originally understood? Line ii can be taken straightforwardly as supplying the meaning for line i so that resurrection is the subject of both. This led Asmussen to make the highly original suggestion that it was the kind of way that Lazarus might have been addressed in the tomb. More probable since resurrection and baptism are closely associated (Rom 6.3ff; Col 2.12) is the suggestion that the hymn was addressed to baptismal candidates (so Bankhead): let them rise from their past dead and sinful life into a new life where Christ will be the light. The connection of light with baptism appears fairly early (Melito *Frag* 8b). Noack suggests that the verse was to be used by a heavenly being to address believers when Christ returns and gives full light to all. While we can understand the singular as addressed to individual believers coming one by one to baptism at baptism, surely the plural would be used at the parousia as then believers would be addressed as a group. Parallels to the hymn have been detected in both the Mysteries and gnosticism but a sufficient number of parallels can be found in Judaism and early Christianity to account for the ideas of the hymn (Gnilka; Schnackenburg; Kuhn; cf Ecclus 24.32f; 1QS 2.3; 4.2; 11.3–6; 1QH 4.27; 1 Th 5.3ff; Rom 13.11ff).

XIII

BE WISE AND FILLED WITH THE SPIRIT

(5.15–21)

¹⁵ **Consider then carefully how you behave,**
    not as those who are unwise
    but as those who are wise,
¹⁶   **making the best use of time**
      because the days are evil.
¹⁷ **So do not be foolish**
    but discern what the will of the Lord is.
¹⁸   **And do not be drunk with wine**
      – it brings ruin –
    but be filled by the Spirit
¹⁹   **addressing one another**
        with psalms and hymns and spiritual songs
      singing and praising the Lord from your heart
²⁰   **giving thanks at all times for everything**
      to him who is God and Father
      in the name of our Lord Jesus Christ,
²¹   **being subject to one another in the fear of Christ.**

This further brief paraenetic section turns from exhorting believers to avoid particular sins and follow certain virtues to more general pleas, though these were not entirely missing earlier (4.27, 30; 5.8b, 10).

The passage is structured around three contrasts expressed through **not** and **but** (vv. 15, 17, 18). There are two main themes: 'wisdom' (vv. 15–17) and 'worship' (vv. 19–20), the third contrast (v. 18) forming the transition from the one to the other.

15. As those who have learnt Christ (4.20) are new people (4.24) and are light (5.8), it is important that believers should **consider** their future behaviour **carefully**. Paul regularly uses **consider** in respect of the consideration of conduct (1 Cor 3.10; 8.9; 10.12; 16.10; Gal 5.15; cf Col 2.8; Mk 13.5, 9, 23, 33).

In the similar verse, Col 4.5, behaviour is related 'to those outside'. The lack of such a reference here does not mean that AE is generalising Colossians (see Beare; Percy); rather its omission is in keeping with the way he discusses conduct only in relation to other believers. He is concerned to formulate an ethic for the internal life of the community and not for the relationship of believers to unbelievers.

Verse 15b contains the first of the three contrasts of vv. 15–18, in this case relating to wisdom. Two kinds of behaviour ('the two ways') are possible, expressed here as wise and unwise (cf 1 Cor 1.18–3.23); the pre-Christian life of readers lacked wisdom; its presence should characterise them now. The contrast was already present in Jewish tradition (1QS 3.13ff, especially 4.22, 24); T Levi 13.7 associates lack of wisdom with the blindness and impiety which in Eph 4.17–19 characterise the Gentile world. Wisdom is a wide term needing definition from its context; here it is not primarily insight into God's workings (1.9, 17; 3.10) but the practical wisdom which, depending on such insight, relates to conduct; it is to this aspect of wisdom that a large part of the Jewish Wisdom literature is devoted. Whereas Jewish thought connected it with a life lived in accordance with Torah, Christian thought connects it to Christ who is the wisdom of God.

16. One aspect of practical wisdom is now described in v. 16a. The difficulty of the phrase of v. 16a, the same phrase as in Col 4.5, has been recognised since at least the time of Chrysostom; it is perhaps this difficulty that led AE to explain it in v. 16b. In both v. 16a and v. 16b he uses words describing time and these should probably be taken in the same general way. We begin with v. 16b.

The 'day' (singular) in early Christian speech meant the day of the Lord, the parousia (cf 6.13), but v. 16b has the plural. Yet that does not necessarily eliminate the eschatological element, for there are phrases like 'the last days' (2 Tim 3.1; Jas 5.3; 2 Pet 3.3; Mt 24.19ff; cf T Zeb 9.5ff; T Dan 5.4; Barn 4.9). Neither the context nor a qualifying phrase suggests that AE thinks here of the evil days as those of the End. He never argues for an imminent End and does not betray the sense of urgency found in 1 Cor 7.26; Rom 13.11; he does not say the time is short, as did much of early

Christianity, but that the time is evil (Knox). For him the world is a more permanent place than for Paul (Lindemann). Why then are the days evil? Not because they are full of natural disasters, earthquakes, famines, floods; nor because Christians are being harassed or persecuted (cf Tertullian, *Fuga* 9.2), of which there is no sign in the letter, though such outside pressure on Christians was then common. AE has not however been slow to paint Gentile culture in the darkest of terms (2.12; 4.17–19, 22; 5.8); in that sense for him the days, his own times, were evil, a period of moral decadence. Of course it is not the days themselves which are evil – time is a neutral category – but the people and events which fill them (cf Pelagius; Origen, *Matt Cat* 134, GCS 41, 67.1; *Judges Hom* GCS 30, 467.15ff), and they are not turned into good days (Jerome) by the wise use of time; the people and events of the outside world remain the same. AE may have regarded the days as evil in another way for they are the period when the evil one is active, and which is under the control of the evil powers (6.10ff). That AE could simultaneously hold both these views can be seen from 2.1ff where he switches between personal sin and the control of evil powers. Perhaps then the best adjective to describe these days is 'godless' (cf Roberts). If some days are described as evil this must imply there are 'good' days; since these are not now they must lie in the future (cf Origen); there is then here an implicit reference to a future for believers lying outside and beyond the existing world.

Excluding then any primary eschatological reference in days we turn to v. 16a. It contains an unusual phrase which is found also in Col 4.5, literally 'redeem the time'. Here **time** in accordance with our initial premise must be taken as a word denoting a period of time like days rather than as indicating a decisive moment or unique opportunity, though both meanings might be present. Here it will have something of the flavour 'opportunity'; 'opportunities' to do good exist throughout believers' lives and are not just rare and occasional moments.

'Redeem' is a commercial term. Dan 2.8 has a similar phrase to that here with the sense 'gaining time', but this cannot be the meaning here, nor that of *Mart Polyc* 2.3, 'purchasing eternal life'. We may take the phrase in a general way as indicating that the believers are to employ their time wisely; it should be used in a disciplined way; opportunities of doing good are not to be missed (Stott; on the use of time cf Prov. 3.1ff; M. Aurelius II 4f). Like a housewife setting out to shop with a limited amount of money, believers have only a limited amount of time and they must spend it wisely (Asmussen). They are not to contribute to the evil of the days, but making the best use of time they will redeem sections of it. In 5.22–6.9 AE goes on to treat three sections needing to be redeemed.

17. This is the second contrast and it is similar in content to the first (v. 15b). **So** probably links it either to v. 16b rather than v. 16a, since v. 16a is a consequence of being wise (v. 15b) and not its basis, or to v. 15b since v. 17 re-expresses v. 15b; it might possibly be linked to v. 15a, though in that case it is not clear why **so** is needed. The readers are not to **be** or 'become' (either translation is possible) foolish; rather they are to continue being what they are already supposed to be, 'wise'. The 'fool' is not someone without a mind but the unthinking person who fails to use the mind he or she already has (for the use of the root in the NT see Lk 11.40; 12.20; Rom 2.20; 1 Cor 15.36; 2 Cor 11.16; 12.6; it is found regularly in the OT Wisdom literature).

The use of **discern** emphasises the need for intellectual effort (cf 1 Pet 1.13) in discerning the Lord's will. Believers have to reason out for themselves what they should do, learning from their personal ongoing experience and the experience of others within their community. This may be why AE moves on in vv. 19f to their common worship, for it gives them the opportunity to learn from one another. The more immediate move is to v. 18, since overindulgence in wine may cloud the mind and render them unable to learn at all.

18. This is the third contrast; it is not made between two entities, wine and the Spirit, but between two conditions, drunkenness and Spirit-possession. In itself the contrast may not be surprising but its introduction at this point is; vv. 15–17 have dealt with generalities of conduct, v. 18a forbids one precise sin, vv. 19–20 again return to generalities. Is there anything in the situation of the readers or in the context of the letter which could have led to the reference to the excess use of wine?

Perhaps it was important for AE's readers to realise that the love feast before a service should not be marred by drunkenness or else the work of the Spirit in the gathering would be hindered. It may be this as well as the connection between drunkenness and ecstasy that forms the bridge to vv. 19f where we move forward to what may have been regarded as charismatic activity in worship.

19. When Christians are filled with the Spirit they worship together. When this happens they: (i) speak to one another in song (v. 19a), (ii) praise the Lord through song (v. 19b; cf 2 Sam 23.2 for the movement from Spirit to song), (iii) return thanks to Christ and God (v. 20), (iv) submit to one another (v. 21) and this finally leads on directly to the nature of conduct in the home.

The use of song in the early church seems to have been extensive; Acts 16.25 provides indirect testimony. Much effort and ingenuity have been devoted to distinguishing and identifying the three names describing what was sung: **psalms**, **hymns**, **spiritual songs**. It is probably better to take them as intended to cover all the singing that went on in worship rather than to differentiate between them. The adjective **spiritual** may apply only to **songs**; this, a more general word than either of the others, might need to be identified ('sacred' not 'secular' songs); yet the term is used without such qualification in relation to religious singing in the OT (e.g. Exod 15.1; Deut 32.44; 2 Kgdms 22.1; and the titles of many of the Psalms) and in Rev 5.9; 14.3; 15.3, which gives it a context in the church in Asia Minor. The word did not then need any qualification in Jewish or Christian circles to indicate the singing as religious. The adjective is therefore to be taken with all three nouns. In view of the use of **spirit** in v. 18 it should be given its full meaning **spiritual** as in 1.3 (cf Rom 1.11; 1 Cor 2.13; 9.11; 12.1; 14.1; 15.44, 46; Col 1.9); it is singing inspired or controlled by the Holy Spirit.

Is it then spontaneous charismatic singing, or the singing, prompted by the Spirit, of existing songs, or the singing of songs whose origin can be traced to the Spirit? The early Christians both used the OT Psalms and composed hymns of their own. AE has just quoted one in 5.14; part of another appears in 1 Tim 3.16. Luke's infancy narrative contains several (1.46ff; 1.68ff; 2.29ff) as does Revelation (5.9f; 7.15–17; 11.17f; 15.3f); adapted hymns are found in Phil 2.6–11; Col 1.15–20. Christians thus continued the Jewish tradition, which itself was still alive (*Psalms of*

Solomon, Qumran hymns); singing was also found in contemporary religious worship. There was thus plenty of traditional material at hand for use. However, few of these early Christian hymns could be regarded as addressed to other believers; they are almost all in praise of Christ or God. Exceptions are 5.14 and Rev 7.15ff, and Phil 2.6–11, if its main purpose, or that of the underlying hymn, was to inculcate humility. Some songs then existed in which believers addressed one another; in 1 Cor 14.26 Paul writes of believers as each one having a Psalm, a teaching, etc.; in the context of the passage he seems to be referring to spontaneous contributions to worship addressed by believers to one another. Singing to one another is just one of the ways believers exhort one another (Heb 3.13). Paul terms such contributions 'spiritual' (12.1; 14.1) and this may be the significance of 'spiritual' here. This neither excludes the 'spontaneous' use of traditional material nor does it imply it. Philo, *Vita Cont* 80, writes of the introduction of new hymns into the worship of the Therapeutae as well as of their use of existing material. AE has probably both in mind. Although 1 Cor 14.15 allows the possibility there is no reason to think of these hymns as glossolaliac in character. Whatever their nature, these songs are a part of communal worship being used either in gatherings of the whole community or individual house churches or within families.

This will also be true of praise offered to the Lord (v. 19b). This clause is not another way of looking at v. 19a, treating inner motivation rather than outer activity (cf Gnilka; Schlier). The praise offered in v. 19b is offered in the course of the same worship as that of v. 19a, but v. 19b speaks of praise directed not to other believers but to the Lord (= Christ, as in v. 17). As we have seen, many Christian hymns already existed, as well as OT Psalms, with Christ or God as object; some may also have been spontaneously created in the course of worship. AE's use of 'Lord' and not 'God' has been held, on the supposition that he used Col 3.15, to be the result of later theological development in elevating Christ; yet this cannot be so, for from the beginning Christ was the subject of creeds and hymns (Phil 2.6–11; Rev 4.11; 5.9, 13).

This worship is not silent worship in the heart (for 'heart' see on 1.18; cf 3.17; 4.18; 6.5, 22) but worship offered from the heart where the Spirit dwells (Rom 5.5; 2 Cor 1.22; 3.3; Gal 4.6); it comes from the deepest level of existence and is not purely emotional ('hearty') froth but contains considerable intellectual content; the singing was singing with understanding (Theophylact). It is often difficult for us to classify traditional material as hymn or creed, since contemporary hymns were deeply imbued with theology. Inner sentiment (the heart) and outer action (the singing) agree; lips and heart are in harmony; this is important for God listens not to the outward voice but to the heart.

20. This verse forms the third clause dependent on v. 18, and, like those of v. 19, relates to communal worship; believers have spoken to one another in song, praised Christ and now as a kind of climax they are to return thanks to God. Thanksgiving, already seen in 5.4 as the alternative to sinful behaviour, has always formed part of Jewish praise of God as the OT Psalms and the Qumran hymns testify, and quickly became a part of Christian worship (1 Th 5.18; Col 4.2; 1 Tim 2.1). This thanksgiving is to be offered, in a typically plerophoric liturgical expression, **at all times** (cf Rom 1.9; 1 Cor 1.4; Phil 1.4; 4.4; Col 1.3; 1 Th 1.2; 2 Th 1.3, 11; Philem 4) and for all. 'All times' are all those occasions when worship is offered. The reference in the next phrase, literally 'for all', is more difficult to determine since 'all' can be either masculine or neuter. It is possible to give thanks for 'things'. It is easy to deduce from his letter some of the things for which AE would wish to thank God: election to be part of God's people, redemption through Christ's blood, enlightenment to understand what God has done, the resurrection and ascension of Christ and of believers with him, the equal status of ex-Jew and ex-Gentile in the church, their relationship to Christ in his body, their new nature, the ability to perform good works. If giving thanks were restricted to giving thanks for people, it would be limited to giving thanks that they believed or that they carried out some Christian duty as prophets or teachers or in the general care of others. In view of this limitation it is then better to take 'all' as neuter and give it a wide sense **for everything**. If this is so, is the list above exhaustive or should it be extended? Some of the Fathers (e.g. Jerome; Pelagius; Chrysostom), instancing Job 1.23, suggest that everything that happens, including unfortunate events, should be included. But while it is certainly possible to thank God for the response of people to evil events (famines, earthquakes, etc.), is it possible to thank him for the evil events themselves? Yet it must be recognised as true that some kinds of suffering, principally suffering for the sake of Christ as distinct from the suffering that comes in the normal course of life (e.g. unemployment, sickness), do bring joy. Meyer, followed by Barth, would rightly include such suffering (cf 3.13; Mt 5.11f; Lk 6.22f; Acts 5.41; Phil 4.4ff; Col 1.24; 1 Th 1.6; Jas 1.2f; 1 Pet 1.6; 4.13).

The next phrase is difficult to translate; it probably means something like 'to him who is God and also Father', 'to him who is at once God and Father', God being presented here as Father of believers rather than of Christ.

These thanksgivings, whatever their content, are offered to God in the name of our Lord Jesus Christ. The clause forms a fitting climax to this section of the letter for it is because of Christ's redeeming life, death and resurrection that God may be approached (2.18; 3.12; cf Rom 5.2; 1 Pet 3.18). After v. 20 we return in vv. 21ff from worship to behaviour. AE slid over easily from behaviour in 4.1–5.18 to worship through the reference to the Spirit; now with a reference to Christ he returns (vv. 21ff) to the way his readers should treat one another in their daily lives. If worship regularly took place in houses then the introduction of the household table in this part of the letter is not unnatural.

Before we leave the subject of worship it is important to ask about its nature. In v. 20 **giving thanks** is mentioned; the cognate noun 'eucharist' became a term for the Lord's Supper as early as *Did* 9.1–5; 10.7; 14.1; Ign *Eph* 13.1; *Philad* 4.1; *Smyrn* 7.1; 8.1; Justin, *Apol* I, 66–7. The verb itself was used by Paul in relation to prayer at the Lord's Supper (1 Cor 11.24) and in the Gospel accounts of the Last Supper (Mt 26.27; Mk 14.23; Lk 22.17, 19). In v. 18 there was a reference to wine. Is then the worship described in vv. 19f to be regarded as eucharistic? However, **giving thanks** is used widely in the NT without eucharistic implication. It seems simpler then to conclude that while vv. 19f refer to community worship they give no clue as to its nature. It may have been eucharistic, it may not. Finally we should note the coming together in vv. 18–20 of the Spirit, Christ and God the Father. This is not a piece of Trinitarian doctrine but as elsewhere in the letter it provides the rough building blocks from which that doctrine was later constructed.

21. That a difficulty exists in relating this verse to the ongoing argument can be seen in the different way it is set out in the Revised Version and the RSV (and most modern translations): the RSV makes a major break after v. 20; the RV after v. 21. As a general caveat it should be realised that authors do not necessarily think in paragraphs when writing. There is at times perhaps a greater flow in the argument than editors care to admit.

In favour of the division after v. 21 are: (1) The participle of v. 21, **being subject**, continues the sequence of participles in vv. 19, 20, all dependent on the imperative **be filled** of v. 18b. (2) 5.21 deals with the relationship of all believers to one another whereas 5.22–6.9 treats only the relationships to one another of those who live in wholly Christian households. (3) The theme of v. 21 is mutual subordination whereas that of 5.22–6.9 is the subordination of individuals (wives, children, slaves) to other individuals (husbands, fathers, masters). (4) Mutual subordination fits well with 5.19 where all believers mutually address one another and there are no hierarchical distinctions (e.g. 'listen to what the prophets say'). It must be allowed however that between v. 19a and v. 21 the material relates not to speaking to one another but to God. (5) Mutual subordination picks up the theme of the introductory verses to the paraenesis, in particular 4.2, and rounds it off before the move to a new area. (6) Vv. 19–21 may form a chiasmus (cf T. G. Allen); v. 19a and v. 21 treat the relation of believers to other believers; v. 19b and v. 20 their relation to God: ABBA.

In favour of the division before v. 21 are: (1) V. 22 lacks a verb and since this must be supplied from v. 21, this would link the verses. (2) 5.22–6.9 deals with a fresh subject, life in the household; nothing in vv. 18–20 suggests AE had the household in mind when writing about worship, apart from the fact that worship took place in houses. (3) The theme of 5.22–6.9 is subordination even though it is not mutual. (4) The participle of v. 21 could be understood as an imperative (see on 4.25); yet is it likely that in a sequence of participles one should suddenly be taken as an imperative? (5) The references to **fear** in both v. 21 and v. 33 (there translated **she respects**) might be taken to indicate

271

an *inclusio*, thus joining v. 21 to what follows; but if there is an *inclusio* it should connect v. 21 and 6.9; the two references to fear may then be accidental.

How is this difficulty to be resolved? **To one another** cannot be deprived of its sense of equality in mutuality along the lines of Mt 24.10; 25.32; 1 Pet 5.1–5 (Maillet: 'to others'). The word carries the idea of equal mutuality in Eph 4.2, 25, 32 and in the vast majority of its occurrences in the NT (e.g. Mk 4.41; 8.16; 9.34; Rom 1.27; 12.5; 13.8; 1 Cor 12.25; 16.20; Gal 5.13; Col 3.9; 1 Th 5.11). V. 22 is not then a special case of v. 21, 'wives in particular should be subordinate' since this would exclude the mutuality which is an essential part of v. 21.

The concept of mutuality between believers is a regular NT theme being found in the Johannine form of the love commandment (Jn 13.34f) and appearing in varying ways in the Pauline corpus (Rom 12.10, 16; 15.5, 14; 1 Cor 12.25; Gal 5.13; 6.2; Col 3.13, 16; 1 Th 3.12; 4.18; 5.11, 13; Phil 2.2; cf 1 Pet 5.5); it is present already in our letter at 4.2. It is the attitude believers as members of the body should have to one another (1 Cor 12.25f) and is closely related to the humility to which all are summoned (4.2). Yet at the same time there are those who are teachers and leaders; all are members of the one body but they have different functions. Early Christianity contains an unresolved tension between authority and mutuality or, in the terms of our passage (taking in 5.22–6.9), between mutual subordination and the authority of some. If this tension has not been thought through by the time of Ephesians (has it ever been?) then it is not surprising to move from mutual subordination in v. 21 to the subordination of one group to another in 5.22–6.9. The possible tension may have been partly veiled from AE because at v. 22 he picks up a block of traditional teaching which began with the theme of subordination. Having written 5.21 under the influence of 5.19, AE had the verb **being subject** in his mind; intending to use the HT in some way, this may have seemed to him the appropriate place to introduce it. The verse is then in part transitional in completing vv. 18–20 and in preparing for the HT. It is however better to associate it with what precedes than with what follows.

The word translated **being subject** is a strong word, frequent in the Pauline corpus (Rom 8.7; 10.3; 13.5; Col 3.18; Tit 3.1; Heb

12.9) and used in relation to the position of slaves (Tit 2.9; 1 Pet 2.18; in the latter case the master is assumed to be hostile). Subordination implies a sense of order in society. Mutual subordination will naturally be voluntary. It is best illustrated by the action of Jesus in washing his disciples' feet (Jn 13.1ff). Jesus associates this type of behaviour, though not using the word, with the nature of true greatness (Mk 10.43–5) and again his own activity illustrates what he says (Mk 10.45). Believers do not fall into mutual subordination easily; the connection of v. 21 with what precedes shows that its attainment is based on the imperative of v. 18b; only when filled with the Spirit do people willingly submit to another and learn not to insist on their own rights. Mutual subordination is of course a necessary basis for democracy.

The connection of fear to **Christ** follows a trend in which the NT transfers statements made about God in the OT to Christ. It also introduces a new element. **Fear** is a word with a wide range of meaning. Here it would be wrong to read into it any idea of 'terror'. It is instead a reverential fear which needs to be balanced by the motivation of love (Rom 12.1; 15.3f; 2 Cor 5.14; Eph 4.32; 5.2). It carries neither a hidden reference to the day of judgement nor even a threat of judgement (pace Schlier; Barth). The attitude Christians should have to their Lord is expressed in many other ways in the NT, above all in the idea of trust. Fear cannot be isolated and discussed on its own but must be regarded as part of a total attitude, and probably not as the most important part.

XIV

BEHAVIOUR IN THE CHRISTIAN HOUSEHOLD

(5.22–6.9)

Up to this point the paraenesis has seemed to jump from subject to subject but now we have a more systematic section centring on the behaviour of those living in Christian households. The style however remains similar to that in 4.17–5.20, the sentences being briefer than in chaps. 1–3, though it must be allowed that they are sometimes longer and more complex than in other parts of the paraenesis since in 5.22–33 theology and paraenesis are intermingled. In large part the style is determined by AE's use of traditional material which in 5.22–33, but not in 6.1–9, he expands to introduce a theological argument. On the traditional material see Detached Note: The *Haustafel*. It contains three sections treating the household groups, husbands and wives (5.22–33), parents and children (6.1–4), masters and slaves (6.5–9).

DETACHED NOTE VI
THE *HAUSTAFEL* OR HOUSEHOLD CODE
The origin of the HT form has been hotly debated; did it arise within the early Christian church, or Hellenistic Judaism, or the Greco-Roman world under the influence of Aristotle, or Stoicism or more widely?

It is now generally agreed that the first theory is incorrect: it was taken over by the church which modified it for Christian usage. We can hazard a guess as to its form prior to its Christian adoption by using the two forms in Ephesians and Colossians:

Wives, be subject to your husbands as is proper [in the Lord];
Husbands, love your wives.
Children, obey your parents;

Fathers, do not annoy your children.
Slaves, obey your [human] masters;
Masters, treat your slaves justly.

The question as to the origin of the form may not be all that important; if people are to live together, there are certain basic areas in which they require moral guidance and Christians must offer them this guidance as much as Jews, Greeks or Romans. One basic area is the household and, though its precise legal definition is unclear, it probably can be taken as including a biological family with their servants and slaves. The household was a social institution in all areas of the Greco-Roman world and especially important for Christians because it was the place where groups met to worship, the base for missionary activity and the place of reception for travelling Christians (Gielen). The baptism of households was also a significant feature of early Christianity (Acts 16.14–16, 34–6; 18.8). However, Greek, Roman and Jewish moralists often include another basic area, that of the state. Paul covers this in Rom 13.1–7 and it is the first area in the HT of 1 Pet 2.13–3.7.

It is difficult to know the correct term with which to describe 5.22–6.9. Martin Luther used the word *Haustafel*, yet it fails to cover 1 Pet 2.13–3.7 with its reference outside the household in 2.13–17. 'Code of social duties' or the briefer 'social code' or 'code of stations (in society)' seem more suitable, but since *Haustafel* is the term in general use we shall use it. Apart from Ephesians, Colossians and 1 Peter, we can trace the form, though not always as clearly, in Tit 2.1–10; 1 Clem 1.3; 21.6–9; Ign *Polyc* 4.1–6.1; Polyc *Phil* 4.1–6.3; *Did* 4.9–11; fragments of it also appear in 1 Timothy *passim* and 1 Clem 38.2. The internal arrangement of the form in Ephesians and Colossians, but not in 1 Peter, is often incorrectly described as reciprocal; 'love one another' is a reciprocal relationship as is that of 5.21; 'rule/obey' is not. It is better then to speak of paired relationships in Ephesians and Colossians. Approximately similar forms are found elsewhere, e.g. Philo, *Decal* 165–7; Josephus *c. Ap.* 2.190–219; Seneca, *de Benef* 2.18.1ff, but never as consistently as in Ephesians and Colossians where in each case one member of the pair is superior and the other inferior. The pair governors–governed was

275

impossible in a Christian HT, for Christians did not address 'governors' about their duties though Jews did. In the paired form both the inferior and the superior are addressed; this is natural in respect of slaves and women since they were full members of the community (cf Gal 3.28; 1 Cor 7.21–4; 12.13; Col 3.11); children are also addressed so they were presumably regarded as members (the pairing is parent-child and not young-old); this would be especially true where a whole household had been baptised. The men are addressed as husbands, masters, fathers, thus giving the HT a patriarchal slant with which no one in the ancient world would have quibbled; this however makes difficult the simple transference of the HT to the modern Western world. In the Greco-Roman world it was normally the adult free male who was addressed but from time to time slaves and women were also. In 1 Clem 1.3; 21.6–9; Polyc *Phil* 4.2; *T Reub* 5.5 wives are not addressed directly but husbands are told to instruct them in their duties.

The HT will have been used in the ethical instruction of Christians, but its precise purpose is difficult to determine. In the wider world it was probably originally designed to assist in preserving the good order of society, the family being seen as a microcosm of society and as a basic unit in its structure. This purpose may well underlie its use in 1 Peter where there is an outward look towards society in 2.11f; free men are to honour the forms of society and wives and slaves are not to act beyond their accepted social roles. Adherence to the counsel of the HT would ensure a stabilising influence on the part of the church. In this way the code could also have had an apologetic function. This may also be true in respect of 1 Tim 6.1; Tit 2.10.

Since the HT was an existing form it does not help us in determining the composition of the communities to which Ephesians was sent, other than that there were some households wealthy enough to have slaves, or the difficulties they were encountering. Its injunctions have an 'absolute' nature like those of the Decalogue and are not contingent. There are two important differences between the codes in Ephesians and Colossians and that of 1 Pet 2.13–3.7; in the latter, unlike the former, advice is given to (i) slaves in respect of angry and abusive masters, and their masters are not addressed, (ii) wives in respect of non-Christian husbands (see 3.1f). It can therefore be assumed that AE and A/Col have in mind wholly Christian households.

AE accepts a HT which implies that all the members of the community lived in Christian households. If he had not done so he could not have moved so easily between marriage and the relationship of Christ and the church. But the rest of the NT belies the idea that all believers lived in wholly Christian households. Much of the instruction given in the Gospels to disciples is addressed to individuals seen as members of the Christian community but not as members of households. In particular Mk 10.29 envisages disciples who have left, or perhaps been driven out from, their families (cf Mk 3.31–5; Mt 10.34f; Lk 12.51–3). In 1 Cor 7.39f Paul advises widows about marriage, seeming to prefer that they should remain unmarried and therefore outside the scope of those addressed in our HT which gives no consideration to single people. In 1 Cor 7.16 Paul assumes the existence of mixed marriages in the community (cf 1 Pet 3.1f; mixed marriages may also be one of the issues in 2 Cor 6.14–7.1). He may have been thinking of single unmarried men, of whom there were an increasing number in this period, when in 1 Cor 6.13–20 he rebukes those who have illicit sexual relationships and yet does not term them adulterers. It must however be allowed that AE has dealt with illicit sexual relations in a general way in 5.3, 5. Tit 2.6 appears to deal with single unmarried men and 1 Tim 5.2 discusses how to behave towards younger women. Incest existed in households in the church (1 Cor 5.1f) but the HT apparently does not see this as a problem. The problems for those living in non-Christian households were much greater than those in Christian households as 1 Pet 2.18–3.7 shows; in addressing slaves 1 Tim 6.1f allows for those with either believing or unbelieving owners (cf *Barn* 19.5–7; *Did* 4.9–11; Ign *Polyc* 5.2); Onesimus prior to his conversion served a Christian master, Philemon; Paul's letter shows that such masters needed Christian advice. A young man converted to Christianity could have had very serious problems over food sacrificed to idols for only such food might be on offer in his home; Paul, but not AE, thinks through the problem of food sacrificed to idols in 1 Cor 8–10. Paul also sets celibacy above marriage in 1 Cor 7.8, 25ff, 40 (perhaps AE may be excused for ignoring this; if he dealt with it, he would have ruined his teaching on the church in 5.22ff!). AE's approach to family relationships is thus both limited (*Ps-Phoc* 175–227 shows the wide range of problems requiring treatment) and simplistic, for he has avoided most of the serious problems that would arise within households. It is thus pastorally unrealistic. Would Paul have ever gone about it in this way? By limiting himself to Christian households AE has failed to address many, perhaps the majority, of his readers in respect of their conduct towards their kinsfolk.

How did AE came to incorporate such pastorally defective material in his letter? Presumably the HT was incorporated into both Ephesians and Colossians simply because it was there. But how did it come to be there? Since Paul shows a much greater realism in his treatment of family ethics he can hardly have composed the HT. It must then have come from outside, and presumably outside the Christian tradition. The origin of many of the difficulties we have seen for the HT derives from its limitation to Christian households; in other households individuals who became Christians would not have been able to participate wholly in the life of the household. Most of these difficulties would have been irrelevant to pagans in a pagan environment; there the obedience of wives and slaves would have been unaffected by a 'faith' difference. Only very rarely would problems arise if a son in a pagan household decided to worship a god other than the principal one worshipped by his parents; normally no exclusive claim would have been made for that god. Husbands would not worry if their wives added another goddess to the number they already worshipped. The HT probably then arose in the pagan, or possibly the Jewish, world where the problems we have discussed would not have been major issues. The pre-Christian form of the HT was simply transferred to Christian households without a realisation of the changes that needed to be made. The form could possibly have originated in Judaism in so far as mixed marriages were not sufficiently numerous in Judaism for their difficulties to have been explored; for the same reason it could have passed unaltered through Judaism on its way to Christianity.

A

HUSBANDS AND WIVES: CHRIST AND THE CHURCH

(5.22–33)

22 Wives, subordinate yourselves to your husbands,
    as to the Lord,
23   for a husband is head of his wife,
    as even Christ is head of the church,
    he being saviour of the (his) body.
24 Yet as the church is subject to Christ,
    so also wives are subject to their husbands in
      everything.
25 Husbands, love your wives
    as Christ loved the church and gave himself for her
26   that he might sanctify her,
    cleansing her with the washing of water
    with accompanying words,
27   that he might present to himself the church
    glorious, without defect or wrinkle
      or anything similar,
    but that she might be holy and blameless.
28 Consequently husbands should love their wives
    as their own bodies.
He who loves his own wife loves himself,
29   for no one ever hated his own flesh
    but (everyone) nourishes and takes care of it,
    just as Christ the church,
30   because we are members of his body.
31 For this reason a man will leave father and mother
    and be joined to his wife
    and the two shall become one flesh.
32 This mystery is profound:

I speak in reference to Christ and the church.
33 **To sum up,**
each one of you is to love his wife as he loves himself,
and as for the wife let her see she respects her husband.

The first main unit of the HT, 5.22–33, treats the relations of wives and husbands. It is much more developed than the similar section in Col 3.18f, especially in relation to husbands. It is sometimes suggested that in 5.22–6.9 AE follows a natural sequence of importance, wife, children, slaves, but though this may appear natural to us, it is neither the sequence of 1 Pet 2.13–3.7 nor necessarily that of the ancient world. 5.22–33 has three main sections: (i) vv. 22–4, where wives, the 'inferior', are the first to be addressed; (ii) vv. 25–32, where husbands are addressed and in which (a) Christ's example is held out to them (vv. 25–8) with a purpose expressed through three parallel clauses **that . . .**, and (b) the point is driven home (vv. 28–32) with reasons for the closeness of husband and wife and of Christ and church, with the motivation sealed through a quotation from Gen 2.24 which is applied to both the marital relationship and that of the church and Christ; (iii) a concluding summary (v. 33) bringing us back to the starting-point, the relation of husband and wife. The passage has in effect two conclusions, v. 32 giving that in respect of Christ and the church and v. 33 that in respect of marriage. The structure is chiasmic for vv. 22–4 and v. 33b deal with wives and vv. 25–9 and v. 33a with husbands: ABBA (Roberts). Throughout the passage the thought swings back and forth between human marriage, 22–3a, 24b–5a, 28–9a, (31), 33, and the Christ–church relationship, 23b–4a, 25b–7, 29b–30, (31), 32. We should note the use throughout of comparative particles, **as** (vv. 23, 24, 28), **so** (vv. 24, 28, 33), another Greek word for **as** (vv. 25, 29). The main comparison is between the marital relationship and that of Christ and the church and operates in such a way that the latter is the basis for instruction about the former, and not the reverse. The result is the alteration of what was a straightforward piece of marital instruction in the original HT into a section whose main theme is ecclesiological, emphasising the relation between Christ and the church rather than that between him and the individual believer. The comparison was made a lot easier because in Greek

church is a feminine and so could be linked to wife; feminine pronouns are normally used in translating this section to preserve the comparison.

Paul discusses marriage in 1 Cor 7 and the relationship of men and women and husbands and wives in 1 Cor 11.2ff; 14.34–6. Nothing here is seriously out of accord with those passages, apart from the absence of the stress on the superiority of celibacy to marriage in 1 Cor 7.8, 25ff. Here, through the comparison made with Christ and the church, marriage is given a more theological basis. While we speak here of the marriage relationship it must be acknowledged that there is some confusion in the passage concerning whether the woman involved is bride or wife, whether it is the wedding ceremony which is in mind or the continuing marriage. In vv. 22–4 and 28ff the latter is the ruling idea but in vv. 26f it is the former. The variation comes about, not because AE wishes to address both brides and wives, but because what he wants to say about the church necessitates the two approaches.

22. This verse lacks a verb and this needs to be supplied from v. 21: **subordinate yourselves** (cf v. 24).

It is not women in general but wives who are addressed. We may contrast this direct address with 1 Clem 1.3; 21.6 where husbands are told to instruct their wives in what is proper behaviour, an approach similar to that of 1 Cor 14.34–6. The subordination of women, literally, is 'to their own husbands' but there is no special stress on 'own' as if it were only to their own husbands that women needed to subordinate themselves. The manner in which they are addressed throughout vv. 22–33 implies that both wives and husbands are Christians.

The verse concludes with a motivation, **as to the Lord**, where the **Lord** is not the husband; if a reference to husbands were intended the plural 'lords' would have been used. The husband is not then depicted as 'lord' of his wife (*pace* Aquinas; Mussner; Gaugler); the introduction of **Lord** however helps to prepare for the following discussion of the relation of Christ to the church. The precise significance of **as** is difficult to determine. It could mean that wives should submit to their husbands *as they would* to the Lord, or, if understood causally, that wives should submit *because of* the Lord. In either case the wife's relationship to her husband is set within the perspective of her relation to her Lord;

the wife's subordination is then a religious act and has a wider context than that of the contemporary patriarchal understanding of the family.

The Pauline and deutero-Pauline letters contain contrasting attitudes to women and in particular to wives. That wives are directly addressed here coheres with Gal 3.28, where women are regarded as equal members of the church with men, and with 1 Cor 7.3ff, where husbands and wives have equal sexual rights within marriage and the husband is not depicted as governing his wife in this respect. Another attitude is partly present in 1 Cor 11.2ff; there women are permitted to take part in public worship but are subordinate to their husbands; this attitude is more pronounced in 1 Cor 14.34–6. In the Pastorals the less egalitarian attitude predominates and the other is excluded.

23. V. 22 could have appeared in a straightforward Christian HT, as does its parallel in Col 3.18, but for some reason unknown to us, perhaps arising out of the situation which led to the writing of the letter, we have an unlooked-for 'diversion' into teaching about the church. **Church** is used nine times in Ephesians; six of these occur in 5.22–33; no other paragraph in the NT has such a high density. The relationship of husband and wife to one another is set in parallel with that of Christ and the church. As in the earlier references to the church in Ephesians it is not individual congregations which are in mind but the whole church.

Verse 23a supplies the basis for the subordination of wives to husbands (v. 22) by re-expressing the superiority of the husband; while it may be right to speak of this relationship as axiomatic (Ewald) in terms of the contemporary culture, e.g. Aristotle, *Pol* 1253B; Plutarch, *Mor* 142E, yet there is insufficient evidence for the use of **head** to describe the relationship. In the passages from Aristotle and Plutarch the comparison is made to soul and body; this is a dualistic relation, and soul does not occupy the same position as head in relation to the body. AE's use of **head** here however enables him to make his transition to his discussion of the church, for he has already used the term in that connection (4.15f); it was used similarly in Col 1.18; 2.19, implying it was an accepted description in the Pauline churches and therefore known to AE's readers. 1 Cor 11.3 contains a sequence God-Christ-man-woman in which each is successively head of the next. This however is not the source of AE's usage for: (i) 1 Cor 11.3 relates man and woman; AE relates husband and wife; (ii) AE does not depict Christ as head of the husband; (iii) the subordination set out in 1 Cor 11.3 belongs to the order of creation (11.8f; cf 1 Tim 2.11–13) but AE, without denying that, for he later quotes Gen 2.24 which Judaism used to found marriage in the order of creation, views it as belonging to that of salvation as the remainder of the passage reveals. Ephesians may then be said to give a new christological sanction to the order of creation.

Headship in the NT embraces a range of ideas including rule, pre-eminence, source, the latter naturally implying priority. While 'pre-eminence' or 'source' are possible in Eph 4.15f, they are unlikely at 1.22 and probably also in 5.23 where the headship of the husband is linked to the wife's subordination.

In the second clause of the verse **as** can be understood either causally (Barth) or comparatively (the majority of commentators): the husband is head of his wife either *because* Christ is head of the church or *in the same way as* Christ is head of the church. Since the comparative element predominates in the passage it is better to choose that meaning here. Its choice implies we see the headship of the husband as one of love, not oppression.

Of the church introduces the dominating concept of the passage. The relationship of Christ and church is wider than that of headship and a brief parenthetical clause presents another aspect: Christ is **saviour of his body**, the church; this aspect is developed in what follows. While 23c may fall in the centre of vv. 22–4, it is certainly not the centre of vv. 22–33. It is better understood as a theological 'trailer' for what follows; it may also provide an explanation for Christ's headship (Bratcher and Nida): he is head because he is saviour.

Christ is not normally described as **saviour** in the earlier NT writings, in Paul only at Phil 3.20 where the context is future and eschatological (cf 1 Th 1.10), but appears in the later writings (Lk 2.11; Jn 4.42; Acts 5.31; 13.23; 2 Tim 1.10; Tit 1.4; 2.13; 3.6; 2 Pet 1.1, 11; 2.20; 3.2, 18; 1 Jn 4.14); the noun 'salvation' and the cognate verb are used frequently of Christ's redeeming work. **Saviour** has a septuagintal background in the concept of Yahweh as the deliverer of Israel and in Hellenistic Judaism where God is

283

saviour (Philo, *Conf Ling* 93f; *Leg Alleg* 3.27). It was also widely used in the contemporary world being applied to the Roman emperor, the Ptolemies, Asclepius, and the Heavenly Man. Our verse is indeed the only point where Christ is presented as saviour of the church, though he is said to be saviour of the cosmos in Jn 4.42; 1 Jn 4.14. '... its frequent employment in the Septuagint as a predicate of God or of the Messiah seems to supply the most natural antecedent for its Christian usage' (Nock). Its meaning varies; for example, it describes day-to-day preservation and care of their subjects by their earthly rulers. However, in the NT it is related normally to the death of Christ (implicit in v. 25), of which the saving significance was set out in 2.14ff. It is thus used both to describe Christ's function and as a title. **Saviour of the body** is a unique phrase in the NT, but Christ as saving and Christians as saved are common ideas and with this in mind it is easy to see how the phrase could appear in a similar way to that in which 5.25 arose out of 5.2. The combination of saviour and body moves us beyond the simple relationship of husband and wife into a discussion of Christ and the church in vv. 25ff where the idea is further developed. Overlordship of itself does not imply a close relation between the head and those he rules but head and body are closely linked; head and body are not however on a par for AE; Christ is the saviour of the body. A clear distinction is thus drawn between Christ and the body (= the church) at the same time as a close relation is created. Saviour and servant (cf Mk 10.42–5) are not far apart; servant and head seem opposed ideas; in a sense also head and saviour indicate very different aspects of the relation of Christ and the church. If he is head the nature of his headship is qualified in that he is also saviour, i.e. he is a saving head (T. G. Allen).

24. After the parenthesis of v. 23c AE returns to his paraenesis and restates the ideas of v. 23b but in reverse order resulting in a chiastic (ABCBA) pattern (23a, 23b, 23c, 24a, 24b). The content of the parenthesis of v. 23c does not affect the thought of v. 24 except by contrast but becomes important from v. 25 onwards. As in v. 23 Christ's headship over the church and its subordination to him is taken for granted and used as basis for an argument by analogy for the subordination of wives to husbands.

AE discusses neither the nature nor the extent of the church's subordination to Christ. Both nature and extent should be seen in general terms and as similar to that of the subordination of individual believers to Christ. AE would then be arguing in the same way as he does in 5.25 where he applies to the church a formula which originally related to the individual (cf 5.2; Gal 2.20 and notes on 5.2). Consequently the relationship of Christ and the church will never on the one side be servile nor on the other tyrannical. His rule over the church will accord with Mk 10.44 and her obedience will be offered in joy (Phil 3.1; 4.4). V. 24b which relates husband and wife in a parallel manner to that of Christ and the church lacks a verb and this is to be supplied from v. 24a; as there it will be in the indicative for both clauses of v. 24 are statements of fact, or at least in the contemporary world v. 24b would have been so taken.

The final phrase, **in everything**, requires explanation and perhaps qualification. It seems an obvious implication from v. 24a and would appear to put the husband on a level with God who must be obeyed in everything. Yet husbands are not sinless and perfect as was Christ.

25. Expanding greatly what must have been the pre-existing form of the HT in the Pauline school (cf Col 3.19), AE now switches his attention to husbands; his counsel for them falls into two brief sections, vv. 25–7 and vv. 28–32, and is more extensive than that to wives. In vv. 25ff Christ's love is given as an example to husbands and not to wives; are they not to love their husbands? AE does not refer to any reciprocal love on the part of spouses as is found sometimes in non-Christian advice (e.g. Musonius Rufus, *Or* XIIIA, Hense, though male superiority is still asserted; cf Frag XIV, Hense, Hierocles the Stoic, Stobaeus, IV 502, 503–7). The absence of any instruction to wives to love their husbands was noticed early and Clem Alex widens what is said to include the wife (*Paedagogus* 3.95.1, GCS 12.29). AE's advice to husbands follows a pattern well known in both ancient and modern counselling, the provision of a role model, here Christ. Yet Christ is not presented as a husband but as a saviour who died. An example of course can at times be more than a model and may exercise a transforming influence. So a causal factor may also be present here: the husband should love his wife because Christ loves him. Apart from Christ never having been a husband he cannot be imitated in everything he did, since the husband is not saviour of the wife as Christ is of him, and he cannot sanctify and purify her or ensure that she is without imperfection (vv. 26f). In fact vv. 26f move away from concern with the husband to deal exclusively with Christ's relationship with the church.

The husband is enjoined to love his wife and his behaviour towards her is not therefore left unrestricted, and, contrasting with the general opinion of the contemporary culture, it is not his 'rights' which are stressed but his obligations. The love referred to here is Christian love and not primarily romantic love. The reference to the husband's love follows surprisingly on AE's instruction to the wife to subordinate herself to her husband; in accordance with the contemporary patriarchal nature of society, the husband might have been expected to be told to instruct, advise and control his wife. Husbands are rarely enjoined in Jewish literature to love their wives (*Ps-Phoc* 195–7; see also *b Yeb* 62b). The Greek word *agape* is not used in Hellenistic literature in relation to households. The verb based on this root is the word used by Christians to denote Christ's self-sacrificing love and the love they should show one another. The husband's attitude is not then to be one of self-assertion or of ordering his wife about but of self-giving sacrifice (Gnilka), the same as is demanded of all Christians towards one another (1 Jn 3.16); a readiness to surrender life is required of husbands towards wives. The solution of marital problems for AE lies in both the subordination of the wife and the love of the husband (Hugedé). AE does not spell out what loving entails; this is done in 1 Cor 13.

Verse 25b introduces either a comparison (the husband's love should be similar to that of Christ for his church, Gnilka) or a reason (the husband should love his wife because Christ loved the church, Zerwick) or both (Schlier).

26. Three final clauses, vv. 26, 27a, 27b, now spell out the purpose of Christ's death for the church; each is introduced by **that**. His death does not leave the church unchanged; though strictly that might suggest the church existed before he died, it would be wrong to push the analogy beyond its limits (see Essay: The Church). An initial act is depicted here in which the church is made holy and cleansed, and the church is now thought of not as wife but as bride at the time of her wedding.

Christ's death has a double effect: it both sanctifies and cleanses. The tense of the participle does not imply that cleansing precedes sanctification (so many older Protestant commentators on theological grounds). The sanctification itself is not to be understood as a continuing process (Salmond). The two verbs, 'to sanctify' and 'to cleanse', are difficult to distinguish in meaning. The former is used here cultically rather than ethically. Those whom God sanctifies are separated from the secular sphere and brought within that of his holiness (cf Ecclus 33.12; 45.4), and are therefore acceptable to him (Rom 15.16). Sanctification has its basis in Christ's death (1 Cor 1.30, where the context is his death). As soon as the readers began to believe and were baptised they were saints, i.e. sanctified; sanctification and baptism are connected in 1 Cor 6.11, a connection brought out later in our verse. 'To cleanse' carries on the connection with baptism for water cleanses, though the link may be indirect (Acts 15.9; 2 Pet 1.9; Tit 2.14; in 1QS 3.4, 9; 1QH 11.10–12 water and cleansing are associated, though of course baptism in the Christian sense is not in view).

The tenses of the verbs indicate that readers have already been sanctified and cleansed. When did this take place? Two possibilities exist, either at baptism or at Christ's death. These two are not unrelated in Pauline theology where baptism is explicitly connected to Christ's death (Rom 6.3ff; 1 Cor 1.13; cf Col 2.12; Heb 10.22; 1 Jn 1.7, 9 where the contexts are the death of Christ). Believers and the church, in the sense that word has in Ephesians, were baptised into Christ when he died, but this only became real for them at the moment of physical baptism; their sanctification and cleansing were then actualised. The baptismal reference becomes explicit in **with the washing of water**; the readers know what is meant and consequently there is no need of explanation. It is only here in the NT that **washing** is used to denote baptism, but see Justin Martyr, *Apol* I, 61.3, 10, 12; *Dial* 13.1; 14.1. Baptism is an individual matter and, though the whole church may have been potentially cleansed in the death of Christ, it is only individuals for whom it becomes real; probably AE is led to speak of a baptism of the church for a similar reason to that which led him to modify the individual nature of 5.2 into the corporate expression of 5.25. The reference to washing may have a secondary meaning.

Marriage is part of the context and prior to marriage the bride in Judaism (Ezek 16.9; *Ab* R. *Nathan* 41; *b Schab* 77b) and in some other cultures had a 'ceremonial' bath. Macpherson is exceptional in seeing this secondary meaning as the sole meaning. Whether the nuptial bath is alluded to here or not the reference to water excludes any thought of a 'blood' baptism or a Holy Spirit baptism.

The final phrase in v. 26, literally 'in a word', has caused interpreters much difficulty. There are two interrelated problems: (i) To which word or words in the verse does the phrase relate? (ii) To what does it refer? Since readers have been baptised and have seen many baptisms they will know what is meant, and AE has then no need to define the phrase (cf Dibelius). It might refer to: (a) the command of Jesus to baptise (e.g. Mt 28.16–20); (b) the words of the baptismal formula, 'in the name of Christ', spoken over the candidate at the moment of baptism (Chrysostom); (c) the candidate's own baptismal confession, e.g. 'Jesus is Lord' (Mitton); 1 Pet 3.21 suggests the candidate did speak something in the nature of a pledge; (d) a sermon, or proclamation of the word, during the baptismal ceremony, perhaps something as simple as a declaration of forgiveness (Salmond); (e) the gospel through which the candidate began to believe (Jerome; Pelagius; Grotius). (d) and (e) are difficult to distinguish since the preaching of the word at the ceremony would also be a proclamation of the gospel. Of the possibilities (a), (c) and (e) may be eliminated: (a) because this, if it occurred at all, would be prior to baptism ('You must come and be baptised because Jesus has commanded it'); (c) because the emphasis in the passage lies on the action of God or Christ and not on that of believers; (e) because this also would be preliminary and because where 'word' means the gospel it is always qualified with Christ or God (6.17; Rom 10.17; Heb 6.5; 1 Pet 1.25). This leaves (b) and (d). Both imply a relation to God or Christ through either the use of a given formula or a proclamation in his name. Protestants have traditionally favoured (d) so that the baptism might not appear to be effective in and of itself without a proclamation of the word to which faith would respond (the sacraments should always be accompanied with preaching); (d) can also be supported through 1 Pet 1.23. There is however no reason to suppose that AE is thinking of the act of baptism as itself, and by itself, effecting redemption; for him it is always God or Christ who redeems (Calvin); there is also no actual NT evidence that at the moment of baptism a sermon was preached. (b) is therefore to be preferred with the great majority of modern commentators. The formula in use at that time was probably not Trinitarian but used only Christ's name (Acts 2.38; 8.16; 10.48; 19.5; 1 Cor 1.13–15; Gal 3.27). Christ's name would remind candidates that the effect of baptism rested ultimately on Christ's giving of himself for them.

In the translation we have used a fairly general rendering in the plural since the singular does not necessarily mean an individual word: **with accompanying words**.

27. The second **that** clause begins v. 27; it has been taken as parallel to v. 26 (Ewald) or as its consequence (Haupt). The latter possibility is the better because it makes the presentation of the bride dependent on her 'washing'; v. 27 is a further step in the argument and not a repetition of v. 26. V. 27 is of course indirectly dependent on v. 25.

In 2 Cor 11.2 Paul had already spoken of the presentation to Christ of the church as a bride yet there are important differences between 2 Cor 11.2 and here: (i) in 2 Cor 11.2 Paul presents the church to Christ; here Christ presents the church to himself; (ii) in 2 Cor 11.2 the bride is an individual congregation; here she is the whole church; (iii) 2 Cor 11.2 depicts a betrothal, the context is eschatological and the marriage is future; elsewhere in our passage the marriage is regarded as already in existence.

Christ presents to himself a bride who is **glorious**, a word whose precise meaning needs to be derived from its context. We should not attempt to understand it etymologically as if it referred to divine 'glory', in particular the glory of the End. In v. 27 it probably means 'beautiful'. Brides are supposed to be beautiful, at least in the eyes of their groom, and the bride's beauty is widely celebrated in literature (Song of Solomon 4.7; Ps 45.8–11, 13–15; 1QapGen 20.1ff; see Isa 62.1–8 for the glory of Israel). The 'beauty' of a bride is normally her own but here it is the groom who makes her lovely; he, Christ, is the beautician who has prepared the bride, as God beautified Israel in Ezek 16.10–14, for he has sanctified and cleansed her (another point at which the analogy breaks down). He created her, and created her 'glorious';

what Christ creates is good just as what God creates is good (Gen 1.1ff). The beauty of the bride, who is the church, is of course not physical but moral and spiritual. Moral and spiritual purity is a Pauline theme (1 Cor 7.14; 2 Cor 6.14–7.1; 11.2; 1 Th 4.3–8).

The remainder of the verse spells out **glorious**, first negatively and then positively. The negative description uses physical terms: **without defect or wrinkle**. The perfect skin condition, suggestive of a young woman, accords with the idea of a bride. The church is young since it only came into existence at the cross yet it is also old as the continuation of Israel. Members are youthful in so far as all have recently been converted but old in so far as they have been the elect of God from before the foundation of the world (1.4). Both the age and youth of the church have been emphasised throughout the centuries (cf Hermas, *Vis* 2.4.1 and 3.13.1).

The verse ends with the third **that** clause giving the ultimate purpose of Christ's selection of her to be his bride. It provides the positive description of the bride repeating the description of believers given in 1.4: **holy and blameless**.

This brings us to the end of the first admonition to husbands, but the section has been much more concerned with the relation-ship of Christ and the church than with that of husband and wife. It has however connected the ongoing life of the church to the once-for-all event of the cross.

28. The husband–wife theme of the HT is now resumed (vv. 28f) from the same basic position that the husband should love his wife; the Christ–church theme is not however neglected and reappears in v. 29c.

Does v. 28 (a) continue what precedes with **consequently** picking this up, or (b) does **consequently** indicate a new beginning, it itself being picked up by the following **as**? In v. 24 the particles move the argument forward but are in reverse order; they also move it forward in v. 33 where they are much closer together. If (b) is accepted, then v. 28 lacks a connection with v. 27 (Meyer). It is thus easier to adopt (a); husbands should love their wives as Christ loved the church. **Should** implies a duty or obligation. The church is Christ's body; he loves it. Husbands should then love their wives who are as their own bodies.

Body, previously applied to the relation of Christ and the church, is now used with reference to the action of husbands towards their wives and AE probably chose it because of its earlier reference, for Christ may be said to love his own body when he loves the church. As well as this AE is about to quote Gen 2.24 where 'flesh' is used of the relation of husband and wife, and it and 'body' can be equivalents in depicting the sexual relationship (1 Cor 6.16; cf 15.39f). **Body** has a wide range of meaning in biblical Greek and does not necessarily carry a strong physical or anatomical connotation. It clearly cannot do this when used of the church and in v. 28 it is interchangeable with the personal pronoun. To say that husbands should love their wives as their own bodies is not as degrading a view of marriage as it appears in English where 'body' is primarily physical, and it is not more egotistical than Lev 19.18 (cf v. 29) to which some commentators see an allusion (see on v. 33). Even if 'body' were understood physically it has to be said that a husband loves his body by feeding and dressing it, and there would be nothing wrong in him doing the same for his wife. But the phrase has here a wider complexion. Whatever a husband would do for himself he must also do for his wife (see v. 29). However, a limitation, absent from v. 25, is now introduced. There because Christ's death indicates the extent of his love for the church it is implied that a man should be ready to surrender his life for his wife; love of oneself can hardly be expressed in willingness to die for oneself! The husband's love in the present context should be viewed more pragmatically as in v. 29. V. 28b with its change from the plural to the singular has been thought to be a proverb (Ewald) but no such proverb has ever turned up. More probably it is a parenthetical explanation of v. 28a. AE may have realised that the reference to a wife as a body might be misleading and so spells it out through the personal pronoun and uses a singular because he is advancing an argument from observation or experience.

29. This verse has been connected both with v. 28a (e.g. Haupt) and with v. 28b (the vast majority of commentators) yet if v. 28b is explicative of v. 28a then it is probably better to relate it to the whole of v. 28 as spelling out the nature of the husband's love towards his wife. As in v. 28b **himself** picked up **bodies** in v. 28a so both are now picked up by **his own flesh** which itself points forward to **flesh** in the quotation of Gen 2.24 in v. 31. Another factor leading to the change from **body** to **flesh** may have been the latter's feminine gender; the same pronoun can therefore refer to it, the church and the wife, so preserving the underlying continuity of the argument. **Flesh** and **body** are different terms but their meanings overlap and so it is possible to interchange them (1 Cor 6.16; 15.39f; 2 Cor 4.10f). While **flesh** (see on 2.3) in Pauline theology can carry negative overtones (Gal 3.3; 5.19–21; Rom 8.9) it takes its meaning from its context and its equivalence here with the personal pronoun signifies that it is not being used negatively (for similar neutral use see Rom 3.20; 2 Cor 12.7; Gal 1.16). Verse 29a expresses a fact drawn from experience, true both negatively, for people do not hate themselves, and positively, for they care for themselves.

The positive care that all people have for themselves is expressed through two verbs in the present tense denoting an ongoing activity. Their background is probably marital as is confirmed by an ancient marriage contract: 'to nourish and take care of and clothe her'.

In the final clause of the verse AE's central theme returns, the relation of Christ and the church. **Just as** is primarily comparative, though it may contain a causal element: husbands should care for their wives because Christ cared for the church. The attempt to discover parallels to the two verbs in relation to Christ's care of the church is probably wrong.

30. How are we to understand v. 30 since at first sight it seems otiose? In v. 29b the argument moved back from husband and wife to Christ and the church. Now it is again people who are at the centre and the first plural replaces impersonal statements. Had the verse read 'because she is his body (flesh)' the sequence of thought would have been explained and the first plural eliminated; but then nothing new would have been said (Gnilka). Up to now, apart from 4.25, AE has stressed the relation of the church as a whole to Christ and not the sociological aspect of the 'body' metaphor in which members are individually related to Christ and to one another (cf 1 Cor 12.12–27; Rom 12.4–8). Has he at this point realised the impersonality of his approach and decided to personalise it? 'Lest his readers should think of this as remote from themselves, the author reminds them of their place in this discussion' (Best, *One Body*). It is only because readers are members of Christ's body that they can be addressed as they are in a HT which deals with wholly Christian households. Christ's care of the church is always his care of the individuals composing it. The emphasis, 'his body', is on the Christ–believer relationship and not on that between believers.

31. This verse is a quotation of Gen 2.24 from the LXX. AE introduces the quotation here without saying he is doing so. At 4.8 and 5.14 he alerted readers to his quotations, but not at 4.25 or 6.2f. In 6.2f which draws on the Decalogue he probably assumed his readers knew it was a quotation; the same probably holds here in view of the widespread use of Gen 2.24 in the Gospels (Mt 19.5; Mk 10.7f) and in Paul (1 Cor 6.16 where he acknowledges it is a quotation). The verse was also widely known and used in Judaism for varying purposes and in varying ways: in CD 4.21 in support of monogamy; Philo uses it allegorically (*Leg Alleg* 2.49; *Gig* 65) and Pseudo-Philo (*Bib Ant* 32.15) typologically. Later in gnosticism it was used of the union of the fallen soul with her brother, the bridegroom (*Exeg Soul* II, 6 132.21–133.11). It is also used straightforwardly of marriage and sexual relations in 1 Esdras 4.20–2 and in the rabbinic writings.

How then does AE use it? One theme of vv. 22–33 is marriage and it must at least apply to this, even though it does not relate directly to the submission of wives or the love of husbands; it would serve to strengthen the marriage bond, laying, because of its immediate context, a greater stress on the duty of the husband; the discussion had of course been individualised in v. 30. In the Gospels Gen 2.24 is linked to Gen 1.27 implying that marriage belongs to the created order; in Ephesians instead it is associated with teaching on Christ and the church; this results in Christian marriage (both wife and husband are assumed to be believers) being given a soteriological basis. That does not mean that marriage is no longer a part of the order of creation for Gen 2.24 lies in the creation narrative.

While the connection of v. 31 with human marriage cannot be ignored there is also, as v. 32 shows, a connection with the marriage of Christ and the church and this has led many past interpreters, using the word 'mystery' in v. 32 as a starting-point, to offer various understandings of v. 31.

32. AE now picks up the biblical quotation of v. 31. In so far as the HT has provided AE with a way into talking about Christ and the church, we have now reached the apex of his argument and, if Gen 2.24 was his 'text', it comes at the end of the 'sermon' rather than at its beginning. There is here a mystery which is important, significant or profound. A disclosure has taken place: something previously unknown, secret or hidden is now revealed.

Not only the word **mystery** but also the final clause of v. 32 where AE says that he is speaking about Christ and the church encourage us to look for a deeper meaning in Gen 2.24. Some have seen in our verse a prophecy of the incarnation (note the future tenses) or of the parousia (future from the point of view of AE), but for both these interpretations the reference to the mother creates an insuperable difficulty; did Christ leave his mother to come to earth or does he return to her? Jerome and Augustine (in *Jo Tr* 9.10, re Jn 2.1–11) thought of the mother as the heavenly Jerusalem, but this is no help. Writers who allegorise normally also give some indication that a meaning other than that of the surface is to be drawn from the passage being treated (cf Gal 4.24). Allegorisation is not then the key to unlock v. 31.

A typological interpretation might be possible. In Rom 5.12ff and 1 Cor 15.20ff Adam is a type of Christ; so the husband and wife of Gen 2.24 have been understood as Adam = Christ and Eve = the church. This is worked out in great detail by Miletic. Jerome drew an entirely different conclusion: as the human race was born from Adam and Eve, so believers are born from Christ and the church (cf Ps-Philo, *Bib Ant* 32.15, where Israel is said to descend from Eve, the rib taken from Adam). It is hard to see this as part of the text. It is probably not the man and wife whom AE says are the mystery but the union of Christ and the church.

An entirely different approach came through the Vulgate rendering of **mystery** as *sacramentum*, which led to the view of marriage as a sacrament. Though many continue to look on marriage as a sacrament they no longer use v. 32 as its basis.

It is probably better then not to attempt to fit what AE is saying into some given hermeneutical method or some predetermined dogmatic pattern, but simply to view him as providing a scriptural basis and theological justification for the drawing together of the husband–wife relation and the Christ–church relation, and at the same time carrying a step further his teaching about the church's close relationship to Christ, a relationship already defined through 'body'. He uses the word **mystery** with its sense of a secret now revealed because he believes what he says is not something which he has thought up on his own but comes from God.

33. This verse provides a summarising resumption and conclusion of the original main point of the HT in relation to husband and wife, from which AE moved away to draw in the relation of Christ and church. The form is chiasmic; husband and wife are now treated in the reverse order to that of vv. 22–32.

In this summary the injunction to husbands is emphatically individualised, **each one of you**, and this individualisation should be understood also as applying to wives. No husband or wife should imagine that what is being said does not apply to them. Though AE has much to say about the church as a whole he is well aware that it consists of individuals who have to relate to one another. This relation in respect of the husband is again defined as love, whose special relevance was spelt out in two different ways in vv. 25–7 and vv. 28–9, but is now varied in one respect; previously his love was to be similar to his love for his body (or flesh) or Christ's love for the church; now it is to be similar to his love for himself (cf v. 28b). Freed from the need to maintain the parallel of the husband–wife and Christ–church relationships, AE drops the word **body** to use the simpler reflexive pronoun. As Jerome observed the expression is somewhat similar to Lev 19.18; for Jewish and Christian understanding of neighbour see on 4.25; here in v. 33 the wife as another believer can correctly be described as a neighbour. The one whom the singer woos in the Song of Songs is described as 'neighbour' (1.9, 15; 2.2, 10, 13; 4.1, 7; 5.2. 6.4). 'Neighbour' was also used in later rabbinic literature in relation to marriage; *b Qid* 41a; *b Nid* 17a; *b Yeb* 37b. Textbooks on Christian ethics discuss the relationship of self-love to love of neighbour and we do not need to enter into this general problem.

Whereas love as the attitude of husband to wife is expressed here in the same way as earlier, a different word is chosen to characterise that of the wife towards her husband. The verb 'I fear' is substituted for 'I obey' (translated as **are subject to** in v. 24); the two were linked in v. 21. The verb 'I fear' ranges in meaning from suggesting terror to respect and reverence. As it denotes here the wife's reaction to her husband's love it can hardly lie in the area of terror; yet reverence would not be an exact rendering, for her attitude includes obedience and submission. 'Fear' is a normal element in all authority structures (cf Rom 13.3, 4, 7; 1 Pet 2.18; Eph 6.5), though if the controlling authority acts unreasonably it may degenerate into terror; in our case the controlling authority is directed by love. As Bouttier points out, all believers are summoned both to fear and love God. **Respect** is probably the best English rendering. What is surprising is the failure to summon the wife to love her husband.

Do we find elsewhere the relation between a single superhuman person and a group of people expressed in marital terms? It appears in the parables of Jesus (Mt 22.1–14; 25.1–13) and as relating Jesus and John the Baptiser (Mk 2.18–20; Jn 3.23–30). Yet though Jesus is featured in the Gospels as bridegroom or husband the disciples never appear as his wife or bride. The husband–wife analogy however is used in relation to the church in Rev 19.7, 9; 21.2, 9; 22.17. In the OT and Judaism Yahweh is depicted as the husband of Israel which more often than not is unfaithful to him (Hos 1–3; Jer 3.8; Isa 54.1–8; Ezek 16, 23). Two writings (Ps 45; Song of Songs), originally composed as poems about human love, came to be applied to the love of God for Israel. 'Bridegroom' however never became a messianic title, yet since statements about Yahweh are often reapplied to Christ in the NT it is not surprising to find the relation of Christ and the church described in marital terms. Philo plays with the image (*Abr* 99ff; *Cherub* 40ff; *Somn* 1.200; see also 1QIs[a] 61.10; 2 Esdr 10.25ff, 40ff; *Syb Or* 3.356ff; *Odes Sol* 38.11ff). The second century provides parallels (see Schlier), especially through the *sophia* myth (so Fischer) or Justin's Baruch (so Batey). It is interesting that Ephesians, 2 Corinthians (probably written in Ephesus) and Revelation which use the image all have a connection with Asia Minor where gnostic ideas were later important. Whatever the source of the image we can be sure that it would have been understood by AE's readers in Asia Minor.

B

PARENTS AND CHILDREN

(6.1–4)

[1] **Children,**
   obey your parents in the Lord
      for this is right.
[2]   **Honour your father and mother,**
      for this is a pre-eminent commandment
         carrying with it a promise,
[3]   **so that it may be well with you**
         and you will be a long time on the earth.
[4] **And, fathers,**
   do not enrage your children,
   but bring them up in the discipline and instruction of the
      Lord.

The second section of the HT covers the parent–child relationship in a manner similar to Col 4.20f; though longer than Col 4.20f it is much briefer than the section on wives and husbands, for AE has no theology to incorporate here. Parents can choose whether they should have children but children do not have a choice and cannot select their parents. The parent and child relationship is thus of a different nature from that between either husband and wife or owner and slave.

Respect for parents was generally expected of children in the ancient world both among Jews, as shown by the Decalogue (cf Ecclus 3.1–9; Philo, *Decal* 120), and among Greeks and Romans (Aristotle, *Nic Eth* IX 2 = 1165a; Plutarch, *Mor* 479f). Christians sometimes viewed lack of respect as an indication of depravity (Rom 1.30) or a sign of the nearness of the End (2 Tim 3.1f). The father was the more important parent. In the Greco-Roman world the mother reared the child until he ('he' is used advisedly for the rearing and education of girls was of much less importance than that of boys) was seven, when the father became responsible for his training and education. The Greek word which denotes children here, though neuter in gender, would have been automatically understood by readers as meaning male children. Children were under the control of their parents, particularly of the father, until either the father died (the normal pattern in Greek society) or was sixty years old (normal in the Roman world). When children are addressed in Judaism they may be adults for no upper limit is put on their age (Ecclus 3.1–9; Philo, *Decal* 120). Indeed in later rabbinic Judaism sermons were delivered to adult children on the theme of obedience to parents. AE offers no clue as to the age of the children he addresses; they must have been old enough to understand what is said, but they could have been small, subteenagers, or older teenagers and young adults. When the church met in a house presumably all its children were present (cf 1 Cor 7.14). What information there is, is insufficient to determine if the children had been baptised. AE says nothing of the actual way in which children are to be reared. In Judaism the real centre of education was the home (Deut 6.7; Prov 13.24; Ecclus 30.1–13; Philo, *Hyp* 7.14; Josephus *c. Ap.* 1.60), though, as with many Greco-Roman households, children would be sent to outside schools for part of their education. Did this mean children from Christian households would be sent to pagan schools? Probably by this time there would have been no question of them attending synagogue schools. The present section on the relationship of parents and children is a kind of equivalent to the discussion of the relationship of older and younger believers in 1 Pet 5.5; 1 Tim 5.1f; Tit 2.6; there was indeed in ancient society a general respect for age.

V. 1 and v. 2 are similarly structured around imperatives with clauses giving the reason for the command. The reason given in v. 1b leads to v. 2 since righteousness and the Law are related. V. 3 supplies a further reason for the injunction of v. 2. V. 4 is differently structured with two imperatives set in contrast with one another.

1. The New English Bible and Revised English Bible follow Marcion and some early manuscripts in omitting **in the Lord**. If **in the Lord** is read, it must qualify **obey** and not **your parents**, and would imply children should obey because they are Christians. If the phrase is not read, then the text says nothing more than any Greco-Roman or Jewish moralist would have said. There is a sense in which the divine reference would have been implicit, for in Judaism, and even more generally, parents came next below God in the hierarchy of obedience, and obedience to them is closely linked to that to him (Philo, *Decal* 119f; *Mos* 2.198; *Spec Leg* 2.225, 235; Josephus *c. Ap.* 2.206; *Sib Or* 3.593f; *Ps-Phoc* 8; *T Reub* 3.8; Stobaeus, *Anth* 4.25.53 = Hense II 640ff; Cicero, *de Offic* I.58; Diogenes Laertes 7.108, 120; Epictetus 2.17.31; 3.7.26; Musonius Rufus *Or* xvi = Hense 82.3–5). AE then has based his injunction on the general moral connotation **this is right** and on the particular connection with the Decalogue; the latter was of course of great importance to his readers and understood by them as a Christian injunction. **Children**, as its use elsewhere shows, implies a biological relationship and offers no clue as to age. It can imply someone old enough to be a believer (Mt 10.21), to work in the fields (Mt 21.28), or to be held responsible for his or her sins (Mk 2.5; cf Lk 15.31), and it can be used metaphorically of people of all ages (Mt 3.9; 23.37; Mk 7.27; Lk 7.35). The children are therefore full members of the community and it is assumed they are of an age where disagreement between them and their parents (biological parents are meant and not 'fathers in the faith') could occur since, though they had attained their majority, they were still under the control of their parents.

Obedience to parents is said to be **right**; although the root of this word is strongly connected in Pauline teaching to justification, the word is used here in a wider way and in common with its use in the moral teaching of the ancient world (cf Epictetus 1.22.1; 2.17.6), a use already met in 4.24 (cf Phil 1.7; 4.8; 2 Th 1.6; Acts 4.19; 2 Pet 1.13; Col 4.1; Lk 12.57).

2, 3. To drive home his point about obedience AE now quotes the relevant commandment of the Decalogue and so provides another reason for obedience. To **honour** is a wider and gentler concept than to **obey**, involving *inter alia* the care of elderly parents. It may also direct attention to inner attitude rather than actual acts of outward obedience; the latter may come from fear of punishment rather than genuine respect. The change of verb cannot however be attributed to AE (*pace* Grosheide) for it is the verb in the commandment.

The commandment is quoted from Exod 20.12 to which it is closer than Deut 5.16; the one significant change is the omission from Exod 20.12 of the final clause referring to the 'land' as good and given by God. The essential section of the commandment is quoted also in Mk 7.10; 10.19; Mt 15.4; 19.19; Lk 18.20 and may be assumed to have been well known to early Christians. Probably converts quickly learned all the commandments of the Decalogue (cf Mt 5.21, 27; 15.4–6; Mk 10.19; Rom 7.7–11; 13.8–10) and in the light of their knowledge AE did not need to use a formal introductory phrase showing the OT origin of the quotation.

V. 2b speaks of our commandment as the 'first' with a **promise**. Is 'first' to be understood numerically or as an indication of significance? The word itself disposes one to the former, an interpretation offered as early as Chrysostom. Yet in the Decalogue the commandment is neither numerically first nor even the first with a promise (see Exod 20.4–6). 'First' also implies a succeeding sequence but there are no other later commandments in the Decalogue with a promise. In an attempt to overcome these difficulties Origen, who appears to have been the first to observe them, followed by Jerome, suggested that 'first' might refer to the whole Decalogue as the first law given after the Exodus or that the promise attaching to the second commandment was not really a promise. Others (e.g. Ambrosiaster; Pelagius) have suggested that the fifth commandment is the first in the second table of the Decalogue. Was it however ever regarded as belonging to the second table? Rom 13.9 does not include it among those generally regarded as belonging to it; in Lev 19.3 it is associated with the first table; Philo, *Decal* 121, regarded it as the conclusion of the first set of commandments which are concerned with the divine. Philo is not however consistent; in *Spec Leg* 2.261 he separates this commandment from those he regards as the chief commandments though in 2.242ff he had associated the fifth with the first four as those for which death is the appropriate punishment and in his general discussion he treats the fifth with the first four. 'First' could also relate to 'promise' and not to the numbering of the commandments in their tables. The evidence is insufficient for taking 'first' as referring to the first commandment of the second table. It has been suggested that since the first thing a child learns is obedience to parents the fifth commandment can be regarded as the first (Abbott). It is difficult to see how the statement (Exod 20.6) accompanying the second commandment can be regarded as anything other than a promise (Lincoln). All these interpretations suffer from the weakness that 'first' indicates a following sequence of commandments with promises and it is impossible to discover them in the OT. If we do not restrict **commandment** to the Decalogue then we have to take into account those that precede it as well as those that follow it. This seems to force us back to accepting 'first' as indicating significance. This has been justified through the use of some rabbinic evidence (*Dt R* 6 on Dt 22.6) which regards the fifth commandment as the 'heaviest' (Dibelius). In the end may it not be simplest to take first as indicating a pre-eminent commandment, one of great importance because it is included in the Decalogue and has a promise?

Whatever the meaning attached to 'first' the nature of the promise is of greater importance. The promise originally referred to the dwelling in Canaan of the descendants of those who entered it after the exodus and was appropriately attached to the one commandment which implied a continuing Israel. Once the Jews began to live in other areas this geographical limitation was no longer relevant. 'Land' (here translated **earth**) was fortunately ambiguous, deriving its meaning from its context. In later Judaism it was frequently omitted in references to the text (it is eliminated in Ecclus 3.1–16; Philo spiritualised it in *Spec Leg* 2.262). AE retains the word but leaves it without a context so that it can be taken as 'earth, world'. In either case it still carries a physical connotation. Since AE has already used 'inheritance' (1.14; 3.6) with a non-physical meaning, does he intend such a significance here (cf Mt 5.5 for a non-physical meaning)? Beginning with Origen (cf Jerome) many interpreters have therefore read a deeper non-physical sense into it, usually one relating to eternal life. It is probably best to take the promise of v. 3 literally. Children who keep the fifth commandment will prosper and live for a long time (Belser; Lincoln). This would accord with much in the OT and with the more prudential ethic of the Pastorals (many have followed Harless in quoting 1 Tim 4.8 to support this interpretation). It is a point of view which contrasts with the immediate eschatological expectation of much of the NT but one into which Christians have regularly declined; it is not surprising to see AE whose ethic rarely touches the deeper levels moving in the same direction.

4. AE now addresses the **fathers** who are as much in need of instruction as the children. In accordance with ancient custom he addresses them alone without mentioning the mothers. It is true that 'fathers' can sometimes include mothers (Heb 11.23) but the change from **parents** of v. 1 is significant; had AE intended to include mothers he would have needed to make this explicit in view of contemporary thought. The admonition to fathers is only about half the length of that to children, but what was said to the latter included a lengthy OT quotation. Since in the ancient world fathers had great authority over their children they might tend to hector them, lay down the law and thus **enrage** them. If fathers enraged their children, this would produce the opposite effect to what they were seeking, for anger is sinful (4.26) and enraged children would then sin. AE's sentiment was not unique in the ancient world (cf Plutarch, *de liberis educandis, Mor* II 8F–9A; Menander in Stobaeus, IV 26.3ff = Hense II, 650.1ff; *Ps-Phoc* 207–17). While the age of the children is not indicated, older children are more likely to be enraged by a nagging father, though the later effects on younger children might be more pronounced.

The positive attitude fathers should adopt is expressed first in a general way through a verb we have translated **bring them up**, used here differently from 5.29 in that it relates to the education and upbringing of children, and then through two nouns, **discipline** and **instruction**, which are difficult to distinguish (so also in Philo who uses them together *Deus Immut* 54; *Spec Leg* 2.239; 4.96); the attempt to distinguish them as referring to instruction through act and word goes back to Grotius but is difficult to sustain. While **discipline** is closely related to the educational process, it should not be restricted to academic learning; Greek education involved moral and philosophical training. In the Jewish world, where the word was associated with wisdom, it came to carry the additional idea of the physical discipline accompanying instruction (e.g. Ecclus 42.5; Prov 13.24; 29.19). Even though the use of physical discipline was common in the educational systems of the ancient world, it is unlikely that this

Jewish nuance would have been picked up in Asia Minor; it is a nuance not found in Acts 7.22; 22.3; 2 Tim 2.25; 3.16; Tit 2.12, though present in Heb 12.5ff (based on Prov 3.11ff); 1 Cor 11.32; 1 Tim 1.20; Lk 23.16, 22; 2 Cor 6.9. Sometimes it is God and sometimes other humans who exercise discipline; normally the context makes it clear when the physical element enters. The word should be given its wider educational sense in v. 4, while recognising that instruction could involve discipline. 'Instruction' is found in the NT only at 1 Cor 10.11; Tit 3.10, though the cognate verb occurs more widely in relation to verbal instruction (Acts 20.31; Rom 15.14; 1 Cor 4.14; Col 1.28; 3.16; 1 Th 5.12, 14; 2 Th 3.15) where obviously the idea of discipline does not enter. The two nouns together denote the process of education though giving no clue as to its content. There is nothing here on which to base an educational theory, except that those theories which permit children to do whatever they like would be excluded.

Instruction is **of the Lord**; the genitive cannot mean instruction about the Lord but could mean either 'with the Lord in view', 'in the light of the Lord' or with the Lord seen as the ultimate instructor who works through the father. The former would result in a meaning similar to that of v. 1, yet if this was what had been intended, we would have expected the same phrase; the latter understanding is therefore preferable: the father mediates the Lord's instruction. The requirement to rear and educate children suggests that AE does not believe the End is about to arrive.

C

OWNERS AND SLAVES

(6.5–9)

⁵ Slaves, obey your human lords
   with fear and trembling,
   in singleness of heart,
       as (if) to the Lord,
⁶   not with superficial care,
       like those who seek to please others,
   but as Christ's slaves
       who do God's will from the heart,
⁷   serving with cheerfulness,
       as to the Lord and not human masters,
   knowing that everyone,
       whether slave or free,
       who does something good
           will be recompensed by the Lord.
⁹ And as for you, masters,
   treat them similarly
       without threats,
       knowing that both their and your Lord is in heaven,
       and that he draws no distinction between people.

This final section of the HT deals with a third important relationship in many ancient households, slaves and their owners. As in the other sections it commences with the inferior group, slaves, and moves to the superior, masters or owners. Both slaves and owners are addressed initially with an imperative which is expanded with participial clauses, those of v. 6b and v. 7 being parallel, and the final participial clause in each case is introduced with **knowing**; these two final clauses set both slaves and owners together on a plane of equality before God. The two subsections are linked by **and** as in vv. 1–4. The whole paragraph is Christ-centred (Stott); it refers to him five times. It was easier to introduce him into this section than the preceding since the term 'slave' could be used to describe his earthly life whereas he was neither husband, wife, nor father.

Several other NT passages deal with slaves (Col 3.22–4; 1 Cor 7.21–4; Philemon; 1 Pet 2.18–25; 1 Tim 6.1f; Tit 2.9f); the frequency of reference raises the question whether there were slaves in the church who were proving unruly in their new-found Christian freedom; more probably the prominence given them in the NT is a result of their numbers coupled with the need to work out a satisfactory relation between them and others in the church. Since the slaves are directly addressed we may assume that at least some were present when the letter was read out in the house where the church was meeting, but would these have been only those belonging to that household? Slaves were of course accustomed to being addressed by their master and given orders, but probably not to being addressed on an equality with their masters.

AE does not question the existence of slavery nor discuss its origin (Augustine, *Civ Dei*, 19.15, attributes it to human sin). It was an essential part of the economic and social fabric of the ancient world and was rejected only by Essenes and similar groups (Philo, *Quod Omnis* 79; *Vita Cont* 70; Josephus *Ant* 18.22), perhaps because members surrendered all possessions on entering the community; members of associated communities living in normal society may however have owned slaves (CD 11.12; 12.11); Jews generally did not object to slavery (*Ep Arist* 15, 12.27; *Ps-Phoc* 223–7). It has been estimated that more than a third of the population of the early Roman Empire were slaves. The great farms and estates of rural areas depended on slave labour and at times slaves on them were regarded as little better than animals, but in the urban areas, to which our letter was addressed, they were often important members of households. Slaves were purchased and brought into the household and could be sold off at any time; children born to slave parents in the household could still be sold off and their relationship to their parents severed. They were the property of their owners; this was at least part of the reason why Paul returned Onesimus to Philemon; he could not then be accused of theft. Aristotle, *Nic Eth* VIII 11 (1161A-B) allots them a very low position but later they were treated more humanely as Stoic teaching shows (Seneca, *de Benef* 3.18–28; Pliny, *Ep* 5.29); yet earlier and cruder views probably prevailed in popular thought (cf Juvenal, *Satires* 6.219–23; Seneca, *de Ira* III 40.2–3). The basic insecurity of slaves is illustrated from the case of Pedanius Secundus, a senator, who was murdered by one of his slaves; after discussion the Senate upheld an ancient law that all the slaves, some 400, in the household should be executed even though only one was the murderer (Tacitus, *Ann* 14–43.5).

In earlier centuries people were enslaved through being taken captive in war or through piracy; however in the more peaceful first century AD most were slaves because they had been born to slave parents (the children of slaves belonged to the owner of the parents), could not pay their debts, were sold by their parents, or exposed as children; a few even became slaves through marrying a slave or sold themselves into slavery because slavery provided some economic security when as day labourers they found difficulty in obtaining constant employment (see on 4.28). This meant that many slaves had talents and skills useful to their owners; they might work at some craft in a business; while in larger households some did the 'dirty' work, others found openings as musicians, medical advisers, educators, stewards, mistresses, companions of the elderly. Sometimes owners hired them out to work for others and were paid for their work. Slaves who held responsible positions would be well treated; though owners had total power over them, valuable assets were not to be wasted. There was little teaching in the ancient world about improving their lot though Seneca, *Ep* 47, does argue in this way. In Judaism masters and slaves were taught how to live together (Ecclus 4.30; 7.20f; 33.31; Philo, *Spec Leg* 2.66–9, 89–91; 3.137–43; *Ps-Phoc* 223ff), though the attitude of owners was not always expected to be humane (Prov 29.19, 21). In society generally if they occupied responsible positions they were often rewarded with their freedom or found themselves able to buy it. If freed they still owed some duties to their owners as patrons. AE, or the HT before him, does not consider the position of freed slaves; perhaps they were few in the churches; Paul did not encourage manumission (1 Cor 7.20–4); he sent back Onesimus to his owner (cf Ign *Polyc* 4.3). Even the Stoics, whose ethical teaching approached most closely to

Christian teaching, did not regard freedom from slavery as important; what was important was inner freedom from the chances and tragedies of life (Epict 4.1; 2.1.27). It is not then surprising that the NT does not condemn the institution of slavery.

Slaves were accepted as full members of the church and included among those termed 'brothers' (Philem 16). Christians were not however unique in according slaves an equal position in religion with free men and women, for they were fully accepted as members of some of the pagan Mysteries and other religious and semi-religious groups. There is no reason to suppose slaves were refused 'ministerial' positions in the church; the Pastorals do not list freedom among the qualifications for those eligible as bishops and deacons. Pliny says he examined under torture two maid servants who held some kind of official position in the church (*Ep* X 16).

5. In vv. 5–8 slaves are addressed and it is assumed they are morally responsible; though the masculine is used it may be held in accordance with normal custom to cover also the feminine; whether female slaves however were ultimately accountable to their husbands (5.22ff) or to their owners is not made clear. Slaves are commanded to obey their owners with a willing and wholehearted obedience. This obedience is developed in vv. 6–8. Tit 2.9f indicates the kind of temptations to which slaves might succumb and so become disobedient. The obedience of slaves to owners was the general expectation of society and AE does nothing to suggest any alteration within Christian households. In these it would be unlikely that slaves would be called on to perform religious duties to which as Christians they objected. By the very fact that he addresses slaves, AE implies that their obedience should flow willingly out of Christian faith and not be forced from them by their master (cf Calvin; Calvin goes beyond the text, however, when he suggests that it was God who imposed on slaves their position as slaves).

Slaves are to obey their **lords**; this is an ambiguous term, used extensively in scripture for Yahweh and Christ; at the end of v. 4 it referred to Christ but this is not its meaning here; to ensure its correct understanding, even though the plural ought automatically to exclude error, AE qualifies it with 'according to the flesh' here translated **human**. Although 'flesh' can have negative overtones it is used here merely to distinguish earthly masters from the heavenly Lord (for the use of the phrase in this sense see Rom 1.3; 4.1; 9.3, 5; 1 Cor 10.18; 2 Cor 5.16). But why did AE use the ambiguous term 'lord'? The most probable answer is that the pre-Christian form of the HT contained **lord** which in a non-Christian, non-Jewish context would have been at once understood as referring to owners; when Christians, or Jews, took over the HT they had to define the word more precisely.

Obedience is to be offered in **fear and trembling**. The phrase is frequent in the LXX (Gen 9.2; Exod 15.16; Deut 2.25; 11.25; Isa 19.16; Ψ 2.11; 54.6; Jth 2.20; 15.2) though the MT has no exact equivalent. Paul uses it at 1 Cor 2.3; 2 Cor 7.15; Phil 2.12. For AE the object of fear is the owner (cf 5.33) and not God as it appears to be in Pauline usage. Since owners are Christian fear is not to be understood in the sense of terror but rather of deference and respect. The attitude of slaves is further described as one of **singleness**. The word signifies both an inner attitude and the corresponding behaviour; it involves purity of intention and dedication to whatever task is being undertaken; it should be practised and exhibited by those who serve God (Wisd 1.1; 1 Chron 29.17; 1 Macc 2.37, 60, *T Reub* 4.1; *T Sim* 4.5; *T Levi* 13.1; Rom 12.8; 2 Cor 11.3; Philo, *Opif Mundi* 156, 170). It is regularly associated as here with a word like **heart** thereby indicating its inner nature in relation to the task in hand: slaves should dedicate themselves wholeheartedly to whatever task their owners set them; vv. 6f develop the idea implicit in the word (Haupt).

A christological orientation, made necessary to show the Christian nature of the HT, concludes the verse. The master does not replace Christ (contrast *Did* 4.11; *Barn* 19.7) nor does he represent Christ to the slave, and Christ is not the pattern for the slave's behaviour as in 1 Pet 2.18–25. Slaves are to serve their owners with the same devotion with which they serve Christ; when they do so they will in fact be serving him.

6. The nature of the service slaves should offer is now expressed first negatively and then positively (v. 6a); the positive side is then expanded in a participial clause (v. 6b); v. 7 follows in parallel with v. 6b.

Slaves though constrained to do what they are told should not do it simply to get by or satisfy the eye of supervisors; they should perform their tasks conscientiously and thoroughly even though their owner's back is turned. Necessarily, of course, owners must be satisfied, otherwise punishment follows; but work is not to be done in a fawning manner merely to gain approval or curry favour but should be sincere. Slaves should display the same attitude in their work as Paul in his missionary activity (Gal 1.10; 1 Th 2.4) for slaves are slaves of Christ just as much as was Paul (Rom 1.1; Gal 1.10) or were Paul and Timothy (Phil 1.1; cf Acts 20.19). Yet there is an essential difference: Paul chose to call himself a slave of Christ, and his use of 'slave' or 'servant' of himself does not indicate social status; this however is the significance of the word in vv. 5–9, and it is a status which slaves had probably not chosen voluntarily. Slaves have both human owners and a divine Lord.

If their true allegiance is to Christ, they will express this by doing the will of God; AE uses here a traditional phrase (cf Mk 3.35; Mt 7.21; 12.50) which qualifies not only the reference to eye-service but the whole life of the slave. All Christians are expected to do God's will, so in effect what slaves are summoned to do is the same as is asked of other believers. Since it is Christian households which are being treated it can be assumed that the will of owners and the will of God coincide; slaves should serve their owners with the same readiness as they serve God. Doing the will of God must of course be inwardly motivated, **from the heart**. **Heart** is a better English translation than 'soul', the literal meaning of the Greek word; it implies here an inner attitude as did the Greek word for heart in v. 6; functioning in this way the two terms are almost equivalent (cf Deut 6.5; Mk 12.30). While a set of laws can be obeyed without inner involvement the whole person comes into play in doing God's will.

7. This verse parallels the participial clause of v. 6b and summarises the previous positive statements about the way slaves should serve. The word translated **cheerfulness**, though regular in Greek from classical times, is a *hapax legomenon* in the NT (for the cognate verb see Mt 5.25); it appears in the later parts of the LXX (e.g. 1 Macc 11.33, 53; 2 Macc 9.21, 26; 11.19; 12.30) and in the papyri. It was sometimes used to describe the attitude of people to their rulers and so could be applied to the manner in which slaves should carry out their tasks (Lucian, *Bis Accusatur* 16; P.Oxy 494.6: cf Xenophon, *Oec.* 12.5.7). These should be done, not grudgingly, but cheerfully, willingly and sincerely; in the Christian household especially, a ready goodwill is required rather than cold loveless service.

8. The final participial clause introduces a motivation for the faithful work of slaves which should strengthen their willingness to serve and thus this clause supports the preceding clauses. Owners might at times forget (since they are Christian owners we ought not to attribute worse failings) to reward the faithfulness of slaves.

Knowing (cf Rom 6.3, 6; 1 Cor 15.58; Eph 5.5) is spoken to the slaves as Christians and implies they are being reminded of something of which they are already aware. We cannot tie down the occasion(s) when they were so instructed; it could possibly have been at baptism (Bouttier) but how much instruction they received then is doubtful; it if better to assume that as they (and their owners) met for worship their attitude to their work would be brought up in periods of instruction or during the preaching of the word; the two cannot be easily distinguished for good preaching is always instructive.

The need to practise active goodness, expressed in different ways, is regularly emphasised in the Pauline corpus (2 Cor 9.8; Gal 6.10: Eph 2.10; Col 1.10; 1 Th 5.15; 1 Th 2.17). The nature of the goodness is determined by the context; here it is willing and faithful service at set tasks which the Lord will reward. Nothing is said about what the reward will be, least of all that it will be the granting of freedom or some other earthly recompense e.g. leisure time or money. The context suggests a non-earthly or eschatological recompense, a spiritual reward for spiritual faithfulness (cf Gal 6.8; Col 3.24 however has a negative outlook), and this fits with the idea of God as the one who recompenses; this also gives another indication that AE's eschatology is not entirely realised. For the proportionality of reward to activity see Mt 16.27; 25.31ff; Rom 2.6; 1 Cor 3.12–14; 1 Pet 1.17; Rev 22.12. The problem of the relation of reward to justification by faith is already present in Paul and AE does nothing to solve it (e.g. is it ethical to persuade people to do what is right so that they may be rewarded?). We note however that AE does not encourage slaves to be obedient and faithful in order to be manumitted. Faithful slaves were often rewarded in this way, but sometimes slaves who already lived in good households rejected manumission, and Christian households ought to be good. By the end of the NT period the manumission of slaves was being advocated (1 Clem 55.2; *Ign Polyc* 4.3; Hermas, *Sim* 1.8).

The final phrase of the section on slaves, 'slave or free', brings slaves and owners together and is suggestive of some kind of equality; AE thereby prepares the way for a transfer of attention to owners.

9. And now for owners; the conclusion of v. 8 provided the transition and the first clause of v. 9 continues the linking of slaves and owners in some kind of equality. The second half of the verse recalls owners to previous instruction in the same way as slaves were recalled in v. 8.

In some respects owners faced greater problems than slaves: could an owner whip, or have whipped, a slave with whom he had shared the bread and wine of the eucharist? Apart from one piece of concrete advice, that owners should abstain from a threatening attitude, the remainder of the advice to them is vague: act towards them, i.e. slaves, 'in the same way'. But what is the same behaviour which is required from owners as from slaves? It certainly cannot imply a reversal of roles and be equivalent to 5.21 (Ernst) with owners serving slaves; slaves remain slaves and owners owners (Masson). The phrase can hardly be linked to **with cheerfulness** (v. 7; so Jerome; Chrysostom; Bengel; Ewald) for it is too remote. The reference to anyone **who does something good** is closer yet it describes behaviour towards owners, and the behaviour of owners towards slaves will be different unless both are incorporated under some general rubric like 'doing God's will'. Perhaps it is best to take the phrase in some such general way with *mutatis mutandis* understood (Alford).

What then is God's will for the way owners should treat their slaves? Only one example is given, the non-use of **threats**. Threats, and the resulting punishment if the threat went unheeded, were the normal way of controlling slaves (Tacitus, *Annal* 14.44); Jewish owners are warned against unnecessary severity (Ecclus 4.30; 7.20; 33.31) and also occasionally pagan owners (Plutarch,

Mor 7E). Threats would be the natural product of the owner's anger at slaves' behaviour (Seneca, *De ira*, 3.24.1; 3.32.1).

AE envisages a solidarity as existing between slaves and owners, not because of their common humanity, as some Stoics might have allowed, but because both have the same heavenly master. Perhaps Seneca approaches most closely to what is said here when he places both owners and slaves as humans under the same *fortuna*. The relevant attribute of God in respect of those in solidarity is that **he draws no distinction**, using a LXX word. At times when the actual word is not used in the OT, the concept still appears, the most famous instance being that of David, 1 Sam 16.1–13 (cf Deut 10.17; Mal 1.9; Ecclus 35.12f; *Ps Sol* 2.16; *Jub* 5.16, and in the NT Gal 2.6; cf *Did* 4.10). The quality is transferred in v. 9 from God (Rom 2.11; 1 Pet 1.17) to Christ. It is also applied to human behaviour (Lev 19.15; Mal 1.8; Ecclus 4.22, 27; Lk 20.21). It means no account is taken of the rank, status, wealth, race, colour, sex, or position, within church or state, of believers.

XV

CONFLICT

(6.10–20)

10 Finally, be strengthened in the Lord,
 that is, with the vigour of his might.
11 Put on the armour of God
 so that you may be able to stand firm
  against the stratagems of the devil.
12 For our struggle
 is not against anything human
 but against the rulers,
  against the authorities,
  against the cosmic masters of this darkness,
  against the spiritual powers of evil in the heavenlies.
13 Therefore buckle on the armour of God
 that you may be able to offer resistance
  in the evil day
 and be prepared in every respect to stand firm.
14 Stand then,
 girt round your loins with truth,
 and clothed with the breastplate of righteousness,
15 and your feet shod
 with the stability of the gospel of peace,
16 in all circumstances taking the shield of faith
 with which you will be able to quench all the devil's
    fiery darts,
17 and receive the helmet of salvation.
 and the sword of the Spirit which is a word of God,
18 praying with every kind of prayer and intercession
 at every opportunity in the Spirit,
 and for this purpose being vigilant
  with all perseverance

and intercession on behalf of all the saints,
19 and on my behalf
that words may be given to me
when I open my mouth with frankness ·
to make known the mystery of the gospel,
20 on behalf of which I am a chained ambassador,
so that I may be frank and bold
in the way I am compelled to speak.

With v. 10 the subject changes abruptly and one of the most original sections of the letter begins. No clear connection exists between the behaviour of members of a household, all of whom are believers and who are not depicted as in conflict with one another, and a struggle between every believer and the superhuman powers. A call to stand firm against temptation or against those who might lead them astray would not have been out of place. But the passage does not deal with human failure in human terms but in supernatural. It is not a question of a conflict within a divided self (Rom 7.7ff) or a battle for the moral life, but a battle for the spiritual. If this is the letter's *peroratio* we should see it then in the light of 1.3–3.21 rather than of 4.1–6.9, for it does not exhort readers to fight against dishonesty or sexual indulgence but returns to the supernatural nature of Christian existence as set out in 1.3–3.21. A failure to stand against the powers would entail for believers their loss of salvation and would not simply be another sin from which they would need to repent. The paragraph resembles the kind of speech with which a general would hearten his troops before they go into battle (e.g. 1QM 15).

The military image is found widely in the ancient world: Yahweh as Lord of hosts, the stories of war among the gods in Greek and oriental legend, initiation in the Mystery Religions (Tertullian, *de Corona* 15; Apuleius, *Metam* 1.13); and it reappears in some Greek moralists (Epict 3.22.69, 24.34; Seneca *Ep* 107.9), though in the moralists the opposition is not necessarily supernatural. Paul depicts the Christian as a warrior (1 Th 5.8; 2 Cor 6.7; 10.3–5; Phil 2.25; Philem 2; Rom 6.13; 13.12), a theme which has continued in Christian use from the Apostolic Fathers onwards (1 Pet 4.1; 2 Tim 2.3–5; Polyc *Phil* 4.1; Ign *Polyc* 6.2; Hermas, *Mand* 12.2.4), and has been expressed especially in the hymns of

314

the church. The immediate background to the Christian usage lies in the OT and in Qumran, for example in the *War Scroll*.

Once the believer has been depicted as a soldier his equipment needs to be detailed. The individual items are conventional and would have been known to anyone in the ancient world. The equipment may be conventional but its metaphorical explanation probably derives from Isa 59.17, a passage which had already been developed in Wisd 5.17–20. Isaiah 59 is one of those passages which are referred, or alluded, to fairly frequently in the NT (see Rom 3.15–17; Lk 1.79; 1 Pet 1.17; Rev 20.12f; 22.12; Lk 13.29; Rom 11.26f). In Isa 59.17 the armour is spiritualised and God is the warrior who wears it; he is described as a warrior in many other places, e.g. Ps 35.1–3; sometimes he is even described as the armour of his people (e.g. Gen 15.1; Ps 3.3; 18.2; 2 Sam 22.3, 31; cf Murray). In 1 Th 5.8 Paul transferred the imagery from God to the believer while continuing to spiritualise the armour.

None of this accounts for the introduction of the supernatural powers as opponents of the Christian warrior. 6.10 is couched in non-mythological language as is most of the rest of the letter. There is a change at v. 11. In 2.1–3 the pre-Christian predicament was described in both human and supernatural terms; the supernatural reappeared, though in different ways, at 3.10 and 4.27. AE's readers would then have been ready to see opposition as coming not only from other people who might tempt them into greed or lust, or might persecute them, but from supernatural powers.

When we ask why at this point AE starts to use mythological language we may be creating a problem for ourselves by the way we phrase the question. Any answer depends on the understanding of 'myth'. If it means the expression of the supernatural in natural terms, the letter is in fact full of this type of language for throughout it behaviour is set in relation to Christ and God. For AE and his readers the devil belonged as much to ordinary language as did God. They envisaged conduct on the one hand as entirely on the human plane of the interrelationship of people and on the other as a part of the struggle between God and Satan. Theological problems concerning the existence of Satan were as unreal to them as those concerning the existence of God.

Christ has attacked and defeated the powers and yet, inconsistently, they are still active. Believers however are not summoned to attack the powers but instead to defend themselves. Thus the equipment God supplies for the struggle is essentially defensive. In keeping with this believers are not ordered to advance but to stand firm, that is, they are to hold the position which had been won for them. While they live there is no end to the need to hold their position.

After the introduction of v. 10 the passage divides into three units: (a) vv. 11f identify the true foes of believers and indicate God is on their side against their foes and will assist them; (b) vv. 13–17 describe how God equips them so that they can defend themselves; it is not the individual items of the armour which are important but what they represent; (c) vv. 18–20 deal with something believers must do on their own, pray and keep alert. The relation of this last section to the first two is not immediately obvious. While the subject-matter changes, the participles of v. 18 depend grammatically on what has preceded.

10. The introductory phrase indicates that a new stage in the argument has been reached.

In v. 10 AE returns to the 'power' language he has already used in 1.19; 3.16, 20; it is appropriate here where a struggle with the 'powers' is envisaged. The verb **be strengthened** is employed of divine empowerment in the Pauline corpus at Rom 4.20; Phil 4.13; 2 Tim 2.1 (cf 1 Clem 55.3; Hermas, *Vis* 3.12.3) and elsewhere in our letter words denoting power are used to indicate divine strengthening (cf Col 1.11; 1 QH 7.6f). **In the Lord** gives the source of strengthening and is probably to be understood here as referring to Christ (cf 2.21; 4.1, 17; 5.8; 6.1, 21), even though in other passages relating to power in Ephesians God is the source, e.g. in 1.19f it is God who raises Christ. The verse is completed with an explanatory phrase.

11. Why AE summoned his readers to be strong is now made clear: they are involved in a struggle with the devil. For this they need both strength and protective armour; God provides both. They need not then go to the fight unequipped.

The equipment is detailed in vv. 14–17; here a general word, **armour,** is used which does not necessarily, but may, carry the sense of 'whole' or 'complete'. This flavour is present in v. 11 and the word means, as often, a set of armour (2 Kgdms 2.21; 2 Macc 3.25; 4 Macc 3.12A; Herod 1.60.4; 4.180; Polyb 3.62.5; 4.56.3; Thucyd 3.114.1; Josephus *BJ* 2.649; *Ant* 7.104; 20.110; Lk 11.22). The actual details of vv. 14–17 do not correspond exactly with the equipment of any particular known soldier in the Roman or any other army, but approach most closely to the heavily armed Roman infantryman. The purpose of the armour is to enable believers **to stand firm against the stratagems of the devil**. AE's emphasis lies on the need of holding on to a position and not of advancing or attacking. It is probably more difficult to stand and await attack, perhaps made with unknown weapons, than with the adrenalin flowing to rush forward in attack. Believers occupy advanced outposts which are always in danger of being overrun by the forces of the devil; they must stand firm as opposed to running away (see Xenophon, *Anab* 1.10.1; 4.8.19; Thucyd 5.101–4; Exod 14.13; Nah 2.9). The need for Christians to stand firm is seen also in Rom 11.20; 1 Cor 10.12; 15.1; 16.13; 2 Cor 1.24; Gal 5.1; Phil 1.27f; 4.1; Col 4.12; 1 Th 3.8; 2 Th 2.15, though in relation to different contexts and situations.

Believers are opposed by the devil (see on 4.27) who has at his disposal a vast array of deceptive ploys (**stratagems** is the best translation here in keeping with the military metaphor). Before conversion believers belonged to the sphere of the devil and he ruled their lives (2.2f); their conversation and baptism did not shatter his power and he now seeks to get them back into his grip, continually patrolling their positions (1 Pet 5.8) and endeavouring to catch them off guard (4.27). For AE and his readers, whatever modern readers may think, the devil was a personal being, an external centre of evil, who is not to be demythologised or explained away psychologically.

12. The supernatural nature of the struggle with the devil is now underlined and his agents in enticing believers from their faith identified, thus justifying the need for supernatural armour.

Struggle originally referred to the hand-to-hand encounter of wrestling but in time was applied more widely to other types of fighting, including battles and war. Philo used the term metaphorically of the struggle against temptation (*Mut Nom* 14; *Leg Alleg* 3.190; *Sobr* 65). AE's use is also non-literal and too much should not therefore be read into the literal meaning of the

317

word. The struggle is literally 'not against blood and flesh', which incorporates a Semitic phrase, though the nouns are usually in the reverse order (Mt 16.17; 1 Cor 15.50; Gal 1.16; Eccles 14.18; *1 En* 15.4; the order of Ephesians appears only elsewhere at Heb 2.14). It denotes humanity primarily as transitory and weak, though here it is not the quality of humanity that is the issue but the nature of the battle as one not with human foes but with those from outside the human sphere. The struggle is not against what may come from human foes: persecution, harassment, temptation, poverty, injustice, or the temptations that may arise out of the self (cf Rom 7.7ff). It is instead against eternal evil beings. Four titles identify these. AE has already used the first two together at 1.21; 3.10; see also Rom 8.38; Eph 2.2; 1 Pet 3.22; 1 Cor 15.24; Col 1.16; 2.10, 15; such terms do not always have a supernatural reference (cf Rom 13.1–3; Tit 3.1) but there is no reason to doubt that reference here. These beings are presumably the agents of the devil (v. 11) and AE probably spells them out because they are names known to his readers.

The cosmic masters, only here in the NT, came to be used in astronomy and astrology and was applied to various gods (the names of the planets show their association with deities). The word is found also in *T Sol* 8.2; 18.2, in both cases qualified by a reference to darkness as in Ephesians. The world rulers belong to the sphere of darkness rather than the time of darkness. The term then indicates in 6.12 a group or class of supernatural evil beings and since these belong to the darkness they will attempt to lure believers away from the light, i.e. from redemption.

The final term in AE's sequence appears to be comprehensive as if he were seeking to avoid omitting any evil supernatural power (cf 1.21; 5.27). Evil spirits are regularly associated with the devil (cf v. 11; *T Sim* 3.5; 4.9; *T Levi* 18.12; *1 En* 15.8–12; 99.7; 1QM 13.2, 4; CD 12.2; Lk 7.21; 8.2; Acts 19.12f). These evil spirits dwell **in the heavenlies** (cf 2.2; *T Benj* 3.4; *2 En* 29.4f; *Asc Isaiah* 7.9; 11.23), and this accords with the association of the powers with astrology. Contemporary Judaism thought of a multiplicity of heavens; do the powers then live in the same heaven as Christ and God? Since AE uses the same plural phrase here as in 1.20, this suggests he thought they did. Such a possibility gave patristic commentators difficulty. Chrysostom, Theod

Mops, Theodoret all understood that the struggle was not *about* earthly but heavenly matters. Some Fathers read not 'in the heavenlies' but 'under heaven'; Theod Mops is aware of this reading though he does not accept it. Jerome believed that the powers were in the heavenlies and this also seems to have been the opinion of Tertullian, *adv Marc* 5.18. The conclusion cannot be evaded that AE presents the powers as heavenly inhabitants and the war between them and humans as taking place there where believers already are (2.6); yet it should also be recognised that heaven is a fluid concept. But, despite Rev 12.7; 13.1ff, can there be war in heaven? To avoid this implication Chrysostom and Theod Mops spoke of a war waged *on behalf of* the kingdom (i.e. heaven). Whatever the precise resolution of this problem, it is important to realise that AE wishes to drive home to his readers that as believers their struggle is of a superhuman nature. AE's emphasis obviously impressed the early church; the first two volumes of *Biblia Patristica* contain forty-three references to quotations of it or allusions to it. It also attracted the attention of gnostics (in the Nag Hammadi library *Hyp Arch* II, 4 86.23–35; *Exeg Soul* II, 6 130.35–131.13; *Teach Silv* VII, 4 117.14–18; *Ep Pet Phil* VIII, 2 137.10–30; *Testim Truth* IX, 3 32.28; cf *Exc Theod* 48.2; the concept of battle with the powers is also found in *Melch* IX, 1 20.22–3).

13. V. 12 was almost parenthetical in expanding on the nature of the enemy with whom Christians contend; v. 13 returns to the themes of v. 11: the need to sustain the fight and the promise of armour. Many of the terms of v. 11 reappear so that v. 13 is in part parallel to v. 11 but in addition it reveals the time of the conflict, **the evil day**. Everything needs to be ready before combat is entered into. Because of the nature of the enemy believers cannot depend on their own resources but require to be divinely equipped if they are to stand their ground and withstand the enemy. The emphasis is on the need to resist the enemy and this readers can do by holding their position.

What and when is the evil day? The same words, but in the plural, were interpreted in 5.16 to refer to the moral decadence Christians believed lay around them outside the church. However, the singular, and often the plural when qualified, normally refer to the parousia, the day of judgement or the end of the world, times which though good for some would be evil for others (Amos 5.18–20; Joel 1.15; 2.32; Zech 14; Dan 12.1; *T Levi* 5.5; *1 En* 55.3; 96.2; *T Moses* 1.18; *Apoc Abr* 19.8f; 1QM 1.10–13; 1 Cor 1.8; 1 Th 5.2–4). Ephesians says relatively little about the End and the conflict is one already in process; the weapons are needed now. Jewish apocalyptic however sometimes envisaged a period of severe oppression leading up to, and immediately prior to, the End, the birth pangs of the Messiah (Dan 7.21ff; 12.1; Joel 2; 4 Ezra 13.16–19; *2 Bar* 25; 68; *Jub* 23.13ff; Mk 13; Rev 7.14; 12.3, 7, 13). In 1 Th 5.8 Paul counsels believers to put on armour in a context relating to the final days, and though in Rom 13.12 the armour is not particularised the context is again eschatological. Perhaps then AE sees the present struggle of believers as part of, or as leading to, the final eschatological conflict (Hugedé); as Schnackenburg notes, AE's eschatology is somewhat hazy.

Some uncertainty also surrounds the verb here translated **be prepared**; the verb can signify either 'prepare' (so the vast majority of commentators) or 'overcome' (Chrysostom; Scott; Schlier). The latter interpretation would render unnecessary the instructions which follow to put on armour (why prepare for battle if the foe is already overcome?). Believers are to be prepared **in every respect** for the present and future struggle so that equipped with supernatural weapons they may stand firm against all the assaults of their supernatural foes.

14. Verses 14–17 list some of the individual items of a soldier's equipment. In part the items are derived from the OT and in part from observation of soldiers. It is not however the weapons themselves which are important, for this is not a physical war, but the explanations AE gives to them; these explanations have no logical connection with the individual items. The weapons are primarily defensive since a position has to be held; any direct attack on the powers is left to Christ and is conceived as already having taken place (1.20–3). The armour is assumed to be even now ready for believers to don; yet only if it is worn can Christian warriors stand against their foes; its putting on is a necessary preliminary to standing firm.

The first item is the 'girdle'; it is by no means clear what is meant; the normal English translation 'belt' gives too precise a connotation and is probably wrong. The metaphor was understood in a wide variety of ways in both the Greco-Roman and Jewish worlds. As to its physical nature 'girdle' could be: (a) the leather apron which was put on under the breastplate and offered some protection to the lower part of the abdomen while leaving freedom of movement and readiness for action; (b) the belt from which the sword hung; (c) the sash over the armour denoting the wearer as someone in authority. (b) and (c) were put on after and not before the breastplate, which is the next item, and as for (c) nothing suggests AE is attempting to give a distinguished position to believers. (a) is then the most probable meaning. However, it is not the identification of the article of military equipment which is important, but the quality 'truth' which is linked to it and this link with truth is probably derived from Isa 11.5. We leave what is meant by truth until we have dealt with **the breastplate**.

This protected its wearer from shoulder to upper thigh level. It is interpreted here as **righteousness** following Isa 59.17; Wisd 5.18; in 1 Th 5.8 it is faith and love. The prevailing meaning of **righteousness** in the Pauline corpus sees it as a gift of God rather than a human quality. It is difficult to see the gospel of peace (v. 15), salvation (v. 17) and the word of God (v. 17) as human activities. Thus it is better to take righteousness here as that justifying righteousness which is the foundation of Christian existence (so Barth). It is this, and not simply moral failure, which is under attack from the devil and his powers.

What then is the significance of **truth**? Most commentators take it as indicating something like sincerity, faithfulness, loyalty, integrity, which keeps it in the area of human activity yet leaves open a wide range of meaning. It could however be God's truth, doctrinal truth, the gospel. Ephesians uses 'truth' both of the human virtue (4.24, 25; 5.9) and of God's truth (1.13; 4.21); the context alone can determine which meaning is intended and the general run of vv. 14–17 suggests that it is God's truth which is in mind. God's truth provides a defence against heresy, false philosophies, pagan religions, all possible weapons used by the devil to lure believers away from their belief.

15. The text does not identify the third item of equipment other than to say that it relates to the **feet**. Lightly armed soldiers who needed to move quickly wore sandals; the heavily armed Roman legionaries wore heavy boots (the *caliga*). Since the other items of armour are those used by the latter probably heavy boots are intended here. These were necessary for long marches and, what is more important in the present context, ensured a firm grip on the ground enabling their wearers to stand firm. Some scholars detect in v. 15 the influence of Isa 52.7 because of its reference to feet in association with the gospel of peace; Isa 52.7 may also have influenced 2.17; Nah 2.1 provides a similar possible influence. Those who discern the influence of these passages have to insert in their translations a word suggestive of movement; the Greek has no such word, but has instead the word we have translated **stability**, a word found only here in the NT, though appearing fairly regularly in the LXX. It has three possible relevant meanings: readiness, preparation, firmness. The majority of commentators accept one or other of the first two and take it to refer to the readiness or preparation for the outward-going movement required for the proclamation of the good news of peace. If proclamation of the gospel is in mind, to whom is it to be made? There is nothing elsewhere in the letter advocating the involvement of readers in missionary expansion; this was only explicit at 3.10 and there it is to the powers that the gospel is proclaimed. This could be said to fit the present context where the powers are the foes; peace needs to be brought to them. Yet the struggle is about neither the spread of the gospel, though presumably the powers would wish to hinder any spread, nor the salvation of the powers, but about the continued salvation of those who are already believers. It may be better then to accept the third sense, firmness. Buscault worked this out in detail quoting 2 Ezra 3.3 and Ψ 88.15 for the meaning 'foundation, basis' (see also Bengel; Lock; Barth). This interpretation accords with the major stress of vv. 11–17 on the need to stand firm and on the defensive nature of the armour. If this solution is accepted it implies Isa 52.7 does not lie behind the verse.

The introduction of **peace** may seem paradoxical since the context is that of warfare but most of the readers were Gentiles; the gospel through which they became Christians was a gospel which made peace between them and God and between them and Jewish believers; hence the appropriateness of the reference. It was believers' knowledge of, and belief in, this gospel which would repel supernatural foes. The gospel of peace would neutralise the enmity of the hostile powers (cf Ign *Eph* 13.2). The gospel of peace falls into the same semantic field as truth, righteousness (v. 14), faith (v. 16), salvation and word of God (v. 17).

16. The fourth piece of armour is the **shield**, spiritualised as **faith**; the importance of taking it is stressed by the initial 'in all', whatever meaning is given to it. It has been variously understood as 'in addition to' (i.e. to all the other pieces of equipment) or **in all circumstances**.

In v. 16 as in v. 15 the OT is not explicitly referred to even though the shield is a frequent OT metaphor; God is the shield of faithful Israelites (e.g. Gen 15.1; Ps 18.3; 33.20). Normally when the OT uses 'shield' metaphorically ('the Lord is my shield') the LXX term is different; our word is only used metaphorically in Ψ 34.2 (cf also Aq, Sm Job 41.7; Aq Ψ 21.7; 83.12). Its use here is then not derived from the OT but from observation of the actual armour of soldiers. It is the long shield of the Roman legionary protecting most of the front of the body against missiles (for its description and use see Polyb 6.23.2; Herod 7.91).

The shield which enables believers to hold their ground is **faith**. This could mean either 'trust' or 'the faith'. If it is trust its object is unstated but is presumably God or Christ (cf 1.13, 15; 3.12; 4.13; 6.23); it is not self-confidence. Trust in God or Christ was operative in the salvation of believers (2.8) and it is through it that Christ dwells in their hearts (3.17). As with the other items of equipment it is given by God. When believers trust God it is as if they had a shield around them. However, since in Greek the word **faith** is governed by the article, faith here could be 'the faith', what is believed. But given this interpretation **faith** lies in the same semantic field as truth, righteousness, gospel and it is best to understand it in this way.

The devil's missiles are described as fiery. Sometimes in ancient warfare arrows, spears, and other missiles were coated in pitch and set alight before being thrown. If they hit home they inflicted deadly wounds; the long shield offered good protection against them, but only while the soldier stood firm; if he began to retreat it was no help. When attacks with fiery missiles were expected, the leather portions of shields were soaked in water since a dry shield would not extinguish a burning missile, only divert it; even a wet shield would not necessarily extinguish one. If the missile did not penetrate the shield it would fall to the ground and be relatively harmless; if it penetrated, the moisture would do something to counteract the burning pitch; a damp shield would certainly not be set on fire. (On the use of burning missiles and on defence against them see Josephus *Ant* 1.203; Herod 8.52; 1QH 2.26; CD 5.13; Sallust, *Bellum Jug* 57.5, 6; Livy 21.8.10–12; Prov 26.18; in Ps 7.13 God is said to use them.)

17. The final two items of military equipment are now listed. The first, the **helmet**, returns us to the OT and Isa 59.17. In Isa 59.17 God as victorious warrior wears the helmet of salvation; now he gives it to believers for their protection. At least here, if not elsewhere, we can see that AE depends on the OT for the significance he imparts to this item of equipment. Previously he had used a sequence of participles to itemise the equipment; now he introduces a new finite verb, **receive**. The soldier, already partially equipped, receives from his armour bearer his **helmet** and **sword**; the Christian receives from his God **salvation** and the **word of God**; this is not to suggest he collected the other items of equipment for himself; all his military hardware comes from God. The helmet is depicted as salvation; **salvation** is rare in the NT appearing only in Lk 2.30; 3.6; Acts 28.28, all passages heavily dependent on the OT; it is found more frequently in the LXX, and is used in Isa 59.17. However, when Paul used Isa 59.17 in 1 Th 5.8 he substituted for it another noun, the normal NT noun for salvation; AE's retention of the LXX word confirms his dependence here on Isa 59.17. Paul had also varied the LXX in another way by speaking of the helmet as the *hope* of salvation, thus imparting an eschatological flavour. AE's stress here on the present nature of salvation is in line with his normal understanding of it.

The final piece of armour is the short-handled **sword**. There is no OT passage from which vv. 11–17 could have been directly derived though all its nouns are found in the OT, with two of them sometimes linked together in the same context, but never closely. What we then have is a play on concepts from the OT and later Judaism, rather than direct dependence on any actual OT passage. The sword is a normal part of a soldier's armour and had to be included; a bare mention was not sufficient; it must also as with the other pieces of armour be related to something which comes from God, and his word meets this requirement. Knox says that sword and word are frequently conjoined in Judaism. Isa 11.2, 4 may have led to the introduction of **the Spirit**; there it is a destructive power and that would be appropriate to a conflict with the powers. The sword is not itself the Spirit, for believers do not wield the Spirit; it is the sword which the Spirit either supplies or empowers; strength is necessary for fighting and power is one of the characteristic gifts of the Spirit; in either case a spiritual sword is intended but not in the weakened sense of a sword which belongs to the sphere of religion.

The sword of the Spirit requires further identification and the final words of the verse supply this. What is **a word of God**? Here it must be a word which protects the user from destruction by the powers. It is not then God's energetic and creative word (Theod Mops), or his prophetic word (though it might on occasion be a word from the prophets), or the OT as a whole (Hodge), though it could be a saying drawn from the OT (1 Pet 1.25; Rom 10.8). It could also be the gospel (Adai) as preached or summarised in a confession or creed. In 5.26 the determination of the meaning of **word** offered some difficulty; there as here it lacks the article. In 5.26 it probably indicated the baptismal formula 'in the name of Jesus'. Here it probably means a saying or formula behind which God stands (Haupt), drawn from the OT and with whose use the devil may be withstood. It could also be a word uttered by a NT prophet fitted to the occasion. All such words of God are powerful for they have been inspired by the Spirit. It was with such words that Jesus repelled the devil in the temptation stories. The Roman short sword was very necessary in close combat; it kept foes at bay. It, or any of the other pieces of equipment, will not kill the devil or any of his powers; only Christ can do that (1.20f), but through the use of a word of God his followers can live through the attacks that they launch on them.

18. This verse, with its fourfold use of 'all', here translated **every**, **every**, **all**, **all**, consists of two parallel participial clauses each carrying imperatival value. But do the participles depend on **receive** (v. 17, e.g. Gnilka) or **stand** (v. 14, e.g. Lincoln; Bruce)? They are hardly wholly independent of what has preceded; if they were, then vv. 18–20 would have to be taken as a separate paragraph (so Adai; Pokorný). It is not a case of 'each piece put on with prayer' as in George Duffield's hymn, and certainly not of prayer only in relation to the helmet and the sword. **Stand** is probably still the controlling verb. Standing firm and praying should go on without ceasing. Prayer is not itself another weapon. Yet prayer has its place in struggle (Rienecker) as the prayer of Jesus in Gethsemane shows. It denotes the attitude in which the weapons are to be used, and presupposes the wearing of the armour. If believers are to stand firm against the powers they need both to pray and to be alert.

In the first participial clause readers are exhorted to pray **with every kind of prayer and intercession**. **Prayer** is a general word covering all kinds of prayer; **intercession** is usually limited to prayers involving requests. The words are found together elsewhere (3 Kgdms 8.45; 2 Chron 6.19; Acts 1.14 (*v.l.*); Phil 4.6; 1 Tim 2.1; 5.5; Ign *Magn* 7.1) and may form a hendiadys. AE probably intends them to be taken as a comprehensive expression for all kinds of prayer, though he only expands the second noun in what follows. Prayer is to be offered at **every** possible **opportunity** (for the phrase see Lk 21.36; cf Ψ 33.1; 105.3; Prov 6.14; Eccles 9.8; Ecclus 29.3); this was Paul's practice and one he enjoined on believers (e.g. Lk 18.1; 24.53; Rom 9.1; 12.12; 1 Cor 1.4; 1 Th 1.2f; 2.13; 3.10; cf 1 Tim 5.5). Believers need to pray continually because their struggle with the powers is never ending. The injunction is not however to be taken so literally as to imply believers should spend all their time in prayer; what is required is a constant attitude of dependence on God. Prayer is to be offered **in the Spirit**; this is not intended to contrast prayer freely offered from the heart with formal set prayers, but to indicate a relation to God's Spirit. AE had previously used the phrase at 2.18, 22; 3.5; 5.18. Though the Spirit and prayer are related, we are not to think of praying in tongues but of prayer which is Spirit-led or directed (cf Rom 8.15f; Gal 4.6; Jude 20; 1QH 16.11; 17.17). Prayer is not to be given up lightly but persisted in: **with all perseverance**.

Prayer in the Spirit is to be accompanied by **vigilance**, watchfulness and wakefulness; this could be a continuance of the military metaphor (watchfulness and standing firm are linked in 1 Cor 16.13; 1 Pet 5.8f) but is probably not since prayer and watchfulness are frequently associated; **being vigilant** however is less usual in this respect than the usual verb 'to watch' (Mk 13.33, 38; Lk 21.36; Mt 26.41; Col 4.2; *Barn* 20.2; 1 Esdr 8.58; 2 Esdr 8.29) and it might be thought to suggest 'sleepless' prayer or night vigils (cf Schlier); vigils became a regular feature in a later period of church life; the first certain reference, and it is to an Easter vigil and not to vigils in general, is in the second-century *Ep Apostolorum* 15. Our passage in conjunction with Ps 119.62; Lk 6.12; Acts 12.12; 16.25; 1 Th 3.10 may have led to the practice.

Prayer can never be aimless but must be directed; here its object is not only that those who pray should stand firm against the devil but it looks outward in stressing intercession for the saints (believers and not angels) and Paul (v. 19). AE had already prayed for the saints (1.16ff; 3.14–19), though not specifically for Paul. The saints, Paul and those who are bidden pray for them are involved in the same conflict with the powers; they must stand together and pray together or they will fall together. When they stand together the church is sustained. Calvin raised the point whether believers were to pray only for the saints; this is probably what AE had in mind; indeed such a restricted sphere of prayer fits in both with the general objective of the letter and the immediate context; there is no prayer here for those outside the church (contrast 1 Tim 2.1–3).

19. The struggle against the powers now appears to slip into the background but it is still present in that Paul's preaching, for which intercession is made, relates to the mystery of the gospel which has to be brought to the knowledge of the powers (3.9, 10). AE, if he is Paul, requests his readers to pray for him, and, if he is not Paul, then to pray for Paul; yet if AE is not Paul, Paul is dead and why pray for one who is dead? The request must then be understood as part of the pseudepigraphical framework. In the similar passage in Col 4.3 it is not Paul alone but Paul and his co-workers for whom prayer is to be made; a reference to co-workers is normal in Pauline letters and its absence may be because AE nowhere else refers to other workers or because he sees Paul as occupying a unique position in the economy of salvation (3.3, 8ff). Elsewhere Paul desires his churches to pray on behalf of him and his co-workers (Rom 15.30; 2 Cor 1.9–11; Col 4.3; 1 Th 5.25;

2 Th 3.1). Assuming AE is using Col 4.3 his omission of a reference to others is surprising.

While believers are to intercede for Paul it is not suggested that they pray for his release from prison; AE, if he is not Paul, may have realised that his readers knew Paul had died during, or at the end of, his imprisonment, and he did not wish to include a prayer which his readers would know had never been granted. Instead what he seeks for Paul, or what Paul seeks for himself, is God's gift (**may be given** is a divine passive) of speech in relation to the mystery of the gospel. Although **words** can refer to glossolaliac speech (1 Cor 14.9, 19) it need not necessarily do so; speech can be divinely inspired without being in tongues (e.g. 1 Cor 1.5; 12.8; Phil 1.14; 1 Th 2.13). The 'opening of the mouth' was a biblical phrase (Ψ 50.17; 77.2; Ezek 3.27; 29.21; 33.22; Dan 3.25; 10.16; Wisd 10.21; Ecclus 5.15; 51.25) which was taken up into the NT (Mt 5.2; Acts 8.35; 10.34; 18.14; 2 Cor 6.11). The prayer is that whenever Paul speaks God should fill his mouth, as once he filled that of Jeremiah (Jer 1.9), and as it is promised that he will do in times of trial (Mt 10.19f; Mk 13.11).

Paul's mouth is to be opened to make known the mystery of the gospel **with frankness**. The wider context of v. 20 which draws attention to Paul as a prisoner might suggest a connotation for the word in the area of courage (cf Wisd 5.1) but the immediate reference to mystery implies the idea of clarity, that Paul should make clear the mystery of the gospel when he speaks. It is difficult to tie the word down to one narrow meaning and it perhaps should be understood as indicating a courageous openness and clarity.

What Paul is to make known is **the mystery**; the total phrase is almost the same as in 1.9 and 3.3. In those passages the mystery was made known by God to believers in general (1.9) or to Paul in particular (3.3; cf 3.4); here Paul makes the mystery known. Of course he could not do this unless the mystery had not first been made known to him. Mysteries remain mysteries unless they are communicated, so there may be in vv. 19f as allusion to missionary endeavour. What is it then that is made known here? In 1.9 the mystery relates to the consummation of all but in 3.3f, 9 to the knowledge that God accepts Gentiles. The latter more restricted meaning seems appropriate here since to readers of Ephesians Paul is especially associated with the preaching of the gospel to Gentiles; the gospel however is more than the equality of Jew and Gentile in God's eyes, though Ephesians stresses this aspect.

20. The argument now appears to be slipping further away from the struggle of believers with the supernatural powers of evil, yet in so far as Paul was preaching to liberate believers from their grip he was involved in that struggle. The strength to defeat supernatural power is called into being through prayer, so the prayer is not one for the loosing of Paul from his chains or for the opening of a door before him so that he can continue his mission work (cf Col 4.3). It is instead a prayer that though imprisoned he may still continue the struggle. Paul, or AE writing in his name, does not bemoan his fate in being a prisoner but seeks to continue his preaching.

The metaphor of the ambassador which in 2 Cor 5.20 Paul applied either to himself and his co-workers or to all believers is now restricted to Paul alone. This restriction may also be true of Philem 9, though there more probably the cognate noun depicts Paul not as an ambassador but as an old man. We cannot be certain AE knew 2 Corinthians but even if he did not the image may have been part of the Pauline school's inheritance; it reappears in Ign *Philad* 10.1. The term was used of imperial legates and clearly represents someone of importance. In 2 Cor 5.20 Paul, and at least his fellow helpers, were Christ's ambassadors; here they are the gospel's; it is however difficult to distinguish between gospel and Christ. Ambassadors are important officials and it is paradoxical for them to be in chains.

Examples of Paul's bold and frank activity are recorded in Acts (9.27; 13.46; 14.3; 19.8) and can be deduced from his letters (2 Cor 3.12; Phil 1.20; 1 Th 2.2). Such bold and frank speaking cannot be restricted to Christians (Dio Chrys *Or* 32.11; Epict 3.22.26f; 4.13.1ff; Lucian, *Demonax* 3). It is however not only in prison but at all times that Paul was **compelled** to courageous proclamation. Stress on divine necessity has not been prominent in Ephesians since the initial eulogy which implied the existence of a divine plan where believers were allotted a position even before the foundation of the world. Paul elsewhere affirmed that a divine necessity was laid on him to proclaim the gospel (1 Cor 9.16f; cf Acts 9.6, 16; 19.21; 23.11; 27.24; cf Bouttier). In

Ephesians his unique position in carrying out God's purpose in relation to the Gentiles meant that the divine revelation given to him (3.3) also laid on him the necessity of making it known (3.7ff). His life is wholly under God's direction and control, even to the extent that he is a prisoner. It is of the very nature of the gospel that to know it means to proclaim it; good news must be told.

In this passage the Christian life has been presented not as a steady progress towards a heavenly inheritance or as a sweeping missionary endeavour to bring all the world to Christ but as a struggle, and this not against conflicting internal psychological impulses or the obstacles and temptations placed in its way by other human beings, but as a struggle against supernatural forces. Though Christ has already defeated these (1.20–3), they are still active in attempting to detach his followers from him. They surround believers in the guise of pagan gods or magical practices, or of unChristian and heretical beliefs cutting away at the core of faith. It is not for believers to attack them in an attempt to inflict another defeat, for believers have not been equipped with the javelins necessary for attack; instead they need to stand where they are; if they hold their line, that itself will be another defeat for the powers. The background to the life of believers is thus expressed in cosmic terms, terms almost wholly absent from the presentation of 4.25–6.9. In order that they should be able to resist, believers have been supplied with supernatural armour which is to be worn with prayer and alertness.

XVI

INFORMATION AND FINAL GREETINGS

(6.21–4)

²¹ So that you may know my situation,
   how I fare,
   Tychicus, beloved brother and faithful minister in the
Lord,
   will make known everything to you,
²²   whom I am sending to you
      with the very purpose
      that you may know about us
      and that he may strengthen your hearts.
²³ Peace and love to the brothers
   from a faithful God the Father and Lord Jesus Christ.
²⁴ Grace be with all
   who love our Lord Jesus Christ
   with incorruptibility.

AE has just requested prayer for Paul; good prayer is always informed prayer, so he moves to ensure his readers do not lack information about Paul. Not that he himself is going to provide the information; Tychicus will supply it when he takes the letter around. This allows AE to avoid any pitfall that might result from the provision of wrong information and protects the pseudonymity. The greetings from and to individuals which are customary at this point in the genuine Pauline letters are missing; Tychicus can be presumed to give and receive greetings in each church. AE may not have known enough about Paul in prison to create a true scenario. If Paul is the author then it may be that he has been held for so long as a prisoner in close confinement that he has lost touch with his local Christian community and so has no greetings to send from them. It can hardly be that he did not wish to betray to the Roman authorities the names of associates for he has no hesitation in supplying names in Colossians. He had no greetings for members in the churches to which the letter will go because he has never visited them and does not know whom to greet; yet if Romans 16 is a part of that letter, Paul greeted Christians in Rome though he had never been there. It may then be that the greeting of individuals would not be appropriate in a circular letter.

21. Tychicus is to inform the readers how Paul is getting on. According to Acts 20.4 Tychicus was an Asian; Paul is said to have sent him once to Ephesus (2 Tim 4.12) and again to Crete (Tit 3.12). All this is late tradition but there is no need to doubt that at some stage he had been associated with Paul who had used him as a messenger. As an Asian he may have been the preserver of the Pauline tradition in Asia (Lindemann); in any case he is a further witness to that tradition. If Ephesians is non-Pauline we do not know whether he was still alive and in Asia at the time either of its writing or of Colossians (see Col 4.7). He was however probably dead, for if he had been alive in the area he could too easily have said he never carried the letter. He is described here as **beloved**, a term of affection used by Paul of others (Rom 16.5, 8, 9, 12; 1 Cor 4.17; Philem 1, 16; cf Col 1.7; 4.7, 9, 14; 2 Tim 1.2); AE has already used it in a more general way in 5.1. It could mean either that those so described were loved by the writer or speaker or that he regarded them as loved by God; the former is probably the case here since the word qualifies **brother** which ties Tychicus to the author; the latter sense would seem more appropriate in 5.1. Believers called one another 'brother' (we do not know what they called female believers), so emphasising their consciousness of being a group. Paul regularly addresses the members of the communities to which he wrote as brothers, but AE has not used the word earlier (if we reject the reading at 6.10) though he does so at v. 23 with this significance. **Faithful** is another term Paul applied to his associates (1 Cor 4.17; cf Col 1.7; 4.7, 9). Here it qualifies **minister** (for the word see on 3.7; 4.12), a difficult word to render into English here. It carries the general sense of the service of others (e.g. Mk 10.43, 45) but later came to denote 'officials' or 'ministers' (1 Tim 3.8); we see the beginning of this in Phil 1.1. Alongside **brother** it can hardly have this significance here. With his use of **brother** AE set up a relationship between Tychicus and Paul, and with **minister** he does the same. Since Tychicus ministers to Paul, Paul can despatch him with the letter. As the varying text of the *subscriptio* shows, Tychicus was eventually assumed by some to have been also its scribe. What is the significance of **in the Lord**? In accordance with its normal paraenetic usage we might have expected the phrase to come at the end of v. 22; in its present position it is perhaps used to link Tychicus to those to whom he is going or, more probably, to tighten the bond between him and Paul. It probably qualifies both 'brother' and 'minister' (Westcott). If a letter is a substitute for the personal presence of the writer then both the letter and Tychicus are substitutes for Paul's presence.

22. Paul is sending Tychicus both to inform readers about how he, Paul, is and to strengthen their Christian resolve; the second **that you may know** clause repeats the subject-matter of the first and extends it; **with the very purpose** is yet another vague phrase. Tychicus will have carried the letter; there was no postal service then for letters apart from government correspondence; they had either to be taken by a friend or entrusted to a complete stranger who happened to be travelling to the area of the addressees. Paul normally sent one of his assistants with his letters. In v. 22, unlike v. 21, Tychicus is to inform readers about us, a surprising plural since no one has been associated with Paul previously in the letter. Paul is in prison but Tychicus is free and able to move around and so would have news of the churches in the area, probably Rome, where the letter was written. What Tychicus was doing would thus also interest the addressees. The purpose of the sending of Tychicus is not restricted to conveying the letter and probably not also merely to giving information; when he arrives in a church he will be received as a distinguished visitor, as one beloved to Paul and his faithful servant; he will then be expected to address the community; this will enable him to inspire, comfort and **strengthen** its members. He will in effect continue what the letter itself is intended to achieve, and apply it more directly to their condition, in solving their local problems, in building up their faith and in encouraging them in all their activities. He will also be an example to them of the Christian life (Origen; Jerome).

23–4. Writers in the ancient world usually concluded their letters with a wish for the welfare of their addressees. Paul turned this wish into a benediction-type prayer and AE follows him in this, except that he supplies not one but two benedictions (yet see 2 Th 3.16, 18). Paul's benedictions vary in length, the shortest being 1 Cor 16.23 (or Col 4.18b if by Paul) and the longest 2 Cor 13.13. The double benediction of 6.23f is much longer than any of these, indeed each of its two benedictions is individually longer than any other Pauline benediction except 2 Cor 13.13. Apart from length it differs from them in one more essential feature, for it is not expressed in the second person plural but in the third (Rev 22.21 is the only NT parallel); this gives it a certain aloofness (Barth), solemnity (Ernst) and impersonality; the use of the third person may arise either from the author's ignorance (or supposed ignorance if he is not Paul) of the addressees or from the letter's nature as directed to a wider circle than one Christian community. It also accords with the way the letter never comes to grips with any actual situation in the life of its readers. The length and style of the benedictions bear the marks of AE's hand though it may be that they had these aspects because he drew them from their existing use in some community with which he was associated. Most Pauline benedictions are built around the term **grace** (so v. 24 here) but can also feature **peace** (Rom 15.33; 2 Th 3.16), grace, love and fellowship (2 Cor 13.13). AE used peace and grace together in 1.2.

23. Peace (see on 1.2; 2.14 for the concept) is the first term in the first benediction. Has AE deliberately given it this prominent position because it is one of his leading themes (cf 2.14–18; 6.15; so Gnilka and most commentators), or because it is one of the leading terms used in benedictions (Rom 15.33; 2 Th 3.16) and is a frequent term near the end of letters (Gal 6.16; 1 Pet 5.14; 3 Jn 15)? Or does chance alone account for its prominent position? At 1.2 grace precedes peace; here it heads the second benediction. It is impossible to answer these questions but at least it can be said that its present emphatic position is not out of accord with AE's theology. Since it appears in a prayer it must be understood as a peace coming from God. God's peace is his salvation (Haupt). AE is primarily praying that the brotherhood should be favoured with God's peace rather than that there should be peace among its members, though the latter would follow naturally from the former (2.14–18); again AE is not praying directly for peace in individual hearts (so Origen; Jerome), though this would be a further consequence of God's salvation. God's peace is directed towards **the brothers**, i.e. the believers (for 'brother' see on v. 21). The term, unlike 'believer','Christian' or 'those who love the Lord' (v. 24), sets up a relationship between those addressed and the writer; they are seen, not as individuals, but as a group, as members one of another (4.25), as belonging to the same household (2.19), as within the one church which has been the subject of so much of the letter.

AE's readers are also to be the recipients of God's **love**. Love is another basic concept of his theology (1.4; 2.4; 3.17–19; 5.2, 25), as it was of all early Christianity. The emphasis lies not on the love of believers for one another but on God's love for them which pre-existed their existence and elected them to be believers (1.4f); God's love should lead those who are brothers to love one another.

Though the precise relationship of peace and love is never defined in the letter, they belong as terms to the same semantic field denoting God's beneficent attitude towards people; the same cannot be said, at least at first sight, of the third term in the benediction, 'with faith'; it instead normally denotes the attitude of believers towards God. In addition it is not introduced with a simple **and** which would set it in parallel with peace and love but with 'with'. Yet to translate, 'together with trust in God', moves it away from their area as gifts of God. As far as the meaning goes it is possible to understand 'faith' as a quality of God (cf Bouttier), for in the OT God is depicted as faithful to his covenant. God's believers are then assured that he will remain faithful to them in peace and love. This interpretation also allows 'with' a normal sense, since 'faith' need not then be taken as parallel with peace and love but as qualifying them as to the manner in which the peace and love are given. The movement is from God to believers. So we translate, **Peace and love to the brothers from a faithful God**. For the terms used here to identify God see on 1.2, 3; 5.20. In v. 23 God is defined as Father and presumably as Father of believers and neither simply as Father of Jesus Christ as in 1.3, nor as Father of all men and women.

24. Grace begins the second benediction; it is the most common word in the terminal benedictions of the NT (Rom 16.20, 24; 1 Cor 16.23; 2 Cor 13.13; Gal 6.18; Phil 4.23; Col 4.18; 1 Th 5.28; 2 Th 3.18; 1 Tim 6.21; 2 Tim 4.22; Tit 3.15; Philem 25; Heb 13.25); it is followed with the usual **with** relating it to the recipients. However these are not addressed with the normal second person plural but identified with a phrase in the third person, **all who love our Lord Jesus Christ**. The idea that people love, or should love, God (the Lord) is common in the OT and Judaism (Exod 20.6; Deut 5.10; 7.9; Judg 5.31; Ψ 96.10; 121.6; 144.20; 2 Esdr 11.5; Tob 13.14; 14.7; Ecclus 1.10; 2.15, 16; *Ps Sol* 4.25; 6.6; *T Sim* 3.6; *Test Abr* 3.3 (Rec A); *1 En* 105.8) and may almost be termed a formula (Gnilka; Schlier); it reappears in the NT, yet in the light of the latter's much greater general emphasis on love comparatively rarely (Rom 8.28; 1 Cor 2.9; 8.3; Jas 1.12; 2.5; 1 Jn 4.10, 20f; 5.1). Perhaps more surprising is the scarcity of references to loving Christ, in view of the fact that to Christ are attributed many of the functions exercised by God in the OT. Our passage aside, there is only 1 Cor 16.22 and 1 Pet 1.8 (2 Tim 4.8 is not a proper parallel); outside the NT there are instances in Ign *Eph* 15.3; *Philad* 1.1; *Polyc* 5.1; Polyc *Phil* 3.3. The idea of loving Christ is then a late development in early Christianity; Paul prefers to speak of a faith relationship with Christ. The love of God for Christians is of course a frequent idea (in Ephesians at 1.4; 2.4; 3.18f; 5.2, 25; 6.23). Our verse provides one of the few places where AE might be thought to define who Christians are, those who love the Lord Jesus Christ; in 1 Cor 16.22, which may be part of a liturgical formula, lack of such love in people prevents them being regarded as Christians. As a definition of being Christian (an alternative and more frequent definition sets Christians out as those who call on the Lord, 1 Cor 1.2; Rom 10.12–14; Acts 9.14, 21; 2 Tim 2.22), these two ideas emphasise the attitude of the persons concerned rather than their election by God as in 1.4. Often 1 Pet 1.8 is quoted here in extenuation; those who have not seen Christ can hardly be expected to love him; yet they are expected to trust him though they have not seen him. 5.1 moreover requires the imitation of God who has not been seen. Thus the fact that Christ is not seen can hardly be relevant.

The final phrase 'in incorruption' is troublesome. The noun is found only in the later portions of the LXX and appears to lack a Hebrew equivalent (Wisd 2.23; 6.18f; 4 Macc 9.22; 17.12; cf Wisd 12.1; 18.4). In the NT it is found at 1 Cor 15.42, 50, 53f; 1 Tim 1.10 (cf Rom 1.23; 1 Cor 9.25; 15.52; 1 Tim 1.17) and in the Apostolic Fathers at 2 Clem 14.5; 20.5; Ign *Philad* 9.2; *Eph* 17.1; *Magn* 6.2; *Mart Polyc* 14.2; 19.2. Its use probably represents a Hellenistic touch on AE's part in an attempt to accommodate his readers. It describes a condition rather than a temporal or infinite continuity and moves in the area of indestructibility and immortality; it is not an ethical term (*pace* Origen; Chrysostom; Theod Mops; Erasmus; etc.) and contains no idea of Christians being freed from moral incorruption, though this itself may be true. There is a problem over the link between this final phrase and the earlier part of the sentence. The solution accepted by many translations (RSV, NRSV, REB, GNB, NIV, Moffatt), 'love with an undying love' is awkward. The connection could however be made in a different way and refer to those whose love is not transitory but persists. This interpretation gives a more suitable close to the letter. The promises of the gospel which it contains are for those whose Christian faith is not a passing whim but stands the test of time. There is a sense then in which this picks up and concludes the conflict of 6.10–17 in which those conquer who stand firm for ever.

Now at the end of our letter we need to look back along the way we have come and summarise our understanding of it. It was probably written not by Paul but by someone strongly under his influence who had also been associated with the author of Colossians. Probably they both belonged to a continuing group of Paul's disciples.

The author's aim was limited. He was not concerned with the wider issues of the life of the church or its members in the secular world but with the internal harmony of individual Christian communities. He thus leaves unexamined vast areas of ecclesiology and his decision not to discuss these areas must have been deliberate; he is not to be blamed for omitting them; they are covered in other parts of the New Testament.

The letter is carefully planned and the author does not wander at random from topic to topic. Its theology and paraenesis serve the same purpose, the maintenance of the unity of Christian communities. The consistency of his thinking displayed in this appears in lesser areas: his christology makes no reference to Christ as the servant of God or humanity, and accordingly the life of believers is not stressed as one of service; Christ's ascension is emphasised and with it the exalted position of believers. Since his main theme is the inner unity of Christian communities, he has no need to refer to the future in terms of the parousia, yet he has an interest in the ultimate unity of all things (1.10). God has given the church its unity yet believers must strive to preserve it or it will be lost. Since the two halves of his letter relate to this unity it is wrong to suggest that one or other is the more important. His moral teaching may lack profoundness, but the causes of division in congregations are rarely great issues but come from the little ways in which people do not get on with one another. He uses one section of a traditional *Haustafel* to explore the relation of Christ and the church which he parallels to marriage, making here an important new contribution to the doctrine of the church. While generally his theology lies within the ambit of Pauline teaching, there is a certain broadening or rephrasing of ideas to meet Hellenistic thinking.

It goes too far to describe the letter as the crown of Paulinism; while it treats the formal nature of the church in greater detail and with deeper understanding than Paul, many areas of Pauline thought lie untouched and the level of moral teaching falls below his. Because of its very general nature the main message of the letter can be easily transferred to the situation of local congregations, for in these there are always factors which would destroy fellowship and break up unity.

ESSAY I

THE CHURCH

1.1. The rise of the ecumenical movement has led in recent years to a deeper study of the teaching on the church in Ephesians. It is not inappropriate then to summarise that teaching. Many commentators indeed hold this to be the central theme of the letter. The word **church** is used more regularly in it (nine times) in proportion to its size than in any of the other Paulines, with the possible exception of 1 Corinthians (twenty-two times). In secular Greek the word indicates an assembly and in the LXX it is applied to Israel as the people of God. Judaism used two words, **church** and **synagogue**, either of which the Christians might have applied to their groups; they chose the former, perhaps because the Jews already used the latter of their gatherings. The Christians used their word in three ways referring to (a) the local Christian community in a town, (b) Christian gatherings in a house, (c) the whole group of Christians in all parts of the world.

1.2. The discussion of the nature of the church may be approached from either the sociological angle or the theological. To adopt the former would lead to an examination *inter alia* of the church in terms of its position among the other social entities of its culture, its relationship to the state, its internal structure, the selection and appointment of its office-bearers, the type of people who belonged to it and the sociological factors which led to its formation. Ephesians is, at least on the surface, not interested in these matters but instead in the relation of the church to God, to Christ and to the Holy Spirit; in so far as the church is defined it is defined in respect of God, Christ and the Spirit, and in terms of its membership, not in relation to other bodies of people. For AE the church is neither the result of the determination of a number of people with similar interests to associate with one another to further a common goal, nor an inevitable development of the historical process; its existence

339

was determined by God prior to the historical process (1.4f, 9–11).

1.3. Even if intending to write theologically about the church AE cannot avoid statements which have sociological significance. Theological theories about social entities must relate in some way to society. If AE has nothing to say about the place of the church in relation to the state yet he sees it as a place of light in a culture of darkness (4.17–19), though of course he expresses what he has to say in theological rather than sociological terms; the result is an almost sectarian outlook, yet there is no sense of a ghetto mentality. He does not lay down limiting barriers by which the church may be distinguished from what lies outside it; baptism is the only such marker; yet he is clearly aware that there is a distinction between the church and the world; in the church is light but in the world darkness (5.8); if he does draw a distinction it is rather between the life of believers before and after conversion (2.1–3; 5.8). AE is also aware of the relation of the church to the supernatural world, for the culture of darkness outside the church is controlled by evil supernatural forces (2.2; 6.10–17). In so far as he writes about the behaviour of members he is making sociological statements. They are not to lie to one another, be abusive, thieve from non-Christians (4.25ff), or sin sexually with one another or with outsiders (5.3ff). In indicating these as sins into which his readers might fall he only does so because he is aware that sometimes they did; in this way he provides a picture of his readers. Yet we must be careful here for when he dealt with household relationships (5.22–6.9) he writes as if all his readers belonged to households in which everyone was a Christian; it is difficult to believe that churches ever existed which consisted only of totally Christian households; AE may not then be very much aware of the actual way in which his readers lived and his depiction of the sins into which they were most likely to fall may be completely erroneous. Yet nothing we know about the early church suggests he was ignorant in this way. Other things he says tell us something about the lives of his readers. They have been baptised (4.5; 5.26), worship together (5.19f) and have some form of ministry (4.11). They also accept the ideas of their surrounding culture on slavery and the relationship of husbands and wives. On the whole however he provides little information about his readers and their manner of life; this is probably a result of the nature of his letter. We learn most about Paul's readers in those letters where he writes to an individual community which he knows; AE is however writing a letter either to a number of communities or more generally to Christians as a whole and he will have had no individual knowledge of the majority of their communities. If however it is impossible to deduce from his letter the proportions of rich and poor in the communities, we can be certain that they contained some wealthy enough to be slave owners and some poor enough to be slaves. Surprisingly however we learn that he did not see membership of the church as restricted to humans on earth for it also includes heavenly inhabitants (see on 1.18; 2.19).

2.1. Since he is writing with either a general Christian audience or a number of congregations in mind, it is not unnatural that he should discuss the nature of the whole church rather than that of local congregations. In doing this he might have conceived of the whole church as the sum total of a number of local communities; instead he thinks of it as the sum total of believers. He has no need then to lay down a set of rules for individual congregations or to instruct them in the steps to take if problems should arise within them; he does not tell them when facing a difficulty in the congregation to summon a church meeting (cf 1 Cor 5.1ff) or to pray for God's help. Sometimes it is suggested that Paul, assuming he did not write Ephesians, lacked a concept of the church as a whole. Yet there is evidence that he did not wholly lack this: he does not write to the church *of* Corinth but to the church *in* Corinth; he has a common policy for all the churches (1 Cor 4.17; 14.33); if Christ is the foundation of the church in Corinth (1 Cor 3.11) he is that for every other local church; if the church in Corinth is God's field and building (1 Cor 3.9) so will every other congregation be; it is not only the church in Corinth that is Christ's body, every community is, and Christ does not have a number of bodies. The rock of the whole church is present as an outcrop in every local congregation. In writing to individual congregations Paul had no need to discuss the nature of the church as a whole and so he did not do so. Colossians is a kind of stepping-stone between the earlier letters and Ephesians, for it contains explicit references both to the local community (Col 1.2; 4.15) and to the whole

341

church (1.18, 24); its author was dealing with one community with a specific christological problem which also had a more general reference. AE, by concentrating on the whole church and on it alone, is able to set ecclesiology more firmly within the divine economy (Schnackenburg). At the same time, though writing of the whole church, he avoids idealising or spiritualising it for in his paraenesis (4.1ff) he has the needs of actual members in mind.

3. There are at least three major theological ways of describing the church: (i) as God's people; (ii) as related to Christ (e.g. as his body), the corporate aspect; (iii) as the realm of the Holy Spirit's activity. The first is rooted in the OT in a way in which the second and third are not. The second is the area in which AE makes his main contribution, though naturally he has much to say in respect of the other two. For him the church is something essentially new which did not exist prior to Christ's incarnation. Judaism thought of Israel as the body neither of God nor of the Messiah, though it did think of God and Israel in a marital relationship and used the image of building in relation to Israel; yet even where continuity of image exists there is also profound variation brought about by the new factor of the incarnation. Images are always flexible and open to modification when new factors and situations arise.

3.1. *The Church as People of God*
This idea is less explicit in Ephesians than in other parts of the NT (e.g. Rom 9–11; 1 Pet 2.9f). Its implicit presence however underlies much of the letter and is seen in the adoption of concepts and images already applied to Israel. Thus AE describes the church as *ecclesia* and believers as **saints**, terms common in the LXX and later Judaism to describe the people of God. Christians are the chosen of God, his elect (1.4), as were the OT people of God. AE draws the images of building and wife from the OT though reinterpreting them in relation to the church. 2.11–22 is the passage where the 'people' idea becomes explicit; Gentiles inherit the promises originally made to Israel (2.12) and though once excluded are now within the people of God. Yet there is a profound change for the people is no longer a continued Israel but a new people, a 'third people', comprising both believing Jews (the first people) and Gentiles (the second people). 2.11–22,

though centring on the idea of the people of God, also provides a link to another leading idea: Jews and Gentiles are reconciled in Christ's body, not his physical body but the body which is the church; the two bodies are of course related since were it not for the dying body on the cross there would be no church (2.16). Paul had already expressed the union of Jews and Gentiles in one body (1 Cor 12.13). The corporate aspect of the one people of God is seen also in the harmonious fitting together of the stones, that is, the people, in the temple (2.21). Other links between the two aspects appear in that holiness, a characteristic of the people of God (they are saints), is attributed to the church as wife or bride of Christ (5.27), and that Gentiles are both fellow heirs (a people of God term) with Jews and within the same body (3.6).

The church as the people of God raises in an acute way its relationship to Israel, God's 'old' people. Clearly there is some degree of continuity, otherwise OT terms used of Israel would not be applied to the church and the church would not have looked on the OT as an authoritative book. Yet nothing is said of a continuing physical Israel after the cross. AE evinces no interest in such an Israel but then he is only interested in the unity of the church. In a sense a continuing Israel would be no different from a continuing non-Israel, the Gentiles; both are sources for converts and members of both need the same salvation that comes through the cross and resurrection of Christ. Ephesians differs at this point from Colossians in that the latter (3.11) sees the abolition within the church of the distinction between slave and free, barbarian and Scythian, as well as of that between Jew and Greek. In Ephesians social distinctions are not abolished, only the religious distinction between Jew and Gentile.

3.2 *The Church of the Spirit*

For Ephesians, as for the certainly genuine Paulines, the Spirit's realm of activity is the church. Neither Paul nor AE had occasion to discuss the nature of inspiration in the arts or in philosophical and scientific thought and thus develop a theology of the role of the Spirit in society as a whole. In fact AE's picture of the world outside the church (4.17–19) leaves no place for that activity except in so far as the Spirit can be conceived as leading unbelievers to see the truth of the gospel. If any spirit is at work

343

in society it is an evil spirit, or evil spirits (2.2; 6.10ff). Within the church the Spirit is one (4.4) and gives unity to the church (4.3). Believers are sealed with the Spirit (1.13; 4.30) and given access to God (2.18); it (we do not know enough to decide whether AE ascribed personality to the Spirit; hence the use of 'it' rather than 'he/she') strengthens (3.16) and fills them (5.18); it controls and inspires their worship (5.19); it leads their prayers (6.18). Believers are equipped in their fight against the powers of evil with a sword empowered by the Spirit (6.17). If they sin against the life of the community (4.25–9) the Spirit grieves (4.30). While in 1 Corinthians and Romans God or Christ may be the ultimate source of charismata, these in fact are depicted more directly as endowments of the Spirit (1 Cor 12–14); in Ephesians, though the charismata are not particularised, they are regarded as the gift of Christ (4.7f); office-bearers are also his gift (4.11). If in that way the Spirit's role may seem to be diminished, it must be recollected that in 1.3 the blessings which God gives to the church, though they are not spelt out, are associated with the Spirit. The Spirit again is a source of revelation (1.17) to the church guiding it through its original leaders into the acceptance of the Gentiles (3.5). God dwells in the church in his Spirit (2.22); this varies in a minor way from 1 Cor 3.16 where it says the church is indwelt by the Spirit of God.

Body (= the church) and Spirit are linked together in the theme of unity in 4.4; this linking provides a suitable passage to the discussion of the more corporate aspects of the church.

4.1 *The Church as Building*

This image, drawn ultimately by Paul from Judaism, came to AE via Paul; despite its Jewishness it was also to some extent present in Greco-Roman culture and so could be readily appreciated by Gentiles. In distinction from Jews, Christians understood it as tied specifically to the Christ-event. He is its angle-stone (see on 2.20 for the word) and his apostles and prophets its foundation. The church has then a foundation different from any that Judaism believed to exist. Consequently it is essentially a new building, and as such can be built with Gentile 'stones' as well as Jewish. That it should be constructed with these two types of stones was not an afterthought when Judaism rejected Christ, but was intended from the beginning, even though Gentiles were not immediately admitted. On the foundation of apostles and prophets with Christ as the angle-stone believers are fitted together so that there results, as we might say, a building secure against rain and storm. It is not however any building but a particular building, a temple in which God dwells. Though this building may have begun in the Christ-event and be envisaged as growing, it has also a certain sense of completeness; if it were not complete God would not dwell in it. This is the tension we have observed as running all through Ephesians; what is to happen is conceived as having already taken place. The building is not then thought of simply as a future heavenly Jerusalem; it exists now. Its growth is moreover not in numbers but in maturity. Linked with this building image, which is not restricted to that of the temple, is that of the family home; believers are the family inhabiting it (2.19) and the family is God's family.

This raises the question regarding the membership of the family of God and of the church. Certainly AE accepts as members those who have faith and have been baptised. He does not provide enough information for us to know if he would have made any other requirement, such as regular participation in the eucharist. The absence of a reference to the eucharist is itself surprising since in 1 Cor 10.16f Paul related it to the unity of believers, a central theme of AE; yet it was probably only because of local difficulties in Corinth that Paul made this link; similar difficulties did not necessarily exist among the Christians to whom AE was writing. Granted his readers meet all of AE's requirements, are they the only members of the church? In 2.19 Gentile believers are described as **fellow citizens with the saints**. Who are the saints? Here and in 1.18 they are probably good supernatural beings, possibly including the believing dead (see on 1.18; 2.19). In 2.6 believers are said to be already in the heavenlies and the church has a cosmic dimension (3.10, 21). Thus the church may have members other than believers on earth but AE is not primarily interested in them; he advises only on the behaviour of those on earth.

4.2   The Church as Body of Christ

(See also Detached Note: The Body of Christ.)

In the two major passages in which Paul teaches about the church as the body of Christ (1 Cor 12.12ff; Rom 12.3ff) he discusses the varying functions of believers, which he relates to their gifts of grace, and their interrelationship. In these two passages the image functions paraenetically. In Ephesians the variety of the charismata of believers is not spelt out though it is said that they have gifts to exercise (4.7); some indeed have special gifts, or are rather themselves special and diverse gifts to the church (4.11f). The paraenetic emphasis is less prominent in Ephesians, being only explicit at 4.25. Three new aspects of the image however appear in Ephesians: the body is said to grow (4.12, 16; cf Col 2.19), is depicted as Christ's wife or bride (5.22ff), and Christ is set out as its head; this latest aspect is present also in Colossians. It is natural to think of growth in relation to organisms; the human physical body as organism is complete in the sense that every part of it is there from birth and yet it grows from infancy to adulthood; its growth is a maturing of capabilities already present from the beginning; it is not a growth out of chaos into unity. In a somewhat similar way the church is one from the begining but matures and in that way grows. Christ is the source of all its growth (4.15f; for the idea of growth see 2.21). The idea of the church as mature person, if this is taken to be the meaning of 4.13, accords with this kind of thinking. An immature church could easily be led into error (4.14).

4.2.1. It was inevitable that once the church was likened to the body of Christ there would be questions about his relationship to his body. Apart from its normal physical meaning as the uppermost part of the body **head** was used metaphorically in many ways of which two are significant for biblical thought, 'origin, source' and 'overlord, ruler'. In theory it would be possible to apply either sense to Christ as head of the cosmos or head of the church. Both the thematic and cultural context of 5.23 imply overlordship as the meaning in 5.22–33; the thematic context of 1.22 requires the same connotation; incidentally we should note that in the latter text head is used without any direct reference to a body, though in some contemporary non-Christian thought the cosmos was regarded as a body. However, the meaning 'source' is possible in 4.15f, though not necessarily so if we take the source of the growth to be Christ rather than the head. There is however no reason why we should not find both understandings of the word within a single writing provided both are possible; where words have more than one meaning the context must decide which meaning is meant. We do not need then to force a consistent significance on AE though in fact he may have been consistent; if so the meaning will be 'overlord'. However, if Christ is ruler this does not mean he holds his position like either an elected president whom voters choose from a slate of candidates or a monarch who becomes ruler through the sheer chance of birth within a royal family.

4.2.2. If Christ is head both of the cosmos (1.22) and of the church, does this imply a relation between cosmos and church? There are other signs that a relationship may exist: Christ fills both (1.23; 4.10); believers already sit in the heavenlies (2.6); the families, or social groupings, of humans and angels have been brought together (3.15); believers are engaged in a continual contest with the powers that are in the heavenlies (6.12ff). All this is surprising since AE does not set church and society in relation and since the cosmos, the totality of existence, includes society within itself, though it is not identical with it. The church is not commanded to evangelise society, yet in 3.10 the church is summoned to make known to all supernatural sentient beings in the cosmos God's wisdom and is at the same time engaged in a continual warfare with these or with some of these beings (6.10ff). A significant difference however exists between the relation of Christ to the cosmos and to the church in that while he is the saviour of the church (5.25) he is the conqueror of the powers in the cosmos (1.21). Despite this difference all things, and this must include the powers as well as all human beings, are summarised or brought to a conclusion in him (1.10).

4.2.3. A further aspect of the relation of Christ to the church, which is not unrelated to the image of the body, is revealed by the terms 'fullness' and 'filling'; these are not used in the earlier Paulines in the same way as in Ephesians; they were however probably terms with a special significance for the Pauline school as their use in Ephesians shows. God fills Christ and Christ fills the church (1.23). Christ is the means whereby God works in the

347

church; Ephesians however tends to stress what Christ does rather than what God does, though God is always in the background. It is not made clear with what Christ fills the church, but it is at least his presence. There is a parallel here to the relationship of believers and Christ, in that Christ fills the church and the church is in him just as believers are in him and he dwells in them (3.17).

The church is Christ's body; he fills the church; he is its head; all this implies a very close association between Christ and church; it is not surprising then that in 3.21 Christ and the church are apparently given equal status in respect of the glory of God. Lest this should appear too high a status for the church in relation to Christ, in the marital image she is called to offer to him her obedience.

4.3. *The Church as Wife (or Bride)*

This image brings out further important aspects of the relation of Christ and the church. Though in the later church the image was transferred to the individual believer, usually a female religious as a bride of Christ, in Ephesians it is always the whole church which is seen as in a marital relation to Christ. The church is never actually termed 'bride' or 'wife' in Ephesians; it is the marital relationship which carries the significance. In using the marital metaphor Ephesians follows an OT train of thought where Israel is presented as bride or wife of Yahweh. There are however significant differences: the church is the wife of Christ and not of Yahweh or God; the unfaithfulness of the church as wife is not discussed as was the unfaithfulness of Israel to Yahweh. Indeed the church is already beautiful (5.27), this presumably in Christ's eyes and not just her own, and there is no paraenetic stress on the church to work to gain its faithfulness to Christ. As noted in the exegesis of 5.22–33, AE's presentation of the image contains an inconsistency; in most of the passage the church is the wife of Christ, but occasionally she appears as his bride, as if the marriage is taking place or is just about to do so (5.26f). As Christ's bride or wife the church is the object of his love; he is her saviour and devotes all his attention to her (5.23, 25); as bride he prepares her for the marriage ceremony (5.26f); as wife he cares for her and provides for all her needs (5.25, 28f). As either bride or wife she is subordinate to him and should obey him (5.24, 33). The distinction between Christ and the church is thus made clear through her subordination in a way which does not always appear in the other images where church and Christ may seem at times to merge into one another.

4.4. These then, the body of Christ, the building, the fullness, the wife, are in Ephesians the main images of the church in relation to Christ. Minor images also exist of which the most important is that of the family or household (2.19; 3.14f). The Jews had belonged to the family of God but now both Jewish and Gentile believers belong to a reconstituted family whose father is God (3.14f; cf 2.18); within the family all are brothers, though AE does not stress this horizontal relationship in the way Paul or Jesus does. The relationship is of course also seen in phrases like 'in Christ' and 'with Christ' (2.6).

Each image presents a different aspect of the relationship. How are they to be reconciled to one another? The image of the body has often been taken as the most important. Can this be sustained? For AE Christ's relationship to the church is real, yet as each image presents it, it to some extent distorts it, for each image brings out important factors not contained in all of the others. When map makers have to depict the globe of the earth on a two-dimensional surface they inevitably distort part of the earth's geography, as can be seen when we examine those atlases which display different projections. When we encounter these differences we are not led to doubt the reality of the earth's existence or its spherical nature. Each image relating Christ and church shows one or more aspects of that relationship yet at the same time distorts or obliterates other aspects. That should not lead to doubts of the reality of the relationship. To ask which is the most important image is then to ask a foolish question. Importance relates to situations; the polar explorer needs a different projection of the globe of the earth from those who live on the equator. So each image of the church has its own importance and this importance relates in a special way to the situation in, or the purpose for, which it is being used. The very nature of variety in the use of the images implies that they can never be fully reconciled to one another. It should be noted also that there may be helpful images, not presented in scripture, which can be envisioned and these may be useful in today's situations. Images excite the imagination and it is open to us to vary and adapt them to our own special purposes; this was already happening in scripture, for the body image is altered between the earlier and the later epistles in that in the latter Christ is seen as head, and in the building image he is changed from foundation to angle-stone. But if we make such variations we cannot claim that they posses scriptural authority. Many theologians and preachers have found it useful to develop from the body image the idea of the church as the extension of the incarnation, but if they do so they should not claim Paul's authority, or AE's, for this development.

5. *The Unity and Role of the Church*

Ephesians is the NT writing which is often held to express most firmly and clearly the unity of the church. It is true that Paul, facing those who would disrupt his converts, regularly argues for the importance of their unity (e.g. Rom 12.3ff; 1 Cor 12.12ff; Gal 3.28), yet the unity of the readers of Ephesians does not seem to be under threat from within their own communities or from outside. The only division to which AE refers is that between Jewish and Gentile believers, and this has already been healed and so belongs to the past. He makes no reference to those other unities between men and women, slaves and free, to which Gal 3.28 and Col 3.11 refer. The diversity in worship which is a prominent feature of the Corinthian church (1 Cor 12.12ff) hardly appears in Ephesians; 4.7 only reflects it in a pale way. There is no trace of parties within the church (cf 1 Cor 1.11ff). Unity on the one hand is an existing fact (4.4–6), on the other there is a need to maintain it (4.2f). In contrast with Colossians which is interested in the unity of the cosmos, Ephesians is interested in that of the church. Although the unity portrayed by AE already exists, it is not a static but a dynamic unity, dynamic not in the sense that it keeps on including more and more previously divided groups but in the sense that it matures. A 'body' is always one, but it can develop by maturing. In his concern for unity AE does not argue for organisational unity (he has no interest in organisation) or remind readers of the leaders to whom they should give their loyalty. No emphasis is placed on a need to search for unity so that the secular world may be impressed by the church's harmony in comparison with the world's disorder and so turn to Christ. AE relates unity strongly to

Christ, but this is not because discordant elements have argued for a unity based on some other centre (Pokorný) for there are few signs of discordant elements and the long paraenesis with its emphasis on the need to avoid sins which would disrupt unity does not stress Christ at all. Unity is not given a focus in the bishop or any other minister as in the Ignatian letters, or, as is so common today, in the eucharist. 4.4–6 might seem to be a focus but contains no single unifying factor. The need for a focus usually derives from external pressures. Perhaps AE is led to stress unity by no deeper cause than the minor frictions which every pastor observes in the way members of his flock drift apart. That minor factors are the cause is confirmed when we notice that AE does not set down boundaries in faith or conduct by which believers might be condemned or even excluded.

6. The Church's Inner Life

6.1. AE's paraenesis shows that he is very interested in the inner life of the communities who will read his letter (4.25–6.9). Despite this he evinces little interest in their organisation, though he allows that there are those who hold office within them and serve them (4.11ff). The lack of interest in organisation is surprising since believers who were or had previously been members in trade guilds, funeral associations and minor religious cults would have been used to work within organisational frameworks. As for a ministry within the communities two of the five groups he names (4.11), the apostles and prophets, have already fulfilled their function (2.19); the remaining three, evangelists, shepherds, teachers, are still active and will continue to be active. AE sees these latter ministries as christological in origin though it may well have been sociological pressure which first led to their creation. Their actual functions as he presents them arise out of the nature of the gospel. AE tells us nothing directly about what they do, except what can be deduced from their titles; probably he did not need to spell out their functions because his communities knew what they were. Special duties, e.g. presiding at the eucharist, are not ascribed to any of them. As a group they are to serve the remainder of their community. We can discern here, more than in the earlier Paulines, the beginning of the clerical–lay division which later came to dominate the internal life of the church. Like the 'officials', the ministry of the 'laity' is directed towards the inner life of the community and none are exempt from this ministry. Directed towards one another it includes both worship (5.19f) and loving service (4.32).

6.2. Though sections of Ephesians are couched in the language of worship (1.3–14; 3.14–21) little is said about its nature. Believers sing and pray (5.19; 6.19ff). Baptism is clearly important for it is mentioned in the piece of tradition quoted in 4.5 (cf 5.26), but there is no reference to the eucharist, which of course does not mean it went unobserved. Baptism is the rite of initiation (cf 1 Cor 12.13), but that does not mean that immersion in water using a defined formula made a non-believer into a believer. Those who come forward for baptism will be those who have faith (1.1, 13, 15, 19; 2.8; 3.17), and prior both to faith and baptism is election by God (1.4).

7. Conclusion

7.1. The church might have been described as the community of the elect, the saved, the baptised, for it certainly consists of these, but it is instead described in corporate terms, body of Christ, building, wife. Yet if it is described in this way it is as the union of believers and not of a number of congregations. Though the church is part of God's plan for the redemption of the universe, it is not presented as the soul or conscience of society. Very little sets it in relation to society, to the nation or to the governing authorities. Instead it is set in relation to Christ as his body and his wife or bride; it is also God's people and the place where the Spirit dwells. It is at all times subject to Christ its Lord and husband. A tension exists between its heavenly and its earthly settings: members already sit in the heavenlies (2.6) and make known the wisdom of God to the powers; glory is given to the church (3.21); yet members have to be instructed how to live with one another (4.25ff). The heavenly nature of the church does not then lead to its removal from history. AE depicts a church which, as we might say, has its eyes directed both upwards and inwards but not outwards. The inward look of course coheres with the ethical teaching of the letter. Despite the emphasis on the behaviour of members towards one another there is no suggestion of a ghetto mentality.

7.2. Traditionally four marks have been ascribed to the church: one, holy, catholic and apostolic. Barth says Ephesians displays these four marks of the church more clearly than any other Pauline letter. Taking these words at their simplest it is not difficult to see that the first three can be applied without hesitation to the church as depicted in Ephesians. The church is one (4.4) and holy (5.27) as are its members (1.1); both its unity and its holiness have been given to it by God. It is catholic for it embraces all within itself, Jews and Gentiles (2.11–22), men and women (5.22–33), slaves and free (6.5–9). The fourth mark, apostolicity, is more difficult to apply. The church is certainly apostolic since apostles are part of its foundation (2.20) and the full glory of the gospel was revealed to them (3.5). Yet in these two texts, the only ones setting out a theology of apostolicity, prophets are linked to apostles and that with a common article which ties them very closely together. If then we wish to use these texts to confirm the apostolicity of the church we are forced at the same time to ascribe to it a prophetic nature (cf 4.11), and there is no reason for regarding the prophetic nature of the church as less important than its apostolic nature. This suggests that proper to the nature of the church is an element of unpredictability, yet an unpredictability guided not by tradition but by the Holy Spirit, an element which in proclaiming God's will may continually disturb the church's accepted order. Indeed if we examine the history of the church we see that it has been frequently subject to prophetic disturbance and that this disturbance has been for its good. Prophets preserve the church from being at ease with itself and settling down contentedly into a routine and conservative way of life; they come from within it and stir it up, directing it into new paths.

Christians have regularly been perplexed by the contrast between what the church is supposed to be and what it actually is, and have attempted to solve this by contrasting the visible and invisible churches. AE seems quite unaware of this problem. What he writes in 3.1–4, 16 might suggest he had the invisible church in mind yet he makes no distinction when he goes on to describe the activities of its members. Believers who are capable of telling lies to one another are members of the one body of Christ (4.25), who can commit fornication (5.3, 5) belong to the bride of Christ who is without spot or wrinkle (5.27), who can steal (4.28) are members of the people of God, who can be drunk (5.18) are in the building of God where God dwells (2.22). AE is unaware of the visible–invisible distinction.

ESSAY II

MORAL TEACHING

1. AE sets out his moral teaching no more systematically than any other NT writer. While the ethical teaching of many sections of other letters is generally, but not always, clearly determined by the situation of their readers as a response to their particular problems, it is difficult to discern the particular situation, if any, to which AE was responding. Yet, while the sequences of injunctions in Rom 12.9ff and 1 Th 5.14ff are difficult to tie in with the main themes of those letters, the apparently similarly haphazard sequence of Eph 4.25–5.2 does go along with the letter's central theological message concerning the nature and unity of the church, and the same is true of almost all the remaining moral teaching in the letter. The sequence of Mk 9.33–50 is held together by catchwords because it was originally oral teaching; Eph 4.25–5.2 is held together by its content relating to life within the church. If the paraenesis of Ephesians cannot easily be related to the particular situations of its intended readers, this accords with the general nature of the letter. Implicit in the way AE outlines his paraenesis is a contrast between the conduct of believers before their conversion/baptism and what it should be afterwards; 4.17–19 (cf 2.1–3) depicts the life of the Gentile world outside the church and fittingly precedes the actual detailing of the new behaviour which AE desires for his readers. None of this means that the ethical instruction of Ephesians is vague or imprecise; it always treats areas of conduct which are the concern of many believers.

2. It may however justifiably be asked whether an ethic is necessary for believers who sit in the heavenlies (2.6). Does this not imply that their behaviour is already perfect? That despite this AE provides moral teaching is part of the tension which runs throughout the letter, exemplified in that Christ has overcome the powers (1.20–3) and yet they are still active in misleading

355

believers (6.10ff). Even though readers are appointed to pre-ordained 'good works' (2.10), it is necessary to spell out what those works are. While they could be defined in general terms as activities which are in accordance with God's will (5.10, 17) this is vague and needs filling out.

2.1. Paul's letters do not follow a single pattern. In the Corinthian correspondence and Philippians ethical teaching is mingled with other material (cf Hebrews). In Romans the ethical teaching follows (at 12.1) a long theological disquisition. In 1 Thessalonians it comes at 4.1 after Paul's discussions in the first three chapters of his movements and personal behaviour. In Galatians it follows at 5.1 his defence of his conduct and theology. Each of these three letters has a precise turning-point where the paraenesis commences. So has Ephesians and its turning-point is 4.1. Preceding it are sections of prayer and devotion and of theology. After it ethical teaching dominates the material, though it contains two theological sections (4.7–16; 5.23–32), but these are integral to that teaching in developing the basis for Christian communal living.

3. Areas of Ethical Concern

Roughly speaking the paraenesis of Ephesians covers three main areas: 4.25–5.2, 6–14 treats the conduct of believers towards one another, 5.3–5, 15–18 the personal conduct of believers which may affect themselves but not others within the community, and 5.22–6.9 the conduct of believers within their own homes. Believers are always envisaged as members of groups and not simply as individuals. For the most part it is all believers who are being instructed though at times smaller groups are addressed. So in the HT men who are husbands, fathers and owners of slaves, and wives, children and slaves are picked out for individual attention. The group of 'ministers' is also singled out in 4.11 and given duties in 4.12. It is not clear why these groups are selected and others omitted such as widows who come in for considerable attention elsewhere in the NT (Acts 6.1–6; 1 Cor 7.39f; 1 Tim 5.3ff). It can be assumed that those specifically mentioned in the HT are also addressed in the more general injunctions of the paraenesis.

3.1. The areas of life in which AE instructs his readers are roughly those of personal behaviour in which individuals relate to

356

one another within the community and by their conduct may ensure or disrupt its smooth running. AE is much more concerned with this than with personal piety. 4.2f are key verses, 4.2 (and 5.21) setting out the essential virtues in this respect and 4.3 indicating their purpose. 4.2f is followed directly with theological teaching about the community whose unity and peace are to be maintained. The theme is then developed in greater detail: truthfulness and good temper towards fellow members are commended (4.25–7); thieving is condemned but only because no good accrues to the community through it (4.28); careful attention to what believers say to one another is important (4.29; 5.4) for bawdy talk would corrupt the community; love towards other community members is stressed (4.32); the examples of God and Christ are set before members (4.32–5.2); those who would upset the community with false teaching are to be avoided (5.6f); in times of common worship inspiration with the Spirit is preferable to drunkenness.

3.1.1. There are also sins to be avoided which may affect people outside the community but not fellow members, fornication, lust and greed (5.3, 5); however no thought is given to the effect of these on those outside the community; the sins are presumably to be avoided only because of the harm they do to the members themselves and through them to the community. In addition the HT lays down positive lines for the mutual behaviour of husbands and wives, parents and children, masters and slaves; curiously fornication is not mentioned as destructive of family life; perhaps AE thinks it inconceivable within a Christian household, though Paul did not (1 Cor 6.12ff). In all this the stress is mainly negative relating to sins to be avoided rather than positive in encouraging the cultivation of particular virtues, though these are mentioned in respect of those which promote unity (4.2), and include love and forgiveness (4.32; 5.2) in imitation of Christ and God. Positive action is however often left very general (4.24; 5.8b, 9, 10, 15, 17); time is to be used in a disciplined way (5.16). This enumeration of virtues and vices may appear to make them unrelated but they are held together through a continued stress on community life.

3.1.2. If the ethical teaching has a main thrust, it is love. It was his love which moved God to act. His election of believers was not arbitrary but came from his love (1.4f) as did their redemption (2.4; 5.2, 25). His love is immeasurable (3.18f). The main agent in his work is Christ, his 'beloved' (1.6), and believers are in their turn termed 'beloved' (5.1). They are rooted and grounded in love (3.17); love builds them up into maturity (4.16). Yet it is strictly the church as a whole which is the object of God's love (5.25); within it believers as individuals are loved (5.2). Though AE refers only to God's love towards believers it may be that had he been asked he would have said God loved all people. Since, as AE presents it, it is his love which has led him to elect those he loves, it is better to assume that AE had never thought out the problem of the relation of love and election. Given his emphasis on God's love it is not surprising that when he turns to the way believers should live almost his first thought is of love (4.2). If the church is to grow it must grow in love (4.15f). 4.32 may not name love but it forms its basis. When AE wishes to describe the behaviour of husbands towards their wives, love is the word he uses (5.25, 28, 33) and this cannot be erotic love because it is identical with the love with which Christ loves the church. Love then for AE is more than one virtue among others; it is the virtue which sustains the others. As far as its content goes love should be understood in terms of self-sacrifice, for it is in that way that Christ's love is described (5.2).

Love was central to the ethic of Jesus as a love which his disciples should show to all people (Lk 10.25–37); love remains the keystone of Paul's ethic. But, beginning with Paul though only partially with him, we find love towards all (Rom 13.10; Gal 5.14) being restricted to love towards other believers (1 Th 3.12; 4.9). This restriction became normal in many of the later NT writings (Jn 13.34ff; 1 Pet 2.17; 1 Jn 3.11, 23); in Ephesians it coheres with the way God's love is expressed in election. However, in writing only of love towards other believers AE does not go as far as 1 Pet 2.17 which distinguishes between the attitude of believers to one another and to non-believers. Love, for AE, binds the community together (4.2) and is expressed through the various virtues expounded in 4.25ff.

3.2. AE's stress on behaviour within the community can be seen even more clearly when we recollect what is omitted in the actual virtues which he emphasises: truthfulness is stressed as important when exercised towards others in the community, but it goes unmentioned in relation to those outside; theft is criticised only because it deprives the community of money, not because of the loss sustained by the person whose property has been stolen; no thought is given to the harm done to the other person who is used in fornication; the HT only sets out duties towards fellow Christians. It is true that most of the other NT letters give greater attention to behaviour within the community than to behaviour towards the outside world, but this largely arises because their writers are dealing with specific problems that have arisen within the community.

To see the narrowness of AE's ethical concern it is necessary to look not only at the areas which he has covered but also at those to which he has given no consideration. Obviously he cannot be expected to cover areas arising out of the complexity of modern civilisation, e.g. trade-union legislation, green issues, social reform. We should not view what he says from the perspective of our times and expect condemnations of slavery or male domination. But there are areas of concern relating to his own time on which he does not touch. The household is clearly important in AE's eyes yet he only considers households all of whose members are Christian, and even then he says nothing about the relation of siblings to one another or the position of widows and grand-parents; he does nothing to resolve obvious points of tension (does the slave wife owe primary obedience to her husband or to her owner?). Divorce was frequent in the ancient world; perhaps AE's failure to refer to it may be excused because it would not be expected to occur in unmixed households. He might however have paid some attention to the victims of wrongful activity on the part of believers, e.g. the prostitute whom the believer has used (5.3, 5, contrast Epict 2.4.1ff, 10.17; 3.24.23), the person whose wealth the thief has taken (4.28, contrast Lk 19.8). When he discusses whether the Christian should eat food which has been sacrificed to idols, Paul takes into account possible occasions of the effect on unbelievers (1 Cor 10.27–9). Interestingly Epictetus comments that adultery has a wide effect on society (2.4.1ff) and renders the victim less than human (2.10.17).

In fairness it is important to remember that Ephesians is so brief that it would have been impossible for AE to treat every problem, yet there are areas of which it is difficult to see how they could have escaped his notice. These relate largely to the interaction between believers and the world outside their community. Every day believers must have been reminded of the dangers of idolatrous worship, yet idolatry is only mentioned in passing in 5.5 and in such a way as if it could be assumed everyone would reject it. If Arnold's claim that magic formed an important element in the background to the letter is correct, and it certainly was a major feature of the ancient world, it is surprising to find it is not condemned (cf Acts 19.19; 8.19–24; 13.4–12; Gal 5.20; 2 Tim 3.8; 3.13; Rev 9.21; 18.23). Christians would have encountered the outside world through the people who lived next door, as shopkeepers who sold goods to all and sundry, as those who bought goods wherever they were on sale. The fornicator met the unbelieving prostitute and the thief the unbeliever with possessions. In mixed households the believer could not avoid daily encounters with unbelievers; AE does not consider even the possibility of broken homes as a result of one member becoming a Christian (Mk 3.31–5; 10.29; Mt 10.34f; Lk 12.51–3).

3.3. The total impression created by the areas of life for which AE provides guidance suggests that his ethic might be defined as a 'church ethic', that is, one applying to life within the church but not dealing with the relationship of either the church or its members to what takes place in the world outside the church. This description of the moral teaching of AE as a church ethic is not out of accord with the way in which when he depicts the church (see Essay: The Church) he stresses its inner life rather than its relation to the world. This does not mean that if AE had been asked he would not have been willing to outline an ethic designed to govern the attitude of Christian communities and individual Christians to the world. For some reason he decided that he did not need to do this. If he had done it something of the way he presents the church and its life shows that his approach would not have been sectarian. He does not provide a list of rules as some Christian groups do today, e.g. do not smoke or dance, attend the eucharist at least once a month, believe Jesus is God; rules like these serve to mark off believers from their surrounding culture and offer opportunities for discipline if they are not kept. AE in his situation might have said members should not eat food that had been sacrificed to idols, attend temple worship or join with non-Christians in business ventures. His failure to provide a set of church rules saves him then from the charge of sectarianism.

4. *Guidelines*

4.1. Neither AE nor any other NT writer is able to provide a sufficient number of injunctions to cover all the situations in which moral decisions require to be made. Those who entered Christianity from Judaism already had guidelines covering a great many possible situations, but most of AE's readers came from the Gentile world with its very varied religious and philosophical backgrounds ranging from those where behaviour was not regarded as important to Stoicism where great stress was laid on it. Gentiles entering Christianity would bring with them the ethic of their previous religious and philosophical culture. In many cases (e.g. truthfulness, kindness) these coincided with what was taught in their new faith, but in other cases there would be slight or wide divergence. It is impossible to deny that AE has taken over a large part of contemporary ethical culture; he retains broadly speaking the patriarchal structure of society and he accepts without query the existence of slavery.

4.2.1. What assistance by way of criteria of conduct does AE offer his readers as they endeavour to live in their new Christian communities? Wide and imprecise statements about doing God's will (5.17; 6.6), pleasing the Lord (5.10; cf Rom 12.2), behaving wisely (5.15), doing what would serve to build up the church (4.2, 3, 15f) or what is fitting (5.3, 4).

4.2.2. More practical criteria are needed, not only for those who as new converts have very recently moved out of pagan culture, but also for those who have been converts for some time yet who continue to live surrounded by that culture. Through the centuries the church realising this has attempted to express what pleases the Lord by stressing variously or together the Decalogue, Jesus as example, traditional Christian behaviour in either its puritanical or catholic forms. Alternatively an appeal is some-times made to conscience (cf Rom 9.1; 13.5). AE however adopts none of these approaches. Yet he has certainly not left his readers to determine for themselves on every occasion what pleases the Lord. The paraenetic half of his letter is a setting out of the kind of conduct he understands as pleasing the Lord. Since behaviour has always to be linked to the actual situation in which it is lived, and he is writing a general letter, he is able to paint only with broad brush strokes. We never find him arguing a case in detail as Paul does in 1 Corinthians in respect of food sacrificed to idols; he leaves his readers to carry out such detailed arguing for themselves. Broad brush strokes entail his seeing everything in black and white; actual decisions are much more complex and often lead only to the choice between two imperfect solutions.

4.2.2.1. As a help to his readers AE offers first of all the precise injunctions given in his paraenesis, but these fail to cover many situations where decisions need to be made. An examination of these injunctions shows that he sometimes bases his counsel on the OT. For a Jew this was the natural place to look for guidance. He brings in Zech 8.16 at 4.25, Ps 4.4 at 4.26 and the Decalogue underlies 4.28 and is explicitly quoted at 6.2f. (Gen 2.24 is not used directly in relation to behaviour when quoted at 5.31.) Interestingly, pagan moralists would not have rejected the content of what he says in any of these instances. His use of the OT is probably intended to enforce the authority of what he says, though at 6.3 he modifies his OT quotation to remove from it a limitation which he would not wish to enforce. If he introduces the OT he has no general advice to give on where its teaching should be followed and where ignored. He never discusses the relation of God's will to the Law of Moses. In 4.24 he gives a general principle for behaviour which could have come from pagan moralists, though he probably draws it from Hellenistic Judaism which had accepted it (see on 4.24). Why did he not use here an OT passage like Hos 6.6 or Mic 6.8?

4.2.2.2. To help his readers he also draws on accepted Christian tradition like the HT and he selects what he wishes from traditional vice and virtue lists. Again in this material there is little with which many pagan moralists would have disagreed. They might not have accepted his development of the marriage metaphor in 5.22ff, but he develops it for theological rather than ethical purposes. Accepted tradition can also change; whereas Paul believed that this world was passing away and the End coming soon and allowed this to shape some of his judgements (e.g. 1 Cor 7.25ff), for AE the world is a more stable place and so judgements on conduct are not made in the belief that all would soon be changed.

4.2.2.3. Role models are a help in ethical instruction, but for Christians they need to be drawn from Christian and not pagan sources. Paul uses himself as a model (1 Th 1.5–7; 1 Cor 4.17; 11.1; Phil 3.17), but only does so to churches where he has ministered; if he wrote Ephesians it would not have been possible for him to present himself as a model since he was unknown in person to its readers; if AE was not Paul he would have been aware not to use Paul as model. In addition to himself, Paul used Christ as role model and this AE could do and did (5.2, 25); he uses God in the same way (5.1). But his use of Christ and God is in very general terms and would not have given much assistance in actual decision making. It would have been helpful if he had referred to incidents in Jesus' life or to some of his sayings (cf §6.3.1). The former of these only appears in relation to Christ's sacrificial death. None of Jesus' sayings are referred to explicitly in Ephesians. Indeed they feature only rarely in Paul. Yet if Ephesians is later than Paul, would the tradition about Jesus not have been more widely known? 4.20f may possibly indicate knowledge by readers of this tradition. If AE knew the tradition he may not have been able to use his knowledge, since in writing to a wide area he would not have been aware what parts of the tradition were known in each particular Christian community. A Christian guideline is perhaps supplied implicitly in 4.7–16 in that within the community conduct which would help the community to mature should be followed.

4.2.2.4. Generally speaking, readers are largely left to make up their own minds and for this, as 5.17 suggests (cf 1 Pet 1.13), some intellectual effort is necessary; the use of **discern** in 5.17 emphasises the need for such effort. When set in a Christian context this is never mere human insight but always insight guided by the Holy Spirit. True understanding of the Lord's will does not remain theoretical but involves it being carried out in practice. This means AE cannot cover every situation, for he does not know the precise circumstances of his readers and does not have enough space to cover everything. He does not even list a set of guiding axioms which believers might apply to their individual situations. They will have to reason out for themselves what they should do, learning from their ongoing experience and from the experience of others within their community. This may be why AE moves on after 5.17 to refer in vv. 19f to their common worship. The immediate move is to 5.18; overindulgence in wine may cloud his mind!

If AE has not been able to give guidelines to meet all the situations of his readers, still less has he been able to do it for us. He may have, and indeed has, much to say to us on many topics of personal conduct but he supplies no assistance on wider issues, for example the environment or social policy. Even if we accepted his advice on personal matters we would be left continuing a patriarchal attitude and accepting slavery.

5. *Motivation*

It is one thing to know what to do; it is another to do it. AE therefore not only indicates the nature of proper Christian activity but also attempts to persuade his readers to behave in the way he proposes. How does he do this? There are many different factors which lead people to act in the way they do: to maintain the integrity of their own lives (I could never look myself in the face again if I did that), the need (hunger, poverty, sickness) of others tore at their hearts so they had to help. It is also possible to ignore such claims. An initial impulse from outside may be necessary. It need not always be Christian (4.25, 26, 28); it could be a negative motivation arising out of not wishing to appear selfish in the eyes of others or out of the fear of punishment.

5.1. Traditionally for many Christians one outside impulse has been the fear of eternal punishment (whether action through fear is morally good or not is another matter), but this is not a significant factor in Ephesians; it appears only at 5.5f, 14; 6.9, and its reverse, a reward for good behaviour, at 6.8. It is noticeable that only 5.5f clearly indicates possible punishing action by God; this action is his response to sexual sin and greed, the former presumably and the latter possibly involving other people outside the community. No divine sanctions are attached to the sins against the community of 4.25–5.2. It is not said that the community does or should act in respect of such sins. Since fornication takes place outside the community its members may have been unaware it was happening. 6.9 reminds slave owners of their responsibility before God; was that because the community itself was powerless in the face of the sin of wealthier members or because slaves would be slow to denounce their owners? That God punishes wickedness and rewards goodness is an almost universal idea; Paul probably derived it from Judaism (cf 1 Cor 3.13–15; 4.5; 2 Cor 5.10; cf 1 Cor 7.29). For slaves fear, not of God, but of their owner, appears in 6.5. Public shame can also affect conduct; for believers this would not be shame in the sight of all but shame before other believers; this idea may underly AE's suggestion that certain conduct is not fitting (5.3f) among the saints. Associated with this may be his stress on the new position of believers; they must not fall back into the old ways of their previous pagan life (2.3ff; 4.17ff); a sharp line is drawn between Christian existence and that of the pagan world (4.17; 2.1ff; cf 1 Th 4.12; 1 Cor 5.1; Gal 2.15).

5.2. Basically the essential motivation for behaviour arises out of believers' own existence, an existence based on, and inspired by, what Christ and God have done for them. It is better to speak here in general terms of Christian existence rather than of some special element within it. Baptism will always have remained a significant event for them, as would also the words of the preacher from whom they first heard the gospel. AE however does not make much of either of these; he prefers a more rounded appeal: they have been called, forgiven, raised to the heavenlies, and are members of the church; the last of these is perhaps the most important in AE's eyes. Significant here is the separation of the earlier theological discussion from the ethical. The transition from the one to the other takes place at 4.1 and contains a plea to believers to live a life worthy of the call they have received. The transition is signalled by **therefore**, as in other letters where we have the separation of the paraenetic element from the preceding discussion on which it depends (Rom 12.1; 1 Th 4.1; Gal 5.1; Col 3.1). The particle throws us back to the theology of the earlier chapters; of these it is only necessary to pick out the highlights of the blessings they have received from God (1.3). He chose them (1.4, 12) to receive redemption through Christ's sacrifice (1.7; cf 5.2, 25) and certified it to them through his exaltation of him (1.19ff). For their part they had not rejected what God had done but believed (1.13, 18), received the Holy Spirit and were given a future hope (1.13f). Once they had been dead in sin and under the devil's control but now they have been made alive (2.1, 5), raised with Christ and exalted with him to the heavenlies (2.6). Nothing in themselves could have brought this about, only God's grace (2.8–10). Indeed, as Gentiles, they could not even have expected this, for God appeared to be interested only in the Jews; now they stand on the same plane with the Jews before him (2.11–22). Their new position was no afterthought on God's part but belonged to his eternal plan (3.2–13). As they understand all this they will be moved to worship (3.14–21) and then to live in the way God wants them to. In theoretical terms the first three chapters set out the indicative of God's action, the second three the imperative in detailing the conduct that should ensue (for the idea see also Gal 5.1, 13; Rom 6.2f, 11ff; 12.1ff; 13.11–14). Yet as we move through the 'imperative' the indicative continually reappears, for believers do not stand alone but have been joined together in one body with one head and are the recipients of the ministry of apostles, prophets, evangelists, pastors and teachers (4.11). Immediately prior to the detailing of their new way of life they are reminded that they are new people (4.24). It is only as they grow into being new people that they will be able to fulfil the demands of their new life. The indicative/imperative concept is repeated throughout the paraenetic section in various ways. They are to forgive and be kind to one another because Christ has forgiven them (4.32) and to live lovingly because Christ has loved them (5.2; note the use of **as** in both these verses and in 5.25, 29). For people to know they are loved helps them to love.

5.3. If there is a specifically Christian motivation, does AE suggest any resources to support his readers in following it up, for it is not easy to walk lovingly and do God's will? The first half of the letter sets out their Christian position; it is one that lifts them out of and beyond normal human inner resources; support comes because their salvation and election have been gifts and they have risen with Christ and sit with him in the heavenlies. They can forgive because they have been forgiven (4.32); they can love because they have experienced love (5.2, 25). God has equipped them with armour so that they can stand firm (6.10ff); they have been given his truth and righteousness, and are at peace with him; they have faith, salvation and his word. They may have to struggle but they do not do this alone, for they are members of the church which is Christ's body and of which he is head; this truth has been the main burden of the letter; thus they are in a network of corporate salvation. It should not then be surprising that AE does not at the outset of his paraenesis encourage them to pray to God for help; they already know that because of their position his help is always present. Only at the end, though not as an afterthought, is prayer mentioned (6.18). Their prayers should not be selfishly directed to their own spiritual needs but should be for all their fellow believers, among whom Paul is special (6.19f). With prayer comes the need to be watchful and alert.

6. *Continuity and Discontinuity*

6.1. Any profound moral teaching not only continues what it finds good in existing teaching but also innovates new teaching; it commences with an existing understanding and modifies it. The teaching of Jesus began with the Jewish tradition in which he had been reared, but he went on to criticise and radicalise it (e.g. Mt 5.21ff). That AE continues what he has received (see Introduction §9.2) can be seen in a number of ways: (i) He incorporates Jewish material into his teaching (e.g. 4.25). (ii) He uses pieces of Christian tradition e.g. the HT, selections from vice and virtue lists, the hymn of 5.14; there is however no reason to suppose he took over an existing baptismal catechism. (iii) While he may have used sections of tradition from his Christian culture, the origin of some of it lay outside both Christianity and Judaism in Greco-Roman ethical teaching. Apart from particular pieces of tradition, in any culture there is also unexpressed material accepted by everyone, and any group with distinctive views within that culture will also draw on what is common in it but modify it for its own special needs. Despite AE's criticisms of his culture in 4.17–19, he draws on it regularly, or at least on its more developed aspects. It is only necessary to note the number of times in the exegesis in which attention is drawn to parallels to Stoic teaching (see index). (iv) At the same time AE gave a new perspective to the teaching which he adopted; thus though the attitude he argues should exist between husband and wife differs little from that of much contemporary ethical teaching, it is seen in a new way through the parallel of Christ and the church. The

367

main difference here between his teaching and traditional ethics lies in the motivation (see §5) arising out of the parallel, and in some areas of his teaching it is the difference in motivation which basically distinguishes his ethic from that of the contemporary pagan world.

6.2. When AE's Gentile readers became Christians they already possessed ideas from their culture of what was good and bad, but they were now brought into the stream of tradition which flowed through Judaism into Christianity. Jewish teaching itself was critical of aspects of pagan teaching, e.g. it rejected idolatry, emphasised humility (see on 4.2) and made a strong and essential connection between religion and morality. The extent of the Jewish element in AE's teaching can be seen in the number of parallels to it to be found in the Wisdom literature, Philo, Pseudo-Phocylides, *Testaments of the Twelve Patriarchs*, etc. With the exception of the **in the Lord** of 6.1, and its reading is not certain, all of 6.1–4 might have been written by a Jew; the sentiment, if not its precise expression, would also have been acceptable to most pagan moralists.

6.3.1. If AE's teaching is in many ways continuous with both pagan and Jewish teaching, it displays discontinuity when he draws on the streams of tradition which took their origin in Jesus and Paul, though of course what they taught depended in part on teaching that existed before them. The streams of tradition flowing from Jesus and Paul were not independent of one another; Paul was, for instance, influenced by Jesus in the primary place he gave to love; Paul, however, rarely acknowledges his dependence by explicitly quoting the teaching of Jesus. In this he is followed by AE, though AE's letter is so brief that it would be unwise to conclude he did not know any of the sayings of Jesus. There are however places where their use would have been appropriate if he had known them. Mt 5.33–7 could have been quoted at 4.25; Mt 5.21f at 4.26f; Mk 7.15 at 4.29; Mk 10.21 at 4.28. Mk 3.31–5 and 10.28f would have strengthened his teaching on the togetherness of believers in the church. To have missed one of these would not be surprising but to miss so many is, and the later the date of the letter the more surprising it is. The restriction of the love commandment to fellow believers is the most striking divergence from Jesus, but it is a divergence in which AE is at one with almost all late first-century Christianity. AE also seems unaware that Jesus recognised that when he called people to follow him this would result in the breaking up of homes, for he provides no teaching for single believers. Rather than suggesting, as AE does, that believers should not associate with those who did not think in the same way as himself (cf Eph 5.6f), Jesus went out of his way to associate with tax-collectors and immoral women (Mk 2.16; cf 9.38f). AE does not challenge his readers to give up all for Christ (Mk 8.34–6; 10.21, 29), to live in faith as children (Mk 10.15), to think of themselves as last and servants of all (Mk 9.35; 10.43–5), to give sacrificially (Mk 12.42–4), or to go out on mission with little or nothing to support them (Mk 6.8).

6.3.2. AE was influenced also by the stream of ethical teaching originating in Paul, especially in his basic approach through indicative and imperative and in his rejection of behaviour as a path to salvation. The details of his teaching also show many resemblances to Paul, as can be seen from our exegesis of his paraenesis where there are continual references to his letters, though this can hardly surprise if AE was Paul. However, if a rounded picture is to be provided it is important also to approach the problem the other way round. If we begin with the list of vices in Gal 5.19–21 we find many of them reappearing in Ephesians but we note the absence of **sorcery** and of **jealousy** and **envy**, which are more destructive of community spirit than any of the vices AE mentions since they represent deeper elements in human sin; AE in his desire to emphasise Christian unity might have been expected to introduce them; more surprising perhaps is his failure to refer to pride and self-confidence (1 Cor 13.5; Phil 2.3; Gal 6.3; Rom 12.16) and to boasting (1 Cor 13.4; 5.6; 2 Cor 10.13–18; 11.16f), all of which are very corrosive to good community relations.

Over and above this we miss the type of thinking found in many of Paul's striking verses; there is nothing in AE similar to the penetrating insights of Rom 12.1f; 15.1f; 1 Cor 10.24; 9.22; 2 Cor 12.9; Gal 6.2; Phil 4.11f and of the hymn to love of 1 Cor 13 (whether Paul wrote it or not he included it). If AE appears as patriarchal in his views on women as Paul, yet he lacks passages like those in Paul which show an approach to equality between man and wife (1 Cor 7.2–5; Gal 3.28). There are also significant differences from Paul; the latter values celibacy over marriage (1 Cor 7.7, 26, 28, 32ff); for AE marriage is the normal and approved condition.

6.4. Granted that AE lies within the stream of ethical tradition emanating from Jesus and Paul, we cannot ignore the lack of their penetration and bite in his teaching. We have already mentioned how he falls below Paul; the same is true when we compare him with Jesus. The pungency of the beatitudes is missing, as is the penetration of sayings like Mk 8.35; 10.42–5; 12.41–4; there is no concern for the victims of believers' sins (cf Lk 19.8f).

7. Conclusion

7.1. AE's moral teaching does not begin from an initial axiom or proposition like 'Love your neighbour', from which it would be possible to deduce proper conduct in particular situations. This is not to imply AE lacks an overall point of view. Whatever believers do should be pleasing to God (5.10), in accordance with his will (5.17), appropriate to a church context and fitting therefore among holy people (5.3). It is this final statement which is distinctive of his approach. His moral teaching is then, as we have said (§3.3), properly termed a 'church ethic'.

7.2. The content of AE's moral teaching for believers within their communities has turned out on examination to be a little humdrum and conventional, reflecting perhaps a period when the initial flush of enthusiasm has died down. It is an ethic for neither ascetics nor an elite of moral athletes. There is no call to leave all and follow Christ as is found in Mk 1.16–20; 2.14; 10.21; it is true that these passages may have originally been summonses to disciples to leave the world, yet Mark has left them in his Gospel which is directed towards those who are already believers; there is no stage at which believers can ignore such demands. There is also no challenge in Ephesians to sacrificial generosity (cf Mk 12.41–4), though the recollection of Christ's own sacrificial giving (5.2) may go some way to balance this. Even if the ethic is a little conventional, and would have appeared so to Jews and Stoics, it may not have seemed like that to many Gentile converts, not all of whom would have been affected by the Stoic ethic; certainly, if 4.17–19 represents AE's real belief about the outside world, he would not have thought of them as previously influenced by that ethic.

7.3. To summarise, the main criticism of AE's moral teaching is its lack of depth and penetration when compared with the teaching both of Jesus and the genuine Paulines. Their most profound insights are absent. On the other hand while Paul envisages only a brief period before the parousia and allows his ethic at times to be shaped by this, AE's teaching is for a continuing situation; it is an ethic which can guide for ever; marriage, for example, is recognised as a permanent institution.

7.3.1. Yet if AE assumes that his ethical teaching is a guide for all time, is it really that? Is it not tied too much to his own cultural situation to be of any help when culture changes? Today in few countries where there is a Christian church is slavery also found, and AE's injunctions to owners and slaves cannot be transferred to employers and employees, least of all where the employers are anonymous financial institutions. The relation of men and women in the culture of most countries of the Western world is profoundly different from AE's time and AE gives no clue as to how believers are to adapt to this, or how to criticise it when they regard it as wrong. Individuals today cannot avoid decisions in political matters; they may have to choose between candidates in elections; they certainly have to decide whether to vote at all; AE offers no guidance for these decisions. While the household is still a basic unit in society its membership has altered; there are no slaves; one-parent families are widespread; grandparents are sent off to old people's homes. New areas in leisure, sport and work exist and may be as influential and important in formulating behaviour as traditional family relationships. AE says nothing which would help us to know whether believers should work primarily to change individuals or to change society; indeed he has nothing to say about changing society, though perhaps he may be excused since in his time believers were so tiny a group that they could not influence society. All this might not matter so much if AE had provided a basis from which an altering social and cultural situation might be viewed and evaluated. He does not seem to see that cultural situations might differ, yet he must have been aware that Jewish and pagan culture differed widely. Though Paul may have accepted the social culture of his time, Gal 3.28

leaves open an approach for judgements in different cultural situations. That AE was writing a general letter and not just responding to particular problems should have made him more aware of the existence of general problems.

7.4. There is however a final and necessary comment to be made in AE's favour. He treats all, women, children and slaves, as well as men, as morally responsible; he addresses them directly and does not tell husbands to instruct their wives in their duties, as very shortly after his time Clement was doing (1 Clem 21.6; it is possible also to read the same limitation into 1 Cor 14.35). Moreover he also sets the same standards of conduct before all; in that way he helped both to increase the sense of togetherness of believers and eventually to prepare the way for greater equality.

INDEX

DATE DUE

DATE DUE